Post-Hindu India

Post-Hindu India

A Discourse on Dalit–Bahujan, Socio-Spiritual
and Scientific Revolution

Kancha Ilaiah

SAGE www.sagepublications.com
Los Angeles • London • New Delhi • Singapore • Washington DC

Copyright © *Kancha Ilaiah*, 2009

First published in 2009 by

 SAGE Publications India Pvt Ltd
B 1/I-1 Mohan Cooperative Industrial Area
Mathura Road, New Delhi 110044, India
www.sagepub.in

SAGE Publications Inc
2455 Teller Road
Thousand Oaks, California 91320, USA

SAGE Publications Ltd
1 Oliver's Yard, 55 City Road
London EC1Y 1SP, United Kingdom

SAGE Publications Asia-Pacific Pte Ltd
33 Pekin Street
#02-01 Far East Square
Singapore 048763

Published by Vivek Mehra for SAGE Publications India Pvt Ltd, typeset in 10/12pt Goudy Old Style by Star Compugraphics Private Limited, Delhi and printed at Chaman Enterprises, New Delhi.

Library of Congress Cataloging-in-Publication Data

Ilaiah, K. (Kancha), 1952–
        Post-Hindu India : a discourse on Dalit–Bahujan, socio-spiritual, and scientific revolution/Kancha Ilaiah.
        p. cm.
    1. Hinduism—Social aspects—India. 2. Brahmanism—Social aspects—India.
    3. Dalits—Social conditions. I. Title.

BL1215. S64I53   294.5086'94—dc22   2009   2009032026

ISBN: 978-81-7829-902-0 (PB)

The SAGE Team: Rekha Natarajan, Sushmita Banerjee, Mathew P. J. and Trinankur Banerjee

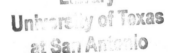

For,

The God who created all human beings—men and women—equal
and in his likeness; prophets who taught and practised equality—
Buddha, Jesus, Muhammad, Marx and Ambedkar; and
my mother and father who were born unequal, lived unequal
and illiterate, and, died unequal.

Publisher's Note

In this book the readers would come across many coinages such as meatarianism, orature, and so on. These words have been used by the author, given his unique methodology and subtleties of argument. The publishers have not interfered with the unconventional narrative structure of this book.

Contents

Acknowledgements

The social masses, who have lived as oppressed castes and communities, suffering for centuries at the hands of the culture of caste, superstition and exploitation—and whose very suffering became the source of this book—I thank them immensely for accepting me as one of them, and sharing their knowledge and experiences.

And, of course, the Dalit-Bahujan movements that have sustained my interest in life and work. I thank all those who are involved in these enduring movements. I thank all my friends for their unsparing criticism of the draft of this book. I have always believed that a good friend is one who, while sharing my broad ideology, does not hesitate to rip apart the bad arguments I tend to develop in any of my writing. Many of my friends helped me in finessing my arguments. My students also gave significant inputs which helped me in writing this book. I thank them all .

I would like to sincerely appreciate the assistance that I got from the SAGE team. Sugata Ghosh, Vice President, Commissioning persuaded me to give this book to SAGE and Rekha Natarajan and Sushmita Banerjee diligently worked on this book to bring it to its present form.

Finally, I thank my family members, who shared the burden of day-to-day life while I was working on this book for more than a decade. Since I am not married, I stay with my brother's family in a small urban apartment. My brother underwent a heart valve replacement surgery 30 years ago, so he falls sick quite often. However, he is able to cope up with life because of the assistance from family members. I am thankful to God for having let me be born in this country, in this wonderful family and for assigning me the job of teaching, reading and writing—that too in English.

Introduction

MAPPING THE SUICIDAL COURSE OF HINDUISM

This book was born out of a gut feeling that the Indian nation is on the course for a civil war; a civil war that has been simmering as an undercurrent of the caste-based cultural system that Hinduism has constructed and nurtured for centuries. The Hindu cultural system is slowly unveiling its self-destructive contradictions, creating tensions in every layer of the caste society. This book covers a wide range of Dalit-Bahujan cultural, scientific and economic knowledge systems, analyses their overall relationships with each other and also with the Hindu religion as a spiritual system. It establishes that Brahmanical Hinduism adopted an anti-production and anti-scientific ethic, compared to the scientific, technological and productive knowledge systems that the Dalit-Bahujan communities have developed and nurtured over the years.

The social, spiritual, economic and educational deprivation imposed on the Dalit-Bahujan castes by the Hindu religious institutions have led, to the organization of different Dalit-Bahujan castes and an articulation of their ideological positions, thereby brewing up tensions. The tensions between the lower and the upper castes are leading to clashes on an everyday basis. On one hand, the spiritual and political aspirations of historically deprived castes and communities are increasing, leading to the expansion of spiritually democratic religions like Christianity, Buddhism and Islam. On the other hand, new political parties are shaping up to fight the hegemony of the upper castes. Thus, the hunger of Dalit–Bahujan castes for power—whether spiritual, political or social—has set the stage for a war of power, of nerves, and also of weapons. These multiple processes have created a degree of tension that might explode into civil war at the slightest provocation. This book aims to highlight the contradictions within the caste layers and map the future course of the Indian nation. It aims to show how the Hindu religion, which is one of the world's four major religions, is on the course of a slow but sure death because of these processes. It is a demise that would reposition the cultures of the world in a major way. It would be impossible to predict how the post-Hindu India would shape up. What this book does however, is dissect the body of the Hindu cultural system and expose the fatal nature of the caste cancer that it has created within itself, show how it is unwilling to undergo a modern medical surgery, leading, consequently, to its suicide. It is a self-constructed disease with a self-determined course.

FOUR SPIRITUAL WORLDS

This book essentially intends to show how Hinduism as a religion is on the course of its death as a result of its own failure to mediate between scientific thought and spiritual thought. In other words, it examines how Hinduism failed to mediate between reason and faith. It draws a particular conclusion about the looming demise of Hinduism, highlighting evidence of everyday clashes of caste cultures and conflict between the productive ethic of the Dalit–Bahujan castes and the anti-productive and anti-scientific ethic of Hindu Brahmanism. Concurrently, it also draws a general conclusion that if a religion does not have the inner strength to gradually move towards institutionalizing the spiritual democratic course of equality and transformation within its inner structures, it is bound to fade away, leaving the available space to other religions that position their relationship between science and spirituality on a positive and democratic route.

The inner strength of each religion has to be examined in the light of the comparative energy of the four major religions that currently govern the cultural realms of the human universe. As of now, the human universe may be said to be divided into four spiritual worlds: (a) the Christian world; (b) the Buddhist world; (c) the Islamic world; and (d) the Hindu world. Though there are other small religions that exist in different parts of the human world, like Judaism, Sikhism, Zoroastrianism, and so on, they did not carve out a spiritual world of their own. Nor did they build nation-states based on a particular religious ethic. They survive as small spiritual cultures in small pockets of the world. They may either survive as small entities for some more time in human history, or they may slowly wither away. But what is important here is to understand that the four major religious worlds have been primarily based on the concepts of spiritual democracy, spiritual fascism and spiritual authoritarianism. This understanding calls for an in-depth study of the internal mechanisms of these religious worlds. This book attempts to undertake such an in-depth study of the Hindu religion from the perspectives of caste, culture and science.

THE HINDU WORLD

Of the four major religious worlds, the Hindu world is the smallest and poorest, with a spiritual base that has no transformative strength. All the so-called modern interpretations of the Hindu religious world, which have characterized it as a great religion, have, in fact, represented its under-developed mind. From Adi Shankara to Sarvepalli Radhakrishnan, the Brahmanic interpreters of Hinduism were appreciative of Brahmanic primitivism and caste-cultural negativism. This negativism was *dharma* for them. It did not occur to them that the existence of caste and untouchability in this country, constructed by that very same religion, has nothing to do with the notion of spiritual justice that the universally positive religions have constructed. If their usage of the term *dharma* alluded to spiritual justice, then we must point out that Hinduism as a religion is fundamentally opposed to the spiritual justice that the other universal religions have developed within themselves through evolution over a period of time. If the Brahmanic thinkers believed the concept of *Varnadharma*—which, in my opinion, is going to be the source of the death of Hinduism—to be an equivalent of the universally valid concept of spiritual justice, then one can only pity their intellectual ignorance. It is this kind of intellectual de-privation, even of the modern thinkers like Vivekananda, Aurobindo, Radhakrishnan, and so on, that has pushed Hinduism towards its death. The Hindu thinkers never realized that in the course of human history, Hinduism would die much before the other religions exhaust their potential to influence the human masses. Now, of course, the largest human mass is available for the expansion of the existing spiritual democracies only in India. The Hindu scholars never realized that the Indian Dalit-Bahujan masses, who constitute a great majority of the national population, are slowly but surely moving away from Hindu spiritual fascism.

The Hindu world mostly encompasses large sections of the population of India and Nepal. The people who identify the most with the religion are the Brahmans, Baniyas and Kshatriyas, constituting about 10 to 12 per cent of the population. The Shudras who fall 'below' these castes in the social hierarchy, have an ambiguous relationship with Hinduism, and— I believe—once they realize that the religion is dying, they will abandon it as one abandons a sinking ship. As I show in this book, the true reason behind the death of Hinduism is its anti-scientific and non-egalitarian ethical values. The Hindu world is the poorest in terms of scientific innovations, and even at the end of the twentieth century, its priestly castes are so primitive in their spiritual approach that there is no possibility of a revolutionary reform within Hinduism. So far, no Hindu scientist has discovered anything that is equivalent to the American or European scientists. Even the claims of Brahmanic *pundits* having discovered the zero and the *Pushpaka Vimana* (the ancient aeroplane) have no substantial evidence, and may in fact be termed false claims. I intend to point out in this book, with substantial evidence from Dalit–Bahujan life experience and history, the basic scientific knowledge known to several 'lower' castes—knowledges that were not allowed to become a part of modern science by Hinduism. The claims, that the Vedic texts are embodiments of all scientific knowledge, have led to the absence of a social base for modern scientific discoveries. It is because of Hindu casteism that India has remained a land barren of scientific discoveries throughout modern history. It has survived on modern science begged and borrowed from other countries, and the Brahmanic intellectuals are solely responsible for this status of the nation.

It was the oppressed productive castes who were largely responsible for the scientific and mathematical discoveries attributed to India in the ancient period, as I shall show in this volume. Present-day advanced mathematics is borrowed from the Christian world. Various technologies, including leather processing, pot making, house construction technology and, more significantly, the technologies of food production, which the Dalit–Bahujan masses built over centuries based on trial and error in their struggle for survival, were forced to remain stagnant. The iron-handed intervention of Hindu Brahmanism stopped the hybridization of scientific knowledge all through known history. Thus, because of Hinduism, India and Nepal remained backward in modern innovative science and the realization of that fact by Dalit–Bahujan thinkers marked a new course of history in this region. The notion of enlightenment never took root in these two nations because of the negative influence; hence, a serious contestation of Hinduism began in the pre- and post-colonial period.

Hindu Identity

Though the so-called Hindu religious identity of India and Nepal is only a few centuries old, the Brahmanism that exists at the base of this religion is much older. The Hindu identity was given to the Brahmanic primitivist spiritual system by Muslim scholars—Alberuni, in particular. He wrote his famous book *Al-Hind*, thereby coining the name that the Hindu rulers and spiritual forces have accepted and made their own. The very name Hinduism did not emerge out of any prophet's life or spiritual work, as happened in the case of Christianity or Buddhism or Islam. Christianity and Buddhism took their name from the life of the great prophets, Jesus and Buddha. The name Islam means 'God's world'. Muslims are also known as Muhammadans, emerging again from the name of Muhammad, the prophet. But the name 'Hinduism' was adopted by practitioners of the religion out of a lack of creativity among Brahman thinkers. It was a name given by the medieval Muslim scholars, who believed that the inhabitants of Sindh (Hind) are primitive barbarians and they did not have any socio-spiritual maturity and cohesion. As the Muslim scholars rightly visualized, the Brahman–Baniya social and market forces built the religion as a caste-ridden, primitivist, superstitious and barbaric religion, and hence they gave a negative name to that religion. Even though the Brahmanic thinkers adopted that name, believing that it is a positive name, they never changed the anti-scientific and anti-egalitarian essence of the *Varnadharmic* system that Brahminism built into it. Even in modern times, they wish to continue along the same path.

Of course, had Hinduism not managed to become a part of the identity of the Dalit–Bahujan population of the Indian subcontinent, the region would have mostly gone over to Islam as the social masses in Afghanistan, Pakistan and Bangladesh did. This would have happened even before the East India Company established itself in India, or at the latest, before the evangelical Christian missionaries arrived. The Dalit–Bahujan population would have found solace in Islam, as the religion offered them spiritual equality within the *masjid* and did not restrict access to the spiritual book. In a way, the arrival of William Carey in 1792 to India changed the course of the nation's Islamization.

The second major intervening event in the religious history of India occurred over 150 years later, when B. R. Ambedkar established Navayana Buddhism in 1956. The largest social mass that remained trapped within the confines of Hinduism after the Islamization of Afghanistan, Pakistan and Bangladesh, and also William Carey's Christianization and Ambedkar's conversions to Buddhism, were the Shudras and Other Backward Castes.

They are 'backward', because they have not moved on to any spiritual democratic religion. Thus, at the end of the second millennium, the Dalit–Bahujan population, which constitutes the majority in India in absolute numbers, stood at the crossroads of a religious competition as the new century began with the process of globalization of the world. This era even opens the spiritual gates through a process of globalization of the spiritual cultures, which has a truly liberative potential for the Dalit–Bahujans of India who were hitherto kept arrested within the caste cultures of the enclosed well of Hinduism. They were like frogs in smaller caste wells within the larger well of Hinduism, with its spiritual culture of not sharing the well water and not allowing 'table fellowship' within castes, even as it kept people confined in their respective caste wells. The cultural and spiritual process of globalization is beginning to bring these Dalit–Bahujan masses out of these wells. This can either lead to a slow, non-violent transformation of the society, or to a civil war over time. In the Indian civil war, castes and religion might play a role very different than what the human history has witnessed so far.

A NEW SPIRITUAL INTERCOURSE

The first interaction of the people of India with a powerful book-centred spiritual democratic religion was with Islam. During the colonial period, they began to interact with Western Christianity and the Bible in a mode considerably different than during the visit of St. Thomas and subsequent times in ancient and medieval India. The pre-William Carey Indian Christianity was Brahmanism of a Southern mode. Jesus was not seen as Baliraja (as the other name for sacrifice), but as Vamana by the Kerala and Tamil upper-caste Christians. Jesus was not seen as a prophet who died to liberate the rest of the world, but as a practitioner of untouchability and casteism. Thus the casteism that operated in South Indian institutions, including the church, kept Christianity a minority religion. This minority status suited the upper caste Christians because that granted them a lot of so-called minority rights. They therefore did not want Christianity to become a majority religion wherein the caste system could be abolished in all forms.

William Carey, in Bengal, started an experiment to establish a 'Kingdom of God' in the tribal regions, following Jesus Christ's prophetic words: *the first will be the last and the last will be the first in that kingdom.* It was from this Christian ethic that the North-Eastern tribes started emerging as the rulers of their own nationalities/states. However, revolutionary conversion processes that challenged Hinduism started with Ambedkar and his Navayana Buddhism in 1956. Between Carey and Ambedkar there was Mahatma Jyotirao Phule, who had seen conversion to spiritual democracies as liberative but had failed to emphasize upon the truth behind this belief by embracing any one of the spiritual democratic religions himself. But what Phule could not do Ambedkar did, decisively and resolutely. By 1956, a spiritual revolution that had taken shape through Christian missionaries, initiated by William Carey, transformed into a Buddhist missionary revolution. The link between the Islamization of Afghanistan, Pakistan and Bangladesh, the Christianization of the northeastern states and parts of southern India, and the Buddhist agenda of Ambedkar is beyond the scope of this volume and needs to be examined separately.

THE INTERACTION OF PROPHETS

Following Ambedkar's modernist Navayana Buddhism, the untouchables, whom I have shown as subaltern scientists and productive soldiers in this book, came in contact with a liberative Buddha in an incarnation of Ambedkar. At the same time, a large section of them found Jesus Christ to be a much more powerful liberator than Buddha. Now the Shudras—the social mass that suffered the spiritual fascist onslaught of Brahmanism for 3,000 years—are standing at the crossroads of the spiritual democratic systems established by the Buddha, Jesus and Muhammad. Like Jesus, Ambedkar also believed in the Kingdom of a Positivist God (the Buddha) wherein the Dalits will be the first and the Brahmans will be the last—in other words, the most exploited social mass will become the socio-spiritual and political ruling class and the class that has historically been the exploiter class will become a part of the ruled social mass. Ambedkar, by virtue of such vision, has come to be seen as another incarnation of Jesus for the Dalit-Bahujan masses of India. This, of course, does not imply that the liberative forces of Jesus Christ's teaching do not operate independent of Buddha and Ambedkar in India—it would be blindness to deny the strength of the winds of his liberative passion, which are much stronger in India than anywhere else in the world now. But at the same time, it appears to me that Ambedkar—who worked resolutely to wash the sin of untouchability in human life—is slowly but surely becoming a part of the long line of liberative prophets of the world. He fought the Pharisees (Brahmans) of India with a determined will and with the same weapon of non-violence that Jesus used without any compromise.

Towards the end of 2007, when this book was on the verge of completion, the caste-centred contradictions within Hinduism were deepening. With three religions—Christianity, Buddhism and Islam, in that order—competing to take as many people as possible into their fold, the demise of Hinduism seemed closer than ever. For a long time in the pre-colonial and early colonial period, the Dalit–Bahujan castes moved towards Islam, which was the only alternative readily available to them with a system of protection from above—the state. Sufi evangelism helped forward that process. Thus the tribal, Dalit and Other Backward Castes moved on to Islam, transforming three major regions into three Islamic nations—Afghanistan, Pakistan and Bangladesh. But once the British colonial state consolidated, the protestant evangelical forces began to work specifically among the tribals and untouchables. Because of the pro-tribal and pro-Dalit spiritual discourses and practices of the Protestants, a significant section of the population began to embrace Protestantism, without confronting the Hindu caste system at an ideological level. This process gave birth to three Christian majoritarian states in the northeastern part of India—Nagaland, Mizoram and Manipur. The expansion of Christianity in tribal regions is still on, and the *hindutva* opposition will not be able to stop that process. But there is a fundamental difference between that mode of expansion of Christianity and Islam and the post-Ambedkarite Navayana spiritual revolution that challenged Hinduism. Ambedkar's confrontation with the Hindu caste system, as a representative messiah of the untouchables, by evolving a conversionist Buddhism threatens the very existence of Hinduism. Quite interestingly, with the emergence and popularity of Ambedkar's brand of Buddhism, Christianity began to compete with the Navayana Buddhism and challenge the Hindu caste system quite openly. There is thus a possibility that in this atmosphere even Islam might revive its Sufi evangelical ethic and compete with Christianity and Buddhism. Therefore, a competitive ethic has clearly entered the spiritual realm. Only when the spiritual democracies compete does the pace of the death of spiritual fascism hasten. We have very positive examples of the quick destruction of political fascism in the World War II, owing to the competitive fight against it by the democratic and socialist states of the world. Similarly, the spiritual fascism of Hinduism must also die when the spiritual democracies compete to take the remaining Dalit–Bahujan masses into their fold and carve out their spaces. As I will show in this book, Hinduism cannot adopt such evangelical methods because of its self-destroying caste system.

THE ROLE OF NAVAYANA BUDDHISM

Ambedkar's Navayana Buddhism became both a builder of a new system of Buddhism and an annihilator of the Hindu caste system and Hinduism itself. He brought back King Ashoka's mode of conversionist Buddhism, which has deeper implications upon the process of the death of Hinduism and also the change in the course of the religious ideologies of the world itself. Very few people in the world know that King Ashoka of India transformed a political army into Buddhist evangelical army in the third century BC. He initiated evangelism before the birth of Christianity. It was in his evangelical campaigns that the present Far Eastern world was converted into Buddhism. Hence, the present-day world must understand that evangelism as a mode of bringing people into a spiritual system that guarantees at least some form of spiritual justice is a positive and necessary course of human liberation and growth. Hinduism cannot become an evangelical religion because of the caste system. The principle of spiritual justice provides scope for spiritual equality amongst people only when a religion believes in equality of all human beings. Hinduism as a religion runs counter to this very principle.

It is established beyond doubt that Hinduism and reason are antithetical to each other as it is based on a casteist and superstitious belief system. If the reason available among the Dalit–Bahujan communities begins to become conspicuous, Hinduism begins to die faster and faster. If William Carey injected an evangelist combination of reason and Christian faith into India, Ambedkar introduced a very powerfully designed intelligence and mass self-consciousness movement that started a different transformative course and made the demise of Hinduism a possibility. His establishment of the relationship between reason and faith in a land of superstition was revolutionary; a relationship that is becoming increasingly competitive between evangelical Christianity and Navayana Buddhism. In the process, even Islam, which took an anti-modernist and anti-evangelical posture is losing out in India as it remains out of the competitive reform, which alone can put spiritualism on competitive edge with capitalism. The Christian nations of the West adopted capitalism as the mainstay of their politico-economic systems and the Buddhist nations like China, South Korea and Vietnam adopted socialism. The reason why socialism survived in these countries is because of Buddhism which is based on a socialistic ethic. Once China realizes that there is a close relationship between Buddhist reason, liberal socialism and controlled capitalism, the world will be put on a different course of development. Even in China, evangelical Christianity is competing with Buddhism and Taoism in this era of cultural globalization. In this atmosphere, Islam, which is on a confrontation course with Christianity on a global plane, will have to evolve an evangelism of its own or find itself trapped by the deadly webs of terrorism that can destroy the moral strength of the religion.

Given this backdrop, evangelical Christianity continues to learn from the Ambedkarite method of publicly challenging Hindu spiritual fascism. As the killing of pastors, raping of nuns and Christian women teachers and burning of churches increase, the process of the death of Hinduism also hastens. In the background of the Gujarat carnage and Hindu–Muslim conflicts, Indian Islam will have to be a friendly ally of Christianity despite the global hostility between the two.

There is a close link between expanding English education and evangelical Christianity, as English kills the linguistic basis of the Sanskrit-centred Indian languages, a trend the Dalit-Bahujan masses are keen to continue. Brahmanic Hindus are powerless to stop the expansion of English because they themselves are mired in it. However, it would be impossible to speculate which spiritual democratic religion will take in the largest number of Dalit-Bahujans into its fold, even though India's development hinges on the direction they take. If English replaces the Indian languages of Sanskritic origin, the liberation of Dalit-Bahujans will take a multidimensional course. Thomas Macaulay, the son of an anti-slavery campaigner Zachary Macaulay, along with William Wilberforce in Britain, injected this tool of liberation, and it first influenced the very protectors and defenders of Hinduism. At the same time it also produced Dalit-Bahujan organic intellectuals who could frame their ideas in the form of globally understandable systematic socio-spiritual and political theories. That process began with Mahatma Jyotirao Phule and reached a certain level of maturity with Ambedkar. And it continues, with some capable thinkers and writers in English emerging from the fold of the Dalit-Bahujan communities. However, English in India still remains an elite language, still under the control of Brahmanic-Sanskritic forces. Once it becomes a mass language, it will take over the roots of linguistic Hinduism. The Sanskritic languages are responsible for maintaining the caste system, and consequently, all Indian languages have a built-in philosophy of casteist cultural essence. The language and grammar is highly Brahman-centred. If English replaces that, the roots of the caste system are shaken. As English continues its expansion, even the Hindutva forces are powerless to stem its course because their own social base, that of the Brahmans, has already moved towards it. The question is how soon the Dalit-Bahujan mass will move into that linguistic world. The English language is a window to scientific thinking. I realize this as I work on this book—if I were to think and write in Indian Sanskrit-centred languages, I would not have been able to see scientific thought in Dalit-Bahujan life at all. That is one of the reasons why the Brahmanic controllers of Indian English education do not want English to become a mass language. A relentless battle needs to be waged to make English a mass language, at least by the end of this century.

HOW RELIGION MEDIATES WITH SCIENCE

It is important to understand how Buddhism, Christianity and Islam mediated with scientific and technological developments. The early scientific discoveries took place in the Buddhist world—China and Japan. The compass, gunpowder, paper and the printing press were discovered by the Chinese Buddhists. Japanese Buddhists also went on contributing to small technologies, ever since the ancient days. By the time early Christianity was shaping its congregative church system, the Buddhist world was positively mediating between faith and science. The rational and anti-fatalist ideology of Buddhist spiritual thought helped the Chinese and Japanese in mediating between science and faith.

The establishment of the Roman Catholic church, where a different discourse was deployed in establishing a nexus between reason and faith, created new conditions for scientific researches that put technological discoveries on a different footing. In the initial days the Church was not willing to accept the discoveries of Copernicus and Galileo; infact, it tried to suppress these scientists. But gradually the Church relinquished their control over the realm of scientific thought. The Newtonian revolution took place in that process. The Christian view of the flat world fell apart, but Christianity reworked its faith to suit the science of the earth being round and the theory of gravitation. In the eras that followed, the Christian world went on a spree of scientific discoveries. Electricity, radio, aeroplanes, television, computers, the microchip, all came from the Christian world, and the church played a very positive role in the course of those discoveries, including the funding of various geographical expeditions. This is not to claim that there were no tensions and struggles between the church and individuals, but in the process, the religious institutions learnt to transform and adjust with scientific discoveries. In this process, the Christian God and prophet became a close associate of science and scientific development.

The Christian world has produced some of the most powerful thinkers in political, economic and sociological theory, and of course in scientific theory as well. From Machiavelli to Marx, it produced thinkers who challenged the church and put the socialist, secular and democratic state in a position of power greater than that of the church. The church reworked its relationship with all these developments. Thinkers who constructed alternative political and social systems were born in the spiritual womb of Christianity. They changed Christianity and Christianity changed them. It was not always smooth sailing, but the very process of reading and rereading the Bible and its new interpretations resolved those contradictions quite progressively. The Bible gave such a liberal scope for interpretation that it even produced a school of Liberation Theology. It produced great mediators like Immanuel Kant, David Hume, Paulo Freire, and so on, who constructed theories that sustained Christianity, modern science and political democracy as comrades in arms. Jesus himself became the synthesizer of all such processes. He became an integral part of every revolutionary theoretician born subsequent to his birth. This is how he remains the most popular prophet, even in the modern world. Unlike the Buddha and Mohammad, Jesus mediated with every situation with a humanitarian will.

The Islamic world has added to that process of establishing a scientific relationship between faith and reason, but differently. For example, Muhammad debunked the myth that God desires the mediation between Him and the rest of humanity by an unmarried saint alone. He established a scientific relationship between sexual engagement between man and woman, as both of them, along with their sexual organs, were created by the same God, who created the universe. When Muhammad realized that both the sexual act and childbirth were not impure processes in God's realm, even the Buddhist and Catholic worlds were shocked. For Muhammad, sexual organs have their own necessary spiritually validated bodily functions. At the same time, he put human sexual relations within certain moral and ethical codes. He did not allow the *Kamasutra* brand of concubinage and free sex experiments in the spiritual and social realms. He allowed sexual relationships only between married couples, and only in exceptional circumstances was polygamy permitted, restricting it to four wives.

Even Christianity and Buddhism, which were saintly and monkish religions, were uncomfortable with the formulations of Muhammad and the spiritual practice he established. His spiritual theory of man–woman relationships as positive and spiritually valid created a tension among the Catholic saintly forces that were living a diabolical life of enjoying clandestine sexual lives while condemning relationships of legally married couples as spiritually unethical and impure. On the one hand, extreme adherence to purity-pollution theory produced institutions such as child marriage and *sati*, on the other hand, the sexist life of some Hindu gods had moral implications on the civil society. Art centred on the *Kamasutra* was sculpted on the Hindu temples, so that all modes of abusing women became spiritually validated. On the other hand, the same religion projected the Brahman life as pure, and claimed to worship celibacy. In this cultural environment, Islam appeared as a liberative religion for the masses because of the absence of such diabolical sexual and moral values. Caste, untouchability and cunningness in everyday life within the spiritual realm of Hinduism pushed millions of Dalit-Bahujans into the fold of Islam. Even in Europe, the new marriage morals and their relationship to Islamic spirituality created a crisis within the Christian ethic. Martin Luther's late marriage and renunciation of his celibate life—with the declaration that he was a man of flesh and sex (but not wood or stone)—repositioned the Christian ethic of sexuality.

Martin Luther's revolt against Papal celibacy and the traditional understanding of sexuality of men in the profession of priesthood came about in the context of expanding Islam and its liberated sexual morality. Taking a clue from the Islamic reasoned relationship between man and woman and their sexual engagement, for satisfying the human sexual need and to continue the procreation of human beings, Martin Luther thought that sexual impurity in Christianity was anti-divine and unethical. He fought for allowing marriage as a process of spiritual practice even for the priestly class. After Martin Luther, the father of reformative Christianity, Protestant Christianity adopted married life as spiritually valid for pastors and the Protestant ethic gave up nunnery and sainthood. Buddhism, however, remained stuck with sexual celibacy and monkish controls on Buddhist spirituality till the middle of the twentieth century. Later, Ambedkar broke that tradition and sanctified marriage in Buddhism. Unlike Gautam Buddha, Ambedkar converted to Buddhism along with his second wife— Savita Ambedkar; Gautam Buddha did not allow his wife Yashodara to join the *sangha* as a wife, but asked her to join as a *bhikkhuni* instead. The classical Buddhist *sangha* did not allow wife and husband to be a part of the *sangha*. Similarly, the views of classical Catholicism on human sexual life are well-known facts. Catholicism held marriage and celibacy as two oppositional modes of life, in the manner of the Buddhist *sanghas*. Muhammad broke all the Buddhist and Catholic myths about marriage, sexual morality and spiritual priesthood. The other religions had to make changes to suit the new spiritual environment created by Islam.

Muhammad had also broken the unscientific attitude of the priestly class towards the dress code and its relationship to God. Muhammad adopted a fully covered dress code with stitched clothes from toe to nail, even for the mullahs who conduct the prayers in the mosques in order to scientifically protect the body of humans from heat and cold in the sandy lands of the Arabic world. The primitivist, naked and semi-naked Brahmanic and Buddhist spiritual mediation process resulted in the death of many people, who lived in the ancient Hindu and Buddhist spiritual realms, due to exposure. The civilizational dress difference between Hindu culture and Muslim culture was observed by William Carey when he reached India. His biographer said when Carey landed in Calcutta he found that Hindus wore clothing that was draped and the Muslims that were tailored. This difference also embodied their differing scientific knowledge. As Muslims struggled to develop the science of stitching, the necessary technology needed to be built up, as a result of which Islamic cultural science surged. Muhammad, thus, played a revolutionary role in the medieval spiritual universe.

Christianity also evolved slowly in adopting changed dress codes for its pastors. Even though Christianity remains the most modern in adopting dress codes, it took a long time to overcome its primitive papal one. The Lutherian reformation helped adopt much more radical dress code than even the Islamic one. The modern Western suit and tie, which has influenced the global dress code, was also spiritually validated in the Christian spiritual world, having developed in the post-Lutherian revolution. Meanwhile, Hinduism remains primitivist with regard to dress and Buddhism has also not fully overcome its semi-naked monkishness.

More than anything else, the Islamic world's contribution to science is in its discovery of oil. Following this development, the living conditions of human beings changed irrevocably. At the present moment, a so-called clash of civilization threatens to breakout between the Christian West and the Islamic East on the question of control of the oil economy. Islam's medieval expansion was based on this kind of strong relationship between reason and the Quranic faith, with a solid organization around the mosque and a spiritually committed army. The Hindu Brahmanic world lost out to the Islamic rulers because of a total disconnection between religion and science. The Christian world realized the possibility of expansion of Islam and it made adjustments with Lutherian Reformation and Copernicus and Newton's scientific revolutions. Since then the Christian world has marched forward by constantly negotiating between Christianity and science, leaving the other three worlds far behind. While the Buddhist world is trying to catch up with the Christian world by adopting a liberal socialist politics, the Islamic one stagnates in medieval kingships politically, and is limping with great difficulty to work out its ways in scientific discoveries. Quite tragically, the Hindu world has remained where it started, not having developed any independent scientific thinking. Economically it has remained a good beggar, and in the political form adopted the British model of parliamentary democracy without building a spiritual democratic base at the ground level. In the scientific realm, the Hindu world still remains a borrower of Western science without developing a criticality of its own.

In case of health sciences, Islam adopted practices like circumcision without any compromise, which played a role in limiting the spread of HIV in the Islamic society. Early Christian society practised circumcision too, but over a period of time it was left to the family. While Islamic society had proceeded in the right path about many things, over a period of time it stopped carrying that relationship between religion and science to higher modernist levels. It refused to work out a transformative method in political science that religion should make several readjustments in modernizing the political systems. They also steadfastly stuck to concepts of political monarchy and dictatorship. Islamic societies refused to adopt democracy as a spiritually valid political system. They saw democracy as a Christian form of government, but failed to develop their own liberating system of political governance. The Hindu world on the other hand has become a good adapter, but not an innovator, even in the political realm.

Christian society, on the other hand, starting with the Industrial Revolution, allowed an enormous amount of revolutionary thinking in socio-political, medical and educational realms. In many fields, the Christian world stood head and shoulders above Islamic medieval science. Today it remains the most powerful world because of its successful mediation between religion, science, liberalism and democracy. It is challenged perceptibly by the Buddhist world, which has developed enough mediating abilities of itself between religion, science, liberalism and socialism. The Islamic world in the recent past, particularly after 9/11, is trying to contest the domination of the Christian world with a combination of spiritual politics of repositioning itself and also by constructing terrorist groups that could attack the Western Christian powers in guerrilla modes. Where this conflict between Christian and the Islamic worlds will lead is impossible to predict. The question then is: where does Hinduism stand in this competitive spiritual politics?

THE DEATH WISH OF HINDUISM

The Hindu spiritual world has kept its masses under an iron fist of super-stitions. Its religious books, from the *Rigveda* to the *Ramayana* (considered to be the last book in the scheme of keeping the Dalit-Bahujans suppressed and oppressed) to the *Bhagvad Gita*, leave hardly any scope for creative interpretation to undo caste and superstition. These, if not abolished altogether, leave no way in which a scientific India could evolve. The science that India uses today is totally borrowed from the other three worlds—of course, mostly from the Christian world. Why did the Hindu world remain so poor in science and technological innovations? One of the main reasons, as this book details, is that the Hindu mind did not allow scientific enquiry into each caste's professional productive fields from the point of view of scientific methods that exist in their productive systems. Each caste had a methodology of its own to build productive science and technological systems, and the Hindu religious system kept them bound, akin to the way in which the Chinese used to bind the feet of women to stunt their natural growth. More fundamentally, the Hindu caste system by force stopped cross-breeding the productive knowledges that existed among different caste communities. This was the crucial death blow.

As Hinduism considered production as pollution, and the productive people as polluted human beings, the productive human self suffered from lack of self-respect, dignity as well as initiative. Second, Hindu spirituality treated reading and writing—textualizing human practices and experience—as the divinely ordained work only of the *dwija* (twice-born) castes. Hence, the productive castes were not allowed to learn reading and writing. The ghettoization of education, of reading and writing of texts, of the synthesization and hybridization of knowledge became a defining feature of the Hindu society, thereby destroying the possibility of growth of science in India. This book shows how that happened in India, from the experiences of each caste. Indian sociological knowledge has failed us by not showing how much science and technological basic knowledge existed among the Dalit-Bahujan communities. And they have not examined how Hinduism as a religion did not allow a proper mediation between science and religion at any point in time in history.

The anti-science Hindu system is mainly responsible for building caste barriers for scientific growth. Since it never worked out its theology properly, it did not build a knowledge system of interpreting any human practice or written text. It adopted a method of reading and reciting spiritual texts without any scope for reflection. It also did not develop a spiritual book of ethical values—all Hindu spiritual texts were constructed around war and sex. Most of the wars that Hindu spiritual texts conducted were either those of invaders against the natives (all Vedic wars show that process) or internal civil wars (*Ramayana* and *Mahabharata*). Of course, some texts were written around the sexual experiments of Hindu gods and heroes. Vatsayana's *Kamasutra* was the first major text of that sort. Unfortunately, in the global book market, it is this book that represents India. This only points to the weakness of Hinduism and not its strength. The book helped in making the caste system more rigid and promoting inequality of women. The Hindu world has not produced a great thinker at any point in time in history. If the *Kamasutra* is a true representative of Indian thought, then it tells a sad story of Hindu creativity.

This book shows that the real strength of India is embedded in the day-to-day productive and innovative life of the Dalit–Bahujan castes and communities. But my aim is not to present the Dalit–Bahujan productive and creative life in imaginary nationalism, but in real nationalism that is rooted in its soil and daily working lives of the people.

HINDU NATIONALISM AND ITS ANTI-SCIENCE BASE

During the anti-colonial struggle, Indian upper-caste leaders made Indian nationalism deliberately representative of Hindu nationalism. Quite naturally, they located that nationalism in Hindu books that constructed the Dalit–Bahujan masses as spiritually impure and historically stupid. Except Phule, Ambedkar and Periyar, no other nationalist leaders wanted to keep the nationalist discourse secular and allow the Hindu anti-science ethic to be critiqued. The mainstream discourse around Hinduism was that it was a saintly religion, but they never examined how it was anti-production and anti-science. This led to a disastrous course of underdevelopment. This book details how the Brahman and Baniya minds built an intellectual tradition of *goondagiri*, which has hampered the scientific and technological growth of the nation.

This book also shows how the Hindu spiritual system created conditions of intellectual poverty and highlights the possible alternatives within the realm of spiritual, social and ethical systems of India. The transition of India from its spiritual fascist and superstitious social base to creative spiritual democracy is a process of struggle. As it involves the transformation of a major society from primitivist idol worship to book reading and book-based spirituality, the course will be a time-consuming one as well. In India, the cultures of reading suffered due to casteist superstition and historical back-wardness. Nationalism should have removed the bottleneck of superstition, casteism and untouchability, but Hindu nationalism became even more superstitious and anti-science. One hopes that this book will help Indian intellectuals to relocate the roots of Indian science and technology. One also hopes that it will aid the Dalit–Bahujan masses to look for a suitable alternative spiritual, social and cultural life process that will bring their historical potential back into play.

Each chapter in this book is written around the cultural and scientific knowledge that each caste possesses within the context of Andhra Pradesh, a south Indian state in India. But it draws general conclusions, as the religious experiences of all Indian productive castes is the same. It also shows how Hinduism at every stage has hindered growth and hybridization of the Indian science, and of historical development all over the country and over a period of centuries. I hope that this book will open a new methodological channel to initiate studies that lead to a spiritual, scientific and social revolution in India.

My appeal to Brahmanic readers is that if they want to read this book they must read it without self-righteousness or self-pity. As they begin to read it, it may generate a warlike situation in their minds which are trained in Brahmanic thought. It may indeed result in a 'war of nerves' between Brahmanic and Dalit–Bahujan civil societies, the latter having just begun to produce its own organic intellectuals. At the moment there is no large-scale Dalit–Bahujan civil society that could take inspiration from a written text and lead a liberation struggle. The main aim of this book is to create the self-respecting Scheduled Caste (SC), Scheduled Tribe (ST) and Other Backward Castes (OBC) into an intellectual social force that can lead a socio-spiritual and scientific revolution. In spite of Phule's writings, my own book *Why I am Not a Hindu* and other writings, the OBCs of India have not realized how Hinduism has historically suppressed their scientific essence. They continue to struggle for political power, not realizing that as long as they are in an oppressed position in the spiritual realm, their intellectual potential cannot be fulfilled and their scientific temper cannot take on a modernist shape. The Dalits, on the other hand, are on a path of spiritual and social liberation, inspired by Ambedkar's writing and practice.

This book is meant to play a positive role in empowering the Dalit–Bahujan forces of India in all spheres of life. It is also meant to show how spiritual democracy and spiritual fascism are opposite systems, and define what roles they play in our lives.

Chapter 1   Unpaid Teachers

STARTING THE JOURNEY

If one undertakes a journey across India through the many layers of its society, the course seems to turn unbelievably torturous. Many foreigners and Brahmanic scholars of India have attempted to undertake such a journey in an attempt to unravel the complexities of its many social, cultural and civilizational systems, but have ultimately failed to understand the essence of India. Studying the Indian society involves living through its processes which also involves a close study of its multiple castes that have constructed myriad forms of suppression and hegemonic relationships. The scholars who belonged to hegemonic castes could not perceive the unique life ethic of these productive castes and thus did not understand the historical contribution of tribal societies to fields such as science and technology. In order to construct a national vocabulary of modernity we also need to understand the internal strength and psyche of communities that have been oppressed for centuries.

I shall make an attempt to undertake a journey through the life of the various castes and communities of India. When a society is composed of extremely complex caste systems, understanding its various cultures is a rather difficult proposition. Yet one has to make an effort in that direction, for it is important to liberate the Dalit–Bahujan masses from the clutches of Brahmanism and from their own ignorance.

I have explored a few questions over the years—Who taught us how to live? Who constructed the humanness of our being, sharpened our sensitivities, and continues to teach us vital lessons? The answer, based on my own long journey across the vast territories of India, is unusual or rather unexpected—for it is the 'tribals'. The moment one refers to these communities—which comprise people from all societies, rural and urban, it immediately conjures images of ignorant, primitive and uncivilized people. Texts—spiritual, secular or scholarly—have constructed them as *Vanavasis* (people who live in forests), or as *Girijans* (those who live in mountains), the implication being that they have not acquired the civilizational standards of the people living in the plains. Their life is not considered as valuable as that of the others who live at the other end of the spectrum of Indian society, that is, the Brahmans. The value of life in India oscillates between the tribals at one end and Brahmans at the other end and these groups constitute the two extreme poles of the Indian society. Thus, the tribals suffer all mundane human tribulations as well as those resulting from not being a part of the civil society. They suffer from the contingencies of nature, the lack of social cooperation, and the brutalities inflicted upon them by other castes. The Brahmans, on the other hand, have lived a life of superstitious faith enclosed by a 'culture of torture' which they inflict upon the others.

The Brahmanic construction of communities, in the context of the many theories of modernity, assumes that the social systems and thought processes of those who live in the villages, towns and cities—those who constitute the non-tribals—are more 'human' than those of the tribal communities. Except the Dalit communities themselves, most other people of India hold this opinion. But my journey which begins right at the heart of the tribal society reveals an altogether different truth about the nature and character of tribals, which the educated Indians are unable to comprehend or acknowledge. The hegemonic power enjoyed by most of the high-caste groups would be at stake once they acknowledge this truth.

Each culture or civilization has its beginnings and growth in particular contextual locations. The cultural claims of the higher castes—particularly the Brahmanic castes—are constructed from a negative experience of humanity; these constructions rely on human interactions that have remained peripheral to the modes of production. The root cultures and civilizations of the human societies have been relegated to the background by the dominant castes. The ruthless cultural hegemonic practices of Brahmanical cultures have demolished the cultural and civilizational base of other caste groups with their particular cultures and have posited the Brahmanic cultural and civilizational self as superior. These practices forced the productive masses to accept the Brahmanic anti-production culture as not only the superior culture but as also the singular historical reality. Because of this lionization of the Brahmanic culture, the origins of the human creative essence are left unknown and undermined, often deliberately. But a careful observation of the tribal culture shows that it still retains traces of the early signs of human creativity.

NAMES AND CULTURE

All cultures are linguistically constructed in the names they adopt for their communities and individuals. Cultural codes are also formed in terms of food habits and dress. In all these respects, the tribals had evolved the earliest human knowledge systems that formed the base of our knowledge systems. Tribals have their own community-names like the Gonds, Koyas, Kondareddys, Chenchus, Nayakapus, Lambadas, and so on. None of the communities desire to be identified as Girijans or Vanavasis—conceptions that show them in a negative light—and want to be addressed by their own specific names, such as the Gonds, the Koyas and the Lambadas. Naming them as Vanavasis is akin to naming the Madigas and the Malas (Dalits) as Harijans, which is repulsive to them. Revolting against this negative construction is a political and nationalist aspiration, since these communities resist hierarchization in the Hindu caste order and wish to assert their cultural identity and establish their space in the vocabulary of linguistic, religious and cultural nationalism. The Brahmanic writers have written innumerable books claiming the glory and greatness of their culture but are yet to realize how humiliating and insulting labels such as Vanavasis or Girijans can be. As one tribal put it, 'wolves assume that sheep are unworthy of living, and hence, just kill them'. Brahmanic cultures consider all other cultures and civilizations unworthy of being written about and glorified and this amounts to cultural homicide. They kill the other cultures by denying them what is their due—their history and social visibility that is required for further advancement and evolution.

The tribal societies are interpreted and constructed in the manner the Brahmanic scholarship wanted to construct them—not in their own image, but in the image of Brahmanism. The tribal communities have many modes of self-construction; the relationship between these tribes and nature is regenerative, where one constantly regenerates and renews the other. But Brahmanic scholarship has relegated them to one monolithic category and has classed their mode of being as 'Vanavasi'. The question then is, why did the so-called 'Hindu' textual knowledge structures classify them using the nomenclature that they did not wish to be identified with? Why was the tribal cultural self-constructed in the image of the popular Brahmanic imagination?

The tribal communities have been classified into groups such as Vanavasis and Adivasis in a typical high-caste Hindu mode of negativism. The primary example of this process could be that of the Chandalas who used to be clustered together at one end of the village while the Dwijas (the Brahmans and the Baniyas) lived at the other end. The Dwija empowerment is rooted in this mode of clustering and assignment of names. Cultural and social markers and locations are indicated by those who have the privilege of naming. For example, Gandhi adopted the specific name of Girijans, who were mountain tribes, to refer to all tribal communities, thus positing their culture and civilization in a particular location. Thus the act of naming is as ideological as one's very being, and accepting a negative appellation is indicative of a process of silent suffering. The revolt begins with inverting that process of naming—in the rejection of the other's language, identities and idiom—and in the adoption of new names, vocabulary, language and identities which challenge the constructions of the oppressors.

Positing the Dwijas as Hindus and the rest—Sudras, Chandalas, Vanavasis—as the 'Others' (but within Hinduism) was a historically de-structive process. The clustered construction of the tribals in the process has all but erased their identity. Casteist cultures have constructed binary notions of opposites—positive and negative, inferior and superior—in the vocabulary of the hegemonic upper caste ideology. Notions like 'superior/inferior' and 'divine/profane' rob the tribals and Dalit-Bahujans of their very humanness. This mode of cultural robbery is more dangerous than the theft of goods and commodities. The theft of people's histories, cultures and civilizations by oppressive forces has had terrible, long-term repercussions that have made whole communities suffer, and many tribal communities were the primary victims of this historical oppression.

THE ADIVASI SELF

What do the tribals or the Adivasis think about their own culture, pro-ductivity, and creativity? Did they teach the people living in the plains their methods of productivity, creativity and knowledge systems? Or were the tribal communities taught by the so-called 'civilized' Hindus? Which group gave to the other, and who were the takers? Who are more human or inhuman? Answering these questions will begin our journey of understanding the Indian society. It will move systematically from analyzing the tribal societies to various other castes that exist in the villages, towns and cities.

Our starting point itself is troublesome, as we are journeying without a map or beaten track to follow, as no such track was allowed to be created and neither was such a map allowed to be drawn. The Brahmans have plundered the tools of writing history as well, and an attempt has to be made to retrieve these tools.

A close examination of the socio-economic conditions and cultural processes of the tribals shows that they taught the 'essence of life' to the rest of the society. That is the reason why they must be treated as our 'teachers'. They laid the foundation of our culture and our civilization. They taught us what to eat and what to drink in order to survive. It is true that human beings do not survive on food alone, but it is also true that they do not and cannot survive without food. Even today, civil society appropriates several aspects of tribal cultures without expecting to be asked to give them anything in return. It does not acknowledge all that it has learnt from tribal societies since such acknowledgement itself is seen as an uncivilized act.

All cultures take birth in the culinary culture of the people. But the Brahmans told us that food is meant solely for eating, enjoying and living on, not to initiate debates or discussions about, and especially not to be written about. Thus Brahmanism created a domain of deceit and lies.

THE FOOD CULTURE

The food structures of all—the meat-eaters, the vegetarians and the pork and beef-eaters—were discovered, tested and standardized by the tribals. The Gonds, Koyas and Chenchus eat a variety of meat, poultry and greens. Apart from eating the flesh of such animals as goat, deer, pig, bull, cow and buffalo, they eat a whole range of forest animals that we do not consider edible. So is the case with greens. Many of these flavours have not yet tantalized the taste buds of people living in the plains. Thus the food tastes of people are socially constructed.

The Brahmanic society projected the vegetarian food as 'divine' food. The taste of vegetarian food has been written about and such food has been eulogized and glorified as pure food, whereas the tribal food culture has been condemned as that of uncivilized people. This is where the tribals lost their identity. The civil society of the people living in the plains never understood the historical process wherein the tribals gave different culinary tastes to the others. In the sociological language of clever scholarship, if a tribal gave up eating meat it was tantamount to getting 'sanskritised', but if a Brahman started eating meat and fish he/she was not 'tribalised'. If at all they are changed, they just got 'westernized'!

Many of us in our normal lives do not realize that the tastes of sheep, goat and chicken meats have been taught to us and standardized by tribals. This process of introducing the taste of different types of meat which the people are not familiar with continues even today. I still remember that day in my childhood when a group of Nayakapus brought an animal called 'Udumu' to my village. Udumu resembles a lizard. The Kurumas competed to make a bid for it. My family finally bought it for a substantial sum. Immediately the 'neck' of the animal that was tied to the 'tail' was untied and it was chopped off. It was then roasted and the skin peeled. At first I was repulsed by its lizard-like form, but when the elders in my family insisted that it tasted much better than the usual kind of meat I tentatively reached out for a morsel. It surprised me to discover that their claim was not an exaggeration. Later, I came to know that the people in the surrounding villages were also taught to eat Udumu by the Nayakapu tribe.

The process described above involves a systematic explanation of the health-value and the taste of each food to the tongue and its utility to the body. The tribals try to explain how eating the Udumu cures certain diseases, but the people living in the plains do not accept these explanations so easily. However, the survival of the tribals in the absence of advanced medical systems was attributable to their culinary culture. Migration of food tastes is a long drawn out process and the tribals kept transmitting their culinary tastes patiently, which were appropriated by the people living in the plains as their own.

Many tribes do not eat monkey-meat, but they savour the meat of the bigger Kondenga that has a black mouth. The tribals experimented with the meat of this animal and soon the village folk living in the vicinity of tribal communities acquired a taste for it. The tribal understanding of the taste of such meat and its effects on human health were based on the long experiments that they conducted on animal bodies, and involved a careful study of the food habits and food systems of various animals.

The modern urban society has no scope to experiment with different types of meats at this stage, and standardize new ones or reject old ones. What the modern culture of food does is that it changes the formulae of cooking which in turn modifies general tastes. This modification is not nearly as original as the early discoveries of the Indian or any other food system, and therefore cannot be said to have the 'primary value' that early discoveries had. Yet, Brahmanism has turned even this aspect upside down.

Brahmanism is perhaps the most dangerous school of thought that negated and destroyed the 'meat culture' of India by pushing the vast masses into a complex process of self-negation. Those who continue eating meat are made to feel that they are 'uncultured'. The Indian tribals not only gave us the culture of eating meat, but also, in fact, gave us the vegetarian food culture. If African civilization can said to be the 'mother civilization' of humankind, the tribals are the 'mothers' of human food culture. The Indian tribals have their own independent contribution to the food culture. It is rich in variety, taste, health and contributed to the development of India's Indian personality.

There are many varieties of roots and fruits that the tribals know as edible. Most have rich protein content. The roots, fruits and leafy foods that we enjoy today as part of our historical food culture are part of the 'heritage foods' that the tribal communities have handed down to us. In my childhood I ate many fruits and roots available in the forest around my village. The reference point of the villagers as to which fruit, root or leaf should be eaten and which should be avoided, and which part of the tree had medicinal value was part of tribal knowledge and experience. What they communicated to the shepherds down the generations gets communicated back to the village. For example, the Pariki and the Tuniki fruits are not commonly known as fruits that can be eaten. Tuniki is a major source of food for several tribes as it is nutritious and can be preserved. It is a summer fruit and the Koyas make a special effort to collect it in large quantities. Delicious when eaten fresh, it can also be dried and stored in *gummulu* (baskets). The dried fruit is eaten during the rains to keep energy levels up. The Pariki is sour-sweet. It too can be eaten fresh or dried.

The *kandas* or roots that we eat, raw or cooked, some sour, some sweet, find their origin in tribal knowledge. Areas which the Koyas, Nayakapus and Chenchus inhabit abound in a particular root-food called Yellerugadda. It is a blackish root with a thick skin structure. Prized for its taste (its digestibility improves when burnt to a particular degree), the inner substance turns white if the root is exposed to the flame slightly. The demand for this root in some villages adjoining the tribal areas is very high as the tribals of the area had taught the local people about its taste and its food value. But that root may not have any demand if it is taken to a distant urban area where its taste and food value are not known.

For a Brahman sitting in an urban office, University, or the temple, the taste and food value of the Yellerugadda would be totally unknown. A Brahman at the University could write that it is a useless and tasteless food; a Brahman at the Secretariat could write a note on a file that growing such roots on co-operative land is a waste; a priest in the temple might say that it is not a divine food—all of which would amount to destroying a great food heritage of India.

The tribals have knowledge of certain root-foods that can sustain them in drought and other difficult conditions. Even poisonous roots on repeated boiling can discard their toxins. The Gonds of Adilabad survive on such roots during drought. Many such roots that the tribals use as food in their struggle for life remained within their own knowledge system. This is because their knowledge of roots and fruits has not been recognized as authentic. We forget that new roots or fruits are discovered by them only at the time of scarcity. Food scarcity at the time of drought forces them to search for alternatives. It is in such search for alternative foods that they experiment with new roots, fruits and other edibles.

THE NOTION OF TASTE

A Brahman in India might die for want of food but he/she will not eat beef. They know that they can survive if they eat it in the time of food scarcity, but the cultural conditioning and patterns set in childhood, drive them to choose death over food. A tribal does not have such dead weight of negative cultural conditioning in his/her mind. Tastes, once acquired and set, do not adapt to new foods very easily. For an average Indian who eats sweets and chillies in the extreme, any Western food is like tribal food and is as tasteless as Gond, Koya, or Kondareddy food that is devoid of oil, burnt or half boiled, and unmixed with proper ratios of chilly, salt and spices.

For most civilized Westerners, food prepared with oil and mixed with spices is considered uncivilized food. Thus, what is considered as civilized by one community is uncivilized for another community. The notion of civilization, therefore, changes from community to community and nation to nation. The food cultures are constructed according to the caste-groups in India. Caste is a colossal compartmentalizer of food culture. This compartmentalization has forced us to lose out on many varieties of food items that would have added to our cusine. For example, there are many edible insects that could not become part of even the kitchen culture of non-vegetarians because of the general fear of the Brahmanic atmosphere.

There are many such edible insects that could have become part of our food culture. The most relished insects by tribals and plain Dalit-Bahujan are Ushillu. The Ushillu live in small mud hillocks called Puttalu. They multiply during the monsoon and the tribals trap them in pots. Within a couple of hours they die, and they are then roasted and eaten.

Ushillu mixed with Yippa (Mohua) flowers filled with nectar is considered a delicacy. Most tribal communities feed their guests on dry Yippa flowers and roasted Ushillu. The consumption of edible insects has now become routine in the plains as well, but not among the Brahmans and Baniyas. Their children think that those who eat such insects are barbarians. But why did the tribals choose only the Ushillu as edible insects? They discovered that eating them in the monsoons (Ushillu appear only during the rains) raises their energy levels. In rainy seasons the hunting grounds turn wet and mushy. The animals that they normally hunt on find lush green bushes and forests to escape. Though they get enough root food in the rainy season, it is not a season of fruits. Hence they discovered the excellent combination of Ushillu and Yippa flowers. Such a discovery was not an act of barbarianism, but it was an act of evolving culinary cultures in adverse conditions. All great things have been discovered by people only in adverse conditions.

SACREDNESS OF ANIMALS

No tribal clan in India considers cows and bulls as sacred. Until recently cattle were not used for agrarian purposes in the tribal areas. The water buffalo was not a very popular animal in the tribal areas. Cows, bulls, and buffaloes were mainly used as food. Thus there is a close relationship between the Scheduled Castes and tribals who have been beef-eaters. Sheep, goat, rabbit, peacock and several other birds do form part of their menu, but the bird that they love and relish is the Guvva (a local bird) and its meat is strongly favoured; it is also said to cure certain chronic diseases. There are a number of stories in the villages about the high protein component of this bird's meat. The meat of some birds according to the tribal communities has a lot of medicinal value too. The Guvva meat is one such medicinal meat. Yet another bird whose meat is believed to cure a lot of chronic diseases is Chamurukaki (oil crow) in the Telugu speaking region. The knowledge of the medicinal value of the bird meat, however, was first acquired by the tribals and then passed on to the villagers.

Even in the civil society there are individuals who know the medicinal value of the meat of some birds. For example, the meat of the Chamurukaki is given as medicine for fits and other related diseases. Most of the lower caste medical practitioners prescribe this bird's meat for many diseases. Brahmanism has negated all such food values and has spread hegemonic propaganda that only vegetarianism is good for society. Vegetarianism has killed the rational element in their beings, since it is not the food of individual choice, but that of cultural conditioning.

It is not that the tribals do not have knowledge of vegetarian foods, roots and fruits, but they also give proper importance to meat in their diet because more energy and flavour. Historically, it gives thus, the vegetarian superiority is proved to be a myth. Brahmanism has destroyed the health of India by propagating the vegetarian superiority and negating the consumption of meat. The Indian society has, over a period of time, turned vegetarian because of the campaign of Brahmanism and Gandhism which has destroyed the general health of the nation.

ESSENCE OF VEGETARIANISM

The tribals are not very fond of vegetables and leaf curries, which does not mean that they do not know the taste of the vegetable curries. They, perhaps, do not know as many varieties of vegetables as the people living in the plains know today, because quite a lot of these vegetables are of a hybrid variety. The non-tribal society has never shared its knowledge with the tribals, so a positive exchange of knowledge between tribals and non-tribals could never take place. The caste hierarchy of the people from the plains has turned the tribal into a victim. Even if the tribals wanted to migrate to the plains and live a civil societal life, it was/is not possible because they could not enter any existing caste. In a caste system, the settlement of any tribal group among non-tribal areas becomes difficult because they must first get a new caste status. Historically all such newly settled groups seem to have been collated as the untouchable communities. In modern society, because of caste reservation and other related subsidies, no group is willing to absorb any new group into any caste category.

No other religion except Hinduism has deemed certain foods as sacred or divine and others as profane/ungodly/diabolic. It is believed that the Hindu gods and goddesses eat specially chosen foods cooked in a particular manner. The preparation of 'puja' food is known only to Brahman families. Since vegetarian foods are defined as divine, Hindu society has acquired knowledge of the various fruits, roots, leaves and nectars from the different tribal groups, but has not exchanged its own knowledge in return. The fact that the civil society has never shared its knowledge with tribal societies makes one wonder why the exchange of knowledge has been one-sided. Why did the caste-based Hindu society take the food systems of the tribals and deemed some systems as divine and the others as profane? This mode of Hindu factionalism not only applies to food but also to alcoholic beverages.

ALCOHOL AND SPIRITUALITY

Integral to the food and drink of the Gonds, Koyas, Lambadas and Kondareddys were natural and artificially brewed intoxicants. In the realm of the tribal knowledge system, the extraction of juice from a tree is not a specialized task. It is part of the routine collection of fruit, roots and nectar. Toddy or (in Telugu language it is called Kallu) and Eata (Kallu) are very popular drinks. The Jeelugu tree, which resembles the toddy tree, yields a superior intoxicant rich in protein. Some tribes are experts in tapping an intoxicant from the Neem tree as well.

The Yapakallu (drink derived from the Neem) is more than an intoxicant. It is supposed to have life-saving properties. It renders a pregnant woman immune to several diseases and tones up one's health. Women drink it like a tonic in the early period of their pregnancy. All types of tree-bound intoxicants—Toddy, Eeta, Jeelugu, Yapakallu—have a tremendous capacity to reinvigorate the body after a hard day's work that can involve food gathering, animal rearing, hunting and fishing. The tribals also brew strong arrack with flowers and tree extracts. Of the several varieties of arrack that are brewed, the one made with the Yippa flower is considered to be the best. The drinks that are extracted from the trees and brewed are not meant only for intoxication. The tribals discovered these drinks and beverages to increase their energy in order to survive in difficult weather and terrain, and for the hard physical labour required to collect food and to fight the natural hazards. Even the most civilized societies in the world improved upon these drinks that the tribal communities discovered and standardized them for the benefit of humanity. Like the aeroplane has been modelled on the birds, similarly all the modern food and drink systems have been copied and improved upon what the tribal communities have given us as an historical reserve. The Hindu religion has humiliated the foods of the world and more particularly the historically evolved knowledge system of our tribals by negating that historical reserve. While tribal spirituality does not interfere with the eating and drinking habits of the people, Hinduism considers consumption of liquor as being against divine dispensation. Hindu nationalism has judged intoxicating drinks as demonic. Brahmanical habits, particularly those of Gandhi, were projected as being representative of the Hindu gods and goddesses. Indian tribalism, on the other hand, teaches us a contrary mode of spirituality. Toddy, Eata, Jeelugu and Yapakallu are very much part of the spiritual fare. So the tribals drink, dance and sing, presuming that their gods do the same. In fact the pre-nationalist Hindutva narratives present the Hindu gods and goddesses as sura and soma drinkers (most Hindu gods in the ancient context were consumed alcohol and ate meat). They are basically located in the spiritual cultures of the tribal people. That dimension of tribalness of Hindu gods and godesses got deconstructed. And now they are being shown as vegetarians and teetotallers. Hence, Hindu nationalism constructed tribal cultures as satanic and hence inimical, and thus negated its own self and constructed the myth as reality.

PODU PRODUCTION AND TRIBAL CREATIVITY

In Telugu country, the Godavari river divides the plains and tribal agrarian knowledge systems. The people of the plains on one side of the Godavari conduct their agricultural operations with the help of tractors while the Kondareddy and Kondadora tribes work in Podu form (if there is any change, it is a recent one) on the other side of the river. Their instruments of production such as the axe, sickle and sticks used for ploughing the soil are made of iron and wood. The sophisticated use of hands is a striking feature of Podu production. All their instruments are designed such that the use of hands is extensive. The deployment of animals such as bull, cow and buffalo for agrarian operations is still an exceptional exercise in the tribal areas. In other words, they have been using bull power only in the recent times. Their knowledge of the use of animal power for ploughing is very recent and for centuries they depended on their own physical energy. The use of the plough made by the carpenter is a recent phenomenon among these tribal communities. The use of these production forces are slowly learnt by them on their own. No civil society of the plains taught them such skills. The evolution of production skills among human beings is a result of collective interaction of people with nature. In the tribal stage of human society their collective interaction with the nature is greater than the people who live their life in the plains. It is in this process that the tribal society evolved our early agrarian technology. In the history of evolution of technology the role of tribals must be estimated with a detailed study of its formations.

THE TRIBAL TECHNOLOGY

The choice of terrain in Podu cultivation has to be made with great care. Land should not be too uneven. The flow of water should correspond with the seed system that is sown for productivity. All these processes are not left to divine dispensation. Not that the tribals do not believe in 'divine powers'.

The forest goddess, the water goddess, the sun, and the rain gods all find a place in their spiritual consciousness. But such gods and goddesses get invoked only after the crop actually appears. The process of production is a consciously interventionist, collective human enterprise.

Podu cultivation involves the selection of a suitable plot of land. Then the modalities are worked out for felling the trees, cleaning the soil, readying the instruments for tilling, and so on. This mode of Podu production involves the use of sickle and axe and an advanced use of the stick for tilling, to make the land conducive for seeding. The energy used for all these processes is not animal energy but human energy, essentially the hands. Using hands as instruments of production was advanced in the tribal stage itself. The Podu production process was the key process in applying the hands to the production system. The Brahmanic Hindu thought, unlike the thought systems of other religions, de-linked itself from the production system and de-valued that whole culture of production. In their so-called cultural evolution, the writing of *Rigveda* becomes central because that book constructed all the tribal production systems as Satanic (Rakshasa) systems. The centrality of this book in building a spiritual culture has regressed human society. The fact remains that tribal communities have built all the early technologies.

The early forms of spade, sickle, axe, crow-bar, bow and arrow, stone instruments have all been built by the tribals. The Hindu Brahmanic forces disrupted that knowledge system, the tribal positive ethic of building technology that helped the productive process, over a period of time. There is a basic difference between the tribals using the technology and the Hindu war heroes like Rama using technological instruments like bow and arrow. The tribals used the bow and arrow to gather food resources and also for self-protection. The Hindu writers converted the basic tribal technological instruments like bow and arrow into simple and pure war weapons. Rama used bow and arrow, which were only war weapons and Parshurama used the axe as a weapon to kill people. This is a travesty of the human evolutionary process and its spiritual culture. The tribal spiritual culture was based on fear and anxiety. The concept of God as a universally accepted spiritual abstraction was evolved with a notion of love and affection, and Jesus, who is considered the greatest prophet of sacrifice across the world, was first evolved by the tribal communities of Israel. Even Gautam Buddha's moral ethic evolved out of Indian tribal cultures. The Indian tribal cultures should have been integrated into the positive spiritual culture. But Hinduism negated that process right from the beginning. Hindu Brahmanism has converted all technologies into war technology. As a result war and violence have become the central life process of Hindu tradition.

TRIBAL SEED SYSTEMS

Though the seed systems of tribal Podu production and that of the plains are similar, there is no evidence to suggest that these systems were transferred from the plains to the tribes. Familiarity with maize, jawar, pulses, and vegetable seeds is common to both, but there are certain seeds known only to tribal societies. Several seeds known to the Kondareddys, Kondadoras, Gonds and Koyas gradually got integrated into the agrarian productivity of the plains. In Andhra, for example, the green jawar and the white jawar were grown by tribal societies much before they began to be grown in the plains. In the tribal societies both men and women handle several tasks. In some *gudems* (hamlets) individuals have also taken to iron smithing. They have, however, not yet acquired the character of a separate caste. Normally, a family does several kinds of tasks. One does the seeding, another looks after the sheep and goats and yet another takes care of the buffaloes, cows and the bulls. A member of the same family may turn out to be an ironsmith and another a pot maker. A religion that allows spiritual equality would have also produced a priest from the same family in which a socio-spiritual and economic collective would have got integrated. Of all the religions only Hinduism did not allow such a process of production and spiritualism to be a familial social collective.

Among tribals certain activities like stitching of clothes did not exist until recently. The natural division of labour that led many civil societies to class formation was stalled in India because it was pushed into caste formations. The attitude of Brahmans, who became the priestly class of India, towards tribals is central to our assessment of them in relation to the whole society. The Brahmanic priestly class seems to have been opposed not only to dignified division of labour within the family and civil society but it was also opposed to egalitarian distribution of resources, leaving no scope for human compassion. As a result compassion has gone out of Hindu diction itself.

Podu productivity is characterized by egalitarian distribution with the co-existence of some private property. A patch of land that is cleared for cultivation is understood to be the private property of a particular family till they move to another place. The notion of private property is subordinated to the communitarian interest of the *gudem* in the Podu production system. It is the moral responsibility of the *gudem* to see that all the families get cultivable land during the season and if the produce is not adequate, then the *gudem* is obliged to go to the rescue of such a family. Podu production and the Brahmanic agrahara production with the system of private ownership of land are antithetical to one another.

It appears that the Indian Brahmans constituted the first community that asked for the right to property without any involvement in production. The Indian tribals are the base community who have always fought for the right to collective ownership of land even today. If the Brahmans stand for selfishness at the one end of the society, the tribals represent selfless communitarian life at the other end of the society.

Both in the realm of production and the social system, the tribals provide us a model to reconstruct our notion of dignity of labour and integrated collective life. And at the other end of the society the Brahmans, even today, provide us a model of moribund private property-centred life without involving themselves in production. The future of India depends on deconstructing one process of life and reconstructing the other process into a futuristic model. The Hindu model, thus, is a negative model whereas the tribal model is a positive model.

A semblance of this communitarian life still operates within the Dalit–Bahujan castes of the plains. But Hindu nationalism from above has almost decimated this structure and replaced it with caste communalism. While the tribal *gudems* are symbolic units of communism in a primitive form, the caste system in the plains symbolizes the degenerative communal life process. The caste-communal Hindu civil society established highly individualized property structures, notwithstanding the joint family system. This Hindu mode of property (or prosperity) produced Sanskritic anti-production knowledge systems. In order to reform the Indian property system completely from being self-centred to a collective and communitarian one, we must learn from our true teachers, the tribals.

This model serves us better than the model provided by Karl Marx in the form of primitive communism based on the European tribal experience. Though the Indian tribal experiences have become part of the life of the people from the plains, the tribal communities continue to maintain their tribal character and communitarian life because of the caste system prevalent in the civil society. Learning from their model of communal life would have implications for our socialistic experiment. Since India is a country of enormously expanding populations, some form of socialistic resource-sharing alone is going to allow the nation to survive. Not only Hindu Brahmanism but Communist Brahmanism too refused to learn from tribal experiments.

TRIBAL ORGANIC LEADERSHIP AND SPIRITUALITY

Like the state, the Hindu civil society never recognized the technological and engineering skills of the tribal social forces. They were regarded as people incapable of building positive institutions, and as a society that could not contribute leadership that is strong enough to inspire people living in the plains. This tension between the Indian tribals and the caste-ridden society of the plains seems to have existed from ancient times. This is also one of the reasons why Indian tribal society from the days of Chandragupta Maurya declined to integrate with the people living in the plains. It was in bitter opposition to the Tribals that Kautilya resigned from his prime ministership and constructed his text of Hindu statecraft–Arthashastra. In keeping with his Machiavellian techniques, he sent teams of Brahman missionaries (they were basically campaign committees) to divide the tribes into castes. Unlike other religions that send missionaries to unite social forces, Brahmanism sent its forces to divide social groups into castes. But these efforts came to naught. From those days the tribals have had inimical relations with the Hindu religion and caste-based ideology. Even in our recent history not many tribals have embraced Hinduism, since Hindu caste-based civil society does not and cannot accommodate them in any form. This is the main reason for tribals to convert to Christianity and Islam wherein they have integrative space. In the spiritual realm, the feeling of being equal to other humans is most important in order to feel one with gods/goddesses. How does caste-centric Hinduism develop such a feeling among the tribals?

NEGATIVE NATIONALISM

Even during the nationalist struggle, the Hindu nationalist ethos never recognised the heroic struggles of the tribals. This is not at all surprising because the Brahman writers never recognized the historical contribution of other communities. It is a fact that the early struggles against the British were carried by the tribals. Nowhere do these struggles find a mention as part of mainstream history. The initiators of the anti-British struggles and the leaders who led those struggles never became part of the school curriculum across the nation. Ironically, history recorded the 'heroic' deeds of those who went from the plains to the tribal areas, but tribal organic leadership never found a space in the pages of popular history. It must however be stated here that the tribals have had a strong sense of natural intellectuality and constructed their heroine/hero images in their oratories (oratures). (I used the concept orature as an antonym for literature). They have their own strong narratives, their own history in oratories (oratures).

Oral literature is an illiterate mode of propagating the knowledge system that the uneducated tribals learnt in order to sustain the past in their social memory. It is a pre-literary form of constructing narratives and communication systems. All literatures have grown out of tribal communication forms. It is absolutely wrong to say that the first form of Indian literature begins with the writing of *Rigveda*. The Indian literature starts in our tradition of tribal orature. Our songs originated here. Even today the Rela songs and Lelle songs which are known as the tribal songs in Telugu country are known forms of literature. Because of the Brahmanical self-aggrandizing modes of propaganda, their literary tradition does not trace itself to pre-Aryan tribal forms of oratures. The Indian tribals are made to feel that their contribution to literature is completely absent. A false impression has been generated that only Brahmans have knowledge and the indigenous tribals and others have no knowledge. This is where the Indian society was misled. The leadership capabilities of the tribals are completely undermined. Even in the modern period the assumption is that tribals are not capable of playing important roles. The Brahmanic forces that invaded India in ancient times claimed that they alone were knowledgeable whereas the native tribes were supposedly not. Progressive leaders of social movements, particularly in relation to ecology and tribal self-respect, like Sunderlal Bahuguna, Medha Patker, B.D. Sharma and others, represent the tribal masses in the national media and public forums. In historicising the Chipko movement and the Narmada valley struggle among others, upper caste migrants from the urban society of the plains garner credit and space in the written discourse of history.

It is a conspiracy of the upper caste media to propagate 'our people as great and their people as meek and weak'. The notion of 'our' has become the notion of the upper caste. The tribals have become the 'other' for all upper castes. The tribals are pushed to the background and rendered as inanimate objects in all movements. Wherever the autonomous states have been formed based on tribal identity, tribal leaders have emerged and have become very efficient chief ministers and administrators, whereas in composite states the tribals are constantly proved to be a failure. At the all-India level, no tribal is allowed to become a national leader with his/her own initiative or capacity. For an average Hindu mind, imagining a tribal in the position of prime minister seems unthinkable.

In the spiritual realm as well, throughout the history of Brahmanism they have not been able to imagine a tribal priest or head of any religious institution which Brahmans are part of. Even today, it is unimaginable that a tribal can run the state where Brahmans and other upper castes live and Hindu institutions operate. So far, history has proved that they can do so only in their own states. But our survey shows that the tribals have enormous abilities to do much if they are provided with creative and rational education.

ORGANIC HEROES

In Andhra Pradesh for example, Alluri Sitarama Raju organized the Kondareddy and Kondadora tribes and mobilized them to fight on his side against the British. The process of historicity glorified him as the only hero while the tribes have got objectified. Books were written, films were made, and he became a subject of study in classrooms. At the same time upper caste society has not recognized the great tribal heroines like Sammakka and Sarakka who became goddesses among the tribal societies. These great women protected the tribal autonomy from the imperial attacks of Kakatiya kings. In fact the Telugu tribal society has given us two outstanding organizers–Sammakka and Komuran Bheem. As said earlier, Sammakka who was a Koya woman belonged to the thirteenth century while Komuran Bheem lived in the early part of the twentieth century.

Sammakka, her daughter Sarakka, and son Jampanna organized the tribals to resist the Kakatiya invasion of tribal areas. The Kakatiyas, though they were Vaddara agrarian rulers, they came under the influence of Brahmanism. For reasons of expanding the state and political control they decided to make inroads into tribal lands and agrarian economies. The catchment areas of the Ramappa, Lakadavaram, and Pakhal lakes were actually tribal lands occupied by the Kakatiyas. The tribal movements against this aggressive expansion were organized under the leadership of Sammakka. She, thus became the most powerful image of tribal self-respect and self-rule and slowly came to be worshipped as a Goddess.

The notions of freedom and independence were always defined in Brahmanic terms in India. The notion of nation was also defined in Brahman terms. But tribal women like Sammakka and Sarakka established their own ideological contours. They saw the Kakatiya expansion in the same way as the modernists saw the colonial expansion of the British. Their battles with the imperial kings and queens were as nationalist as the struggles of modern nationalists.

Nationalism, thus, is historical and evolutionary. The Indian Brahmans not only constructed it in their own image, but also destroyed the other images as if all other social communities were their enemies. Sammakka was a great warrior-strategist and an organizer. She is said to have mobilized thousands of tribals who fought a bloody battle with their bows, arrows, cudgels, axes and other lethal weapons near the Jampanna rivulet.

Many lost their lives in this struggle to protect their land. The Koya consciousness is centred around Sammakka. There are narratives and songs on her struggles; she is worshipped on festive occasions. This image is so potent that nobody remembers Rudrama Devi, the Kakatiya woman ruler against whom Sammakka is said to have pitted her wits. Once every two years, a jatara is held in the name of Sammakka and Sarakka. Lakhs of people from all over the state throng to worship them.

After Sammakka's image underwent a transformation from heroine to goddess, her spiritual base expanded to include the Dalit–Bahujan castes living in the plains. For centuries the Scheduled Castes (SCs) and the Other Backward Castes (OBCs) name their children after them and participate in the jatara. This is the only instance when a tribal heroine turned deity has become acceptable to the Dalit–Bahujans communities.

During the jatara, women and men go into a trance or a mood of *Shivam* (divineness). They jump and dance in a state of enthrallment. But the Brahmans have never treated them as their own divine figures. In return, the tribals also do not care about the Brahman priestly class. Brahman priests do not find place in their worship. The puja or prayer between tribal priests and Sammakka can take place in different languages. Sammakka is a deity who can understand many tongues. She is also said to eat all kinds of food that the tribals eat, from vegetarian to meat.

Sammakka's transformation from an ordinary tribal woman to a warrior-heroine and later a deity clearly indicates that the tribal mode of establishing a dialectical relationship between the human being and the spiritual being is essentially human-centred. In the image of Sammakka the tribals construct their cultural self and their spiritual being. Whatever they eat and drink is offered to Sammakka. Even in the years of prohibition, tribal priests in the face of serious opposition from government officials asserted that no worship could be considered complete without offering arrack to Sammakka. A few years ago, the Andhra Pradesh government officials maintained that they would not permit drinking by priests and the offering of arrack to the deity at a public gathering. Tribal priests insisted that without offering the drink, the deity could not be brought down the tree. The government had no choice but to give in. This instance demonstrates that the exclusivist mode of worship, so typical of Hinduism, has no place in the tribal relationship between the people and the divine.

In the 1920s and the 1930s, Komuram Bheem had organized the tribes against the Nizam's (the Muslim rulers of Hyderabad State) forest policy and revenue system. The anti-tribal forest laws were meant to assist the revenue officials to aggrandize the Gondwana land and devastate their agrarian production. The officialdom terrorized the Gond tribes. The Sahukars (Baniya businessmen) used the situation to their advantage by establishing a nexus with the officials of the Nizam. The tribals were being exploited by the forest officials with the administrative support of the Nizam government. Bheem organized a struggle against the oppressors with the support of the tribals.

Bheem, a brilliant boy, attacked Siddiqui, an usurper who had plundered his family. He fled to Chanda via Ballarshah and from there to the Assam tea gardens. Here he learnt to read and write and also to struggle against the autocratic rule. He returned and began to organize the Gonds against the Nizam at Jodenghat which comprised 12 villages. His initial strategy was to negotiate with the Nizam and work out a democratic solution but the latter refused all overtures. Komuran Bheem died fighting the state in the late 1930s and became a martyr and a spiritual hero of the Gonds. Even today the people celebrate his jatara. Bheem has become a god to the Gonds as Rama became a god of the Brahmans and Kshatriyas in North India.

The stories of Sammakka and Komuran Bheem bring out the striking difference between Hindu and tribal divinity—the tribal deities emerged out of martyrdom and not out of hegemonic killing. In their spiritual discourses, violence does not get hegemonized. Tribal cultural ideals evolve from their own organic heroines and heroes. Of all the religions in the world only Hinduism has deified killers as gods. As it happened among the tribals of India, only martyrs have become the prophets and divine figures of different cultures the world over. The barbarity of Brahmanism starts with the worship of killers.

WORSHIPPING THE SELF

The tribal consciousness does not worship all modes of martyrdom. As against these organic leaders whose martyrdom turned into divinity, the martyrdom of an upper caste Telugu man who died in the tribal areas in the Rumpa region was never glorified as tribal divinity.

Let me elaborate the story of this upper caste man in some detail. During the nationalist movement a Kshatriya man called Alluri Sita Rama Raju went from the plains to tribal areas. He organized some tribal youth into a militant outfit and fought against the British. He died in the process of that struggle as the British police caught hold of him and killed him. This man's image was constructed as a great nationalist image. In the socio-cultural realm he was projected as a cult figure.

In all Telugu nationalist books he occupied a very important space. A cinema was made on his nationalist struggle by the upper caste people themselves. In many cities and towns his statues were erected. But the tribals themselves never gave him importance. Whomever the tribals respect they project him/her into their own divinity. Sita Rama Raju never became their god like Sammakka and Komuram Bheem. He was not spiritualized as their own leaders were; tribal children were not named after him. The Communist movement tried to project many non-tribal heroes who died in the tribal areas. But they too did not achieve the status of Sammakka or of Komuram Bheem among the tribals. The inability of the Communist-Naxalite movement to operate outside the Hindu paradigm blinded it to the inner urge of the tribals to construct their organic leadership. The tribals have tremendous consciousness of their own self. This gets reflected in their spiritual and cultural symbols. No tribal community has projected any non-tribal as their spiritual symbol. All their spiritual heroes and heroines are organic persona that have been constructed as divine agencies, with a definite philosophy of their own. Tribal societies have a very strong sense of history, tradition, culture and philosophy which gets reflected in their orature. The Indian nationhood must recognize all these unwritten but living processes of our multi-layered civil societal histories. The notion of tribal innocence and ignorance is a constructed one. They have their own knowledge system, which the upper caste societies must study in order to build on it. What the Hindus thought and did to the tribal ethos was the opposite. Their discoveries, struggles and their systems were judged to be that of devils. Hindu books portray the images of the devils in the image and social self of the contemporary tribals.

MAN–WOMAN RELATIONS

Tribal society offers a different perspective on gender relations rooted as they are in notions of productivity and labour. The tribal man–woman relationship is fundamentally different from the ideal Hindu man–woman bonding that controls female sexuality as epitomized in the Rama–Sita or Radha–Krishna relationship. In this respect, both Hinduism and Islam share a cultural context. Though Christianity too subordinated woman to patriarchy, it has begun to grant autonomy to women in many ways. The practice of pardah has become common to both Hinduism and Islam, and both exclude women from public life and production. Their value systems de-legitimize female expressions, and in this regard the Hindu ethos is the worst. In the case of Sita, it was suspicion of her sexual morality that put her through the test of fire and banished her to the 'forest prison'. Radha, on the other hand, was marked out for perpetual sexual separation that robbed her of her very humanness. Every Hindu text has enslaved women in sexual bondage. Islam and Christianity on the other hand saw women as social dependents. But the contemporary life process of tribals shows that the autonomy of women is integral to their societal evolution, which has more progressive characters than the other three religions put together.

The positive woman–man relations in tribal communities have a basis in materialism and positive spirituality. Collective participation in harnessing nature, procuring and producing food made such relations essential. Though these communities still retain primitive modes of production and cultural formations, most of them are underwritten by socio-economic equality. Their social and political institutions have not yet yielded space for women to be manipulated by men, or lower castes by higher castes. Child marriages in tribal *gudems* were/are virtually non-existent. Boys and girls live in intimate relationships, both within the *gudems*, at food collection sites and at the Podu production sites. The man–woman bonding forged during the hunting and fishing period eases into a relaxed and friendly spirit in the fruit-gathering and root-digging seasons. However, familial bonding expresses itself in activities such as digging the roots or hunting the fish or of readying a patch of land for agrarian production. The physical intimacies and sexual interactions take place in the process of their teenage formations and also in the process of the collective struggle for hunting, fishing, root and fruit gathering and the Podu production process. They learn all forms of coupling expressions from the different birds and animals they watch on a day-to-day basis. They are animals among animals, birds among birds and nature among nature. Brahmans are the first social group who separated from this mode of child and adulthood interaction with nature. Despite the Hindu injunction that tribals should not learn any form of written expression, their languages display linguistic equality. In the civil society as we go higher up the social ladder, the women as a social being begins to lose equality in a greater degree. This becomes evident in the terms of address for the wife and husband, father-in-law and daughter-in-law and other kinship terms. On the contrary, the reference codes for both men and women in tribal societies remains the singular 'you'. Women do not use the Telugu mode of 'meeru' or its Hindi equivalent 'aap' to address their men folk. The language that operates between men and women, particularly the wife and husband, is an indication of the degree of equality among them. The degree of equality between men and women among tribals is more than any other upper caste social group.

TRIBAL MARRIAGE

Marriages among Tribals, are also far more egalitarian as compared to the civil society in the plains. Pre-marital sexual experimentation does not invite social ostracism among the tribals. In the Kondareddy and Kondadora tribes, when two young people decide to marry, they inform the parents who then ask them to live together in a chosen place possibly for a week or so. Among the Lambadas, after the marriage is fixed, the groom has to live with the bride's family for a month or so and prove his mettle. The burden of adjustment is not on the woman but on the man. His ability to work and maintain positive and sensitive human relations with his future wife's family comes under scrutiny. In this notion of marriage, the woman is not a subject of rigorous patriarchal moulding as a sexual slave but a human being with cultural and economic autonomy. The female body is, to a large extent, within the woman's control. Among tribal societies the system of dowry does not exist. At the time of marriage, a Lambada groom has to gift bulls and cows to the bride's family. If dowry and other patriarchal controls are entering into the Lambada community, it is a new Hindu evil.

Among the Lambadas, women are considered to be doubly productive. They produce children and also engage in work that involves interaction with nature and other people. It is normal for tribal women to fell trees, carry logs, swim across rivers, plough the land, and participate in activities that are normally considered to be the domain of men. Hence, men must pay when they take away a girl from her parental home. Lambada women, for instance, are seen driving ploughshares, bullock carts, or the mota (irrigation buckets pulled by bulls). Non-Lambada communities regard these as male tasks. It is this functional productivity of Lambada women that structures their marriage and familial relations. In the recent past, as they began to live around caste-based Hindu society, the evils of casteist Hinduism have spread to them as well. Studies of the tribal societies show that men carry the patriarchal values into their own civil societal structures from outside, and what Lambada men are doing is a case in point.

In my childhood I used to see Lambada women and men sing on their way to the fields, or on the way back to the *tandas* (a Lambada hamlet is known as *tanda*), and also dance sometimes. This is quite uncommon, for I have not seen people of my caste or the Mala and Madiga castes sing and dance on their way to work or back. Dwija or upper caste communities could never think of doing so. Tribalism has enormous flexibility in the physical interaction of men and women, since they know that the human body remains quite healthy when involved in work, dance, and performance. Lambada women dress up in gorgeous *langas* and jackets. They sing about heroines and heroes, about the sun, moon and the flowers, about ordinary men and women. Their collective dances are rhythmic and involve vigorous body movements. Compare, for example, the Bharatanatyam with the Lambada dances. A striking difference is that one is collective and relates to production and strengthens the relationship between the community and nature; the other is individualistic, with the woman whose existence is defined in relation to the divine. The alienated, solitary woman keeps longing for human (male) company. In Bharatanatyam, the Radha solo is an expression of a perpetually deprived woman. No Brahmanic cultural form presents a confident woman who longs to live an autonomous life. India, therefore, has a very powerful base in tribal modes of thinking, creativity, economic and cultural production and also the modes in which man–woman relations are articulated in the tribal societies.

The transfer of tribal knowledge systems took place over several centuries. It did not happen in a structured way either, for the tribals did not commodify such knowledge. The knowledge was basically transferred through social interaction, however occasional such interactions might have been. Therefore, the tribals are our early teachers, or to be more precise are our 'unpaid teachers', unlike the Brahman teachers who were paid for not teaching us. Now the tribals are becoming conscious of their role in nation-building. They are now demanding that recognition and are asking to be paid back that historical reparation.

Chapter 2   Subaltern Scientists

As we step over the threshold of tribal societies to continue our journey into the plains, we enter the village from the eastern side. Any representative village in the Telugu country (and in the rest of India as well) begins with the Madiga *wada*. The Madigas are the Chamars of North India. Beyond that is the Mala *wada*, the equivalent of the Mahars in Maharashtra and the Paswans in Bihar (every state has similar castes), and from there onwards, we climb up the caste hierarchy. In every village, both the Madiga and the Mala communities may not be there. But almost every village would have any one of them, or either of them. In the contemporary discourses, the Madiga *wada* is known as part of the Dalit *wada*. The Dalit *wadas* were supposed to remain only on the eastern edge of the village society because it was believed the winds that blow from the western side of the village should pass over the Brahmanic castes and move on to the rest of the village before it touches the Dalit *wada*. Such a location of the Dalit *wadas* became a necessary condition because Hinduism ordained it to be so.

On the fringes of the village, it is quite common to find makeshift tent shelters. These belong to the Dekkalis, Chenchus, Chindus, Badubukkalas or occasionally to the Bandivaddaras (wandering stonecutters and ironsmiths). I shall call them the 'cultural castes'. If the Madigas were the first major productive people of India, the castes mentioned above were the propagators of the culture that emerged out of productivity. There are such cultural castes all over India. The Madiga creativity and socio-economic influence on civil society has still not been acknowledged in written discourse. Hindu texts describe these *wadas* as belonging to the untouchables—Chandala, Mleccha, Antyaja, Panchama, or *antaranollu* in Telugu, and so on. Some of the dehumanizing nomenclatures that Hinduism had given to these people to express contempt and repulsion have, unfortunately, come from the Hindu spiritual texts. No nation or ruling class in the world has condemned its own people for as long as these people have been condemned. They do not figure in any of the so-called ancient Indian literatures—as though they have never talked, never walked; as though they never lived on this soil at all. For the Brahmanical writers, literature means tales of war and love but not of productivity, creativity and science. The Madiga life still remains in oratures, but not in literatures.

ORATURES AND KNOWLEDGE

The Madiga oratures and their organic intellectuals contested the caste-centred consciousness of mainstream historiography by configuring images of their selves and their expertise in a manner that should, paradoxically, make the Hindu scholars rediscover themselves as parasites to these productive classes. In their philosophical realm, the Brahmans and the Baniyas had existed as beasts amidst humans for centuries. In fact, several social anthropologists believe that the main difference between animals and humans lies in the latter's propensity for labour. Marxist psychologists have thoroughly researched the conflicting social position of those who produce with labour and those who live as parasites. They conclude that the anti-social and criminal behaviour of forces (like that of the Brahmanical castes) is rooted in the historical process of alienation of people from labour, which is the chief source of humanizing social beings. Life regenerates in production, not in parasitism. This principle is unknown among Hindu priests and writers.

A Russian psychologist said that in the absence of other personality moulding conditions, particularly labour, the possibility of earning satisfaction of one's needs leads to a deterioration of the personality. Parasitic needs that are not controlled by labour may become a source of anti-social behaviour. The mother of all parasitic cultures is the culture of Brahmanism. Among the reptiles and insects, parasites look for a strong support base among the birds and animals. All parasites perfect the art of deceptivity and construct a permanent support base for themselves. Among humans, the Brahmanic forces constructed parasitism as knowledge, and the mechanism to work out the parasitic processes as culture. Culture here is not a condition of intimate human interaction, but a byproduct of isolationism, humiliation and the rape of human essence.

The post-Hindu nationalist textuality is a process of restructuring the consciousness of the Brahmanic forces that condemned the productive people, and hailed the hegemonic, exploitative and parasitic social forces as civilization. It is a reflection of a self-empowering process, which is at once subversive and organic. The Dalit textuality expresses itself in two rather complicated processes. One school of Dalit writers—the Madiga writers, to be specific—work to subvert the very meanings of the words and concepts which have hitherto portrayed the Dalit self as low and mean. For instance, words like *chandala* and *mleccha* have been reinterpreted to point to their historical worth. Used as a suffix to their names, the word *madiga* is deployed by the Madiga Dandora activists in Telugu country to connote a positive meaning. It invokes subaltern science and development as the way of their life. With several such movements cropping up all over the country, the meanings of many words that the Hindu scholars used to demean the Dalit–Bahujan masses are changing to mean the very opposite. The names that had hitherto been used in an abusive sense are now being inverted with a sense of veneration. The gods that the Brahmans praised seem to be turning into devils and vice versa.

The Dalit press, in general, is producing a whole range of oral and written arguments that are going to establish Brahmanic writing as cruel jokes upon history. The Dalit press dissects the social process by inverting language, order and hierarchy, sparing none, even those who consider themselves to be progressive and revolutionary. All knowledge systems—literary, cultural, or of the social and physical sciences—are being restructured. The social layer that had been marked as 'polluted' is being highlighted as scientific and socially useful, while the so-called 'pure' is being reconstructed as unskilled, parasitic, anti-social and anti-national. The Dalit press constructs itself in its own language, upholding the productive ethic of the Dalit–Bahujan masses as the central force that mothered all cultures in India. It looks at its own self in a manner that is the very opposite of the way Brahmanism has constructed it so far. For Brahmanism, the Dalits were a social mass who were incapable of producing great ideas of society, economy, culture and politics. The contemporary Dalit writing on the other hand shows that they can very capably construct their own beings and produce great thought in all spheres, including philosophy, economics, politics and diplomacy. It has been proved historically that the self that has suffered is not a weaker self—it is, in fact, a stronger self that has always been the backbone of all nations.

The second stream of the post-Hindu nationalist textuality gets accentuated in the displacement of the old language. It formulates a countertheory in terms of socio-economic and political equality. Though Ambedkar's writing's gave the impetus for both theoretical formulations, the first mode searched its alternative language in the day-to-day living processes of the productive castes. Their interaction with the world of nature, with productive tools, with animals and birds, with all human beings cutting across castes has therefore been brought into textual discourses in the recent past. In this mode, the language of writing was the same as the language of speaking. The written text was not a commodity delivered by the divine force as an abstract absurdity, but the handiwork of living beings. The second school seeks to interpret and re-interpret the writings of Ambedkar in order to empower themselves. Its dilemma lies in its failure to locate the social source of the egalitarian society that it wanted to construct. Organic intellectuality is not a superhuman process. After a great debate on Ambedkarite thought, an agreement seems to have emerged that the assertion and the subversion of identity, as well as the demystification of their mystified history is an integral part of building the post-Hindu society. We must, therefore, learn to acquire a different framework to understand caste society now.

Caste was created by Brahmanism in order to sustain its parasitical existence. It was hitherto used to exploit, control and manipulate the masses so that a system of consent could be evolved. In this movement, however, the very same caste has become a tool of revolutionary transformation. The exploiters are being attacked as culturally decadent, inhuman and socially unworthy to be accepted as superior. The notions of inferiority and superiority are being subverted as the new discourse tells us that which is useful, is comprehensible to all and is shared by all is not only socially useful but also spiritually liberating. That which is hidden, which is confined only to the chosen few in the name of god is, in fact, devilish.

UNDERSTANDING THE MADIGA SELF

How, and from where, does *Madigatwam* (the philosophy of the Madigas) originate? Its historical and scientific character is contained in the very tasks for which it is condemned as Chandala, Mlechha or untouchable. The removal of carcasses, peeling of skin from the body of the carcass and eating beef was made central to the process of rendering the Madiga self as 'untouchable'. For centuries the socio-economic responsibility of removing dead bodies fell on the Madigas/Chamars, because Hinduism regards the dead as untouchable. The question that must be asked here is: did burying or cremating the dead pollute the villages, or did they make them clean, livable spaces? If Indian society purges itself of its casteist mindset and cleanses the pollution from its mind's eyes, the removal of carcasses will not then be shunned but regarded as a scientific activity of keeping the villages clean and disease free. Indeed, it is because of the Madiga/Chamar communities that the nation has survived contagious diseases, and these communities must receive due credit for that. In fact, they must be rewarded for their labour and their sense of cleanliness. Consider the following possibility: if they too had been irrational and unscientific and treated this task as polluting, the dead bodies would have rotted and would have become the source of deadly diseases. Every family of the present generation must acknowledge its debt to the present generation of every Madiga and Mala family, because at some time or the other, their ancestors shielded people from dreadful epidemics by removing bodies, even at a great risk to their own lives.

The Madigas/Chamars have been traditionally condemned because they are involved in the peeling of the skin from the bodies of the dead animals. But was that very skin which was transformed into leather, which, as Jambhavantha (the ancient Madiga god) rightly said, became the early protection of all human bodies from both natural hazards and dishonor. We shall see later how the science that transformed skin to leather and from leather to commodities remains one of the earliest science and technological systems of India. It is important to know how it became possible for Indian Brahmanism to construct a philosophy of superstition that legitimizes the survival instinct to live without working, to eat without involving oneself in the process of the production of that very food itself. Though this instinct is common to all human beings, the Brahmans of India acquired it in an uneven proportion. This caste constructed for itself a genetical self, which saw everything upside down. It saw knowledge as ignorance and ignorance as knowledge. It branded what was divine as that of the devil and embraced devilishness as divinity.

ANIMALS AND FOOD

The Madiga and Mala castes nurtured all domestic animals, for they knew that the village could be productive only when human beings and animals were able to co-exist. A village becomes a village only when the animals, humans and birds live together in that space. Living automatically follows death. When animals and humans die, their bodies must be removed and buried—otherwise, the village would suffer. This process of removal of dead bodies is both scientific and spiritual. Those who understand the process and handle it are wise, and those who do not understand it are fools, or crooks. The Madiga/Chamar communities understood the significance of this and began to execute it as a socially useful and scientific process. And that is where the survival of this nation lay, and still does.

In Hindu India, these communities have been traditionally condemned for eating beef. The Indian civil society must learn that all human beings have always been beefeaters. Engels, in a summation of L. H. Morgan's *Ancient Society*, said that after human beings learnt to eat beef, there was an enlargement of the brain. Scientific experiments and studies have proven that only beef has 21 per cent protein. It is possible that before beef became the staple food, human beings died of hunger. It is a known fact that the whole world eats beef as a preferred food, whereas the Brahmanical society condemned it as the food of the unworthy. While some people are well within their civil societal right not to eat certain varieties of food, if they construct negative theories about positive experiments of people in the course of human evolution, the entire society suffers as such theories stall the development of the society. This is precisely what Brahmanism has done. No god in the world condemned beef as spiritually inferior food. No god said that vegetables do not have life. The Brahmans constructed this hierarchy of food out of thin air, for the purpose of construction of a social hierarchy. Therefore, we must ask—how can some people's food cultures be constructed as polluting? What is the significance of such principles of purity and pollution in a spiritual theory? How does one describe this 'purity' and 'pollution' anyway?

It is important to note how and why the Dalits of South India, even in villages where there were no Muslims, retained this food economy and culture, despite opposition and abusive rejection from the other castes. Was it merely economic compulsion, or was it a sense of self-respect and the conviction regarding their tastes and life processes that made them persevere? It is clear from their writings today that within their own *wadas*, they dismissed others for their ignorance of the taste of beef. They said, *brahmanlaku yemi eruka batuku ruchi*, or 'what do brahmans know about the taste of life?' Jambhavantha, who is considered older and greater than Brahma—the god of the Brahmans—in the oral spiritual discourses, explains how their civil societal relationships were positive, and superior to that of the Brahmans. Jambhavantha, in this discourse, is of the opinion that it was leather work that initiated industrial work in the whole universe. The culture of eating beef, according to him, was the most divinely ordained culture of people. There was no house where there was no leather, he narrates.

Neither the Brahman nor the Baniya house was leather free. All gods desired to be beefeaters and leather goods were loved even by them. The whole narrative of Jambhavantha, thus, runs counter to the Brahmanic cultural history. It constructs, in a remarkable way, the inclusion of the beef and leather economy of the Dalits in the divine world.

The beef culture of the Madigas and Malas—of all Dalits—of India is pre-Islamic and pre-Christian. In the rural areas in particular, the people had no knowledge that people in other parts of the world eat beef as well. While it is possible that the Dalits of India who embraced Islam and Christianity acquired cultural friends (for similar food cultures make friendships easy, and dissimilar ones keep people away from one another) after their conversion, but Islam and Christianity did not introduce them to beef. Rather, these communities familiarized them with the Indian variety of beef. The Hindu hatred of beef and the Islamic and Christian internationalization of the same might have resulted in the large scale conversion of Dalits into Islam and Christianity. Even in the face of condemnation and complete negation, they retained their food culture, with beef at its centre. In this sense, they are a perpetual link between the present and the past cultures of India. The post-Hindu nationalism, therefore, reframes the terms of discourse about Indian culture being not that of parasites but of producers and subaltern scientists.

THE MADIGA/CHAMAR CREATIVITY

The philosophical mystification of the economic process started with the construction of the Hindu socio-cultural myth around leather being considered unclean and anti-divine material. The Madiga *wada* had a contrary perspective on leather economy. In this perspective, the processing of leather was central to human existence and development. Rural civil society had always been a synthesis of agrarian production and village-centred industrial production, and the culture and art forms that had grown around these two productive processes. These techno-economic and science-oriented attitudes seem to have had their origin in the act of peeling off of the skin from the carcass and converting it into leather. Fierce resistance to this techno-economic, proto-scientific process and creative philosophy, as evidenced in the technique of making leather, came from the 'self-centred spiritualism' of the Brahmanical forces, expressing itself historically in the form of caste.

A study of community and cultural discourses make it apparent that the war between the Brahmans and the Madiga/Chamars was bitter and long drawn out. It was a war of cultural economy, for the institutionalization of two opposite modes of cultures, civilizations and economic systems. It was a war between productive spirituality and parasite spirituality. The parasitic spirituality acquired more sophisticated war weapons because its whole thinking was centred only upon war. The Brahmanical forces perfected methods of killing the other by making war a divine dispensation. Its culture was produced out of a war-mongering spirituality. Its gods believed in killing the others and its writers believed in eulogizing beings who perfected the art of war and sex. The Madigas/Chamars, on the other hand, developed an expertise in making instruments and using them for human welfare. It is natural that all those who developed an expertise in war and diplomacy established their hegemony over those who built productive instruments and culture. The play of Jambhavantha that gets repeatedly enacted within the Madiga *wadas* constructs this narrative in a different way. This story tells us that war is inhuman and building war weapons is the task of a destructive mind. Of all the spiritual schools of the world, only the Brahmanic school portrayed war as a divine process—all other spiritual cultures, view an anti-war ethic as truly spiritual. Gautama Buddha and Jesus Christ are two great anti-war spiritual heroes, whereas Rama is the very opposite of them. Jambhavantha too believes in an anti-war ideology. The story of Jambhavantha quite elaborately relates an anti-Brahman narrative and tells us of the great Dalit culture of production and humanitarian values. It makes the leather economy central to its philosophy, and includes labour as the central agency of human development. Any protracted form of production survives in a combination of philosophical perseverance and the socio-economic necessities of existence. The Madiga/Chamar continuation of their leather economy is a part of the same tradition.

CONSTRUCTION OF LEATHER INDUSTRY

The Madiga *wadas* evolved a full-scale procedure for the transformation of skin into leather and of leather into a commodity. This process needed a mind that could cut through the myth of leather being impure and set it up as a cottage industry in India. The Madigas/Chamars achieved the skills to establish this industry over a period of thousands of years. It involved, of course, some mind-boggling experimentation with animal bodies and the methods of peeling the skin off the bodies. My discussions with Madiga tanners living in remote villages revealed that they kept experimenting, proving and disproving until a common theoretical formula could emerge for a prototype. Verifiability was an integral part of the

Madiga experimentation, as opposed to the ritual mode of Brahmanical spiritualism. Offerings of water, ghee and other foods are made to the gods with no verification of what is happening to the offered substances. On the other hand, the efficacy of ingredients like salt, bark, lime had to be established first in order to turn the wet skin—which would otherwise rot—into sustainable leather. This process has a humanitarian dimension. It becomes a process of survival for all.

The rapid entrenching of the caste system denied the Madigas/Chamars the facility of writing down that formula, which, in itself, is quite complicated. If Brahmanism had not banned education for these subaltern scientists, they would have recorded that process several centuries ago. In the absence of a written mode of communication among the Madigas/Chamars, they used their memory to transmit the formula to future generations verbally, as oral tradition. This was the main difference between the science of the Indian Madigas/Chamars and that of the cobblers of the West. The latter had the advantage of a written formula, codified by their ancestors. This fact is at the heart of the major advances made by the Western industrial economy. The leather bags, buckets and ropes, which were the primary requirements for agrarian operations, found their formations in that knowledge system. In India, that knowledge system was forced to remain in the form of orature, which curtailed the scope for advanced synthesization and hybridization.

The mode in which the skin gets peeled from the dead body of the cattle involved a whole process of building up of knowledge, which required certain skills. Peeling the skin without making holes in it required proper cultivation of hand- and knife-usage skills in a highly advanced manner. It was perfected in generational experimentation. Once a standard procedure was established, teaching that procedure to the next generation involved another mode of training skills. This teaching was not merely theoretical but also practical. The lab of a Madiga/Chamar community was the open field where he/she would post-mortem the body of a cow, a bull or a buffalo in order to acquire and impart the knowledge of peeling skin from the body of dead cattle. This, in itself, is a sophisticated and dynamic process. The skill of full use of knife and hand to peel off the skin from the body involves a method of training. This method was standardized centuries ago and was handed down from generation to generation.

The scientific role of salt in keeping the wet skin from rotting was discovered by the Madigas/Chamars several centuries ago, and it still remains the primary condition of tanning in the Madiga/Chamar *wadas* of the remotest villages where nothing is known about modern tanning processes. The salted skin is dipped into the powdered mixture of the bark of the *tangedu* plant. This process continues for about 15 days. The tanners taste the sourness of the water every day. With each passing day, the skin absorbs some of the chemical content in the *tangedu* water and begins to stiffen into leather. The semi-leatherized skin is then put into a tub of lime. Within another week, it transforms into leather. It is then washed clean in a stream or a pond. This four-stage process of salting, dipping in *tangedu* water, soaking in lime and washing is the normal way of treating skin to change it into leather. To obtain a more sophisticated kind of leather, one final step remains. The Madigas use the dried and powdered fibre of a fruit called *karukkaya*. This fibre is boiled in oil and on cooling, it is systematically applied to the piece of leather in order to give it a polished, smooth and black look.

An odour, rather odd, is generated during the process of leatherization. But it is equally true that any industrial process, whether modern or of the Madiga classical type, has a dual outcome in the form of a commodity for human benefit and the release of pollutants. The Brahmanical knowledge systems failed to assess this fact objectively and hence condemned the process. While civil societies in other parts of the world worked out a notional understanding of commoditization, which has an inherent tendency to release pollutants, the civil society in our country adopted a hostile stand. Due to the anti-science ethos of Hinduism, human beings who managed this process were labelled untouchables, condemned to social isolation and subjected to untold misery and indignities. Despite the social negation by the Brahmanical order, the Dalits of India understood the historical significance of keeping this process alive, as the very survival of human society depended on it. The price they paid for this was indeed heavy. But the battle with the casteist mind, on the one hand, and hostile nature, on the other, helped them build a strong philosophical fortress around them.

The Madiga/Chamar worldview is the epicentre of the Dalit–Bahujan philosophy. Mud and food are interconnected, just as pollution and purity are. One does not exist without the other. The narrative of Jambhavantha emphasizes that Brahmanism fashioned divinity out of nothingness, whereas Madigatwam forged it out of the conflict between purity and pollution. Divinity in this discourse comes to life in the form of commodity: leather. Life is not comprehended in terms of eating what exists in its pure form but as a constant struggle between separating the impure from the pure and commoditizing it for human utility and consumption. While Brahmanism advocated the notion that suffering should be avoided, Madigatwam believed that pain and pleasure go hand in hand in the process of life. There is no notion of pleasure without the notion of pain—they are closely interconnected. The night is not to be shunned but to be understood as a re-energizing period, for the day cannot exist without night. Extending the same logic to work, it can be said that there is both pain and pleasure in removing the dead body, in peeling the skin off and converting it into leather. For Hinduism, these are repulsive tasks. Dalitism on the other hand would consider them as acts of labour that give pleasure, for they exercise both the body and the mind. Besides, the process of the commoditization of skin has a dimension of spiritual attainment that is not individual but social. Leather, therefore, is a social commodity—purified by the community in the interest of the entire society.

The whole exercise of converting skin into leather, which is executed within the Madiga/Chamar *wada*, might involve some limited interaction with the Malas or other castes. This activity is conducted in a general atmosphere of civil societal hostility. Instead of constructing a textual basis for this knowledge system (which other religious societies of the West and East have done) Brahmanical textuality negated it, abused it and set ethical values against it. The roots of Indian economic development are embedded in this mode of Dalit interaction with the dead and the living. The dead in the Madiga notion come to serve the living by making their body or parts of that body a usable commodity. For them, they neither are ghosts nor devils. Brahmanism, on the other hand, treats every dead as potential danger to every living being. Hence, touching them is seen as carrying the deadly spirits of the dead along with the living, leading to untimely death of the living too. It is this mythical notion of all dead being dangerous that made the Brahmanical philosophy to be the most superstitious philosophy that the world had ever seen. The very opposite Madiga/Chamar notion of the dead, be it human or animal, which advocated interaction with the dead bodies in order to transform them into usable commodities, is the first form of science witnessed by the humankind. This understanding became the first foundation of our economic activity. Thus, the Madiga notion of development is both economic and socialistic, as opposed to the Brahmanical idea of development, which is measured in terms of self-survival, with a constant fear for one's life. Their struggle with nature to survive has been a natural one, because the fear of caste and untouchability has haunted them throughout their living history, the account of which they were never allowed to share with other human beings for centuries.

Leather and Agrarian Production

It is not an exaggeration to say that the agrarian revolution in India centred around leather instruments. The leather economy achieved two things that were crucial to human development. One, it produced instruments with which multi-dimensional agrarian development became possible, and two, it produced instruments that enabled human beings to harness nature and hence facilitate human life. The human effort to wage a war on nature—forests, uncultivable lands and mountainous regions—began with the confidence that the human body had a protection of leather clothes which the early humans wore. The war against nature was the most difficult war that the humans fought. To do so, what was essential was the confidence that one's own body has protection from the incisive attacks of nature. The leather-based household industry that the Dalits established provided human society with that confidence.

In transforming leather into a commodity, the Madigas used knowledge that is both creative and scientific. Along the way, they also fashioned their productive instruments. Even before a sophisticated knife system emerged, they worked with the hand and a wooden stick in tandem to separate the skin from the carcass, taking care not to tear the skin. It is an acknowledged fact that the evolutionary jump from apes to human beings took place with the effective use of the hand in the process of production. In India, the Dalit mode of using the hand in an advanced form and in a manner that establishes an early link between household industrial process and agrarian production seems to be reflected in stripping the skin off the carcass. Even today, a Madiga/Chamar has the training to separate the skin from the dead carcass with the help of a small stick. However, knives known as *chinna katti* (small knife) and *pedda katti* (big knife) are commonly used nowadays. The use of stone, then of wooden knives and finally, of iron knives, seems to have developed in India around the Dalit *wadas*. The specialization of wooden knife and iron knife made by carpenters (Vadrangis) and iron-smiths is a consequent development.

The most important instrument that the Madigas designed and developed in the process of advancing the leather economy was the '*aare* (a needle used to stitch shoes, etc) '. This instrument also passed through the phases of stone and wood and finally stabilized in form of iron. This instrument played a key role in shaping the leather into an agrarian usable commodity like leather ropes, bags and buckets and leather instruments like *chappals* and shoes. Its final form was that of the *dappu*, which might be termed the first musical instrument. They also took the help of carpenters and ironsmiths in shaping these tools. Division of labour among the Madigas, carpenters and ironsmiths was a progressive step, as it meant assignment of skilled work to different groups of people. If the caste system had not come to perpetually separate them, they could have become inter-marrying social groups. That would have resulted in an exchange of professional skills by hybridization of their knowledge system. Brahmanism forcefully stalled this process. The construction of advanced *aare* made a sophisticated stitching process possible. Over a period of time, the *aare* was developed in such a manner that it could be used to stitch leather by passing the thread through the holes made in it.

The other key instruments like the *rampe*, the *gutam*, the *teedgal*, the *sandan* and the *martole* require enormous designing and engineering skills. The Madigas struggled to fashion their instruments and make them more sophisticated. This process was far more complex than the construction and use of systems like *yagya mandapam* and *yaga kumbham*. While *yagya* involves self-negating processes, shaping leather instruments was a process of creating, re-energizing and developing the human essence. The human essence gets generated and regenerated when something is being transformed from one form into another. For example, there is in the process of transforming a piece of leather into a pair of shoes a transcendental experience of giving shape and birth to a new thing. A man's life becomes meaningful only in the process of giving shape, and finally giving birth to new things with the help of labour, whereas a woman's life becomes much more meaningful because she gives shape and birth to a new human being itself. This she does in addition to producing things with the use of labour. Patriarchy destroyed the human ability to advance in all fields by subordinating the doubly capable human being called woman. The whole process of leatherwork, which created a new thing from the body of a dead animal, is the most creative thing that happened in India in antiquity, perhaps the first creative thing that happened in this land and later elsewhere.

MARRIAGE BETWEEN IRON AND LEATHER

Another important achievement of the Madigas/Chamars was their struggle to connect leatherwork with iron technology. In order to melt the ore, the Madigas designed a very special and crucial instrument called the *kolimi-tithi* (this is the Telugu name) or the leather blowpipe around which iron smithing was done. The leather blowpipe was an advanced instrument, the making of which involved an essential principle of physics—that empty space sucks in air. The earliest blowpipe consists of a roundish leather sac, with its tail end getting extended into the hearth wherein a constant supply of air needs to be provided in order to keep it burning. The blowpipe sucks in air from the atmosphere and pushes it in a controlled manner into the hearth so that the iron ore rod that is placed under the coal gets heated at more than 200 degrees. After this it is beaten with another instrument (called *sammeta* in Telugu) in order to mould it into a useful agrarian implement. This process is followed in Indian villages till this day.

A major breakthrough in the design of the *kolimi-tithi* came about when a small hole was cut on the underside of the sac and a leather valve was stitched from inside. When the sac is pressed from outside it lifts the valve up and air gushes in. Air is pushed into the hearth once the valve closes. This technique ensures a constant and controlled flow of air. As a matter of fact, the leather blowpipe system gave a new turn to agrarian operations. This is the mechanism that operates in the human heart, which can constantly pump blood in and out. The Madiga scientists discovered such an air pumping mechanism several millennia back. And they applied that method to blowpipe in order to advance the production process and to develop an advanced technology of production.

Gradually, the blowpipe system was modified to reduce human labour within the cottage industrial process. There exist about four or five varieties of blowpipes, which are a combination of wood and leather. The principle, however, remains the same, with Madiga/Chamar scientific skills being central to the whole operation. Many industrial mechanisms were worked out based on the very same principle of physics, that if an empty space is created in the sac, that empty space gets occupied by air by pushing the valves arranged to the small holes. To understand this mechanism several centuries back was not ignorance. In fact, it was a process of pushing primitive science forward to post-primitive stages. A community that had acquired such knowledge would have been treated by other spiritual texts as God's chosen people—Brahmanism, however, treated them as the lowest of the untouchables, and constructed a false spiritual theory wherein it was said that the Madigas were fated to leatherwork because they had been condemned to ignorance by the gods. The fact is that when compared to Madiga/Chamar knowledge, the Brahmans pale out as the most ignorant people that India has produced.

LEATHER AND AGRICULTURE

The other important agrarian instrument in which leather played a central role was the irrigation bucket. The earliest form of irrigation in India was well irrigation, and the buckets used for that purpose were made of leather.

The Madigas designed various types of buckets by stitching leather into a round shape, with a tail to pour out the water. In fact, the Madiga leather buckets are the ancestors of the modern day buckets, tubs, and so on. These buckets made human settlement in villages which are far away from rivers possible. Digging of wells and drawing of water from those wells with the help of the leather bucket improved living conditions, and also agrarian production. In several villages, the process of drawing water with pure leather buckets, or with iron buckets having a leather tail to pour the water into a structured canal system is in vogue even today. The *mota* system of Telangana is based on this leather tailed buckets drawn by bullocks. The most effective use of underground water for the purpose of irrigation was done with this leather-centred technology.

The role of leather ropes in establishing a sustainable land tilling process has never been studied. Even today, the rope that is used to keep the plough and the yoke together, as the bulls drag the plough and furrow the soil, is made of leather. In Telugu country, it is known as the *varena*. The leaf blades or *baredakulu* with which the bulls are tied to the plough are also made of leather. The leather belts that the peasants use to tie up the cattle to a pole and varieties of leather belts that peasants use to decorate their cattle have enormous social and cultural value. Culture is a by-product of the process of utilization of commodities. Brahmanism defined culture in its own image, wherein the relationship between the Dalit productivity and peasant productivity were never examined. Indian culture was tragically shown to have existed in and around temples, but not in the image of those who built the temple—it was shown instead in the image of the Brahman, who occupied the space only to further his spiritual fascism. The essence of Indian culture in this mode became a laughing stock in all the books that the West had produced, except in the writings of Max Muller, who himself was an Aryan racist.

Apart from the agrarian ropes, the Madigas also made a hundred different varieties of leather bags for procuring and preserving grain. The use of such bags went beyond the caste barriers. Jambhavantha repeatedly says, 'There's no human being who doesn't use my leather. The Brahman and Baniya houses have no escape from my leather. Show me a house without use for my *vaar* (Telugu name for leather).' Leather bags were made for keeping water cool. Shepherds, cowherds and foresters would store water in leather bags. In ancient days, the leather bag was the only source of storage for oil, rice and all other grains. Whatever was stored in leather bags survived for a longer period of time, while retaining quality. Leather bags were the best refrigerators with regard to liquids. Shepherds, even now, use leather sacks for carrying water for longer distances. Who discovered all these utilities of leather bags? Naturally it was the Madigas/Chamars, the makers of such suitable sacks that refrigerated water. In our village system, the makers of the commodity were themselves the discoverers of their utilities. Brahmanism had little access to these knowledge systems—and yet, as a people, they took pride in the fact that they were people of knowledge.

The most commonly known, but as yet unexamined, instruments that played a revolutionary role in Indian human and agrarian operations are the *chappal* and the shoe. It would be interesting to consider the scientific skills that would have gone into the making of the shoe/*chappal* so that they suit the Indian weather conditions. While Indian conditions vary from region to region and from season to season, there are some common characteristics. In each region, the shoe/*chappal* makers made designs that were most suitable for that particular region, while retaining certain commonalties. In South India, which hardly faces severe winter, one sees a greater prevalence of open feet *chappals*. In North India, where the winter is quite severe and extends up to six months in some places, the Chamar community developed a great expertise in making several types of shoes and *chappals*. It was this knowledge of weather and geography that made them subaltern scientists, with a futuristic imagination. Without their knowledge of weather and geography, making suitable shoes/*chappals* would have been impossible. Even today, an average Brahman's understanding of geography and weather is not good and the weather department (that mostly has Brahman officials) has proved to be a national disaster.

SHOE AND SCIENCE

At the time the Hindu gods—Brahma, Vishnu, Indra, and so on—were waging wars against the *sudra* agrarian producers for not surrendering to their politico-spiritual autonomy, the Madigas/Chamars were producing a very advanced shoe/*chappal* which was worn even by the gods. Why did the Hindu divinity demonize the chappal/shoemakers? No other society seems to have produced human beings whose productive skills were as sophisticated as those of the Indian chappal/shoemakers, especially in the ancient period itself. If the textual descriptions and the paintings of Hindu gods are to serve as an indication, then the Hindu gods did, indeed, wear shoes. Who had made the shoes that the Hindu gods wore? Did the Brahmans make them? The Brahmanic knowledge system and written texts do not show that they possessed such a skill and knowledge at any point of time in history. The so-called *rishis* were said to have worn only wooden *chappals–padakollu*–as they did not want to touch the leather shoes made by the Madigas/Chamars. Such a social process of constructing sainthood is not an indication of spiritual wisdom but an indication of social stupidity–one only has to look at the spiritual culture they constructed. All the Hindu gods wore the very shoe that the Dalits made, and yet these gods had no respect for their labour and creativity. If the shoe/*chappal* was so untouchable, why did the Hindu gods deign to wear them? The *sanyasis* (hermit; often used in a similar connotation as 'sage') condemned the leather shoe and wore the wooden *padakollu*. But the *padakollu* could not be used by the peasants as they had to till the land, thus they had to wear leather shoes. But being influenced by the saintly class the peasants too started believing that leather shoes would pollute them. Since the Hindu saints were not engaged in productive work such as tilling they could wear the *padakollu*. The Dalit philosophy constructed the shoe/*chappal* not in order to go about indulging in gluttony and hoodwinking the people who build the very economy of the nation, but in order to increase production. The Hindu *sanyasi* life is a social negation of this philosophy. Brahmanism used everything as a mode of personal comfort–at the same time, denying that comfort to others was its ultimate objective.

The shoe/*chappal* invented by the Madigas/Chamars about 4,000 years ago fulfilled a key function in winning the land over for cultivation and habitation purposes. Tropical forests are difficult to penetrate without footwear. The making of the *chappal* involved a careful study of the foot structure of human beings, and the relationship between the foot and the toe. After much experimentation, they finally realized that it is the *gooda* and the *ungutam* that enable the footwear to stay in position. The production of the shoe that covered the whole foot was possibly a later development. If the vast and varied spread of the shoemaking Dalit communities across India and the available information about the shoe/*chappal* in ancient India is any indication, India was the most advanced country in the world in leather technology. But unfortunately, academic Brahmanism has never allowed Indian research to focus on such a serious area. In no nation does research operate in such a vacuum as it does in Indian laboratories, because Brahmanism treated research as a threat to its continued existence and dominance. As a result, a positive inquisitive mind did not develop in the Indian universities headed by Brahmanic forces.

Indian priestcraft delegitimized the *chappal* as *chandala padartha*. It never acknowledged that the skill and human energy demanded by *chappal* making was far more complex than the *puja* process. Due to this spiritual delegitimization, the Komati *shahukar* (literally, a person dealing in money) in the village never stocked the *chappal* as a saleable commodity, regarding it as un-Hindu; the Brahmin priest never allowed it around the temple. In fact, Komati shops did not sell leather goods at all. The Madigas had to sell these from their own shops. No other religion considered leather anti-spiritual in the way Hinduism did; no other religion rendered the shoemakers untouchable. Institutions may certainly frame rules for leaving shoes/*chappals* outside, so that the dirt carried by the footwear is not carried inside, but a nation that renders leather—which is one of the key ingredients of the economic development of the nation—socio-spiritually untouchable cannot progress very far. Such perverse spiritualism killed the scientific temper of the nation and hampered the whole developmental process.

The Madigas/Chamars suffered a double alienation due to this negative spirituality. Their scientific energies did not gain the enormous social support they deserved; instead of becoming the most respected of all social beings, they were forced to be the lowest of even the untouchables within the civil society. Their social alienation forced them to become more and more withdrawn from the civil society. Their skills in science and technology were stilted. Furthermore, they were alienated from the history of their own scientific knowledge because for several thousand years it was not considered respectable enough to be chronicled in written texts. Because of this social untouchability, the hybridization of the Madiga knowledge system did not take place. India as a nation needs to become aware of the fact that it is because of this alienation that the West—which at one point of time possessed little knowledge of leather science in comparison to India—managed to overtake Indian leather production, leaving the country far behind global standards.

DAPPU: INDIAN MUSIC, ART AND CULTURE

Contrary to the popular notion, which claims that language, song, music and art were developed for leisure, music and art are organic expressions of the processes of labour and production. The Dalit–Bahujan belief that *pani* and *paata* (work and song) are part of *shudra* philosophy or Dalit philosophy, and *chaduvu* and *sandhya* (reading and praying) are defining features of Brahman philosophy has significant philosophical implications for the formation of culture. Song and dance, which became a part of human existence in the tribal stage, was meant to lighten the burden of work and to re-energize people so that they could get back to creative and productive work again and again. These cultural instruments emerged in the productive communities as an organic process of expression of human productivity and creativity. A production process is not a social process, but a creative process. At each stage, the process needs to discover and rediscover the instruments of production, and also the instruments that sharpen human skills and sensibilities in the process of the humankind's struggle with nature.

A revolutionary achievement of the civil society of the plains was that it created an instrument of music along with many other instruments of production. The most creative manifestation of that process is the *dappu* (drum). This does mean that the tribals did not construct musical instruments. They too constructed musical instruments, but those instruments remained within themselves, whereas the *dappu* became an instrument of all communities, including that of the Brahmans. The *dappu* is an ancient instrument—the most ancient, in fact, in the formation of Indian art and culture. The *dappu*, again, emerged out of the Madiga *wadas*. The Madiga mode of *dappu*-making and its social use indicates how Madiga philosophy built an ideology of 'love all, hate none', as opposed to the Brahman philosophy of 'hate others and love the self'. It is this philosophy of 'love all and hate none' that made the Dalits the most humanitarian of all social servants. For this greatness of theirs, Brahmanism punished them by imposing untouchability upon them.

The technological know-how of *dappu*-making was both complicated and simple. The initial breakthrough was perhaps difficult, but later it became a common sense process within the Madiga *wadas*. For caste-cultural reasons, however, *dappu*-making remains a Madiga techno-economic activity even today. Since the Dalit *wadas*, in their struggle for self-sufficiency, could not depend on anybody within the village for exchange of cultural instruments, they constructed several such instruments on their own, which in the process became socially useful instruments, cutting across all caste boundaries. The castes above them used their instruments, but did not respond with adequate humaneness, despite what they took from them. Their outlook was essentially exclusivist. Thus, while the Brahmans produced their first book called the *Rig Veda* and made it a highly exclusive commodity, the *dappu* serves as a good example of a socio-cultural practice that is the very opposite. The Madigas constructed it and made it a commodity for all communities. It is this human value that expanded the cultural realm of India, and not the *Rig Veda*, as per the Brahmanical claims.

DAPPU AND SOUND

Dappu, as it is still used in villages, is entirely made of leather and wood. Its form indicates that it is a pre-iron age instrument. A strip of wood is bent to form a ring, with a leather rope that holds both ends together. Holes are made in the wooden ring and a highly processed piece of leather is stitched onto one side. As the leather dries, it becomes taut and produces a musical sound at the slightest touch. The *dappu* is slung over the shoulder with a leather rope, and with a *chitkana pulla* (a very thin stick) in the left hand and a *chirra* (big stick) in the right, the player beats the *dappu* in a rhythmic manner. The playing of the *dappu* is an artistic process. *Dappu* playing is mostly a collective process, but even individuals can play it with a single rhythm.

The *dappu* produces a melodious sound that spreads to a vast area along with the wind. Its rhythmic melody makes the social atmosphere very sacred and sensitized. In a village environment, in the company of green crops, swinging mildly in the breeze and birds singing their own melodious song, the music of the *dappu* produces an impression of social collectiveness. With the rhythmic sounds of *dappu* the whole village becomes alert, brought to its cultural orgasm. This is the only instrument which gets played both by men and women—overcoming barriers of patriarchy—for the excitement, pleasure and relaxation of all communities. Despite being treated as 'untouchable' in their day-to-day life, the Dalits open up their heart in social events, ignoring the arrogant behaviour of all the other castes who continually mistreat and humiliate them. In weddings, in house warming functions, in festivities of child birth and lamentations of death, the *dappu* becomes a social mobilizer, an instiller of the energy lost in the routine work of production and reproduction. Without the constant intervention of *dappu* music, people may very well have become mental wrecks given the kind of casteism that is practised in villages in day-to-day life.

The *dappu* serves an enormous social purpose even today, when so many modern musical instruments are available. *Dappu chappudu* (the music of drum) is considered auspicious on happy occasions like a wedding, or a festival or when a girl attains puberty. It remains integral to funeral processions. The *dappu* music reminds the mourners of the cyclical process of life. For all those born, death is inevitable—hence they weep for the dead and return afterwards to the normal processes of life. The mourners surrounding the dead body, when tempted to ponder over the futility of production and procreation in the face of the inevitability of death, are reminded by the *dappu* music that the feeling of *vairagya* (detachment from everyday life, renunciation) will not last long. Everyone will have to come back to the intercourse of production and procreation as a necessary part of life. The philosophical strength of the *dappu* music, thus, is immense. For centuries it brought people back from the depths of despair and restored the everyday processes of life.

The drum is also played on collective village occasions like driving evil spirits out of the village. The *dappu* is used to make public announcements (*dandora*); it was the only mode of announcing the dates of village functions, official announcements by the government, and so on. Thus it was/is an instrument of music and mass communication. Village folk working in the fields or grazing their cattle in nearby pastures and forests could figure out from the sound of the *dappu* whether it was celebrating a wedding, mourning a death or making a proclamation. No modern musical instrument can send such distinct messages through sound and music. If the announcement was about someone's death, people left their work and got ready to participate in the funeral procession. The whole Dalit *wada* participated in funeral processions of people of all castes, in spite of the fact that they were treated as untouchables, even during such funeral processions.

The humanness of human beings is truly expressed only at the time of the death of a person. The Dalits mourn the death of even the cruelest of their oppressors with a forgiving heart. Both *dappu* music and the participation of Dalits in funeral processions, even that of their oppressors, is the greatest communitarian heritage in India. The Brahmanic culture on the other hand is the very opposite of this Dalit cultural life. A Brahman does not participate in the funeral procession of others—he weeps for no one. But after the dead body is taken away with melancholic drum music, and after the family of the dead person is made to reconcile with the fact of the death of his/her dear kith and kin, the Brahman makes an appearance. He comes in the form of a priest to take away the products of the labour of the dead person, left behind for the wellbeing of his dear ones. He tells the family that it would be necessary for the satisfaction of the departed soul. By feeding the priest, he says, they would also feed the dead person. He recites the *mantras* incomprehensible to all and asks for *dakshina* (payment) in the form of rice, pulses, vegetables and finally *godakshina* (payment in the form of a cow). He does not stop there—he asks for money, and sells the cow for money as well. And as the kith and kin of the dead starve, the Brahman keeps eating in the name of God. A *dappu* playing Madiga does the opposite. Money is not important for the Madiga collective who play the drum and dance in front of the dead body, taking the burden of death upon themselves. They, thus, perform a divinely ordained function, and the drum thus becomes the most divine apparatus in the village economy.

In weddings and other family functions, *dappu* music is meant to enhance the pleasure of the people involved in the function. There is a philosophical understanding among the Madigas that the music of pleasure is important for enhancing human energies. They have, thus, developed multiple modes of music that develop human personality. In this regard the *dappu* played a key role in constructing cultural values among village folks.

Ironically, while the Hindu social system used the *dappu* for all collective and individual purposes, the *dappu*-maker and the player had no socio-economic value. Its scientific design was never accredited, its artistic value never acclaimed. Though the instrument was designed by the Madigas and they are the ones who play the *dappu* (in Tamil Nadu they are called the Pariahs), it served the socio-cultural purposes of all castes. The sound was used to sustain the social spirit of all. While the makers and the players of the *dappu* and the instrument itself were defined as untouchable, the sound, nevertheless, was considered pure and used for divine and spiritual purposes by the Brahmanical castes as well. Even the Communist school of thought, dominated as it was by the upper castes, deployed the *dappu* for political propaganda and cultural movements but never thought it important to attempt to bring about a change in the social value of the maker and the player. There is a grand cultural narrative in the history of the *dappu*. The art historians, most of whom were from Brahmanical backgrounds, missed out on that grand narrative.

SINGING AND DANCING

Playing the *dappu* is not an individual activity in the Madiga *wadas*. Everyone, right from a child to an aged person, knows how to play it. The sound of the *dappu* lends itself with great ease to singing and dancing. Brahmanism did not allow group singing consisting of all castes and group dancing because they saw a danger to the caste system in group activity. If group dancing and singing, consisting of members of all castes, was allowed, then the subsequent social intercourse would pose a serious threat to the spiritual sanctity of social untouchability that Brahmanism had constructed over time. Brahmanism thus injected a deadly fear into the process of humans entering into close social intercourse. With a fear of touching the other, they cut short the human life itself. But the Dalits sustained it and developed it. This is known as *dappu kotti darveyyi* (dance and play the dappu). A Madiga combines several skills and arts with himself/herself. The

Malas also participate in these arts, and that is the reason why even among the Communist parties, the cultural activities are left to the Madigas and the Malas while the ruling of the party and of the state is taken over by the upper castes. The *Hindutva* parties, of course, use all the skills of the Dalit people for their own spiritual, social and political ascendancy, without granting them any human dignity.

The status of the Madigas is thus akin to that of the shoe and the *chappal*. If the *dappu* is used as an instrument of liberation, the status of Dalits working in all these parties—Communist as well as *Hindutva* parties—may change slightly, but they will not be completely liberated till they overthrow Brahminism in all walks of life.

Many of the musical instruments of the other castes have their roots in Madiga leather technology and designing skills. The *dolu* and the *jaggu* that the Yadavas/Kurumas use have a kinship with the *dappu*. The *maddela* (the drum instrument used in Carnatic music), the *tabla* and the harmonium, regarded as Brahmanical instruments, owe their existence to the *dappu*. These caste-specific instruments do not have any downward mobility. They are used by people within their own caste functions. It is interesting to note that caste hierarchy created a system that alienated even the leather instruments that were produced by Madiga skills. But once the scientificity of this community is realized, many social forces may galvanize around these subaltern scientists.

The Brahmanical attitude to leather instruments, whether of agrarian production or of cultural recreation, was to use these instruments for their own advancement, even as they delegitimized their value and the knowledge used to make them. Art, music and culture deriving from the Hindu worldview centre on love, lust and violence, and images that are involved in such processes. The Brahmanic notion of love and divinity are casteist and based on individual-centred pleasures. Even the musical instruments that are played to express these emotions, such as the *veena* (plucked string instrument used in Carnatic music), the *mrudangam* (a kind of drum; the primary percussion instrument in Carnatic music) and the *murali* (the flute) do not send aesthetic messages to create egalitarian cultures. *Brahmanatwam* hegemonized the *veena* and dance forms like the Bharatanatyam, which express Radha's unattainable desire to unite with Krishna. In this mode of aesthetics, there is no scope for liberation, even at the spiritual level. On the contrary, *dappu* music and song have a communitarian appeal, and its aesthetics do not hinge on man–woman love in the patriarchal mode.

In the present context of the identity formation of the Dalit-Bahujan castes, the *dappu* has become a powerful symbol for decasteization and egalitarian values, as evident in the manner in which Dalits deploy it and the Madiga Dandora movement uses it to carry forth their politico-ideological struggles. But these movements did not utilize the social mobilizational ability of the *dappu*. It still commands the consciousness of the Indian villages, but it must be played by projecting its own image. As long as socially oppressed forces do not construct their own image with all their strength, they will not challenge the enemy. The cultural realm plays a key role in challenging the Brahmanic forces, and the *dappu* plays an important role in the socio-cultural and ideological struggle.

During the struggle for independence, the *veena* and the *murali* were projected as cultural instruments of inspiration. Children were named after them. The Dalit struggle to reformulate national cultural symbols is going to have serious implications for Indian material and spiritual development. The Dalit–Bahujan aesthetic that is expressed through the *dappu*, *daruvu* and song have a tremendous potential to rebuild the scientific spirit of the nation. The *dappu* must, therefore, become the cultural symbol of India. If Dalit politico-cultural movements establish their hegemony, then children might also be named after the *dappu*. The names of people indicate the direction of the society. As long as Brahmanism remains at the centrestage of the Indian society, the society will never acquire the strength to mobilize all its scientific abilities. To re-energize ourselves, we have to read and re-read the history of the socio-economic energy of the Madigas/Chamars of India. The Indian society must understand the subaltern scientific basis of this caste community. Based on this new understanding of the role of Madigas, we shall examine the role of Malas in the next chapter.

Chapter 3   Productive Soldiers

In our journey, we enter the Mala (Mahars in Maharashtra; there are equivalent castes in all north Indian states) *wada* immediately after crossing the Madiga *wada*. They inhabit the same social space as the Madigas—untouchables—as Hinduism has termed them. How did the Malas, who, for centuries, have been treated as untouchables, contribute to our rural socio-political economy, culture and philosophy? A consideration of the narratives and dictums that form the Mala societal discourse, however, has the potential to reconstruct the Malas as a community involved in a whole range of tasks, such as village defence, agrarian production and weaving—activities meant to sustain, stabilize and develop the village system. In other words, they functioned both as soldiers and as agrarian engineers, assisting the village community to forge strong bonds with nature. The Malas were crucial in achieving this balance, thereby creating the essential conditions for living and the institutionalization of the village system.

In its earliest phase, the village economy hinged on common land. The Malas were not only opposed to private ownership of land, but also showed a strong inclination for collective property. One may find sufficient evidence of this in their contemporary living process, and also from their day-to-day discourses. The Brahmanical system, on the other hand, set up its hegemony by creating private property in the form of *agrahara* land that had the sanction of the king who resided far away from the village. Strangely, the Brahmanic books spiritually and legally permitted the Brahmans to own any amount of property. And the very same books denied the right to property to those who brought the land and labour into a procreative alliance. The Mala mode of life shows that the early village economy was structuralized with their innovative involvement. This early village economy needed a group of committed people who would protect the demarcated boundaries and prevent others from laying claim to the land and crop—an attitude that had its moorings in the philosophy of collectivism. The Malas seem to have been the people who, in their constant interaction with nature and natural beings, developed an understanding of the agrarian processes and of the fact that the whole process needed a collective struggle against nature. Winning a battle against nature was more difficult than winning any battle against fellow human beings. They believed that human collectivity alone was the essential prerequisite to win battles against nature.

THE VILLAGE SOLDIERHOOD

The village formation required a defence mechanism. This mechanism, in the beginning, was probably meant to protect the human collective—the village—from deadly animals. It is perhaps at a much later age, after the invasion of Indian land by the Aryan invaders, that it evolved into a mechanism to defend the productive villages from the war-mongering Brahmanic forces. The responsibility of the defence was shouldered by the Mala communities. The extreme inimical relationship between Brahmanism and the Malas—in which the Malas were brutally pushed to the lowermost rung of the society and branded untouchable—is an indication of this history, rooted perhaps in the early resolve of the Malas to defend the village system from Brahmanic invasion and from the anti-production philosophy they were setting in motion. Otherwise, how does one explain the reduction of an entire agrarian community—whose identity remains, even today, centred around agrarian labour—to untouchability? The Madiga untouchability was justified by the Brahmanical texts by constructing a theory of ritual impurity around leatherwork. Assuming, for the sake of argument, that such a stance on leatherwork was indeed (following the Brahmanical theories of ritual impurity and leatherwork), how does one define the relegation of the Malas—a community which was never very intimately connected with leatherwork—to the status of untouchability? The most fundamental reason for this seems to be the inimical mindset of the Brahmanic forces towards the productive process. The Brahmanical self, historically, has been constructed with an anti-productionist bias. The militant Malas played a key role in opposing the anti-production ritual campaigns that the Brahmans as a people and Brahmanism as ideology undertook over a period of time. Even today, defence squads like *ellollu*, *kavalollu* and *talarollu* (these are Telugu names for such squads) comprise largely of people from the Mala community in Telugu villages. Where there is no Mala presence, the Telagas and the Mudirajus take the responsibility of protecting the villages. The collective defence of the Mala mode does not express itself in violent methods. In their philosophical realm, weapons were merely symbols, not instruments for creating conditions of violence. In actual fact, the weapons used by the *kavalollu* were made of wood and were meant to induce a sense of security and infuse confidence within the village community. The marked preference for Buddhism displayed by the Malas of the Telugu country and the Mahars of Maharashtra after 1956 is a reflection of their anti-violence and egalitarian culture. The *karra* or *katte* (lathi) is both a defence weapon, as well as a service instrument. It has a double-edged knife at one end that transforms an ordinary staff into a deadly weapon called the *kathi-karra* or *barsha*, which can kill both by piercing and hitting. The *barsha* is also used to clean irrigation canals in order to ensure the smooth flow of water. Many also deftly wield the *kathi* (knife). Even the *kathi* is a weapon with double utility, which can be used for self-defence as well as hunting. But a slightly modified mode of the *kathi* becomes the hook, which is used to cut the crop and weed out waste plants from the crops.

MALA PHILOSOPHY OF DEFENCE

The Mala notion of defence was radically different from that of the Kshatriyas. The Kshatriyas believed in *rajya rakshana* or in the protection of the royal kingdom, not of rural communities. The role of Kshatriyas was akin to that of a standing army. The Kshatriya understanding of defence—endorsing the notion of full-time soldiering—found its parallel in Brahmanism, which assigned the task of full-time priesthood to the Brahmans. The Kshatriyas had, in the name of defending the state, built a war-mongering standing army to invade the neighbouring states. The Brahman priest was a constant instigator of war, and the Kshatriya king was a constant killer. The Hindu Kshatriya killer gods were constructed in this process, in order to grant spiritual sanction to wars and killing. Over a period of time, these two castes specialized in an exploitative mode of governance and distanced themselves from any form of productive activity. Anyone who dared to suggest the involvement of the Kshatriya–Brahman combine in production activity was considered to be a violator of *dharma*. *Dharma* in Hindu thought, thus, may very well be termed as a mode of protection of the parasitical upper castes. If the spiritual weapon in the form of *dharma* did not work, they forced the ruling political agency to invoke *danda* (literally, law of punishment)—a brutal method of punishing the enemy. This method was constructed in the civil society in the name of defending the spiritual purity of the Brahmans, the Kshatriyas and the Vaisyas from the attacks of the Chandalas and the Shudras. Philosophically, the notion of *dandaneeti* (the mechanism for administration of punishment) was constructed to keep the Chandalas, the tribals and the Shudras out of the realm of reading and writing. The Malas or their equivalent communities all over the country seem to have fought against the system of *dandaneeti* quite militantly. As we have seen in the 1990 and 2006 Mandal struggles, the Brahmanic society, being more organized, and more ruthless in attacking the Dalit–Bahujans, also succeeded in every war that preceded the Mandal struggle. They involved modern form of *dandaneeti*.

Philosophically, the Mala system of defence had a very broad base. In addition to strengthening their physical prowess, they also had the responsibility of keeping the village clean, expanding agrarian lands, preparing cattle for agriculture, harvesting and threshing grain. Weaving was undertaken during non-agricultural seasons. The cloth weaving process seems to have been perfected by this community, much before a specialist caste called the Shalas (Padmashalees in the Telugu society) took up that job. Hence, the reference to 'Mala *neta*' (Mala weaving) is very commonly seen in many villages. The proverb 'Mala *neta* is older than Shala *neta*', indicates that the earliest weaving technology was developed by the Malas in India.

As part of their productive agrarian skills and weaving work and defence needs, the Malas evolved their own special brand of gymnastics-cum-martial exercises. These communities were involved in sports like *kabbadi*, long jump and high jump, climbing trees, target shooting of birds and animals and walking long distances. They assumed that sports, besides keeping one's muscles in excellent condition, would also strengthen one's productive energy and other commercial activities. The *karrasamu* or the stick-rolling exercise was central to this system. Most Mala men (though women are not excluded from acquiring this skill), are expert *karrasamu darulu* (stick rollers). In this routine, the muscles are trained to withstand extreme physical assault and strenuous work in the fields. It is an extraordinary technique that trains the individual to escape rain by rolling a stick and leaping about constantly. Though the early teachers of such martial arts were the Malas, they did not make this knowledge caste-centered. These arts were taught to anyone who wanted to learn. Admission to the gymnasium was free in this communitarian life.

The cultivation of such village arts made the village holistic. This, in essence, means we have had the culture of developing martial arts and gymnastic exercises around the Dalit *wadas* much before the Greeks developed them. But as time passed by, the communities that developed those processes were forced into untouchability; in the spiritual and social realms, their activities were constructed as Chandala activities. The whole Indian civil society, thus, lost the spirit of sports. Sports itself was seen as a Shudra and Chandala activity, and the Brahmanic forces condemned all such sports as unworthy of respect in the spiritual realm.

The Brahmans and the Baniyas as communities are anti-sports, both mentally and physically, even today. A true sports culture still survives only among the tribals, the Dalits and the Shudras of India. Since that activity itself did not have any spiritual and social status, the very culture of sports among the educated social forces did not find any respectability till the Muslims and the British came to India. The Brahman entry into sports is a very recent phenomenon. This trend was coupled with the forceful delinking of education from the social groups that have historically been skilled in sports, leading to their failure to modernize these skills. They could not propagate whatever skills they have in sports as the mass media was completely out of their reach. Furthermore, the culture of sports and gymnastics suffered a heavy blow with the campaign of vegetarianism. Even now, the social groups that are the best suited for high energy-consuming sports are the beefeaters. But even now, the Brahmans of India, as the latest debate on beef food culture has shown, are dead against granting spiritual and social dignity to the beefeaters of India. Because of this Hindu mindset, the best of our Dalit–Bahujan and Muslim youth do not get any place in the sports arena.

The Mala philosophy of defence was a holistic one. It defended the villages from plundering enemies. It believed in constructing a culture of sports and exercise. Historically, with the forceful entry of Brahmanism into villages, all such activity was rendered untouchable. And when the Brahmans began a campaign for vegetarianism, the consumption of meat—beef in particular—as anti-Hindu untouchable cultural philosophy, the very energy in India began to die. The Dalit-Shudra ideology fought against it, but because of the lack of the principle weapon of propaganda—education—in their hands, they lost the battle.

SPORTS AND FOOD CULTURE

The development of global sports and health systems is intimately linked to eating habits and cultures of exercise. It is a known scientific fact that of all meat products, beef contains the highest amount of protein. The Dalits of India, even in the face of opposition from the Brahmanic communities and the ruling Kshatriyas, retained that food culture, for physical requirement as well as for the sake of national health. India has the smallest sports base in the world because the upper castes and many Shudras had given up eating beef, owing to the massive campaign that Brahmanism took up against it. Those who persisted in maintaining that culture were condemned as 'uncultured'. But in fact, it is Brahmanical culture that promoted what might be called an 'uncultured' life. Brahminical lifestyle still remains detrimental to national health. Through the discourses that the Brahmanic writers have produced and reproduced, a mythical hegemony of vegetarianism has been constructed. The South Indian Dalits persist with their beefeating culture in opposition to this mythical hegemony, along with Muslims and Christians in the larger civil society. Beef is still treated as spiritually sanctioned food and a basis for good social health in the Dalit *wadas*. The whole of India needs to turn to this mode of holistic and energetic food culture. This process should be understood as Dalitization. It is Dalitization, and not Sanskritization, that remains the best course for the development of India in all fields.

The Malas appear to have been forced into untouchability by the Brahmin–Kshatriya communities after they specialized in the martial arts, because all such arts were rooted in day-to-day labour. The development of Mala expertise in certain war strategies was viewed as evil and harmful to upper caste interests. They therefore decided to limit every caste within a sphere—no community was supposed to go beyond the confines of their particular sphere. Many stories set in and around the Dalit *wadas* show that they had fought battles every day to philosophically sustain their Dalitism. The stories of Jambhavantha and Bethala in Telugu country exemplify this struggle. Similarly, the tribal youth Ekalavya had to cut his thumb as punishment for excelling in *banavidya* (bow and arrow fight). Beerneedu, a Madiga and the commander-in-chief of Katamraju's army, had defeated Khadga Tikkanna—a Brahman—but it is the latter's name that figures in history books as a hero. This is the diabolical design of Brahmanic historiography. The Hindu gods become heroes because they kill, but a Dalit who defeats a Brahman in war is not fit to be considered a hero. Truth, thus, becomes a victim in this kind of historiography. The ruling caste combine of India declared that only the Kshatriyas and the Brahmans could acquire proficiency in *bana-kathi vidya* (bow and arrow and knife wielding). The Brahmans, not being very warrior-like as a community, avoided war and preferred secure and risk-free work like priesthood and guruship to the Kshatriyas. The Malas went against the Brahmanic spiritual dictum in various ways, by learning even reading and writing clandestinely. The social roots of emergence of Ambedkarism lie in this mode of Mala anti-Hindu ideology, and a well spread network of covert and overt activities.

COMBINING PRODUCTION AND SOLDIERHOOD

While 'soldierhood' continued to be the main socio-political activity of the Malas, their present skill structures indicate that they also possess a vast knowledge of agriculture. There is enormous evidence to suggest that the Malas were also involved in developing the earliest techniques of agriculture. Hence, they are considered a caste of agrarian labour. After the village economy came into existence, food grains had to be produced repeatedly on the same patch of land. This required a systematic study of materials that could be used as manure to increase the fertility of the land. Mala women were adept at seeding, planting, weeding and cutting the crops. In fact, early village settlements were entirely dependent on their skills. The knowledge of soil–seed relationship and deploying the energy of buffaloes, bulls, cows and other animals for tilling the soil did not emerge out of the Brahmanical written texts or their oral tradition. Neither their written texts nor their present knowledge systems contain any evidence of their involvement in agrarian production. Any caste or community that wants to live off the productive activity must invariably become an expert in manipulative politics—the Brahmans provide the finest example of this. The only matching instance in world history of a social force practising such deceptive socio-spiritual politics is that of the Pharisees of Israel. Jesus Christ fought a heroic battle against them. Similarly, Ambedkar staged his own heroic battle against the Brahmans of India.

Like the Madigas, who were experts in the process of transforming skin into leather, the Malas specialized in understanding the relationship between the seed and the character of the land. Mala agricultural science was more advanced than the tribal *podu* production, which was a shifting system, and its productivity levels were not high. Neither the hybridization of seeds nor the use of buffaloes and bulls in agriculture or the fertility of land was known to them. There is a proverb that says that the Mala hand turns the soil into gold (*Mala cheyyi matti bangaram chese cheyyi*). This is an indication of the centrality of the Malas in the agricultural process, which was so crucial to humankind's survival. This is the reason why the Malas appear to be a community that does not have a craft of its own. All the communities which turned to agrarian production appear to be non-artisanal in their skill base. The agrarian evidence available in the village system shows that the Malas possessed multiple skills, which made their role integral to the functioning of the village economy.

SCHOOLING ANIMALS

It is commonly known that the advancement of agriculture was closely linked to the training of cows, bulls and buffaloes to carry out agrarian tasks. The Malas had a central role in the schooling of animals according to generally applicable principles, so that other castes could also adopt the same methods. Such training required extremely specialized skills. This would have been violently opposed by the Brahmanical forces, as is evident from the differing attitudes of the Dalit-Bahujans and the Brahman-Baniyas towards the cow. For the Malas, the cow had a socio-economic function to fulfill. It was not only useful for agrarian tasks, but also provided milk and procreated. Therefore, the cow was nurtured with greater care than the bull. Brahmanism took a contrary view—the cow was considered a sacred animal, and hence barred from the performance of any task. Within the animal kingdom, thus, the cow was constructed as a Brahmanic animal by the Brahmans in their own mirror image. They never assigned any productive labouring work to the cow. They claimed that it produces wealth from nowhere. The false stories—that mere worshipping of the cow leads to immense wealth—were in fact constructed to take the cow out of the process of labour. The irony, of course, is that though they consider it a sacred animal, they do not nurture it. Feeding and washing the cow, cleaning the sheds and removing dung is again a Mala task. The proverb *Malintiki poyina aavu manchigai vastadi, brahminintiki poyina aavu batiki radu* (the cow that goes to a Mala home returns healthier and the one that goes to a Brahman's house does not come back alive) is illustrative of their differing treatment of cows and the hostility existing between the two castes. The former does not worship the cow but nurtures it, while the latter worships the cow and takes the milk but does not nurture it. The Hindu philosophy of animals runs counter to all other religious philosophies, for it projects the cow as an animal that does not require human care at all.

In reality, the Brahmanic treatment of cows is violent and brutal, and Dalitist or Shudra treatment of the cow is humane. The latter's killing of cows to use their flesh as food is a natural relationship between plants, animals and human beings. The greatest expression of humanity lies in the care and nurturing of cattle and plants from birth to death. The Brahmanical sin against the plant and animal kingdoms, as well as the human society lies in their refusal to participate in this nurturing, even as they live as parasitic consumers. It was this parasitic consumerism that lead to the evolution of a dominant Brahmanical culture that worshipped violence. The Mala life, on the other hand, provides an instance of an alternative mode of living, wherein human beings continually interact with nature and life in order to reproduce it again and again.

The wellbeing of the society is intricately connected to the well-being of all cattle—buffaloes, bulls, cows, pigs, chicken, and so on. The progress of human life is dependent on the progress of animal life as well. At the same time, using the flesh of animals for food is part of that progress. The practice of killing animals for food does not endanger the species so much as the culture of not nurturing them does. *Malatwam* does not differentiate between the cow and the buffalo, for both have their uses and serve humankind. *Brahmanatwam*, on the other hand, abhors the buffalo for its dark skin but loves and drinks its milk as it is white. This kind of differential treatment of both the milk-producing animals, even as they consume the milk of both without hesitation, is rooted in the Aryan racism of the Brahmans. The Aryan race, after all, believed that the colour white is beautiful and sacred while black is ugly and symbolizes the devil.

Training Cattle

Training cattle requires special skills and knowledge of animal psychology. Calves, bulls and buffaloes have to be handled with care. The cattle learn every task bit by bit. A Mala trainer puts a log across the bull's neck in order to train it to be a tiller. Animals resist this training to begin with. Sometimes they take fright and bolt or they simply sit and refuse to move. In the process of training, the animal has to be habituated to use its neck to carry weight for long periods of time. A cattle trainer needs to know the various mechanisms to train cattle to draw ploughs. A boil may erupt on the neck and develop into a wound. In such a case, the wound should be treated so that it does not weaken the animal. Once the yoke is placed on its neck, the animal has to be disciplined to walk. Initially, the trainer walks along with the bull—gradually, it gains enough experience and becomes a regular tiller by itself. The Mala tillers deserve special mention for they not only push the plough deeper and very close to the earlier furrow, but also drive the cattle in the right direction. But in spite of such training, if an animal misbehaves, the iron rod (*kaalu karru*) at the end of the plough hits the leg. Thus, the animal has the double burden of functioning within the discipline prescribed by the tiller and also investing its energy to drag the plough.

The cattle are also trained to pull the bullock cart loaded with grain and people. They have to be made sensitive to the driver's signals that are communicated through ropes called *paggalu*. For instance, they must understand when the driver wants them to turn, move forward, or stop. The Malas were, in fact, expert *paggalu*-holders as they were rope makers too. Many people from other castes are capable of training cattle today, of course, but the earliest trainers of cattle appear to be the Malas, who should also therefore, be seen as a productive agrarian caste.

Making the cattle draw water from agrarian wells is a difficult part of their training. This is indeed a central activity in arid and semi-arid regions. Bulls have to walk back and forth in order to fill buckets with water from deeper wells. This is known as *mota* driving. *Mota* poses an everyday challenge to the animal and to the man or woman who is handling it. A small error can land both the person and the animal into the well. This work process also demands double the energy that other agrarian activities require, which is why both the human and the animals which constantly perform this task end up looking frail. Though the Malas and the Madigas originally specialized in these tasks, people of other castes also handle them now. Except for the Brahmans, the Komatis, the Kshatriyas and some of the artisan castes like the Salas, the Kammaris and the Ausalas, all other castes have knowledge of cattle rearing, training and agrarian production.

The Malas did not believe in confining their knowledge systems to themselves. In fact, they are known for their openness, as is evident in the proverb *Mala noti mata neella muta* (the word of a Mala is like holding water in cloth). It indicates their willingness to communicate and disburse their knowledge to all. In the Indian caste system, knowledge from the below moved upwards without any hindrance. The Malas were willing to share their experience with all the castes above them. But the Brahmanic castes were never willing to learn from them. At the same time, they were not willing to allow the Brahmanic knowledge to flow downwards.

SOURCE OF THEIR KNOWLEDGE

Where and how did the Malas learn these methods of training cattle and developing agrarian science? There is enough evidence to show that their knowledge evolved out of a constant struggle with nature. Concepts relating to agrarian productivity were not handed down to them from the Vedas or from the Shastras. These were texts that addressed only the Brahmanical castes and did not seem to comprehend the organic relationship among soil, seed, humans and animals. Assuming that some Shastras did speak of agriculture, the language used was Sanskrit, which no Dalit–Bahujan could possibly understand. Thus, Sanskrit as a language never seems to have evolved the vocabulary of production and production-related science. The agrarian productive knowledge has grown within the languages of the masses, and to some extent Pali, which had some relationship with the production process. Sanskrit became the language of the elite. This is the reason why Sanskrit must be rejected as national language, as it has no productive ethic built into it. The Dalits and Shudras, in fact, can better relate themselves to English as a national language than Sanskrit. They must look up to English as a language of liberation instead of looking up to Hindi or Sanskrit. The Mala or Mahar experience in Andhra Pradesh and Maharashtra has enough evidence to show that once they could access English education through the means of the Church and Buddhist networks, quite a few leaders emerged from among them in many fields of life. Ambedkar himself had lead the way by learning English quite effectively.

BRAHMANISM, PRODUCTION AND POLLUTION

Brahmanical philosophy tended to categorize productive tasks as polluting. Conversely, the non-productive *puja*, with all its associated activities, was characterized as pure. For instance, the whole procedure of *puja* is based on consumption rather than production. The Malas had to battle almost on a day-to-day basis against the Brahmanical mode of spiritualism, which promoted a culture of consumption rather than that of production. Those who struggled to produce food from the soil were condemned as dirty, and their knowledge system was made invisible in written discourse on the pretext that there was nothing philosophical about it. The Malas contested this mode of Brahmanical oppression with a philosophy of production that was tellingly contained in the expression *okkithulo rendithulu* (two seeds in one). Their socio-cultural knowledge of the plant system told them that a seed could produce innumerable seeds, while human beings can produce only one child at a time (only occasionally more than one). The philosophical discourse of production survives in numerous proverbs that exist as a source of communication among them.

THE SCIENCE OF MANURE MAKING

There is a saying in the Mala *wadas*: *penta lenide panta raadu* (without dung-manure, no crop is possible). Contrast this saying with the Brahmanical attitude: *penta manushula antaraadu*—that is to say, 'those who interact with dung-manure should not be touched'. Both convey diametrically opposite notions of cultural economy. Malas, and other communities who lead similar lives, believe that *penta kuppa* and *panta chenu* (manure and crop) are inherently linked. *Malatwam* reasons out the close connection between mud and food, realizing the simple fact that humans must engage with filth (dirt, slush, slime) in order to produce food. This constant engagement with the outside world characterizes the Mala philosophy of existence. For instance, the producer of manure or the irrigator works in the larger interests of the society—their function is crucial for achieving socio-ecological balance. The Malas performed this task with tenacity and consistency. They saw manure as the source of crop, and began their task with that perspective—it was, therefore, inevitable that they had no qualms about soiling their hands.

On the other hand, the Brahmanical civil society would expect a good crop, but without being polluted themselves by the *penta kuppa* (manure system). In the name of divine purity, the *penta kuppa* was negated by Brahmanical philosophy as a pollutant that marred spirituality. A *sanyasi* who withdraws from society for his personal ends—that is to say, the achievement of *moksha* (freedom from cycle of birth and death)—epitomizes *Brahmanatwam*. The Brahman does no productive work whatsoever, but somehow expects that food should come to him from the very same civil society that he abuses as impure. This mode of human existence denies all advancement, and that is the reason why texts written by *sanyasis* do not contain any positive productive knowledge. Whatever knowledge they constructed pertains to self-aggrandizement and self-attainment, but never involves the consciousness of a social collective. The productive social collective is an untouchable, invisible mass for them. Thus, the Brahmanical philosophy operates in opposition to all other religions—Buddhism, Christianity and Islam. In those religions, a full-time spiritual activist works through regular intercourse with the productive social collective, as that is also taken as a work of God. The more he/she becomes a servant of the social collective, the more spiritually liberated he/she becomes. But in Hinduism, the philosophy of a spiritual saint works in opposite direction. A Hindu saint should not touch and should not sit with the productive social collective.

WHAT IS *PENTA KUPPA*?

What is the *penta kuppa*? How does it take form? It is interesting that animals also have a major contribution in the making of the *penta kuppa*. It is closely related to keeping the living space—home, the street or the village—clean. *Penta* is a classical form of manure that is prepared in deep pits. The main ingredients that go into it are—dung from domestic animals; their fodder remains, such as dry grass, green grass and *choppa* or jawar stems; human excreta; and other organic wastes that decompose to form manure. Leftover food that could not be consumed is also dumped into the *kuppa*, in sharp contrast to the Brahmanical attitude towards leftovers, which believes that they are pollutants and should therefore be shunned. Most of this work is handled by the Malas (and also the Madigas) in Andhra Pradesh.

The process of decomposition inside the *penta kuppa* releases odorous gases with a higher percentage of carbon dioxide and carbon monoxide, which do have harmful effects on the human body. The solution that *Brahmanatwam* offered to this problem was to reject the idea of *penta kuppa* itself. Negating this interaction with *penta kuppa*, however, is a negation of life itself, for the *penta kuppa* is symbolic of the relationship that exists among manure, soil, plants, humans and animals. *Malatwam* sought the assistance of logic and reason to find ways and means of reducing the ill effects of these gases. Within the limits of its own knowledge of science and hygiene, it stipulated that hands, legs and feet should be washed clean after any interaction with *penta* and *panta* (crop). The relationship between *penta* and *panta* is an organic relationship. Human society, spiritual or otherwise, cannot abandon or hate that process. A positive spiritual philosophy has to deepen that relationship. At the same time, the ill effects that this involvement with crop and manure has upon the human being who performs these tasks must be overcome. This must be done with the help of science, which is also an integral part of a positive, progressive religion. This is where Hinduism as a religion has failed to move towards the direction of becoming a positive religion. The Dalit life process provides a positive direction to evolve and adopt a positive religious course as well, as it does not see any contradiction in production of manure and its link with God's spiritual realm. Further, a spiritual ideology has to interact with scientific processes, as spirituality and science are closely related. The Mala mode of thought possesses that understanding of the relationship between science and spirituality—that is why the Malas spent their days working in the fields and making manure and went to the temples that they built near the village in the evenings. The Hindu temples, on the other hand, do not allow any productive community to set foot inside them.

MALAS AND IRRIGATION SCIENCE

Much before the tank or canal irrigation system evolved, paddy crop was grown close to the village through a system that was devised to channelize used water flowing through the village into the fields. Hence, the saying, *vurenbadi polam karchuleni phalam* (a paddy field near the village yields fruitful crop without any expenditure). It is this 'dirty water' that yields the crop. The Malas are referred to as *neeratikandlu* (those who water crops), or those who monitor and channelize water in the fields. Working in this kind of muddy water mixed with manure must have had serious implications upon their health. But this irrigation process was central to the survival of the village. The Malas, thus, persisted in doing the work, with the futuristic vision that the society as a whole was larger than any individual or community. Thus, they have historically invested their labour in a work of hazardous nature, in the interest of the society at large.

The Malas were experts in tank construction, which involved heavy labour, both physical and mental. Their engineering skills can be gauged from the location of the tank itself. The tank was always between two hillocks with space for irrigation. The *ayacut* (*chikham*) was on the periphery of the village, and the irrigated land under that particular tank covered the maximum possible area of village land. The *tumulu* (water releasing gates) were arranged at places where the downward flow of the water becomes easy. It was also ensured that the water gates were capable of drawing the entire water from the tank bed and irrigating most of the land. Even today, expert knowledge in production of manure, canal construction, monitoring irrigation and understanding the land demarcations called *gatlu* or *voddlu* lies with the Mala and the Madiga communities. The Mala *neeratikandlu* know better than any other agrarian workers how much water level should there be in each paddy patch with *gatlu* on all sides.

MALA WEAVING

Besides engaging in food production, evidence available in Telugu villages shows that the Malas also discovered the method of weaving cloth. The earliest producers of cloth were the Mala *netagandlu* (weavers). They were alienated from the process of cloth production when caste demarcations became evident in civil society. The Salas, who are an advanced community of cloth weavers, came into existence later. Cloth production went through several stages in India. In the first phase, jute cloth or *nara batta* was produced; the second phase involved the making of *pathi batta* or cotton cloth; and silk or *pattu batta* was woven in the third phase. In the Telugu country, the knowledge of weaving all three types of cloth and also building up the relevant technologies for their production was developed by the Malas.

The Brahmanical knowledge system did not recognize cloth production as a significant skill. Their concern for cloth was merely at the level of consumption. Quite interestingly, the best cloth in every age was used by adherents of Brahmanism. All Hindu deities are shown to have worn silk *dhotis*, while the upper part of their body remains uncovered. Some *sanyasis*, even today, live naked in their pursuit of Hindu spirituality. The Brahman priests and Shankaracharyas also remain semi-naked. For a long time in Indian history, the Dalit masses remained semi-naked for they did not have clothes to wear. Brahmanism, with the help of legal codes like Manudharma, prohibited them from wearing clothes. Till mid-nineteenth century the Dalit women in Kerala were not allowed to cover the upper parts of their bodies. In the Dalit spiritual sphere, however, the images of gods like Jambavantha, Pochamma, Katta Maisamma exist neither in nakedness nor wearing silk clothes as indicators of spirituality. No Dalit priest needs to present themselves in semi-naked form. Just like Islam, clothe in Dalit philosophy are seen as necessary to human existence and wellbeing.

DALIT PHILOSOPHY OF DEAD BODY

The Malas have a definite philosophical position on the human body, whether living or dead. In fact, their position is an extension of the Madiga mode of understanding of the body. Though they were relegated to untouchability in the society, the Mala and the Madiga discourse on the human body signifies a positive attitude. They believe that since all human bodies are constituted of flesh and blood, no body can be considered untouchable. They repeatedly ask: 'Is water, instead of blood, flowing in our bodies?'

For the Malas and the Madigas, all bodies are touchable and all living bodies have a language and a psychology. All these bodies can touch and exchange goods, commodities and ideas with one another and live in a state of social unity. Brahmanism takes a contrary view. It claims that some bodies are spiritually different from others, and hence their physical existence should remain exclusive and distinct and others' bodies should remain untouchable to them. Though there was (is) no rational basis for this exclusivity, it was imposed on social communities in a hierarchical order. The idea of this mode of separation must have originated in the Aryan notion of colour difference. Historically, segregation by colour was the first form of segregation, and all other forms of segregation followed. Caste, too, emerged out of this mode of segregation. The untouchability that the Malas and the Madigas suffered is an extreme form of segregation that Brahmanism created in order to delink all forms of science, spirituality and productivity. It was in this process that Brahmanism made even the dead human body untouchable, by prohibiting all forms of anatomical examinations.

Dalitism (of the Malas and the Madigas), with its broader philosophical and humanitarian worldview, came to the rescue of the rest of the society by their timely disposal of the dead bodies. But for Dalitism, neither the Brahmans nor the neo-Kshatriyas (Reddys, Velamas and Kammas) or the Bahujans (Other Backward Castes—OBCs) would have remained safe on this earth. Even the Bahujans were influenced by Brahmanism as they lost the courage to handle their dead during epidemics of cholera, small pox and other dreaded diseases. It was the Mala and the Madiga castes that showed tremendous courage in removing the dead from villages and urban centres. Quite ironically, all such life-saving labour processes and scientific thinking were hugely devalued and these people were paid meagre wages as well. These twin processes were set in motion in order to kill their body and their soul. Brahmanism worked out a strategy, in which the most useful and scientific forms of work would be paid the least wages. These social communities invested their labour for the long-term benefit of the rest of the society, in adverse conditions, in the face of social humiliation inflicted upon them—Brahmanic Hinduism ruthlessly kept them in a state of poverty and destitution in order to kill their creativity and their energy.

It is common knowledge that in Hindu thought, the dead are regarded as untouchable. Even the Bahujan castes considered them *sudakam*. The Malas defied such notions by burying the bodies before they began decomposing. They dug *bondalu* (pits) a little away from the village to bury the dead. Even today, it is the Malas who dig burial pits. Like the Buddhists, the Dalit civil society believes that the human body is composed of earth, water, fire and air and on burial, the different elements in the body mix with the corresponding elements in nature. The chemical decomposition of the human body, in turn, re-energizes the soil. In fact, this method of disposal of dead bodies proved to be an invaluable source of information both from archeological and anthropological point of view to understand the evolution of the human body and brain in India.

Hinduism, for reasons of its own, favoured cremation of the dead body, which destroyed the possibility of a serious examination of the human skeletons and skulls that are available underground post-burial.

Dalit-Bahujan understanding of Brahmanism offers two explanations for this preference: first, Hindu *dandaneeti* used violent means of dispute resolution, such as public flogging, breaking of limbs and cutting off of the tongue and the nose. Cremation of bodies killed in the process of such torture would leave no evidence for the future generations to consider. Before this unscientific practice had been converted into a religious custom, the Shudras preferred to bury their dead. However, over a period of time, the OBCs and the neo-Kshatriyas adopted the practice of cremation. Second, the argument that cremation does not consume land and is therefore economical does not hold in the light of the fact that burial, as practised by the Mala, Madiga and some other Shudra castes, did not demarcate separate burial land; the same land was used for agricultural purposes. The Dalit-Bahujan masses did not use the Christian or Muslim mode of exclusive allotment of land for building tombs or special burial markers in each dead person's memory. This, certainly, was a scientific mode of thought at work.

It is also possible that the Hindu notion of the impurity of the dead body made cremation a more attractive method, because it leaves no traces of the impure body. Furthermore, Brahmanism looked upon every dead body as a potential ghost, and it was believed that with the burning of the body, the ghost also gets destroyed. However, this practice seriously impeded the advancement of medical sciences in India, especially that of anatomy. Consequently, unlike the Chinese, we did not have our own system of medicine until the British introduced one in our country. Now, the Brahmanic forces have entered the system, made it a profession of moneymaking and not of service, and rendered it inaccessible to the Dalit-Bahujan masses.

The Mala practice of burying the dead body indicates that they were dealing with the dead bodies in a rational manner. They operated outside the purview of superstition. From making the *pade* (wooden structure for carrying the dead), to digging the pit or setting up the *costam* (bed of logs on which the body is placed for cremation), to burying the bodies, the Malas do everything. The Madigas performed these tasks in places where there were no Mala communities. The Malas also beat the *dappu* while carrying the dead, a task that normally belonged to the Madigas. The exchange of roles between the two communities in certain areas is quite common. The Malas and the Madigas do not perform the tasks relating to the dead casually. It is not a commercial activity for them, for it does not result in any substantial monetary benefits. They do not get the advantage of any kind of special food on that occasion, either. Historically, even on such occasions, they were forced to eat the leftovers. Yet, they do these tasks keeping in view the interests of the larger community—it is common sense that if a dead body is left untouched out of fear of being polluted, it will rot and endanger the entire village or town.

The Malas and the Madigas weep for the dead and share the sorrow of the family, even though they do not belong to their caste or community. They also carry the news of the demise to the dead person's kith and kin. As *vaarta haarulu* or *kaburu cheppetoliu* (those who carry the news), they risked their lives, for they had to go through thick forests, cross rivers or climb mountains in order to convey the news. They also worked as *kati kaparis* or watchmen at the cremation ground. While ideologically they are at odds with the Brahmanical system of disposing off the dead, they still work as guards to ensure that the entire body is consumed by the flames and that wood is not stolen by others during the process of cremation.

The Malas narrate the story of Veera Bahu who spent all his wealth in order to save Harishchandra from the nefarious designs of Vishwamitra. Gurram Joshua's—a famous Dalit poet—poems on Veera Bahu are very popular among the educated Madigas and Malas, for he is an embodiment of a just and brave person. The Mala–Madiga or Dalit notion of justice, therefore, has an opposite social value. The Dalit communities all over India need to realize that their historical potential has been destroyed by Brahmanism. A day will come when these communities will have to ask for reparations based on their contribution to science, technology, engineering, productivity and how and by what means Hindu Brahmanism tenured them through the means of untouchability and social humiliation. Though the Shudra castes, who occupy a higher position than the Dalits in the caste ladder, had a role in the repression of the Dalits of India, the main political and ideological responsibility for this crime falls upon the Brahman intellectual force, which used the spiritual domain to carry out its agenda of oppression. It was Brahmanism that defined science as ignorance and superstition as Shastra.

In the following chapters that deal with the Shudra castes, we shall examine what kind of productive relationship exists historically between the Dalits and the OBCs in terms of their day-to-day existence.

Chapter 4   Subaltern Feminists

Our journey of 'walking through truth' is fraught with barriers of untouchability as we pass the Madiga-Mala civil society and enter the Shudra civil society. The Shudra civil society begins with the Chakalis, who are known as Dhobis in several parts of the country. Both men and women of this community wash clothes of the whole village civil society. The Dhobi women play the key role in the whole process of collecting clothes and washing them, while the men play a supporting role. This is the only country where a particular caste/community took up the task of washing the clothes of all communities, including that of the Dalits, whom the Shudra is not supposed to touch. This is the only caste community where women lead the creative humanitarian work and cultural process. Also, the men operate within the realm of work traditionally defined as feminine only within this Chakali/Dhobi community. This is in sharp contrast to the Hindu mode of life, where, historically, women could not play any significant role in the society. But it is also true that as of now, this caste—particularly the women of the caste—have no recognition whatsoever. Their social being, except at the time of washing clothes, is as untouchable to the Hindu gods, to the priests and to the *dwija* social life as a whole. The rest of the Shudras also have a love-hate relationship with the Chakalis.

Washing of clothes as a social process does not receive any social recognition. No so-called respectable social gathering discusses the social process of cloth collection from every house for the purpose of washing.

No pundit talks about this process in a social gathering; no Hindu writer wrote a word about the value of this work. In the ancient Hindu literature, the Dhobi life figures only once in the Ramayana. In other texts, there is no reference to the Dhobis at all. And the only mention of the Dhobis in the Ramayana is where they are said to have discussed the spoiled *sheela* (chastity) of Sita at the Dhobi *ghat* (a place by the river where the clothes are washed). Rama is upset by the fact that even the lowly Dhobis believe that his wife has lost her chastity in the company of Ravana, and therefore sends her to the forest. Thus, the Dhobis in the Ramayana are portrayed as the reason why Sita was forced to go to the forest when she was pregnant. The implication of this narrative is this: if the situation is such that even the Dhobi women—who themselves have little or no notion of *sheela*—are critical of Sita's conduct, then she truly is worthy of Rama's condemnation. Such a portrayal is not only a condemnation of Sita but also of Chakali women. Even in the modern period, not a single book written by the *dwija* writers speaks a positive word about the Dhobis. No text book at the school level informs the students that there exists such a community called the Chakalis/Dhobis, as though such information somehow spoils the child's well-being.

WHAT IS CLOTH WASHING?

Professional cloth-washing involves washing all kinds of clothes, from clothes shat upon by children to the dirtied clothes of men to the menstrual clothes of women and clothes worn by those suffering from diseases—all of which fell upon the Chakalis. The Brahmans, Baniyas and the Kshatriyas would not touch their own soiled clothes, following the Hindu belief that cloth-washing is a process of spiritual pollution, and those who wash clothes are tainted by the activity. On the other hand, the Chakalis/Dhobis did not collect the clothes of the Dalits, as they were untouchable to the whole village and their clothes were not meant to be mixed up with the clothes of the touchable communities. For a long time, the Brahmans, Baniyas and Kshatriyas would demand that their clothes be kept separate from that of other castes. This total exclusivism of the Brahmans exists even today. If the Chakalis did not wash the clothes of the subaltern scientists and the productive soldiers of society, the reasons behind it was located in Brahmanism. If the Chakalis too thought that touching the clothes of these productive castes was polluting, the rationale behind it was located in the spiritual culture of Hinduism.

How and why did the disease of untouchability enter into the domain of the social community that washes the clothes of the whole society?

This disease of untouchability was indeed injected by the Hindu sacred scriptures, which were named the Dharma Shastras (scriptures of justice). The barriers of untouchability between the Dalits and others stood as a wall, not allowing their skills, values and knowledge systems to have any meaningful social intercourse. Brahmanism constructed negative and hierarchically inhuman social processes in the social consciousness of all the communities that start with the Chakalis/Dhobis and move upwards in the caste order. The castes below the Chakalis/Dhobis are untouchable for all castes above the Chakalis and the Mangalis (barbers), and the Chakalis/Dhobis and the Mangalis themselves are untouchable for the rest of the Shudras and *dwijas*. This is a strange and complex system that Hinduism constructed.

THE BEING OF SHUDRA

The civil society that starts with the Chakalis/Dhobis and moves upwards in clusters was/is named the 'Shudra' society in the Brahmanic texts. The Shudras were said to have been people who do not have any knowledge, people whose brains are not capable of thought. They were also the people who interacted with soil and animals—the people who interacted with production and productive instruments, which were considered spiritually polluting and socially degrading. In other words, the Shudras were the people who possessed qualities which were the very opposite of the notion of the Brahman. As it is well-known, the notion 'Brahman' was associated with the highest form of knowledge. We know that the meaning of terms are normally constructed in the image of the constructors—the Brahman writers defined themselves as highly knowledgeable, and the people whom they wanted to use as their slaves were given names that meant the very opposite of their own. The Chakalis/Dhobis thus became the first rung of the Shudra society who bore the stamp 'stupid' irrespective of their abilities. The knowledge base of the Chakalis, however, is the prime base which the whole Shudra society should be proud of. They had a unique culture and a sense of service but, people with inhuman values treated them as untouchable. We shall see in this chapter what *Chakalatwam* is all about.

CARRYING THE BURDEN OF HEALTH SCIENCE

What do the Chakali/Dhobi women actually do in everyday life? They wake up early in the morning and perform their household chores. They go to every house and collect the clothes that are meant for washing. The men are also assigned some houses for collection of clothes. Once the clothes are collected from every house, they are arranged in bundles. The whole family, including the children, carries the clothes bundles on their heads. As they carry heavy loads of clothes every day, the Chakalis are known as 'donkey's load bearers'. Of late, Chakalis in certain areas are using donkeys to carry the burden from the village to the *Chaki revu* (Dhobi *ghat*). But historically, the Chakalis carried the clothes on their heads as a social responsibility of the individual Chakali family as well as the entire caste.

Once the Chakalis reach the Dhobi *ghat*, they dip all the clothes in the water. For a long period in history, they must have washed the clothes with plain water alone, and later realized that washing clothes with water only was not cleaning the clothes to their own satisfaction, as well as that of their customers. In the whole struggle to overcome the problem of washing clothes to their own satisfaction as well as that of their customers, the Chakalis/Dhobis might have discovered the soil soap several centuries back. Such a discovery of the soil soap must have been the earliest in the world. In Telugu country such a soil soap is known as *choudu matti* (a kind of soap). The *choudu matti* is not just ordinary soil available all over. It is a specific soil that has light brown colour and contains the chemical character of a detergent. The *choudu matti*, on touching, produces a burning sensation and washes dirt off one's hand at once. The Chakalis mix the *choudu matti* with water and stir it so that it completely dissolves in the water. Some Chakalis heat the *choudu matti* water and dip the clothes in it and some dip the clothes without heating it up. Before settling upon this soil as the best, the Chakalis/Dhobis must have gone through a process of experimenting with several kinds of soil which have less chemical elements. It was a process of elimination of the not so useful soil soaps and adaptation of the most useful soil for the purpose of washing the clothes clean. Such a process needs not only the ability to search for a soft soil that contains detergent quality, but also a comparative grasp of various kinds of soil and their detergent qualities. Experimentation and elimination of less useful soils, with a careful examination of their detergent qualities seems to have gone on for generations, and the final selection of the soil soap seems to have been done with a precise knowledge of the detergent character of the *choudu matti* that they use even now.

The second major breakthrough in the process of washing science in India was the process of heating the clothes after they are dipped in the *choudu* water. Why and how did the Chakalis/Dhobis discover the process of heating clothes? The soil soap they discovered was obviously not killing the germs that carry diseases from person to person. The clothes that

Chakalis/Dhobis collected from the entire village were mixed up with each other, which might have led to the spread of germs. Further, the germs that accumulate in soiled clothes slowly enter the body of the person using the clothes and make him fall sick. The Chakalis/Dhobis realized that using merely the soil soap in itself would not guarantee the good health of the person wearing these clothes. In the process of the intellectual struggle to overcome this problem that was related to the well-being of the whole village, they discovered the process of heating the clothes dipped in the *choudu* water. As a result, even now at village tanks and streams, we can see the *Chaki revu*/Dhobi *ghats* that have permanent cloth boiling structures. Thus, the process of discovering *choudu matti* and heating of clothes at the Dhobi *ghat* was a result of the scientific thinking and struggle of Chakalis/Dhobis to invent new technologies to develop the human society.

Who must have played the leading role in this whole process of searching for the soil soaps? How did they work out the techniques of eliminating the relatively less useful and adopting more useful soil soaps until one reached a stage where one found a soil soap over which no further improvement could be made? The Chakali/Dhobi women might have played an important role in discovering and improving the technology of soil soap. Even in the process of discovering the boiling technique, the women seem to have played the central role. In the realm of science, a practitioner alone can make further improvements of technologies and the methods of using them. A distant observer cannot create the idea of improvement and cannot evolve the necessary technology for a particular economic function. It is those who are involved in the day-to-day process of work alone who can discover newer and newer things. For example, in no way a Brahman could discover the soil soaps and hand it over to Chakalis/Dhobis—not only was the science of washing unknown to them, but was considered not worthy of observation either. The Brahmans were superstitious and did not give importance to empirical research as they considered the process of observation and analysis an unworthy act. Hence, they refused to interact with nature in a creative manner. The invocation of God's will does not work in this field—rather, it would go against the development of the basic science. Development of science is not an act of superstition, and also not of religion. It is a process of negotiation with reason and faith.

Furthermore, Brahmanism constructed religion in a negative philosophical mode. No religion opposed scientific experimentation in the way Hindu Brahmanism did. Did God say that washing clothes is an unworthy act? Did He say that one who performs the function of washing other people's clothes should be treated as unworthy of being divine? In fact, true spiritual philosophy constructs all those who serve others as the ones who would be loved most by God. The Brahmans of India stood against the advancement of all modes of science and spirituality, and they constructed the science of washing clothes as the most unworthy human act. This is a part of their larger ideology of opposing creative interaction with the nature. Except at the stage of consumption of the products that come from nature in the form of food, natural products—in all preceding stages—are untouchable for the Hindu Brahman. Similarly, in a patriarchal society, the men who do not participate in the process of cloth washing or any of its peripheral activities could not have made substantial contribution to new discoveries in that field. Even the Chakali/Dhobi men, who participate in washing activity in a marginal way, could not have contributed much to the advancement of washing technology. Hence, it could be easily concluded that the discoverers of soil soaps and the technology of dipping clothes in hot water in India were the Chakali/Dhobi women themselves. Why did they participate in this kind of activity related to health science? Did they—do they—have any philosophy of their own in undertaking this activity, or was it a work of foolish women who had no philosophical notion of health, economy and the aesthetics of human life, and its relationship with nature as a whole?

PHILOSOPHY OF WASHING

The philosophy of washing one's body or one's clothes is rooted in the developed notion of human health. The understanding of good health and social cleanliness is a part of the evolution of health science. Since the evolution of the science/art of wearing clothes, health science acquired two fundamental dimensions. One is the basic health of human beings, which is related to the consumption of food and washing one's own body. The second dimension is related to the cleanliness of clothes. Human beings wore clothes both for the protection of the human body and for increasing the human productive energy. A whole range of ideological constructions evolved around the practice of wearing clothes over a period of time. The type of clothes people wear and the method of wearing clothes became a part of the concept of beauty and other aesthetic notions. From the notion of protection of one's body to body make-up—a whole set of cultural aesthetics began to be constructed around clothes. The whole ideology of cultural aesthetics is netted around the way the people wear their dresses and the kind of colours they choose and the kind of cleanliness they maintain. From among the Shudras, three communities dealing with the science and aesthetics of wearing of clothes came into being: at the level of weaving, the Padmashali community; at the level of stitching of clothes, the Durjy or Mera community; and at the level of cleaning clothes, the Chakali/Dhobi community. But for the historical knowledge of these communities, cloth technology and the aesthetics of dress would not have evolved in India. Of these three communities, the Chakalis/Dhobis have been assigned the lowest social status by the Brahmanical system. They are considered as untouchable as the soiled clothes they wash. Why is it so? To find our answer, we must understand the role of Brahmanism and Hinduism in the subjugation of the Chakalis/Dhobis.

HINDUISM, SCIENCE AND AESTHETICS

All religions worked out their own dress codes. But some religions used the dress code as an oppressive instrument against the people who operate around that religion. The evolution of human dress codes is a scientific process. Hindu Brahmanism negated that science at the level of its discovery and at the level of its advancement. But when it came to wearing clothes, they used the cloth market quite heavily. All religions worked out subtle suppressive aesthetic values around the dress code. But Hindu religion seems to have worked out far more suppressive methods to humiliate the productive masses, by establishing several methods of hegemonic and subordinating structures using the colours of the clothes they wear, the method of wearing clothes, and so on. The relationship between God and people and the relationships among people were determined using the false philosophy constructed around clothes. The Hindu God is said to love a particular colour (saffron) and wearing one's clothes in a particular manner, that of the *sanyasis*. A religion that prescribes one colour destroys the aesthetic culture of people. The Chakalis/Dhobis have developed a culture of cultivating the aesthetic value of multiple colours. The seven-colour rainbow is highly respected among all the productive castes. The productive castes loved—and loved equally—all the colours that nature has constructed in the process of its evolution. The Hindu philosophy went against all that was loved by the productive communities.

Hindu Brahmanism constructed its own philosophy of clothes and spirituality. In fact, all religions constructed their own philosophy of clothes in relation to their own religious philosophy—but Hinduism clubbed its philosophy of clothes with its philosophy of caste, in the process banning the wearing of certain kinds of clothes by the Shudras, Chandalas and the Adivasis. They were not supposed to wear colourful dresses and get an aesthetic and cultural status at par with the Brahmans. Certain kinds of clothes and certain colours that the Brahmans wear were not supposed to be worn by others, and if they did, brutal punishments were invoked. The colours and modes of dressing themselves construct hegemonic and subordinate caste orders. The politics of colour gets reflected in the brutalizing saffron colour, which is symbolic of the Hindutva ideology that validated the caste hierarchy. The oppressiveness of Madi expresses the dehumanizing nature of the food culture of Brahmanism. What is this Madi? A Brahman woman is supposed to wear a wet cloth around her waist while cooking food for the consumption of God and her family. Actually, in the name of God, the food is cooked for the family's sensuous consumption. But the tragic part is that the cooking activity of the woman—that too of the Brahman woman—has to undergo a torturous course, with wet clothes on her body as long as the cooking activity keeps going. Thankfully, such bad cooking processes were not practised by the Shudras, Dalits and the Adivasis. Where do we place the Chakalis/Dhobis in this realm of the science of wearing clothes and the aesthetic values of beauty? Was the knowledge of the science of washing clothes socially useful? Did they develop the knowledge of looking well, the notion of beauty and a sense of aesthetics, or did they destroy the aesthetic and ethical values of the society? Why did Hindu Brahmanism construct Chakalis/Dhobis as the most disrespectable among the Shudras? It appears that Brahmanism assigned the most disrespectful social status to those castes and communities that made a fundamental contribution to our basic knowledge system. The Chakalis/Dhobis made a fundamental contribution by working the systems of basic health science—hence they seem to have been given the lowest status, even within the Shudra society.

The Hindu aesthetics constructed a hegemonic status for *sanyasi* culture. The *sanyasi* is one who does not believe in washing clothes and cutting hair. The so-called spiritual bath that Brahmans as people and *sanyasis* as their representatives take is not meant for cleaning the body. There is a proverb in Telugu villages: *Brahman snanam vadalani banka* (the Brahman mode of bath is not meant to clean off the dirt on the body, but is meant to only satisfy the spiritual ego). If anybody finishes bath within a few minutes, it is called a 'Brahman bath', because in the common sense perception of Dalit-Bahujans, a Brahman finishes his bath within minutes because he does not take the bath for the sake of his own health. He just pours water on his body and believes that the very wetting of his body satisfies God, and then he runs out of his bathroom. A Brahman remained the permanent priest of the God of Hinduism, and both Hinduism and Brahmanism constructed their cultural aesthetics outside the realm of science. This is in sharp contrast with the Chakali/Dhobi mode of washing that satisfies both the temporal needs of health and economy and the spiritual needs of absolute cleanliness. Thus, Hindu Brahmanism and *Chakalatwam* stand on opposite philosophical grounds.

CULTURAL AESTHETICS AND WOMEN

While all patriarchies have brutally suppressed the relationship between the culture of women and social aesthetics, women have always played a leading role in the construction of a society's aesthetic culture. This is clear from the day-to-day discourses of women and the process of family life in India. The decoration of households, looking after the physical beauty of children along with their well-being and their mental and physical growth have traditionally been women's activities. The process of washing clothes is not just an economic activity, but also a cultural and aesthetic activity. Neatness and cleanliness not only have health value, but also have an aesthetic value. The Chakalis/Dhobis have made individual beauty as well as social beauty their objective. The collective beauty of the village takes shape only when the whole village is clean in terms of the clothes that its inhabitants wear. The proverb that 'a village that does not have a Chakalis is a village of ugliness' clearly indicates that the Chakalis/Dhobis have constructed an aesthetic consciousness among the Indian villages.

GENDER RELATIONS

While examining the cultural economy of the castes, we must also see how caste has constructed gender relations and also locate sites that provide positive examples within the Dalit–Bahujan (Shudra, Chandala and Adivasi) civil society so that some stepping-stones of civil societal transformation can be seen. Since caste has constructed gender relations in a compartmentalized form, the most positive and equalitarian sites of gender relations exist within the caste communities that have productive social relations. They must therefore be studied, and the universally applicable living processes of such caste groups should be theorized. *Chakalatwam* (the life and thinking process of the washermen's community) becomes a junctional point by setting an example for synthesizing different modes of woman–man (in Telugu discourses, the sequence is always Aada–Maga) relations, and also by attempting to erase social barriers of untouchability among different castes and individuals.

Chakalis were/are the only caste, which, by washing the clothes of all castes remained the most active social link among various castes in the village system. The social interaction of Chakalis/Dhobhis is nothing but a rejection of the Brahmanical notion of keeping Dalits completely away. Brahmanism ordained that the social relations between the touchables and the untouchables should be delinked by all means, and yet this community retained its social linkages. The Chakalis, while being part of the Shudra community, quite consistently and over a period of centuries, violated the dictum of the Brahman priests and of the so-called Brahman pundits by maintaining social intercourse with the untouchables as well. This connection has historically maintained cultural communication between Dalits and Bahujans (all Shudras, for that matter). These linkages are very important to heal the historical wounds of untouchability between the Dalit and the Shudra communities. Added to this, the capitalist market and urban employment, along with the enforcement of Ambedkarite reservations, are assisting in the erasure of the barriers of untouchability in urban centres. So, urbanization or modernization of the mind and economy of the Shudras and the Dalits, even in village settings, will change the future course of Indian society in a big way. The future of this nation, and for that matter, any nation, depends on the total restructuring of man-woman relations in spiritual, social and economic realms by re-examining the positive spiritual, social and cultural contribution of women. The lives of the Chakali women will show us a new direction of life in reframing man-woman relations.

The most important contribution of the Chakalis lies in internalizing a feminist practice within the caste—a practice that was neither talked nor written about till today. Nor was there any search for such a site of feminist theory and practice, for the simple reason that no upper caste female scholar could think of searching for a site among the Dalit-Bahujans, as they were the 'others' whose family, caste and man-woman relations were seen as unworthy of emulation. It was assumed that learning new relations was possible only by observing the Western societies. So far, the study of family—a social unit that became the centre of the discursive debate—was a study of the Brahmanical family, which was a socially negative unit. The Dalit-Bahujan families and the social structure that they built contain many positive values within themselves. In order to achieve women's liberation and to depatriarchize the Indian social system, it is important to study the Dalit-Bahujan social relationships like that of the Chakali/Dhobi community quite closely.

CLOTH WASHING AND FEMINISM

The Chakali mode of feminism is related to washing clothes—a task that is not even mentioned in the scriptures of Hinduism, except occasionally to show how feminine it was and hence, how polluting. Pollution and womanhood always went hand-in-hand in Hindu spiritual thought. The Brahman writers constructed the female body itself as polluting, and a body that washes a child's body, that washes clothes and dishes and one's house, as even more polluting. A Brahman God remains distant to such bodies, and more so to female bodies. In Ramayana, as we have discussed earlier, a Chakali/Dhobi was shown as an immoral being. Rama repeatedly says, 'After all a washer person, the lowest of the low, keeps talking about the unfaithfulness of my wife. She then deserves to go to the forest.' The God of the Brahmanical forces, thus, insults the most positive community in history. This was again a paradox—a man whose sensibilities were more feminized, who had been trained to have no respect for the patriarchal mode of man–woman relations was seen as immoral. A Chakali man is more feminized than the average Indian man. His understanding of female sexuality is more radical than that of any average Hindu man. But such an understanding was/is treated as unworthy of respect. It did not find social visibility and economic viability.

The Chakalis, as people, are not only subalterns but are also people whose relationships of cultural economy have not acquired any visibility. There are various questions that have not been answered so far, such as, who discovered the soil soaps? Who discovered that the washing of clothes was an essential process for improving the health and the energy of human beings all over the world? Why, and by whom, has washing been constructed as a female process? How does one invert such historical processes and re-frame the relationships? Such questions have never commanded social respect, even among the upper-caste women. Caste has made the consciousness of Indian women so disoriented that even as victims of patriarchy, they have never searched for spaces of liberation. This mystification of the life of the Hindu women needs to be located in the Brahmanical family system. Brahmanical patriarchy constructed all modes of washing as pollution. The theory of 'female body pollution' and 'male body purity' had a deep impact on both men and women, and they never tried to go beyond the frontiers of that Brahmanic patriarchal knowledge. They never seem to have realized that Brahmanism, viewed from the point of women, is self-destructive as well. For the liberation of all women, including that of upper caste-women, an understanding of subaltern feminist structures is as essential as an understanding of the global structures of man–woman relations.

UNDERSTANDING FEMINISM

If feminism is understood as women existing in their own image, constructing their self in their own consciousness, their being, labour in their own historical realms, *Chakalatwam* has a great potential for female liberation. If human relations should be seen within the available models of life and social relationships, *Chakalatwam* has the necessary qualities to be defined as feminism of a subaltern mode. This is because of the fact that the sexuality of Chakali women is not manipulated, controlled and exploited by the men of their own family as much as that of woman of other castes/classes. Within the Chakali caste, the practice of 'male roles' being taken up by women deconstructs the gender roles. Men, too, are trained to take up 'female roles'. Chakali women molded the psyche of the Chakali men so that they see washing as a work for both men and women. All patriarchal notions about washing the body and the kitchen stand redefined in the minds of both Chakali men and women. Training men in collecting clothes, washing them at the *Chaki revu* (the washing place at streams and tanks) and returning back to the respective houses needs definite feminine skills. In all these tasks, the Chakali women played a leading role, and the Chakali men followed their women, in negation of the patriarchal family. Among the Chakalis, the family is defined in female self. This mode of definition itself stands in total opposition to the mode in which the Brahmanic family is constructed.

The Dhobi *ghat* is a feminine place where washing of clothes and the washing of the Chakali women's own bodies takes place in open air, as the process of washing the body is considered as public—and not private—as the washing of clothes. This process of bathing in the open, in the presence of men, constructs the female body as a body as respectable as the male body, and not a mere sexual object. In such gender-neutral public domains, not only does patriarchy stand negated but a new social relationship is also built. As of now, the Chakali women have such a public space where the body of the woman is not treated as totally different from that of the man. Washing of clothes and the washing of one's own body, in the Chakali mode of thinking, are functions to be conducted in a public space. This becomes clear if we carefully examine the familial understanding of the notion of washing of clothes in other houses, in the so-called modern families. Households where modern and postmodern washing processes

(I treat bathroom washing as modern and machine washing as postmodern) are now prevalent are mainly Brahman, Baniya and neo-Kshatriya houses, and even in these houses, washing continues to be a female activity. While even an office-going woman (who works both at home and at the office) handles washing machines at home, the man (who works only at the office) keeps watching the wonder world of television. While his wife performs all the so-called dirty tasks such as washing after returning from office, he keeps on reading the newspaper or watches the television. Her office work is discounted at home and her household work is discounted in office.

The Chakali women are known for their memory. They know which clothes belong to which family by memory. A well-known proverb in the Telugu villages is *Chaduvukunnoni kante Chakali melu*, that is, the 'Chakali is several fold better than an educated person, that is, a Brahman', as the memory of a Chakali is so perfect that not a single dress is misplaced while distributing the clothes. Several households may possess similar clothes, but the Chakalis know which dress belongs to which family. Chakali children also learn the method of counting clothes from the very childhood, because every day they are required to count the clothes belonging to the entire village which they have collected for the purpose of washing. If these skills were harnessed with literacy, the Chakalis would have been a great national asset.

For Indian men, even their Brahmanized workplaces are not places of work but places for collecting bribes. Since women, by and large, are incapable of collecting bribes as ruthlessly as men do in the form of money, commodities, bottles of alcohol, and so on, there is still place for honesty among Brahman women who, of late, have been joining these modern offices. But even those Brahman women who work in the modern offices do not tend to be as corrupt as the Brahmanic men are. A Brahmanic wife works not only in the office but also at home. So the office-going Brahmanic women carry a double burden. To compensate for her incapacity to collect bribes and to see her children grow in the image of their father, she must work more at home as her husband and the other male members of the family insist on immersing themselves in the world of television. The difference between the Brahmanic women and Chakali women is that a Chakali woman trains her children in how to be good washer persons, whereas the Brahmanic woman trains her children—particularly male children—in how to survive on soft bribery. The cultural essence of the Brahmanic women and the Chakali women differs in many basic ways. The Brahmanic women suffer the day-to-day oppression of the Brahmanic men as they are acculturated to regard this oppression as divinely ordained.

Even the modern English education has not emancipated them from this cultural superstition. If the Chakali women get modern English education, their creative experimentation of free and democratically productive life would be fundamentally different from that of the Brahmanic women. They can change the political and cultural essence of the Indian family itself. They would innovate several technologies that would make home management far easier. They would also work towards changing the political and cultural life of the Indian family itself. Though Hinduism has been operating as an external agent of suppression on them, they have been able to sustain the subaltern feminist essence. If only these subaltern feminists transform themselves into modern feminists, the life of Indian women would change. But Hinduism as a religion and Brahmanism as a modern ideology of that religion have been impediments in this process of change.

FEMINISING MEN

In all modern houses, washing (clothes, dishes or the house itself) is considered to be a female task. For that matter, all tasks of cleaning are considered female tasks, which reduce the masculinity of the men (reduce the *magatanam* or *purushatwam*) who enter those spheres. The Chakalis are the only caste whose notion of *aadatanam* (femininity) and *magatanam* (masculinity) are not constructed around the tasks they perform. The biological differences and the functions of the female–male bodies seem to be separated from the socio-economic tasks of individuals. This does not mean that the effectiveness of their sexual functions is dissociated from labour. They seem to have de-gendered the notions of labour. For example, in any other agrarian caste, plough driving is seen as a process of increasing one's manliness (*magatanam*), and seeding is seen as a process of increasing femininity (*aadatanam*). The former is considered more important. Man's work is considered to be potent work. Female work is considered impotent work. Here the notions of potence and impotence relate to the sexual energy of men and sexual servitude of women. Wage structures too are defined in a differential manner—male labour is costlier than female labour. In other words, masculinity is considered more important than femininity. The Chakali mode of washing clothes, on the other hand, positions the potence/impotence discourse in different terms.

The *Chaki revu* is not a masculine site. It is essentially a feminine site, with men participating in the activities of that site, performing tasks designed by women themselves. In patriarchal Brahmanical households, some men may suddenly turn 'shameless' and begin to participate in the activity of washing, but in such cases, the wife herself rejects such a participation, as it would have implications on his *magatanam*. This is very unlike the Chakali women, who have had no hesitation in drawing their men into washing work. *Magatanam* and *aadatanam* in other castes (more so in the Brahmanical castes) are not understood as a constantly regenerating process within the mechanism of male–female bodies, but are seen as a social construction by separating male tasks from female tasks. Though construction and transmission of this consciousness was done in the domain of the patriarchy, women of many castes internalized the language and the essence of such discourse. If a man washes clothes, his *magatanam* dwindles; if he washes the house, it dwindles further. If he washes his own plate it dwindles even more. Therefore, the man refuses to do these tasks even if the wife asks him to do them. She gets beaten up, or at least, abused. In many cases, the wife herself refuses to allow the man to do such tasks because the patriarchal civil society, including the women of the neighbourhood, begins to suspect her *aadatanam*. More significantly, her *aadatanam* is suspected her own peer group, as all such peer groups operate within the ideological parameters dictated by men. These groups accuse one man of becoming feminized, and another woman of being masculinized—the actors in the work process, thus, are more concerned about this form of social gossip than about the energy that work generates.

The gossip centres (what we call the *adda*) of men are constructed in the image of masculinity. Among the Brahmanical castes, the *sanyasi* (the most useless person from the Shudra perspective) gatherings, the temples and shops, and among the Shudras, the caste panchayats, the places of tilling and cutting trees, areas where women are not a part of the activity in an integrated manner, become the social law-making centres. Women also have their own centres of gossip. The water-drawing wells, the crop-cutting places and the crop-weeding fields, the marriage *pandals*, and so on, become the social *addas* of women. These centres constructed their own laws, their own customs and conventions, but the philosophical structures that women (of all castes) constructed did not find many places for themselves in a world dominated by patriarchal authority. As a result, the philosophical understanding of washing among all men except the washermen themselves holds a very different meaning. The Chakali *wada*, thus, evolved a different discourse of law and man–woman relations.

These discourses are very important for reframing social relations at all levels of the society. So far, the upper-caste society thought that working women's discourses have not contributed to any knowledge system, but in fact, the larger productive society evolved its familial laws, its social norms and its ethical codes based on the discourses that these women had constructed in their workplaces. Their workplaces were also sites of construction of their social laws. The marriage laws, the divorce laws, the social norms of behaviour—all are evolved in the process of productive work, and more so that of women. The laws that the Chakali women evolved had slowly entered into many layers of the society, and that is the reason why man–woman relations among Chakalis acquired several democratic values. But in Hinduism, which is a highly patriarchal religion, the negative aspects of patriarchy were considered as ideal; it checkmated the permeation of such subaltern feminist values amongst all the castes.

If men begin to perform tasks such as washing clothes, their own women begin to ask: is it manly to wash clothes? The internalized consciousness of self-negation thus begins to operate as a social destroyer. This is akin to the lower castes themselves refusing to enter upper-caste households, after a certain stage of internalizing their inferiority complex. Chakali women, however, never allowed such consciousness to settle among themselves. They never saw the washing of clothes by their men as an action that undermined their *magatanam*, just as many Lambada or Mala women do not see any danger to their *aadatanam* in driving the plough or bullock cart or drawing water from the well.

All patriarchies (Hindu, Islamic, Christian, Buddhist, and so on) constructed femininity as passive and masculinity as an active element, and they were considered pathological in nature. For political reasons, and also to increase the passivity of women, more labour was assigned to them and less food was apportioned for their consumption (eating less in quantity and quality). Even in Brahmanical consumption, there is a difference between male consumption and female consumption. Men have to eat more to be strong, and women have to eat less to be delicate and slim. To institutionalize such living processes, the Hindu gods were constructed as strong war heroes and the goddesses were constructed as delicate dolls. To some extent, Buddha and Jesus differ from this mode, as they too seem to have had unheroic and delicate feminine bodies. *Chakalatwam* operated in all spheres essentially in the feminine mode. Its mode of collection of food from the customer's houses and the manner in which men and women eat in collectivity and share work equally was a condition of feminine family.

The task of cooking for the family, and feeding both the gods and the male members of the family has imposed a double burden on the Brahmanic women. The Hindu family is thus an institution that promotes destruction of the female self, as cooking for unknown husbands called gods to feed them delicacies is a destructive process. In this respect, prayer-centred religions like Christianity and Islam reduced the burden of women, as the gods worshipped in these religions are not food-eating creatures. Second, the social utility of food suffered very much in Hinduism owing to this practice of offering food to the gods—starving human beings have no value in this philosophical system, and the offerings to the gods require more food than the humans do. By evolving a method of social collection of food, the Chakalis have evolved a subaltern feminist method of food gathering that does not require cooking. Because of the caste system, this process has left the Chakalis with many humiliating experiences, even though they did this in order to facilitate their social responsibility of washing clothes. The same deed, when performed by a Buddhist *bhikkhunis*, acquired more respect, because they gathered food with some spiritual authority.

Do the Chakali men wash utensils at home as they wash clothes along with their wives, mothers or daughters at the *Chaki revu*? Do they do tasks like pasting the house with red soil (*erramatti*)? Though there is no affirmative evidence available as such, one might say that as the Chakali men do not hesitate to wash clothes at the Dhobi *ghat*, they do not have much difficulty in performing other tasks as well. The psychological barrier, therefore, is undercut as and when it is required, as their mental makeup allows the performance of such tasks very easily. But this does not mean that the Dhobi men are completely feminized in relation to the tasks performed by them.

Though the Chakali process of collection of food from customers' households was similar to that of the Brahmans or of Buddhist monks collecting alms, it was much more devalued for two reasons: (*a*) the food collection of Chakalis operates within the female domain—a standard mode of asking for food in an abbreviated form was/is *Chakalidannavva* ('the Chakali woman has come'), and the Chakali women were/are allowed to address the women of the household, but not the men; (*b*) it is in the exchange for labour, not in exchange for spiritual deception. A Brahman never takes cooked food, whereas a Chakali always takes cooked food from all castes, like the Buddhist monks do. This positive humanitarian culture of collecting cooked food from all the customers was not treated with kindness by the Hindu society due to its caste consciousness.

The subaltern status of women becomes clear if one considers the kind of food offered to the Chakali women by the upper-caste women themselves. The Chakali women, however, have shown two remarkable solutions to overthrow the household burden of cooking—limited cooking at home, and consumption of food collected from all houses by men and women alike. Women from the Brahmanical castes and all the other Dalit-Bahujan women never taught their men to wash their saris and blouses, their plates and other utensils and their houses. They, therefore, think that the Chakali women, who taught their men to wash saris and blouses in a public place, at the *Chaki revu*, without feeling bad about it, made their men womanly (*aadabokilla* man). But the Chakali women, by teaching their men to be expert washers of clothes, made a tremendous contribution to feminist practice. The Brahmanical and Dalit–Bahujan men must learn from the Chakali men to be good washermen than to be good rulers, workers in male spheres or writers. In restructuring human relations, it is important to transform women, especially subaltern feminists like the Chakalis, into parliamentarians, administrators or writers. It is important to redefine woman–man (Aada–Maga *sambhandalu*) roles, drawing lessons from the everyday engagements of Chakali women and men. More significantly, it is important to acknowledge that subaltern women are capable of providing theory and practice for reshaping the whole society.

THE IMPLICATIONS

The implications of this discourse are that the de-genderization of the sites of work will reframe the spiritual and material relations of women and men on the one hand, and the whole of the civil society on the other. While work-based gender discrimination is universal, the Hindu Brahmanical order conditioned that relationship with its particular modes of 'Spiritual Fascism' that conditioned the Indian consciousness much more rigorously. Hindu spirituality constructed the notion of feminine beauty around the sari and blouse culture. Any change in the dress code that seeks to introduce easily washable and maintainable clothes is resisted by the carriers of the Hindu culture. Religion operates through rituals. The rituals construct particular modes of relations between men and women. When the religion does not provide any scope for spiritual democracy and constantly conditions consciousness within the framework of spiritual fascism, the women find no channels of liberation at all.

Hindu spiritual thought sees women's bodies as the site of sexual gratification for men. The subaltern feminism of the Chakalis emerged out of their fieldwork-based productive ethics, over a period of centuries. This does not mean that the Shudra castes above the Chakalis and the Chandala castes below them do not practice oppressive patriarchal culture. While the *Shudratwam*, because of its productive ethic, constructed a democratic patriarchal process, the Brahmanical spiritual system, coupled with a lack of exposure to fieldwork even after the emergence of a section of Brahmanical office-going women, did not de-gender the labour process at home and also in the larger civil society. This does not mean that the office-going upper-caste women do not shake the old boundaries of Brahmanical patriarchal relations at all. They have done so in many spheres. The Brahmanical women who acquired English education—that foreign language which carries a different culture with itself—liberated the Brahmanical women from the Hindu dress code and their insulated food habits, exposing them to cross cultural dress and food habits. This is one post-Hindu mode of life that has entered into our civil society.

The Chakali mode of feminism offers much more radical notions of life as it is intrinsically linked to interaction with nature—soil, forests, streams, rivers, tanks, and so on—and also with the civil society at both village and urban levels. The husbands (or other related men) of the office-going women are more suspicious about the social relationships (including physical relationships) of their women than that of the Chakali women. This is because of the simple reason that for the Chakali man, the body of his wife is not just a site for sexual gratification which can be hidden or protected by constructing barriers around her workplace. It is not possible for a Chakali man to prohibit his wife from taking up washing work. And that is not a measure of a truthful life between husband and wife, either. As one goes up the caste hierarchy, one also sees an increase in the notion of the woman's body as a site of sexual gratification for the man. The structure of the Hindu religious system is such that it considers the woman's body to be a commodity. It may not necessarily be so in the mind of other men, but it is certainly so in the mind of her husband. It is a part of the culture of the Hindu men. Thus, de-Hinduization, either by learning lessons from subaltern feminists like the Chakali women or by westernizing through English education and the office-going lifestyle, seem to be necessary conditions for women's freedom in India.

However, the Chakali mode of feminism with its 'work equal, live equal' philosophy is, as of now, insulated due to the lack of education, modernization and exposure to the larger world. For the liberation of Indian women, the native modes of liberative work and skills should be combined with cross-cultural linguistic intercourse, which will take India to the post-Hindu modernity.

Chapter 5   Social Doctors

The Mangalis (barbers) and the Chakalis (washerfolk) live as neighbours in the Telugu country; perhaps they live like that in all states. The Mangalis, though numerically small, constitute an essential social force in the Telugu civil society. They are not an untouchable community like the Madigas or Malas. They shave heads and other parts of the human body as part of their work. They touch all men except those who live in Brahmanical seclusion. Brahmanism labelled the Mangalis as a polluted community, just as they did in the case of the Chakalis, Malas and the Madigas. Brahmanism knows how to brand people; seclude them layer by layer.

SOCIAL DOCTORS

In reality, the Mangalis were social doctors, who possessed knowledge of the human anatomy and knew how to keep the human body clean and healthy. The knowledge available with them indicates that they considered themselves as social doctors ever since human civilization shed its savage instincts to transform itself into a civilized social structure. They knew a great deal about health at a time when human beings were hardly aware of the importance of washing one's body and shaving body hair. The elders of the Mangali community mention that the individuals and communities—whose health the Mangalis have traditionally protected—treated them with disrespect, without understanding the value of the health science that they developed. When I was discussing the importance of shaving one's body hair with an old barber in a village he said, 'shaving is meant to keep the body clean and healthy, but how can we believe that this art was taught to us by Brahmans. They do not have any respect for this work. Other castes also despise this profession. But we have high regard for our profession. Had we disrespected our profession we would not have been able to improve upon it'. Many barbers are of the opinion that without them, the rich would have fallen victim to several diseases that originate in unwashed and unshaven armpits and other parts of the human body. Shaving the body is the first form of protecting the human body from diseases.

The practice of cutting hair, shaving the body, cutting nails and filing them were services that the barbers offered for centuries. This work distinguished humans from animals, as animals cannot shave their own body. Even a cursory look at the work ethic of the barbers, their expertise and their philosophical moorings, indicates that the barbers contributed enormously to social progress by setting up the basic philosophy of health and well-being. In fact, the word 'mangali' means 'that which is good and positive'. Why, then, did Brahmanism treat *Mangalatwam* (barberhood) as the pollution of the body and the soul?

Throughout history, the Mangalis were treated so badly that they had to name themselves as neo-Brahmans (the educated Mangalis call themselves *Nayi Brahman*, which means neo-Brahman) in order to acquire some social status. This, however, did not improve their condition, and even today, they live by and large without any substantial property. In Telugu country and perhaps all over India, the barbers live in dire poverty and suffer from all the indignities that the Scheduled Castes undergo except that of untouchability. They cannot sit with castes higher than them. Their cooked food is not shared by the other castes. They have to beg and borrow food from the castes that are higher than them. Their seclusion is as tragic as that of the Dalits.

A systematic survey of this caste's creativity, the instruments that they use and the philosophy that they developed to further human culture and civilization, and also its marginalization by Brahmanism, urges a close and radical re-examination of the discourse of nationalism. There is a need for constructing the post-Hindu discourse of nationalism in an altogether different terrain, with altogether different epistemological tools. The nationalist, Marxist and subaltern historiographies focused on the struggles in Indian history. These were texts written by hegemonic social forces, who did not see the critical role of the instruments produced and services provided by the Dalit–Bahujan castes in the advancement of human history.

Till recently, the socio-economic contribution of the productive masses was not the content of Indian historiography and political sociology. This study of the barber community shows that the study of Indian history, sociology and political economy needs to undergo a significant change. To make this shift possible, we need to adopt a different approach.

THE BARBER'S DISCOVERY

As India entered the civilizational stage, a group of people discovered that growing hair can also sap a lot of energy. In fact, it can become an impediment to good health. It was the barber community that discovered the relationship between constantly growing hair and declining levels of human energy. However, it is not clear as to why the science of shaving differentiated between male and female bodies. The patriarchal norms dominating the civil society conditioned the notions of aesthetics and beauty even with the Mangali community. Though all religions created cultures that differentiated between the hairstyles of men and women, the Hindu religion rigidly prohibited a woman from shaving her hair. Hence, this health-improving activity of getting one's hair cut remained the prerogative of the male. The hegemonic social system appears to have forced Indian women to construct a self-negating notion of beauty by nurturing long hair. The concept of the long-haired beauty seems to work more in the interest of men than women. Hindu epics like the *Ramayana*, the *Mahabharata* and the *Prabhanda Kavyas* described women as a 'lathangi' or a creeper. Such a portrayal invariably went with a description of a delicate body and long black hair. The longer the hair, the more beautiful they were supposed to be. But in reality, the longer the hair, the weaker would be their bodies. There is a proverbial understanding among the Mangalis that long hair causes mental weakness.

Hindu hypocrisy allows Hindu men of all castes to wear trousers and shirts—which were fashioned by the Europeans—instead of the *dhoti* and the *kurta*, even as Hindu women are expected to wear a *sari* and a blouse. Some men even wear the three-piece suit topped with a European-style haircut. However, it would be considered anti-Hindu for Hindu women to sport similar attire and hairstyle. In the modern world, only China has developed a cultural process which sanctions both men and women to get their hair cut and allows women to wear trousers and shirts like men. Europeans and Americans are quickly moving towards a similar culture of dressing—after the jeans arrived in the American market, the dress culture of women began to radically change. But the Chinese women are the first to move towards uniform dress code and hairstyle. To achieve that level of civilization, the Chinese women have had to wage a war against patriarchy time and again.

BUDDHIST SHAVING

A careful observation of the history of hair-cutting shows that Brahmanism, through the practice of sanyasihood, negated this practice of cutting of one's hair, because Brahma was supposed to be looking into all aspects of human health. *Sanyasi* Brahmanism, therefore, set up barberhood as being anti-divine and barbers as people who should not be allowed to touch the body of the *sanyasi* Brahmans. *Mangalatwam* was constructed as socially polluting. The classical Hindu texts regarded the *rishis*, *sanyasis* and the *sadhus* as the most sacred and knowledgeable persons. All of them are portrayed as people who did not allow the hair on any part of their body to be cut—the longer the hair on one's body, the greater the sanyasihood; more unwashed the hair, more divine. Even in contemporary society, *sadhus* and *sanyasis* working as an army of the Hindutva forces remain totally unshaven. This *hindutva* mode of spiritual negation of barberhood found its antithesis in Jainism for the first time in Indian history.

As far back as the seventh century BC, the Jain school revolted against *sanyasi* Brahmanism and practised the shaving of one's head, one's face and other hairy parts of the body. The early Jains did not discriminate between men and women. In fact, even now, the Jain male and female monks keep a clean-shaven body.

However, a much more powerful revolt against the *sanyasi* school of Brahmanism came from the Buddhist school of social cleaners. The *bhikkhu sanghas*, in opposition to Samana Brahmanism, opted for the shaving of the head, face and other parts of the body. The women members of the *bhikkhuni sanghas* could also shave the head if they wished. Textual evidence also indicates that they encouraged women to be mindful of their health. Upali, a barber, was in charge of the *sangha* discipline and he greatly influenced the *sangha* system of cleanliness. For the Buddhists and Jains, barberhood was a social mechanism to keep the body clean and healthy. For the Jains, the presence of the barber within the vicinity of the spiritual congregation was not only permissible but worthy of encouragement. The fact that Upali, a family barber of the Buddha, was elevated to the level of top leadership in the *sangha* shows that Buddhism adopted barberhood as an essential process of human development. Here spirituality was a collective process of all human beings, not an exclusive prerogative of a handful of people, as it was among the Hindu Brahmans.

In contrast to this mode of spiritual health, Hindu *sanyasis* grow hair all over their body, including pubic hair. During the Kumbha Mela of 2001, Brahman *sadhus* and *sanyasis* roamed naked with their hair grown to the point of touching the ground. There were *sanyasis* whose long hair measured three metres. *Mangalatwam* is strongly opposed to this barbaric mode of Hinduism. The heads of the *sanyasis*, *sadhus* and *rishis* are full of unwashed and untrimmed hair that the productive masses, who believe in culture of hair-cutting and washing, find shameful. The unwashed hair and body gives out an offensive odour. India must overcome the barbarism of sanyasihood.

THE DALIT–BAHUJAN NOTION OF SHAVING

The spiritual processes of Dalit–Bahujans, even in contemporary society, are not only closer to the Jain and Buddhist practices, but also more barber-friendly. During the Bonalu festival, spiritual offerings are made to goddesses like Pochamma, Maisamma, Maramma, Gangamma, Yellamma, or to gods like Potaraju, Beerappa, and so on. Every male member in the family has to shave their face, their head, and so on. Of course, women in these communities are also governed by patriarchal notions of the long-haired beauty.

In the spiritual culture of the Dalit–Bahujans, the barber becomes part of the spiritual interaction with the divine. The notion of cleanliness is more pronounced in the Dalit–Bahujan festivals than in the Brahmanical festivals. Apart from the inevitable rinsing of the head, the shaving of the male body is part of the ritual culture. The shaving of one's head is considered the highest form of purification. The barber is also part of the ritual offering of the sacrificial goat or sheep. He gets his share of meat and toddy. Thus, in Telugu village culture, the Mangali is an organic being, but his place in the Hindu religious rituals is that of an untouchable. Unfortunately, what the Brahmans believed and practised became a norm for the Brahmanical life through ages and is prevalent even today .

THE HINDU PRIEST SHANKARA AND SHAVING

The Brahmanical notion of barberhood and health underwent a change after the emergence of Shankara of Kerala in the seventh century AD. His modified medieval Brahmanism in the seventh century AD was characterized by the shaving of the head of the Brahman priest as well. Perhaps, he was the first spiritual Brahman to have his head shaven clean. However, the essential understanding of social pollution of barberhood remained intact even after Shankara's Advaita Brahmanism became popular in the medieval period. The Brahmanical notion of the social indignity of *Mangalatwam* (barberhood) continued even in the modern period. At the same time, modern images of the Hindu gods portrayed them as clean shaven. One can assume from this that the gods too interacted with barbers. How is it that the same Hindu gods constructed barberhood as pollution? Thus emerged a paradox in Hindu thought—the Hindu gods, from Brahma to Krishna, had clean shaven faces, but the *sanyasis* who worshipped these gods regarded any interaction with the barbers as polluting. It is interesting to note that the priest who mediates between God and the Brahmanical forces is expected to have a shaven head except for a tuft of hair called *pilaka juttu*. In spite of such a relationship of the Hindu civil society with the barbers, their social status was kept low, both legally and through civil societal means.

SAMSARI VS SANYASI DISCOURSE

The social discourse about the skill of cutting hair and shaving the head or face is such that while the barber's knowledge is used for the social purpose of the Brahmanical communities, his being is despised. Contrarily, in the Dalit-Bahujan *wada*s, a *sanyasi* is not viewed as a respectable being but as an idle creature, a parasite who consumes commodities produced by the productive society constituted of the Sudras and the Chandalas. The *sanyasi*—a word used as an abuse by the Dalit-Bahujans—symbolizes those social forces that do not work but consume the resources. The Dalit-Bahujans attached a great deal of importance to the concept of a *samsari* (a disciplined householder) who lives a collective life within a social framework of producers and reproducers. The Dalit-Bahujan *samsari*s did not extol the living processes of the social secluders. For them, *moksha* (spiritual liberation) could be attained within a social collective. According to the Dalit-Bahujan discourse, the main social source of all forms of knowledge is *samsaram* or familyhood, not *sanyasam* or sainthood. In their perception, *sanyasam* is a process of life that was constructed to negate the productive and reproductive processes of *samsari* life. The *samsari* life is a life of social union of the male and the female for facilitating the process of acquiring knowledge about nature and human beings. *Sanyasatwam* negates the very process of interaction with other human beings and nature. While *Samsaratwam* is oriented towards the continuation of life, *Sanyasatwam* works towards terminating it. The social production of human life, of goods and commodities, of human culture becomes possible in the process of *samsari* life but not in *sanyasi* life.

The Brahmanical forces fabricated the meaning of *Sanyasatwam* in the most respectable terms. Though the *sanyasis* do not do any productive work, do not lead a life of cleanliness and survive by begging, they are said to be the most divine of people. Of all the religions in the world, only Hinduism regarded begging, that too only by the Brahmans, as the most respectable way of life. But the Dalit-Bahujans considered such a philosophy of existence as the most disreputable mode of living. The cutting of one's hair, a significant aspect of human life, differentiates between *Sanyasatwam* and *Samsaratwam*. In Dalit-Bahujan philosophy, a *samsari* is one who lives life with a social purpose, by both producing grain and commodities and reproducing human beings. In their view, the *sanyasi* has no life of social purpose. It is a life that exists for one's own self. That self negates the life processes of all others.

The *sanyasis* are highly political beings. They sustain themselves by delegitimizing all forms of labour and labour power. For instance, those who protected the village from dreadful diseases by removing carcasses, or peeled the skin off dead cattle to convert it into leather (the Madigas in Telugu country); those who defended the village from external threats (the Malas); those who washed clothes (the Chakalis); those who reared cattle, sheep and goats (the Gollas); those who made pots (the Kummaris), were totally delegitimized and made to feel as if they weren't human beings at all. But those who were involved in these tasks rejected the Brahmanical definition of *Sanyasatwam* as divine and posited their divinity within the frame of *Samsaratwam*. The Dalit-Bahujans constructed their spirituality in conjunction with productivity and creativity, to which Brahmanism was opposed. Though *Samsaratwam* was practised by the Brahmans (they call it *grihaprastha*), the *samsari* life was supposed to involve only in the reproduction of their future generations. Even during the *grihaprastha* period, a Brahman, a Baniya or a Kshatriya is not supposed to participate in the social and economic activities of production of wealth—but at the same time they must participate in the social accumulation of wealth. Such an existence was central to Brahmanical spirituality.

How does one characterize the anti-barber philosophy? While their birth into non-Brahman families is itself sinful, essentially, it is their involvement in the business of cutting hair—which, in Brahmanical understanding, is polluting—that is the real reason behind their social condemnation. The irony of this philosophy is that when the hair is on the Brahman body, it is treated as divine, but when it is touched by the barber it becomes polluted.

The barber's notion of human hair is, in fact, the very opposite of this. Barbers constructed a philosophy based on the common sense that hair is one of the organic elements, and because of the systemic relationship and conscious consumption of food, hair on the human body grows and needs to be cut for the well-being of the body. The process of hair-cutting or shaving the head or other parts of body emerged out of their common sense philosophy, that longer the hair on the human body, weaker would be that body. But Brahmanism ensured that both the work of shaving or cutting hair and the people doing that work should be despised in the spiritual realm.

THE BARBER'S SKILL SYSTEM

What is the nature of the barbers' skills and how do these skills operate? A barber's knowledge begins with an understanding of the relationship between skin and hair. The next stage is to learn to operate a very sophisticated knife, which, if not wielded correctly, could cut and badly injure the body. This skill has to be learnt in childhood itself. Learning to shave and to cut hair involves enormous skill. Some inexperienced barbers try their newly acquired skill first on buffaloes. Some others are straightaway put on to human beings. But such a beginning means that the learner must first observe for a long time and have detailed theoretical discussions with the teacher. In most cases, the teacher is none other than the father of the trainee. It is in these theoretical discourses that the teacher teaches the pupil about the importance of the human body, the nature and characteristics of human skin, and the dialectical relationship between the skin, hair, knife and scissors.

At the field level, we have no knowledge as to who designed the barber's knife. My assumption, therefore, is that the Mangalis themselves must have designed the knife, scissors and other instruments. Those who interact with hair and the human body alone would know what sort of sophisticated instruments are needed. Who could have discovered that there is a contradiction between freely growing hair on the body and human health? The Mangalis must have found this out with the improvements in human health science. The attempts to understand this contradiction must have been made even before Indians began to wear clothes. The Jains provide the best example of being unclothed but at the same time possessing a clean-shaven body. Wearing clothes is an external mediation into human life, whereas the relationship between human hair and the human body is an organic factor. Hence, producing cloth, stitching and wearing it became part of our civilizational development, whereas hair cutting, shaving and dressing of human hair became part of our cultural heritage.

The science of shaving the human body seems to be one of the major issues around which the spiritual battle between *sanyasi*-centred Brahmanism and *bhikkhu*-centred Buddhism was fought. Brahmanism seems to have contested the Buddhist mode of human intervention on two grounds: one that it was against divine desire and second, that the impermanent body does not require purification processes. In their view, what needs to be purified is the soul, which is understood to be permanent. The question that arises is that why did a Brahman *sanyasi* indulge in food consumption, which prolonged the life of body? In their philosophical realm, the soul exists, with or without the body. Since he (a *sanyasi* is mainly a male) wants to free himself from that body as soon as possible, the best way to do so is to stop eating. But the *sanyasi* does not do so—the modern *sanyasis* eat more and more and continue to live for long. Buddhism, on the other hand, argued that the difference between soul and body is a myth. The discourse of *Mangalatwam* has many things in common with that of Buddhism. The human body needs regular attention and constant cleaning in order to acquire physical and spiritual energy.

The discourse of material and spiritual synthesis in order to construct a civil societal relationship is an integral aspect of Dalit–Bahujan life. The barbers say that when they shave the human body to the satisfaction of the person being shaven, they attain a spiritual satisfaction that encourages them to improve their skills further. Not only that, in the process of shaving the human body clean, their own life becomes meaningful. One barber said, 'We do not live for ourselves, we live for others.' This notion of living for others challenged Brahmanism, which encouraged living for one's own self. Another barber said,

> The relationship between me and the head of the other in my hand is sacred but this sacredness does not involve denying the other any skills of mine or the pleasure I derive when I'm involved in beautifying the body of the other. I'm a greater artist than any other artists that the Brahmanical pundits talk about.

The Brahmanical pundits saw skill where it did not exist and did not see where it actually existed.

THE BARBER'S KNIFE: A SYMBOL OF CIVILIZATION

The barber's knife is the most important symbol of Indian civilization. If our culture is constructed through our behaviour, manners and habits, our civilization is reflected in the structures of our instruments and the methods of use. Perhaps the most sophisticated, the sharpest and the most creative instrument that ancient India produced was the barber's knife. Its definite existence could be traced back without any difficulty—as I said earlier—to the period of the Jain societies. Even women could shave off their hair in these early Jain societies. While in India the Brahman *sanyasis* refused to recognize the historical importance of the barber's knife, there is no evidence of the existence of such an instrument in the West or in ancient Greece as far back as seventh century BC. The human images that are available to us from the times of Homer and Socrates do not show any signs of shaving of either the head or the face. As we all know, the age of Socrates was about 200 years later than the Jain period in India. The existence of such an advanced form of shaving science would not be possible in an under-developed society. It would be possible in a civil society where one group of people closely interacted with the other. For instance, the intimate relationship between barbers and ironsmiths was essential in developing such a sharp knife and an advanced pair of scissors. The initial recognition of barbers' skills and trust accorded to those skills among various sections of the society were necessary for social expansion of the shaving operations. All this must have taken place in the pre-Brahmanic period.

Surprisingly, in the Hindu cultural claim, there is no invocation of the barber's knife (*mangali kathi*) or the potter's pot (*kummari kunda*). The Hindutva school claims its historic greatness based on the Vedas and the Upanishads. But these texts are parochial, racist and casteist. They extol the Aryan hegemonic wars against the native Indo-Dravidians. These texts do not reflect the advanced civilizational roots of the barbers or the potters or a host of other instrument-makers. In fact, for the civilization-makers like the barbers, pot makers, leather tanners, shoemakers, producers of meat and milk, and so on, these texts did not exist. What existed for them as symbols of the civilized world were their own tools and instruments and the methods of using these tools and instruments for the advancement of the Indian society. Their discourses are about the historical greatness of their tools and instruments. The history of the Mangali community is spoken of in terms of the generational transformation of their skills and advanced instruments of shaving that they used. It is also discussed in relation to the changing models of shaving. Shaving remains central to their socio-spiritual discourses. That does not exclude women.

WOMEN AND SHAVING

The Aryan Vedic texts are patrilineal and condemnatory of the female social forces of all castes, as well as of the tool designers and the tool users. The civilizational tools and the tool users, on the other hand, have a gender-neutral system of thinking. The life of barbers shows that the civilizational modes they constructed were gender neutral. The Brahmanical cultural constructions, more often than not, came in the way of the fullest use of these civilizational instruments. While the non-Brahman women had traditionally practised shaving of one's head, the Brahmanic women too began to discover the use of shaving tools with the decline of the influence of Brahmanism. The Hindu idea of the long-haired beauty was a negation of a sound body. In this context, other Indian women may derive a lesson from the Jain and the Buddhist women, in whose culture women were allowed to cut or trim their hair without being considered unethical or ugly. Women's beauty was seen in terms of their social usefulness.

In the modern context, when men mostly wear their hair short, women too could go for such a style. After the 1911 revolution, the Chinese women had given up wearing pigtails and preferred to wear their hair short. They also changed their dress code, and now wear trousers and shirts as men do. After adopting this new style of dressing, the mental and physical faculties of Chinese women have improved considerably. Indian women can overcome their limitations in the physical and mental sphere by following their Chinese counterparts. Indira Gandhi had set an example by wearing her hair short. The rural women admired her courage and confidence and voted her to power. Now Mayavati, a female Dalit leader of our country, has adopted a similar short hairstyle, for which the oppressed masses adore and not oppose her.

As it happens, in the case of individuals, there are heroes and villains; similarly, in the case of communities too, there are positive and negative communities. The classical Brahmans were the best instances of such a negative community. A clear indication of this negative process is reflected in the very lifestyle of the *rishis* and the *sanyasis*. Of course, the anti-shaving culture of the Hindu *sanyasis* became highly visible after the BJP came to power. The Hindutva forces believe in *Sanyasatwam* as sacred, and hence they want to construct the culture of anti-production as a great culture.

THE BARBER'S KNIFE AND INDIAN SURGERY

The barber's knife had many uses, the evidence of which is extensively present in villages even today. It served a socio-medical purpose. Apart from being an instrument for shaving the body, it is also a surgical instrument. In the absence of sterilized surgical knives and scissors, the barber's knives and scissors were the main source of surgery in our village system. These were the only available semi-sterilized instruments for operating on the human body. The knife gets sterilized when it is constantly rubbed against the leather sheet and the soft stone called *palugurai* in Telugu language. The Mangalis were the first medical practitioners who worked out methods for treating diseases with herbal medicines and also the first surgeons who discovered the proto-scientific methods of curing diseases through surgical intervention. For snake-bites and scorpion stings, the Mangalis were the best medics. They acquired the knowledge of treating many diseases with herbal liquids. Even today the Mangali's knowledge of plant medicine is extraordinary. They know hundreds of plant medicines. Their knowledge is the main source for Indian Ayurvedic medicine. Brahmanism has destroyed such great knowledge of the Mangalis by condemning it as ignorance, and by constructing *mantra* as a great source of curing diseases. The Brahmanic notion of curing diseases with *mantra* has made the whole Indian society superstitious.

Human nails collect dirt and filth. Traditionally, the Mangalis also perform the task of keeping human nails clean. At the time of a marriage, a barber shaves the groom's body, cuts his nails and massages his body with turmeric and oil. In fact, the Mangalis are considered to be the best masseurs. The fee they charge is less than half of what a Brahman priest charges for reciting *mantras* that no one understands, and yet people pay huge sums of money, rice and other things to Brahmans. Apart from these, the male barbers also work as messengers, carrying messages about births, weddings and deaths. In combining so many socio-medicinal practices in their profession, the Mangalis served as the most useful social doctors.

BARBER WOMEN

The Mangali women were the best midwives, who had perfected the method of making a woman's labour easy and bearable. They were experts in cutting the umbilical cord after delivery. While the Shudras and the Chandalas sought the services of the Mangali women for delivering and cleaning the infant, evidence shows that Brahman and Baniya families did not take advantage of this expertise. In the Brahman and the Baniya families, the woman was expected to deliver by herself in a room while the priest would begin the *puja* outside. Allowing Mangali and Chakali women into the house, even for the purpose of assisting in the delivery, was regarded as ritual pollution. Brahman women did not allow them into the house, as ritual purity-pollution was central to their consciousness. The Shudra–Chandala consciousness and the Brahmanical consciousness of both men and women had two separate, perhaps parallel, formations. The Shudra–Chandala consciousness combined spiritual and material sources of solving the problems of life. Brahmanical consciousness, on the other hand, was conditioned by the superstitious spiritualism which was not supposed to be mediated by any form of material (medical or otherwise) processes of life. Barring entry to women barber and washer women is a clear indication that the Brahman women had internalized the theory of *paraloka prapti* or entering heaven. Historically, the Shudra–Chandala women had a certain degree of autonomy because of their involvement in agrarian and household industrial production. This could have been one of the reasons why practices like *sati* did not enter these communities. The women of these communities would have resisted them.

The utility of the social-medical practices of the barbers was opposed by the Brahmanical forces. From the *Rigveda* to *Manu Dharma Shastra* to modern Brahmanism, the Mangalis were assigned a very low status. They were told to beg and borrow the leftovers from the upper castes. If they interacted socially with castes higher than theirs—except for the purpose of cleaning their bodies—they were meted out with harsh punishments. The Mangali's social doctorhood was treated as ritually polluting and Brahmanic superstition was treated as ritually purifying. The nation thus lost a great knowledge and value system because of the disrespect of the Brahmanic forces for social medicine.

BARBER MORALITY

Despite Hindu ideological attacks, the Mangalis persisted in constructing a positive social consciousness in order to help the civil society develop its health and spiritual modes of living. Spirituality is not only embodied in *pujas* and *yagyas* but also in cleaning the bodies of others. The shaving process is a spiritually re-energizing process. It is as significant an activity as that of saving a life by a doctor. Spiritual energy is accumulated when human beings live for one another.

The Mangalis were a community possessing advanced skills, who could handle highly sophisticated instruments like the knife, scissors, nail cutters, and so on. Even children could shave without injuring the most significant parts of people's bodies. Had the barbers developed vengeful tendencies, several heads would have rolled—but they did not. Every barber was in control of the head and neck of even the most barbaric person of the upper castes at the time of shaving. After Shankara adopted the shaven head as the necessary condition for Hindu priesthood, the Mangalis had to shave the head of the enemy of *Mangalatwam*—the priest. If they wanted to take revenge for the insults that they suffered at the hands of Brahmans, they would have used their knife as a weapon to cut the priest's throats—but the barbers set up an altogether different social morality. They endured social torture but never paid back in the same language and actions as the Brahmanical forces did.

During my field work, I came across the story of a Mangali boy who was walking on the street wearing trousers, full shirt and shoes. When a Reddy, the lord of the village, saw the boy walking with his head held high, he became furious. He caught hold of the boy, abused him and beat him black and blue. The boy pleaded guilty and fell at his feet. The Reddy warned him and let him go. After a couple of days, the Reddy sent his servant to call the barber for shaving his face. As the father was away, the boy decided to take the place of his father. The moment the Reddy saw him, he wanted to know if the boy had learnt his lesson. The boy nodded.

'Can you shave well?' the Reddy asked him.

'Yes,' said the boy.

The Reddy *dora* sat on a *gaddi* under a tree in his compound. He asked the boy to shave him. The boy applied the newly introduced shaving cream on the *dora*'s face and brushed his face and his throat. Then he held the *dora*'s head and began shaving his face. The *dora* was happy with the boy's work. Suddenly, the boy turned the knife around and slit the *dora*'s throat in a matter of seconds. The *dora*'s family hushed up the matter, lest every barber take revenge in a similar fashion for the accumulated indignities.

This story indicates how Mangali morality can change when one's identity is in a crisis. As the Telugu proverb goes: *Mangalollu talusukunte talakayaluntaya* (If the barber wants to cut, how can heads survive?) If they had taken revenge as the Brahmanical castes did, the system would have suffered enormously. A barber once said, *Mangali neeti samaja rakshanaindi* (Barber morality has saved the society.) If only Mangali women were to act unethically, they would have killed many children at birth itself. A Mangali activist once said,

> If we were to resort to the Brahmanical immorality of cutting Eklavya's thumb for learning archery, or killing of Shambhuka for practicing penance, we would have killed many upper caste persons after their

head came into our hands for shaving. But we didn't stoop to their level of immorality. Even now our educated persons working in offices suffer indignities at the hands of the upper castes, yet we have not given up the morality of people respecting them.

The Indian society is still a repository of this kind of Dalit–Bahujan morality. But it is also a repository of Brahmanical immorality. The Dalit–Bahujan morality is its strength and the Brahmanical immorality is its weakness. Hindu Brahmanism as a religion survived and maintained its hegemony by reinforcing violence through divine means as well as through day-to-day spiritual practices. Many of the Hindu gods are warrior gods and many Brahmanical rituals worship violence. Non-violent human beings like the Mangalis—men and women—have had to suffer enormous indignities and violence. If that suffering needs to be stopped, if the positive non-violent culture needs to acquire a hegemonic status, the Mangali community has to turn its knife to the neck of casteism—not to use violence as a creed as Hindu Brahmanism does but in times of need, as the Buddha suggested.

CHANGING THE STATUS OF SOCIAL DOCTORS

If scientific temper needs to be put on its legs—as it is standing on its head now—the social doctors need to gain a very respectable social status. The Indian system of medicine cannot develop without understanding the knowledge systems of the social doctors who developed our early knowledge of medicine and social morality. If all communities were to be selfish like the Brahmans of India, the Indian society would have ended long ago. The real strength of this society lies in its social communities like the Mangalis. The culture of such a community is a social capital in a dormant form. It is this social capital that needs to be seen as our social reserve.

Chapter 6   Meat and Milk Economists

YADAVAS AND BUFFALOES

Our journey from the Mangali *wada* takes us straightaway to a caste community which is an enigma of history—the Gollas or the Kurumas, who, of late, cutting across sub-caste divisions, are adopting a pan Indian name: Yadava. Unlike many Shudra castes, this caste had a peculiar place in the history of production and mythology. In economic terms, they are known as *gopalakas* (cattle grazers), which was central to the formation of the Indian agrarian economy. The cattle economy is centred around four types of domesticated animals: cows and bulls, buffaloes (both male and female), sheep and goats. Among these animals, the buffaloes as milk producing animals were introduced to the Indian civil society by the Yadavas. The Yadavas played an important role in domesticating these animals. Even in Brahmanic life and mythology, buffalo milk has acquired a spiritual and divine space, but the very animal itself, because of its black colour, never acquired spiritual acceptability in Hinduism. Hinduism, thus, is a religion of the Aryans and the Aryan identity is racist in nature. They humiliated people who were not a part of their (Aryan) culture, colour and norms of life. In Hinduism there is enormous respect for the white colour. Thus cow nationalism was constructed around the image of the white cow. The buffalo is despised because of its black colour.

However, the cow was not loved for its nurturing role in day-to-day existence by the Brahmans; it was declared instead as a divine animal. It is thus occasionally worshipped by those superstitious Brahmanical elements which were influenced by spiritual animalism (a primitive notion of treating certain animals as God). It has come to be described as *Kamadhenu*–an animal that gives whatever one asks for–in the so-called epic literature written in the socio-political and historical interests of the Brahmanical forces. Although the concept of *Kamadhenu* refers to a mythical cow, but over a period of time it has become a nomenclature for cows in general. Even if one makes a journey from Kanyakumari to the Himalayas, not a single Brahman boy or girl can be seen grazing cows in the fields, but modernist paintings of the cow as cultural animals hang on the walls of their rich 'nationalist' houses. The poor buffalo, for being a black animal, has never acquired either divine or the modern nationalist status in their discourses. But this does not mean that buffalo milk (two-thirds of the milk consumed in India is buffalo milk) has no utilitarian value for Brahmanism—it has high food value but the entire milk economy is under the control of Brahmanic forces.

The sheep do not have any respectability in the Hindu ethos. No Hindu text, from the *Rigveda* to the *Bhagavad Gita*, gives any respectable space to the sheep and the goat. In fact, for being shepherds, the Yadavas had to suffer all kinds of social humiliation. Though the Yadavas were called *gopalakas* in ancient days, now they are known as *pashu sanskriti manushulu* 'people of cattle culture'. In an abusive mood, the Brahmans call them *barre sanskriti manushulu* 'people of buffalo culture', and they are also known as *gorre vasana manushulu* 'sheep smelling beings'. Thus, buffaloes, sheep and the Yadavas have become synonymous. For being animal grazers, they have been condemned to be animals possessing no knowledge about the ritual processes that the Brahmans and Baniyas are said to have.

BUFFALO BEAUTY AND YADAVA SKILLS

The buffalo represents Negroid–Dravidian black beauty among animals. It sustained the Indian milk economy. Innocent and peace-loving by nature, the buffalo should have been the most respectable animal within the animal world of India. As I said above, though the buffalo, the sheep and the cow are associated with the Yadavas, only the cow has been constructed as a divine animal by Brahmanical literature, without drawing from the knowledge of the Yadavas themselves. The buffalo and the sheep on the other hand were treated as devilish animals, and the Yadavas themselves were treated as uncivilized beings. The buffalo was condemned because it is black in colour and its presence in any sacred activity is considered undesirable even though its milk is as white as cow's milk and has always had the highest food value in a tropical country like India. The sheep, which is a symbol of positive values and social collectivity, and has great utility in terms of meat and wool, has also been relegated to cultural background as they too did not serve the white racist purpose of Aryan Brahmanism. Even now, the Brahmanical forces do not consider sheep and goat as animals that need to be talked about positively at all. From among the many Hindu gods, Krishna alone was portrayed as a shepherd. Of course, there is a definite connection between his Yadava link and his projection as a cow-grazing god. Neither Brahma, a Brahman by birth, nor Vishnu's incarnation Rama, who was a Kshatriya, unlike Krishna, was said to have anything to do with cow or cattle. They conducted wars which were considered to be the highest spiritual activity in their literature. Of course, the recognition of Krishna's godhood also came from his successful conduction of a war, which is where he also composed the Hindu religious book, the *Bhagavad Gita*.

The *Bhagavad Gita* was interpreted and reinterpreted during the Indian struggle for freedom, as it left some ambiguity about the role of labour. But finally, all Brahman and Baniya leaders interpreted it to suit their Varnadharma theory. Krishna was not adopted as the main hero of modern Hindutva for two reasons: *(a)* He was identified with the Yadavas, who also hailed him as their nationalist hero, and cattle-rearing; *(b)* Krishna did not operate within the Brahmanic paradigm. He did not work as per the directions of the Brahmans, as Rama did. He declared himself to be above the Brahmans. Though he accepted the principle of Varnadharma, he would not have indulged in the killing of the Shudras at the behest of the Brahman gurus. He put himself above Dronacharya and Bheeshma, whereas Rama was always under the control of Vashista and other Brahman gurus—the killing of Shambhuka was done at the behest of the Brahman gurus themselves. This was the reason why the Sangh Parivar presented Rama as the main hero of its idea of Hindu Akhanda Bharat and Krishna was kept at the margins. The result of this historical trajectory of the Yadavas is that they remained the enemy of the Hindutva forces all over the country. The emergence of Laloo Prasad Yadav, Mulayam Singh Yadav and a book like *Why I am not a Hindu* being written by a Yadava writer are a part of that historical antagonism of the meat and milk economists and the parasitical Brahmans. Even in the modern period, since the Brahmans—no matter which ideological school they belong to—remained outside the realm of production, they never assessed the history of the productive masses the way it should have been done.

In spite of being descendants of Krishna, the Yadavas did not possess the highest status in the society. Their social status should have been above that of the Brahmans, and cattle-grazing should have been portrayed as the most spiritually respectable in the divine book that Krishna himself is said to have written. If that were so, the Yadavas themselves would have been the priests in the temples reciting the *Bhagavad Gita* morning and evening, and the rest of the day they would have been grazing cattle in the field as Krishna did. Thus, cattle-grazing could have become a spiritually respectable activity. If Krishna, being a cattle-grazer, could have written the *Gita*, every Yadava should have had the right to education and the right to write books. The Indian *gurukulas* (centres of education) would have been headed by the Yadavas and would perhaps be named 'shepherd schools'. Perhaps they too would have opened 'field schools', where grazing cattle, sheep and goat and learning to read and write would have become a pleasant activity for all of them. Most of the Indian population would have by now been educated, as every shepherd and cattle-grazer would have been educated—as was the case with any other country in the world where human beings were equal at least in the realm of spirituality. The result, therefore, would have been that not only the Brahmans and the Baniyas but all Indians would have been eligible for education. In the absence of that, the Dalit–Bahujans—including the Yadavas—remained enslaved under the grip of the spiritual fascism of Brahmanism till the British came and liberated them from the bondage of illiteracy.

After the British came to India, the most enslaved untouchable communities learnt about prophets who loved all humans equally by embracing Christianity; they also acquired proficiency in the English language so that they could embrace modernity along with Christianity. The Yadavas, in spite of being shepherds, do not see the relationship between their own beings and Christ and Muhammad, even though the latter were shepherds themselves and loved the sheep as the Yadavas do, even now. As a result, the Yadava leaders—Mulayam Singh Yadav, Laloo Prasad Yadav and Sharad Yadav—who consider Hindu Brahmanism to be their own religion cannot speak in English and cannot provide an alternate vision to the Yadava community in terms of their spiritual, cultural and political existence. The English language and the cultural history of the Yadavas are conveniently inter-marriagable systems—English as a language has enormous pro-productive ethics; Yadavas all along have been involved in productive work thus they can learn English with ease because of their productive cultural roots. Though Krishna was one of the Yadavas and a larger number of Yadavas remained outside the fold of the Brahman-headed *hindutva* forces, they did not historicize their own tradition or theorize their own experience. They did not even homogenize their relationship to sheep and other cattle. Hence, they still operate within the domain of Indian primitivism. In the spiritual realm, they remain at the feet of the Brahman. This contradictory consciousness does not liberate them from the historical bondage of Brahmanism. They, thus, need to locate their self in the context of universal socio-spiritual forces and put their self in the realm of universality.

JESUS AS A SHEPHERD

We have a great example in Jesus Christ, who loved and lived among the sheep. He loved the sheep and described himself as a shepherd, even though he was born in a carpenter family. In the whole of the Bible, therefore, the shepherd became a highly respectable social and moral being. In spreading the message of the Bible and that of Jesus, shepherds played a very important spiritual role. They could easily combine grazing animals and learning reading (as they all needed to read the Bible) and writing as part of the field activity. That is one of the reasons why the Christian religion constructed enormous dignity around labour, and all animals have equal rights in the realm of spirituality. Hundreds of books were written about the human essence emphasized in Psalm 23, where the Psalm of David says:

> The Lord is my Shepherd, I shall not be in want.
> He makes me lie down in green pastures,
> He leads me beside quiet waters,
> He restores my soul.
> He guides me in paths of righteousness for his name's sake
> Even though I walk through the valley of the shadow of death,
> I will fear no evil, for you are with me, your rod and your staff, they comfort me.
> You prepare a table before me in the presence of my enemies.
> You anoint my head with oil
> My cup overflows.
> Surely goodness and love will follow me all the days of my life,
> and I dwell in the house of the Lord
> forever.
> Source: NIV Study Bible, p. 800.

This kind of relationship between the sheep and the shepherd both in the spiritual world and the social world has no meaning for a Brahman and his religion called Hinduism. The shepherd, in the spiritual world, happens to be God himself, and in the material world a human being who wishes 'goodness and love' for both humans and animals. There is no place for such a God or such a human being and the animals he cares for in Brahman life and religion. His God hates the shepherd and the sheep. The modern English-educated Brahman intellectual forces did not change this cultural environment of Brahmanism. Even the Communist Brahmans hanged on to that very same ideology of spirituality. They established the relationship between the Brahmanism of such inhumanity and modern intellectuality. Even in the domain of Islam, the relationship between God, the shepherd and the sheep exists in a manner that is similar to the Biblical understanding.

Prophet Muhammed was a shepherd as well. God is said to have granted him prophethood while he was grazing his sheep. It is for this reason that he is referred to as the 'Prophet of the Black Blanket' (Kale Kambali Wala) with great reverence. In the Brahmanical worldview, a person with such a 'black blanket' would be a fool, whereas in Islamic culture, such a person could become a prophet. This is a great cultural difference. The innocent Yadavas not only believe the Brahmanic forces in all sincerity but also function as the nuts and the bolts to the Hindu *rathas* (chariots), even though they are not given the right to sit in the *rathas* at all—such is the tragic situation of the community. This does not mean that they have completely surrendered to the Brahmanic political ideology. They, in many ways, contest the Brahmanic ideology in the political realm, but in the spiritual realm they remain at the feet of Hindu Brahmanism. Thus their success in other fields becomes limited. This is the reason why they have failed to produce an intellectual class of their own which could play a critical role in the society.

SHEEP AND THE WOLVES

The Brahmans of India deceived the Yadavas so brazenly that they took away the Yadava God and made him serve their own purpose. The book that Krishna wrote was rewritten to suit their sinful life of not working in the fields and at the same time consuming away the food resources garnered by other sections of the society. This is evident from the fact that in *Bhagavad Gita* the Yadavas have a low social status. The book as it exists today serves the interests of the Brahmanic forces. Even if it was written by Krishna, it must have been rewritten by the Brahmanic forces at a later stage. If the Adivasis, Madigas, Malas, Chakalis and Mangalis were plundered and rendered spiritless in the fight against the Brahmanical forces, the Yadavas lost everything—their God and their book—by believing in the truthfulness of the sinners. The end result is that though the *Bhagvad Gita* exists today in the name of Krishna, it is in fact the most anti-Yadava book. It has been reduced to a book that praises the laziest and the most deceptive social forces as the most sacred people, and it condemns the most hardworking believers of the Hindu God to be slaves of the Brahmans, Kshatriyas and the Baniyas. The book loses all spiritual dignity as it says, 'I have created four Varnas. In which the Brahmans are meant to read books and perform rituals (*pujas*).' The right to read books, including the *Gita*, is granted only to them. The Kshatriyas are granted the right to rule the state and the Vaisyas the right to earn money by doing business. All Shudras, including the Yadavas—the community Krishna belongs to—are assigned the duty of working hard by grazing cattle, tilling, irrigating the land and producing food, and, above all, developing science and technology, only to hand over the 'fruits of all labour and knowledge' (*karma phala*, as the tricky Brahmans wrote in the Gita) to the three aforementioned castes. The Shudras, of which the Yadavas constitute the single largest segment, were thus made the slaves of the Brahmanical forces. As of now, the Yadavas stand as the innocent sheep, whereas the Brahmans may be termed wolves and the Baniyas, foxes.

How can the Yadavas accept this position as God-given? If the Yadavas want to get out of the slavery and humiliation, they should simply reject the *Gita* while claiming Krishna as a great *gopalaka* or as a shepherd, one among them, and make him walk out of Brahmanism. As long as the community does not reject the book in which it lost its self-respect, it cannot gain any social position at all. The Yadavas slaved under the Brahmans, believe that what the Brahmans wrote in the *Gita* in the name of Krishna was the truth. When the book praised the Brahmans in the name of praising Brahma—the god of the Brahmans—the Yadavas thought it was a divine truth. They never knew that no God in the world condemned one community to serve as slaves to other communities. The gods sent their prophets only to liberate the people from slavery and spiritual and material oppression. Gods or prophets condemned individuals for their spiritual omission and commission, but not communities as a whole. The writers of such books—the Brahmans— sinned against God by telling lies in the name of God as well. All these years, the Yadavas lived like sheep, and now the sheep must revolt, not merely in the realm of politics but also in the realm of spirituality.

After some Yadavas emerged as counter-cultural force in the country, the Brahmanic press constantly constructs the Yadava social forces as 'people of buffalo culture'. The Brahmans, on the other hand, are portrayed as hapless sacred cows in the changing world. The sheep does not have much space in Hindu mythology for reasons not known. Even during the nationalist period, the sheep did not find any space in literary works as they were associated with Christians. The shepherd, in Christian discourses, is a most humane person, who cares for the safety of one lost sheep even if there are 99 others in the flock. This is because he/she sympathizes with the miseries of the one that got lost. Jesus (known as Yesaiah in Telugu country) himself is known as the 'shepherd of people'. The Brahmanical gods, on the other hand, are haters of animals like sheep which are symbols of innocence and collective life. Brahmanism remained an enemy of collective life as well as the human beings who represented socio-spiritual innocence. The Yadavas, being a socially innocent caste, lost their social status because they themselves were shepherds. In the Brahmanic discourses, God never identifies himself with a shepherd who nurtures sheep, even though it is an economic animal that sustains human life. Brahmanical discourse constructs the Yadavas as a flock of people who deserve to be disrespected in the public sphere and used for hard labour in the economic sphere.

THE UNHINDU FOOD CULTURE

Brahmanism has constructed an unusual contradiction between meat and spiritual life. Meaterianism (*mamsaharam*) and vegetarianism (*shakaharam*) are, oddly, constructed to be enemies of each other. It is a contradiction that emerged out of Brahmanical superstition and manipulative strategies. No religion in the world used this superstition and manipulative strategy to destroy the health and cultural heritage of people as Brahmanism has done. The cattle economy of India was centred around a beef-eating culture. Krishna was a cattle-grazer at a time when beef was the main staple food of all people, including that of the Brahmans. Beef was a spiritual food in the pastoral economy in which the Brahmans seem to have written the Vedas.

During the three anti-Brahman phases in history, the Brahmans fell into the practice of vegetarianism. The first was the Buddhist period, which opposed the superstitious Brahmanic killing of agrarian cattle and resisted the use of cattle 'agrarian productive energy' (bull power). If Europe operated its agriculture with horse power, India operated its agriculture with bull power. The buffalo was a great mediator between agrarian operations and the milk economy. Its meat, however, was never favoured by the Indians. The Shankara of South India organized the Brahmanic forces against the Buddhists and propagated a pure vegetarian food culture to hegemonize the spiritual domain.

The second anti-Brahman period was the Muslim period, which had brought in a highly organized religion to India, which shelled superstition and idol worship. The Quran prohibited eating only three things, on grounds of hygiene: dead animal flesh, blood, and pig meat (pork), as pigs at the time of Muhammad ate and survived only on human excreta. The third such period was the British period, who liked beef more than any other food. They were considered to be the cultural enemies of Brahmanism.

The Brahmans considered all the three aforementioned socio-cultural forces as enemies, and gave up eating meat with a cunning theory of 'spiritual purity' to go with it. Subsequently, Gandhi, a Jain–Baniya who wanted to lead the Brahmans during the freedom movement, constructed vegetarianism as part of nationalism. He, in spite of being a Jain–Baniya, pretended to be more Hindu than the Brahmans themselves, and used vegetarianism as a cultural stick to beat the beef-eating British rulers. However, that stick hit the Indian beef-eaters harder than it could hit the British. While all this was happening, the food-cultural ground between the British and the Shudras, Chandalas, Adivasis, Muslims, Indian Christians, Sikhs, Buddhists, and so on, remained common. In this regard, the British and the various beef-eating communities of India had something in common, whereas the Brahmans stood alien in their own land. In the process, even the Shudras lost a great food-cultural heritage of their own, but they retained the meat-eating culture with a vengeance. For this, at least, the Yadavas are responsible.

YADAVAS AND MEATERIANISM

The Yadavas always remained enemies of vegetarian Brahmanism. They protected the meat-based food culture and it was linked up to their spiritualism, though they too did not come out of the realms of superstition and idol worship. They challenged Brahmanism all through Indian history. In one major respect the Yadavas became victims of Brahmanical diabolism. When the Brahmans were getting westernized and learning English to become a part of global capitalist modernity, the Yadavas remained backward. The Yadavas remained a big source of the Brahman money mobilization (collectors of *dakshina*) process by reciting *mantras* for marriage, death, childbirth and housewarming ceremonies. Unfortunately, no *mantra* was understood by them. In fact, through each *mantra*, the Brahman was only fooling the subjects for whom the *mantra* was being recited. The Brahmans, even now, have the spiritual audacity to fool the family that gives them money, rice, vegetables, oil, and so on. There are very few *mantras* in the Vedas that ask God for the welfare of all. A Shudra, as per the Vedas, was a fool borne out of Brahma's feet. How can such a book pray for the welfare of the Yadavas, who were considered to be the centre of the Shudra society?

The single Yadava caste alone must have invested most of its labour on the Brahmans, who never had any respect for them. Nor did they get any spiritual salvation out of the labour that they invested on the Brahmans. They lost the real battle, as we have discussed above, when they lost the book and the place for their food and production culture in that book. Now they remain bookless beings. This is a pathetic situation for a hardworking and socio-spiritually obedient community. This was done, as modern Brahman sociologists argue, because of their 'impure' food culture. The eating of meat, fish, and so on, was constructed as unclean, and eating of vegetables was constructed as clean. The Brahmanic discourse of clean and unclean is not related to clean washing or clean maintenance, but to spiritual purity and pollution. The theory of spiritual purity and pollution is a theory of primitivism.

When someone asked Jesus to define what is clean and what is unclean, Jesus replied, 'what goes into a man's mouth does not make him unclean but what comes out of his mouth makes him unclean'. He further added,

> Don't you see that whatever enters the mouth goes into the stomach and then goes out of the body. But the things that come out of the mouth come out of the heart, and these make a man unclean. For out of the heart come evil thoughts.

The Brahman writers put across their thoughts as divine books. In fact, all those thoughts were unclean. They characterized all the meat products that the Yadavas produced as unclean. The Yadavas, thus, lost the socio-spiritual and political essence of life by believing what the unclean mouths spoke as truth. It is only by distancing themselves from those unclean mouths and their unclean books that speak lies about every community that they will get liberated. The process of spiritual liberation is a process that needs to negate the Hindu essence. The Yadavas have to face this challenge if they really want to liberate themselves and become modern.

SHEEP, GOAT AND HUMAN HEALTH

The Indian health sustained because of the production of quality sheep and goat meat by the shepherds. As of now, the largest quantity of meat that the Indians consume is that of sheep and goat. Since its production does meet the requirement of most of the meat-eating population, it is also the costliest food in India. Except the Brahmans and the Baniyas, it is also ritually venerative food for all the other castes. Meat still remains central in the worship of goddesses like Pochamma, Maisamma, Maramma, Potaraju or a host of other goddesses and gods that the Dalit–Bahujans worship all over India. Even in the worship of Krishna in certain regions of India, offering meat still remains a convention. Though the Brahmanic propagandists, during the nationalist period attributed the massively meat-eating culture among the Shudras, Chandalas and the Adivasis to Islamic cultural expansion, the meaterianism is in fact pre-Aryan. The Indus valley civilization presents us with a massively sheep- and goat-eating culture. Among all the Oriental cultures, Indian culture is very rich in sheep and goat economy, because the availability of the very protein-rich green grass for the consumption of sheep and a variety of plants for the consumption of goats made India very suitable for raising sheep and goats. And because of the good grass and plants available on Indian soil, the meat of sheep and goats raised in India is very tasty. It was this tasty meat of sheep and goat that was responsible for the development of an Indian variety of cuisine called the Biryani.

The rice- and meat-based Biryani, though originally standardized by the Dalit–Bahujans who converted into Islam, spread across the country as a special dish of India. It now remains a cultural link between the Muslims and the non-Muslim Dalit–Bahujans. Because of such strong food-cultural linkage between Indian Islam and the Dalit–Bahujan mass, the Hindutva forces could not succeed in destroying the Islamic forces and their cultural heritage in India. In fact, the cultural affiliation between Indian Muslims and the Dalit–Bahujans is much more friendly than that of the Dalit–Bahujans with the Brahmans and the Baniyas. Food culture played a key role in developing that relationship, and within that food culture, the meat-eating culture played a fundamental role. The meat food products remained in the market because the shepherd community refused to get

Brahmanized, and to a large extent, refused even to get Hinduized. From among the historical Shudras, the Yadavas, as an Indian community will play a key role in either dismantling or sustaining the Hindu religion in the future. The Brahman domination and sustenance of the superstitious Hinduism became possible for all these years because the Brahmans succeeded in keeping this community illiterate and ignorant of its own greatness. Once this community gets educated across India and sees the greatness of its culture in the global mirror, Brahmanism will collapse as a house of cards.

Goat meat has more medicinal characteristics than lamb meat. The Indian goat is a leaf- and herb-eating animal. According to the butchers who sell meat and have a lifetime experience in dealing with goat and sheep meat, meat is the only food that is not adulterated and unfertilized with chemicals. Of all the meats, goat meat is not only rich in protein but also a food that has the highest medicinal value. Goat eats plants that have the highest medicinal value. In fact, most of the plant medicines were discovered by shepherds themselves by carefully observing the plants that goats were eating. Thus, the shepherds combined spiritual knowledge with medicinal knowledge in their long voyage of life that mediated between animals and nature.

In my interaction with butchers, one of the butchers said, 'Each part of the goat meat is good for that part of human body—thigh meat is good for thigh, intestine is good for intestine, brain is good for brain, and so on'. The discovery of meat and milk as humanly useable commodities which can be harnessed from the bodies of the animals is one aspect of the Yadava science, and discovering herbal medicines along with technological cures of the diseases of humans and animals is another aspect of it. The Yadavas seem to have played a very important role in these two tasks—in discovering and propagating both aspects of animal and plant life and food; the medicinal value out of both plants and animals. It is true that the tribal discoveries were the most fundamental discoveries in the Indian society. The Yadavas, however, seem to have played an additional role in many discoveries, and as wanderers with cattle and sheep, they were very powerful agents of propaganda as well.

ANIMAL HUSBANDRY

There is enough evidence that the basic animal husbandry was started by the Yadavas themselves. Even today, the treatment of animals in villages is done mostly by the Yadavas. Had there been no knowledge of the treatment of the diseases of the cattle, would the animals have survived illnesses? Much before the emergence of modern animal husbandry, where the upper castes have made their entry and made money, the cattle-grazers prepared herbal medicine themselves and worked out the process of burning sensitive nerves with iron rods, so that some of the nerve-centred diseases could be cured. That knowledge is still in the hands of the Yadavas in our villages. Cattle-rearing is a holistic economic and humane activity. The animals need day-to-day care, and the care cannot be taken if the activity is devoid of love and affection towards the animals. But, love is a necessary condition, but not a sufficient condition for animal protection. The overall improvement of the bovine population was possible only when enough healthcare mechanisms were developed by the social forces involved in the cattle-rearing activity.

Animal husbandry is not like the hobby-based upper-caste environmentalism. It is a lifetime job that comes with all kinds of hardships. The animals live not only in the larger environment but also in a cultural context. Human culture does not evolve only in the social interaction of human beings—animals contribute a lot to our cultural growth. Our habits, our likes and dislikes, our human love-hate relationships are formed in interaction with animals as well. This form of animal interaction is nothing akin to that of the Brahmanical forces with their pet dogs. The natural mode of interaction between humans and animals is a deeper process, wherein animals are taken into the natural setting where they eat, drink, play and have sex when the season demands. Many human instincts have evolved out of animal instincts in the long association of humans with animals.

The Yadavas were the main mediators between animals and nature. This mediation becomes possible only when the love of animals reaches a spiritual height. The husbanding of not just one—as the Brahmans occasionally involve themselves in worshipping the cow—but many animals, such as cows, goats, sheep and buffaloes, and especially dogs to protect the domesticated economic animals, have serious implications upon the human psychology. Animal grazing also involves a constant mediation between animals and ecology. In this mediation, the individual taking care of the animals also has to be an expert reader of ecological conditions. There are earth wounds and swamps which swallow the animals the moment the animals reach there. There are snakes that bite the animals in some areas of wild reptiles, the remedy of which is available only in the herbal medicines produced from certain plants—the Yadavas developed great expertise in curing such snakebites in time. The notion of God gave them enough courage and confidence to face hardships, but that does not mean that they did not make material efforts to find solutions at the human level. This is where the Yadavas acquired the culture of conquering nature in order to sustain the relationship between animals and human beings. On one hand, they believed in the Brahman's status as the spiritual pundit, but on the other hand, they never surrendered there investigative efforts to the superstitious recantation of the so-called Vedic *mantras*. Though the Brahman went on telling them that his recitation cures all ills of all beings, the Yadavas seem to have realized that it was not a substitute to medicine. But they hardly realized, as the Buddha said, that Brahman *mantra* consists more of lies than truths. The Brahman *mantra* is not like the prayer of other religions, for prayer has a liberative element—a Brahman's *mantra* is an agent of enslavement, which meant to mobilize money and food for the reciter. While being the victims of Brahmanical superstition, the Yadavas, out of their own compulsions, operated outside the sphere of Brahmanism with regard to medicine, food and science and technology as well.

SCIENCE AND TECHNOLOGY

The Yadavas have a powerful scientific and technological basis of their own. Two instruments that accompany the Yadava life process have acquired historical significance. The first is the fire-producing stone, along with cotton and the iron pieces that are always kept with a cattle-grazing Yadava. The collective combination of this instrument is called 'fire producer' (*chakamukha rayee*). The Yadava shepherd always carries with him this fire producer, day in and day out, in rain or in blistering heat, because fire is an essential element of life for him. It is his companion to save himself and also his animals. He evolved his scientific mechanism to produce fire whenever he wants, as a ready reckoner to save him from the cold, heat his milk, cook his food and save his animals from the sudden diseases that attack them.

Many Yadavas involved in the task of grazing animals smoke, as that works as a stress reliever. In the biting cold of winter, the fire producer serves to create an instant fire to warm them up. As and when the cattle are attacked by sudden seasonal diseases, the Yadava instantly cures the disease by burning the key nerves of the animals. The fire producer thus is a self-discovered technology of the Yadavas, developed in the process of struggling with nature and their historical devotion to the animal wealth of this nation.

The second technological instrument that the Yadavas perfected and used effectively to serve the human and animal purpose is the axe. It is an instrument that is carried on the shoulder of a Yadava as long as he follows the animals. The axe is an instrument of protection for both humans and their beloved animals. The axe has never been used as a weapon of human destruction, but it has been used as a weapon of social construction, of both the animal and the human worlds. It was used to cut the trees to feed the goats. It was used to prepare logs to construct houses for human dwelling and cattle housing. Unlike the Brahman community, which cannot claim to have built shelters for housing the animals who needed protection as much as the human beings needed, the Yadavas built an umpteen number of dwellings for both humans and animals. The housing of animals served two-fold purposes. It served a spiritual purpose, that of keeping the innocent beings in a condition of happiness—all gods and goddesses, except the Hindu gods, were concerned about the happiness of animals. Among the Dalit-Bahujans, serving the animals that have no tongue to communicate is known as the most divine and humane activity in ones lifetime. The other purpose, of course, is to help them grow healthy, so that they can serve the human purpose better. These people serve both purposes by investing their labour in the productive activity; they serve the society by producing milk and meat. The belief that God created the animals to serve the human purpose has been there in all spiritual thinking processes. Thus, the technology that humans—in this case the Yadavas—constructed served the purposes of both humans and animals.

The Yadava cultural discourses show that the animal is an economical, as much as it is a spiritual, entity. Science and technology are agents that serve the purposes of both human beings and animals. Human beings and animals serve each other's purposes. The Yadavas, as a community, put into practice the notion of keeping the animals happy as long as they live and use them to serve the purposes of higher beings—humans—in a manner that causes them less pain. A good shepherd is one who loves and takes care of his animals. This is the reason why all the great prophets wanted to become good shepherds.

The axe as a technological instrument was effectively used by the Yadavas all along their cattle-grazing life. Apart from these instruments, they used wood to construct all modes of dwellings for lambs, sheep, cattle, buffaloes, and so on. As they had to live in forest areas, they constructed all kinds of wooden artifacts for sleeping, preserving one's belongings, and so on. They also constructed wooden dwellings to take care of young lambs and baby goats, as these animals could not travel along with their mothers. A Brahman pundit would have no idea as to how to protect baby animals from the deadly beasts on the prowl. It was the scientific mental faculties of the animal husbanding communities that developed technologies that protected the species of socially useful animals. In fact, the Indian Brahmans, as a literate, intellectually negative community, did not allow these scientific processes to grow within an environment of social dignity.

THE NUMBER SCIENCE

The numbers have been a part of the shepherd life since time immemorial. Since the shepherds and cattle-grazers were wanderers, it is unlikely that they gathered their knowledge of numbers from the other social forces in the village system. The possibility of the shepherds learning the number science from the Brahmans, who claim to be the source of all knowledge, is therefore quite puzzling, because the Brahmans seldom interacted with the sheep- and cattle-grazers. The Brahmans never treated them as human beings who could be taught any letter-based knowledge at all. In fact, there is no evidence to show that the Brahmans acquired the knowledge of numbers before the shepherds. It is a necessity for the shepherds to count their animals on an everyday basis. Perhaps, even before agrarian production started—where the counting of seeds was a necessity, because agrarian production must multiply the seeds, and counting therefore has to go into the multiplication of seeds—counting animals became essential among shepherds. It is a known fact that the animal economy was a pre-agrarian economy.

The animal herding process transformed into a fully matured economic process only after the herding of animals had become a part of the civil societal operation. The process of herding animals or humans invariably involves counting. In other words, the knowledge of numbers is an inevitable condition for herding. Herding in itself is a number game. The herding of animals could not have become an expanding economic system unless the counting mechanism did not acquire a cultural character in the civil society. The use of numbers is as much a cultural process as it is an economic process. For the shepherds and the cattle-grazers, the knowledge of numbers is a fundamental mechanism of the herding economy. In fact, for the Brahmans who were composing books like the *Rigveda*, there was no need for the knowledge of numbers as much as it was for the shepherds. If we carefully study the life of the shepherds from the present to the past, we realize that the earliest instances of counting can be located only in the animal economy.

Since the sheep- and cattle-grazing activity all over India is associated with the Yadava community, the number science could be easily traced back to the Yadavas themselves. Every Yadava child starting with his/her fifth year begins to learn how to count the sheep. The father teaches the child counting as the most essential aspect of shepherd life. Only by counting the total number of sheep—even before the child becomes familiar with everyday shepherding activities, such as calling each sheep either by name or by its colour combination—can the child ensure the safe return of every sheep in the herd. If there is a huge herd, even the most experienced shepherd must rely on counting, because even such a person cannot identify all the sheep by name. This is true even in the case of a huge cattle herd. The herder cannot identify all the cattle by name or by its colour combination or any other way. Hence, the only basis for his/her verification of all the cattle is counting. Thus, the number science in the Indian context is much older than the Indus Valley civilization, because the animal economy was not only pre-Aryan, but it was also highly advanced in other parts of the country. The number science, in terms of race, was discovered by the Dravidians, and in terms of caste, by the Yadavas. The claim of the Brahmans that the number science was Vedic and Aryan is not only false, but is also an un-Indian claim. The Aryans must have had their own counting mechanism. But before the Aryans came to India, the buffalo and sheep economy was quite advanced. Thus they must have been aware the number system. The Aryans destroyed quite a lot of that economy. Quite ironically, the discovery of zero is attributed to Aryabhatta. If Aryabhatta discovered zero in the fifth century, was there no counting beyond ten before him? The shepherds had to count their cattle, sheep and goats every day! Thus, the science of counting that was developed by the productive masses must have been appropriated by the Brahmanic writers. Linking up Aryabhatta's name with number science is a clever design of modern Brahmanism. It is impossible for a community which has no relationship with animal husbandry and agrarian production to develop the number science.

Even if we look at the modern Brahmanic life from one end of India to the other, we see that it does not have any innovative link with the productive mathematical process. Communities such as that of the shepherds, the pot makers, and the washermen on the other hand, have a day-to-day need for counting. Without knowing the zero, their counting would not have gone beyond ten. These communities dealt with hundreds of animals, pots and human clothes, and so on. If you look at Indra's life in the *Rigveda*, it appears as though he used numbers only to count dead bodies. This is evident from the fact that people worshipped Indra so that they could kill their enemies (usually Asuras) with ease. Subsequently, the Brahmans seem to have used numbers to count the number of cattle they killed in *yagyas*, but they had definitely acquired this positive mathematical knowledge from the productive communities. The Brahman counting, in essence, was negative counting. Any claim of the Brahmans in terms of productive science and the science that develops in the process has no verifiable objectivity. It is not supported by the living process of that community in the contemporary world, either. Most of their books were re-written to suit their hegemony in the modern world. The productive castes and communities simply should not believe in them. Thus, the Yadava community has every right to patent the Indian mathematical knowledge and reject the Brahman authority over that knowledge.

WOOL, TURMERIC AND NEEM

The production of wool and the weaving of blankets has been part of the Yadava economy for a very long time. Sheering of wool from the body of the sheep and preparing it for production of blankets for human use was one of the main economic activities of the Kurumas/Yadavas. All the instruments and the techniques that are required for the production of wool and blankets have been evolved by the Yadavas themselves. The Kuruma/Yadava women have played an important and skilled role in building up the wool economy. Preparation of wool and the process of weaving blankets involves various stages and highly sophisticated instruments, and this community worked out all the knowledge that goes with that activity. The Hindu Brahmanical culture, out of its ignorance, humiliated the Yadavas for building up this knowledge, as it was derogatively described as 'blanket culture' (*gongadi sanskruti*) .

The Yadava women have been as active participants as the Yadava men in constructing the meat and milk economy in all its dimensions. Apart from that, the women made their own discoveries. The most important discoveries that saved the lives of many human beings and animals are the use of turmeric (*bandari* in the Yadava language) and neem as medicinal plants. The Yadava women could integrate both turmeric and neem into their spiritual and material life process. These elements have become a part of their cultural life. Even now while the Brahmanic women use *kumkum* as *tilak* on their foreheads and mango leaves for ritual offerings, the Yadava women use turmeric for *tilak* as well as making up their body. They use the neem leaves for the purpose of spiritual offerings. The neem leaves and turmeric are totally integrated into their ritual practices.

Turmeric is not only used as an antibiotic medicine for human beings and animals, but is also extensively used in the Yadava houses for decorating the wooden gates of the houses. Turmeric, thus, has become both a spiritual and an aesthetic material. It is used for cleaning wounds, washing the body of newly-born babies and pregnant women, as well as those women who have just-delivered. One does not know whether turmeric is originally an Indian plant—but ever since its discovery by the Yadavas, they have made a close study of its usages.

Similarly, the value of the neem tree might have been discovered by the Yadavas. This is just one plant whose properties they studied in-depth—they studied the properties of many such plants. Neem is one of the most useful medicinal plants that India, as a geographical landmass, has produced, and it was the animal husbanding communities who truly discovered its use value. It was used by these communities to cure many diseases in humans as well as animals. It played a key role in curing a disease like small pox, in cleaning the human teeth and in producing a very useful intoxicant called *yapa kallu*. For a long time, children, and even adults, are made to sleep on beds made by neem leaves. It is not a medicinal plant that a specialist would use, but it is a plant that the popular mass uses both in the medicinal as well as the spiritual realm. It does not appear much in the Brahman Hindu rituals. It is not a plant that the Vedic texts refer to much. Many of these medicinal treatments were worked out by Dalit-Bahujan women.

The sophisticated task of milking animals, and transforming the milk into curd, buttermilk and *ghee* have also been great contributions of the Yadava women to the Indian society. Among the working castes, the women interacted with nature and played many key roles too. No Brahman woman can claim that they discovered how milk could be transformed into curd since they were not actively associated with milk production and distribution. The Yadava women were a part of the milk economy and would have played a key role in discovering the process of making curd and *ghee*. Unfortunately, their contribution to the milk economy has not been documented so far.

THE MOTHER HEN CULTURE

The metaphor 'Mother Hen Culture' (*Tallii Kodi Sanskruti*) seems to have been constructed around the life experience of the Yadava women. It is a culture built exclusively by women, who, while leading a life within the traditional marital structure, constructed an autonomous administrative and civil societal space for themselves. Like all other women, the Yadava women get married and lead a female-centre life, where the man is always away with his animals. In fact, other women who fit very aptly into this metaphor are the temple dancing women, who never got married but produced children, and lived a civil societal life of their own. But the temple women were considered to be sex workers, never involved in productive work. The shepherd women lived within the framework of the marriage system and were, in most cases, faithful to their husbands, but the entire civil societal struggle to bring up their children and to construct an independent economy of their own was undertaken by them alone.

This economy, centered around milk and agrarian operations, also gets an independent recognition in its own name. In this economy, the husband does not claim any major say. In fact, a shepherd husband concedes autonomy to his wife. He knows that she is a being who makes a house for him. For a long time in the village civil society, the children are identified with the name of the mother, and the father has no problem whatsoever with that mode of recognition in the civil society. Thus, the mother is a 'Mother Hen' who procreated children in cohabitation with a husband who plays very little role in the day-to-day struggle of bringing up the children, in a manner akin to that of the cock and the hen where the cock plays very little role in the upbringing of the chicks.

This Mother Hen role of the Yadava women did not result in very frequent divorces, either. It evolved a process of understanding between men and women about the roles that they need to play in a social and historical context. If the man worked around sheep, goat, buffaloes, and so on, constantly invading the world of nature, the woman built a civil societal culture of collective living. The shepherd community does have its cultural occasions where they, as a caste, gather together, cook together and eat together. The Brahmanic communitarian life, on the other hand, is man-centred on a day-to-day basis. Though the child-rearing process is entirely in the woman's domain, they are not supposed to take any credit for that work. In the shepherd community, the woman always receives due credit for the work that she does. Hence, in most of the families, the modern education of the children is mother-driven. The father's role in the process of modernization is minimal.

THE GEOGRAPHICAL DISCOVERERS

Sheep- and cattle-grazing involves enormous amount of wandering. The need for discovering pastoral lands for grazing the sheep, cattle and buffaloes, invading the territories hitherto unknown, is a concomitant process of the profession. The love for the animal, which made a shepherd bold and humane, comes from this process. The needs of a shepherd are that of the sheep themselves. The needs of watering and sheltering them, and keeping them safe from water-logged areas and keeping them away from dry spells forced the Yadavas to keep on discovering good grazing spaces and dwelling spaces for both humans and animals. Even today, the Yadavas have the highest knowledge of landscape and terrain, rivers, mountains, forests and wild animals. The expansion of our village systems was based on such shepherd discoveries. Among the Yadavas, the good shepherd is one who can spot the green pastures that are surrounded by streams and water bodies, free from wounded earth, dangerous wild animals and reptiles. A good shepherd discovers such landscapes in order to nurture animals to start with—these places are slowly turned into places of human settlement, as what proves to be good for animals also turns out to be good for human habitation and productive settlement.

The process of geographical discovery also goes hand-in-hand with the discovery of several useful plants, fruits and seeds. The argument that maize has come from America may or may not be true, but the life of a shepherd is associated with many seeds that the human beings have learnt to consume. With this knowledge, the shepherds must have contributed to the cross-breeding of seeds in many ways. The knowledge of maize seed among shepherds is quite old in India. Let us examine the source of seed hybridization in relation to cattle and sheep hybridization. Katama Raju, a famous cattle-grazing Yadava, who also possessed adequate knowledge of Yadava medicine, migrated to the Nellore region in Andhra Pradesh with his cattle and sheep. He seems to have crossbred his migrant cattle and sheep with the local variety of cattle and sheep. As a result, today, the variety of cattle and sheep available in that district are not available in any other district. Katama Raju must have also found out that the topography of that area was best-suited for sustaining hybrid cattle and sheep. Even now, the cattle and sheep that are raised in the Nellore area, in spite of being the best in height, weight, colour, and so on, have a lower survival rate in other areas. Thus, cross-breeding of animals has been an occupational aspect of the shepherd communities all over India.

The shepherds and cattle-grazers, being nomads, were the ambassadors of cattle, seed and plant hybridization in the Indian sub-continent. Such hybridization processes require a detailed knowledge of soil systems which are conducive for certain animals, for certain seeds and certain plants. The Yadavas did all this, without staking their claim over these knowledge systems.

ARE THEY ECONOMISTS?

An economist is one who knows about production, distribution of food resources and also who knows about the intricacies of food processing and marketing. The knowledge of all these processes involves a close association with the production process itself. The Yadava men and women, over a period of centuries, developed an expertise in the production and distribution of meat, milk and wool, using the science of numbers in order to synthesize the process. The Brahmanic economists of India describe these very people, who made the fundamentals of the Indian economic system, as foolish. However, a Yadava man, in loving animals and living all his life among them, serves a twofold purpose. First, the shepherds or herdsmen, by taking up the task of animal herding, expand the populations of those species which have developed an intimate relationship with human beings. At a time when there were more animals on earth than humans, saving all animals was not an economic activity. It was therefore necessary to choose animals that would become necessary for human sustenance. In this process, sheep, goat, buffaloes, cows, and so on, became the dearest and most useful animals to man. The expansion of the population of these species was in the interest of human beings. Secondly, the optimal use of animal resources by humans for the development of the human civilization was a scientific process in itself. The Yadavas constructed the fundamental knowledge system as to how to use and expand that animal resource for human advancement. Is this not enough to characterize them as economists? They developed the whole meat and milk economy in this country.

GOOD SHEPHERD VS BRAHMAN *RISHI*

Many great prophets of this world, be it Jesus Christ or Muhammad, described themselves as the Good Shepherd. They told the world that God wanted his people to be Good Shepherds, caring for the innocent humans as well as animals, by constantly interacting with all human beings and good animals that have been serving the human life process. The sheep has become a metaphor for the good, useful and innocent people who keep struggling with the nature in order to establish heavenly conditions on the earth, in order to establish a meaningful and comfortable standard of living for all. The Good Shepherd cares for the crippled and wounded and the animals in pain and even those going through the painful process of delivering offsprings. He/she applies medicine on their wounds so that they can heal, binds their broken legs so that they can heal and restructure again, and so on. He helps the delivery process of animals by playing the role of the midwife.

The Good Shepherd goes in search of the lone missing sheep, leaving the entire flock for themselves because in the course of searching for the fellow sheep, it remains alone. It is in a helpless, distressed condition, and reaching out to a lonely, distressed animal is the essence of the good human life. When he/she finds the lost sheep crippled or wounded, having been attacked by wolves or other animals, the Good Shepherd holds it in his/her arms as he/she would hold his/her child and brings it back to the flock. In performing such tasks, the shepherd empowers himself/herself. It is a process of liberating oneself from the bondages of selfishness of the Brahmanical variety. Such liberation is a self-learning process. The Good Shepherd combines spirituality with materiality. For example, a Good Shepherd woman in every village is known for carefully milking the buffalo, sheep or cow, without hurting them or beating them. She is also known for properly boiling the milk, converting it into curd, buttermilk and *ghee*. But these are all her technical and skill-based qualities—the best known Good Shepherd woman is the one who does not send those who ask for buttermilk empty-handed. All Yadava women were/are known for this generosity. This process of treating an available resource as collectively shareable by all members of the civil society is a truly magnanimous gesture on their part. The Good Shepherds, thus, fed the Brahmans and Baniyas of India with all the milk, curd, buttermilk and, more than anything, the *ghee* that they produced, only to be spiritually deceived. On the other hand, the prophets who emerged in other societies felt that the best mode of serving God is that of the Good Shepherd—therefore they chose that metaphor.

A Hindu Brahman *rishi* hates to be a shepherd, as this duty involves touching and caring of sheep, buffaloes, cows, and so on. The rishihood that Brahmanism constructed isolates itself from all other human beings, whether they are in distress, and diseased and struggling to reach that very God whom the *rishi* wants to reach. The rishihood, as constructed by Brahmans, does not believe in teaching all, caring for all and curing the diseases of all. It is an institution that works for self-liberation at the expense of others. Take, for example, our medical profession, which is not based on the principle of Good Shepherdhood. Unlike Good Shepherds, the doctors do not believe in the concept of treating all human beings with care and concern. It has been turned into a modern Brahmanic profession. The civil societies that believe in the principle of Good Shepherdhood evolved better humanitarian values. The societies that adopted the Brahmanic concept of rishihood and worked according to that ethic turned selfish and socially destructive.

A Brahman *rishi* does not believe in curing the wounds of humans or animals—even an animal like the sheep—because the self of the *rishi* hates human life and animal life. While the Good Shepherd, in the process of loving the sheep, produces meat and milk for the consumption of his own self and for the well-being of others, the *rishi* believes in grabbing the milk and other food items that other humans produce for his survival. Thus, while the notion of Good Shepherd is socio-spiritually positive, energizing and liberative, the notion of the Brahman *rishi* is negative, selfish and destructive.

Good Shepherdhood, as I said earlier, is not a prerogative of Yadava men alone (as rishihood was that of the Brahman men); the Yadava women have an autonomous space for themselves. Good Shepherdhood is not a patriarchal institution. There have not been women saints in the Hindu religion, but there have been Good Shepherd women among the Yadavas. Any institution that comes into being in the process of human life should be able to liberate men and women. Thus, the concept of the Good Shepherd is liberative for both men and women.

The shepherds of India believed that the Brahman priests and the *rishis* who plundered them economically and socially were doing so in the interest of all. They never suspected them all these years. Though Krishna himself is a Yadava, the Yadavas possess none of the dignity that they deserve owing to the Brahmanic projection of Krishna as written in the *Bhagavad Gita*, a text which only empowered the Brahmans, Kshatriyas and the Vaisyas. Now not only the Yadavas, but all the Dalit–Bahaujans should start their own Good Shepherd schools, which stand for different values. The *gurukulas* and Saraswati Shishu Mandirs that the Brahmanical Hindutva forces are running are meant to hoodwink the Dalit–Bahujans in the modern period. The Dalit–Bahujans can establish their own Good Shepherd social institutes and research centres to study the importance of the meat and milk economy that the shepherd communities produced by investing their mental and spiritual labour power. They can study how Brahmanism can be driven out from their lives and how the Brahmans themselves could be converted into Good Shepherds, so that the negative spirituality and self destructivity that they infused the system with could be rooted out. If they see God as a Good Shepherd, then they should not follow the spiritual fascism that kept them under-developed for centuries. Let them rebel against their own ignorance and see the world around them.

Chapter 7   Unknown Engineers

Once we cross the Yadava civil society with its contributions and complications, our journey enters into the domain of the artisan castes (in Telugu country—Gouda, Kamsali, Kammari, Kummari, Vadrangi) of India, who have their own love-hate relationship with Hindu Brahmanism. Other such castes, with similar skills, exist all over India. They all form a part of the larger civil society that Brahmanism constructed as forces born from the feet of Brahma to serve the Vaishyas, Kshatriyas and the Brahmans, in upward order. They were/are all treated as social forces incapable of receiving equal status as that of the Brahmans, Kshatriyas and Vaishyas. They too were prohibited from studying Sanskrit and from becoming Hindu priests. Some of these castes attempted to *dwija*-ize themselves by allowing their men to wear the sacred thread across their body, their women to cook food while enwrapped in a wet piece of cloth, and so on. But this did not change their social status much. Their attempts to Brahmanize themselves did not attribute any respectability to their historically built skill and knowledge systems. The men in these castes wear a thread across their body in an imitative mode of Brahmanism, but that did not convince the Brahmans to treat them as equals.

The artisan castes have built enormous knowledge of engineering in several fields. The Indian civilization, owing to the Brahmanic Hindu cultural onslaught of anti-production, was made in the image of these castes. If India had not been invaded by the Aryans, Muslims and the British colonizers, then perhaps the engineering skills of Indians would have been credited with a philosophical vision of an un-Hindu mode, right from the ancient pre-Aryan days. More than the Muslim and the British invasion, it was the onslaught of Brahmanic Hinduism that debased the skill system of these castes by not granting them any spiritual status, and also by not allowing their knowledge to take shape, expand, synthesize and hybridize itself. These castes have not formed any resistance to Brahmanism and did not carve out any visible space for themselves in the Indian history. We shall take a cursory look at their basic engineering skills, which do not find place in the spiritual and literary books written by any Brahman writers at any stage of Indian history.

TODDY TAPPING

The toddy tappers (Gouds in Telugu country) in some states are middle-Shudras, and in some states like Tamil Nadu (Nadars) and Kerala (Ejavas) are ex-untouchables. As of now, they have acquired a middle caste status almost in all states. Brahmanism had constructed this caste as ritually polluted, as they did with the Yadavas. They, in my opinion, form the first stage of the engineering knowledge of our society. Their engineering skills operated around the discovery of trees that ooze fluids that human beings can consume and keep their health in balance. These drinks work as an intoxicant, acting as an agent of relaxation for the tired human body. The whole process of toddy tapping, till this day, remains natural, as it does not involve any process of brewing. From the written sources of other countries, as per the best of my knowledge, we do not have any evidence of harnessing such fluids from trees that function as intoxicants—Europe and other Western countries did not harness drinks from trees, except, perhaps, nectar. The Bible and the Quran talk about wine made of fruits like grapes and *kaju*, but not of toddy drawn from any tree. Those involved in wine-making in the Euro-Arabic societies acquired the highest social status, and performed the role of a priest or a *mullah*. In Christianity, wine is a spiritual offering even today. Such a spiritual practice exists in all Dalit–Bahujan communities. Nowhere in the world was the tapping of a natural drink from a tree considered a spiritually unworthy task. Its socio-spiritual status had nothing to do with the drinking practises of the spiritual agents like the Pope, the priests and the *mullahs*. Islam prohibited drinking of brewed liquor, as the question of health is involved in it. But neither the Quran nor the Bible condemn the consumption of toddy. The drink did not exist in the societies where these texts evolved. But no religious text disallowed equality for human beings who perform an activity like toddy tapping or brewing liquor. Hinduism, however, did not allow any respectable status to toddy tappers. It oppressed them for centuries. At a time when the Brahmans were writing their *Dharmashastras*, all the Hindu gods drank both toddy (*sura*) and milk. In fact, there are not many references to the drinking of milk in the basic books of Hinduism—the *Rigveda* does not mention milk, assigning it no spiritual status at all. On the contrary, the *Rigveda* praises Indra, saying, 'You scattered to side the ones that did not press *soma*; as *soma* drinker you are supreme'. While Indra, who drinks *soma*, is praised, the *soma*-tappers, who worked out all the necessary technology for the tapping of *soma*, were considered socially undignified people. Hinduism constructed people as clay dolls in the hands of Brahman writers. The truth was shown as they wanted to show it. The truth in their hands became worse than a doll of clay.

Toddy tapping has two important components: one, the art of climbing the palm tree which is one of the tallest trees in India, and does not have branches on the stem. It needs to be climbed like a lizard climbs a wall in order to harness the fluids. This requires highly sophisticated training and advanced mechanical skills to climb and operate at the top of the tree. Before they engineered the *moku-mutthadu* (two instruments used to climb toddy trees till today), they must have climbed the palm tree with the help of their limbs, which is as good as walking into a death trap. Every toddy tapper uses highly sophisticated knives, and pots of different sizes while remaining on the top of the tree. The way the tapper cuts the *gela* (that portion of the tree from which the toddy flows out), holding the balance at the top of the tree with the help of the *moku* and the *mutthadu* highlights their astonishing skill. Second, their main engineering skill lies in handling the knife to blade out *gela*, which is a tender growth at the (neck) top of the tree. The toddy tapper uses his hands skillfully to carry out this task; a skill that is transmitted from father to son. This whole process of extracting toddy nectar from the tree involved, at least in the initial stages, a systematic study of the tree. Toddy is not just an intoxicant but also a health drink. Toddy tapping, thus, is a living link between humans and nature, by building technology required to tap the toddy. These early engineers are kept outside the ritual frame of Hinduism, as the drink that they produce and the engineering skills involved in the process are seen as polluted.

ENGINEERING AND AGRARIAN ECONOMY

The most serious engineering skills of India are located in three communities—the ironsmiths, the carpenters and the goldsmiths. These communities brought in a revolutionary change in agrarian production.

All these caste communities suffer from the social stigma of Shudra existence. Iron smithing seems to have pre-Aryan existence, hence it continues to be a Shudra occupation all over the country. Historically, the skill of using metals to make tools must have been perfected much before the onset of Indus Valley civilization. One can see the link between the present mode of smithing technology that exists in Indian villages even now carrying with itself some of its ancient pre-Aryan characteristics as well as its legacy from the Indus Valley civilization. Like the books of religion, even human professions carry a whole lot of history with them. The artisan communities and their tool-based engineering skills work as a record of their own history. The knowledge and the technology of iron smithing still existing in our village agrarian economy provides us enough clues to write a new history of engineering and its relationship with Hindu spirituality.

The process of smithing iron has several stages. The process of smithing has contributed to the process of agrarian revolution in several ways. How the Indian social forces, before the Aryans invaded the country, discovered the importance of iron is a part of history. In other words, the discovery of such a process had been done before the Aryan gods like Brahma, Vishnu, Rama, and so on, became part of the Hindu pantheon, and before the technology was advanced to the level of building an urban civilization. There is no evidence to show that after these social forces that follow and worship the Hindu gods emerged, they contributed in any way to the advancement of this engineering process. But the very diabolical declaration, that such creative forces were born out of the feet of the Hindu god, was enough to maul their moral strength and historical energy. Their feet-born status was dehumanizing. We must, therefore, look at the scientific skills that these spiritually dehumanized forces possess within themselves.

The process of melting iron and the working out of the smithing process, especially in terms of caste and the Indian civil society, has not been discussed in any significant way in any of our historical writing. The entire development of the smithing technology is a part of the knowledge system of the ironsmiths (Kammaris in Telugu country, and equivalent castes in all the linguistic states). In the Brahmanical civil society, they too suffered a stigmatized life, so much so that their full energies could never be explored. Any knowledge that gets stigmatized by the manipulators of history causes enormous damage to the whole process of history itself. Indian Brahmanism, thus, has done very serious damage to the Indian engineering process by elaborately talking about *agni* (fire) as an agent only of sacrifice. But they never realized that *agni* also worked as a powerful instrument to melt iron in the ironsmith's hearth. No text discussed the importance of fire in this process of engineering. Neither did any text talk about how these communities discovered the methods of negotiation between fire and iron in order to melt it.

THE MELTING HEARTH

The first stage of the smithing process of iron and the development of iron-related engineering starts with well-established 'iron melting spot', which is connected with two pipelined leather sacs that keep supplying air into the hearth in a channelled manner. The manner in which the blowpipes are made with the combined knowledge of the cobbler and the smith is amazing. Down below the blowpipes, a soft leather valve is fixed from inside as a carefully made whole. As the sac gets pulled up, the vacuum inside the sac absorbs air through the valved whole as the valve moves up because of the pressure of the air from outside. Once the air gets into the sac, the valve blocks the air inside the sac. As the sac is pressed from above, the air filled through the iron pipes that are connected to the hearth and the sacs gets blown into the hearth. On repetition of the process, the air is pushed into the hearth quite fast, so that the burning coal in the hearth keeps heating the iron to the required degree. This process was discovered in the pre-Aryan period itself—this highlights the engineering skills of the Shudra, condemned as foolish people by Hinduism during the Vedic and post-Vedic periods. The same trend continues, even now.

The iron hearth spot is attached with an erect and heavy iron pillar for shaping the hot iron burnt almost to melting point at a high degree of heat generated in the coal, among which the raw iron is kept. This entire village-based iron-melting spot is known as Kammari *kolimi* in Telugu. The Kammari is a highly knowledgeable person who knows about the properties of iron that he (iron smithing in the villages is primarily a male task) has to handle. He knows at which point of heating the iron melts in the hearth, and knows how iron should be moulded to build agrarian instruments or early industrial tools like the sickle, the hammer, the spade, and so on. The hammer that was made out of this process has been the most powerful industrial instrument that shaped not only India but the whole world. The Indian smiths have their own share in working out this historic instrument that caused the industrial revolution in the world, but that link was never properly established. The Communist movement all over the world used the sickle and the hammer as their ideological symbol. Both these symbols were also used to boost the social status of the proletariat of the world. But in a caste-ridden society like ours, proper assessment needs to be done of how Brahmanism has degraded the very builders of that industrial economy. The Communist leadership that had its roots in the Brahmanical families never understood how such anti-industrial essence of Brahmanism destroyed our human development over a period of centuries. Since the Indian Communist movement was also headed by Brahmanic theoreticians like E.M.S Namboodiripad, they too never assigned the role of engineering to these communities.

As is well-known, the roots of industrial revolution in all societies lay in the agrarian tools that were shaped by the very same ironsmiths. Given the negative history of Brahmanism, it must have resisted all such experiments in working out our knowledge of engineering and productivity in order to develop our agrarian and industrial economic systems. For them, the only technology that was useful was the war technology. Since its spiritual heroes are war heroes, it reads all human relationships in the language of war. Brahmanism never located itself in agrarian and industrial production, which was the main driving force of human life. All other un-Hindu prophets like the Buddha, Christ and Muhammad talked about agriculture and industrial economic process, but none of the Hindu gods discussed these issues. This is simply because the Hindu gods—whichever caste they were said to have been born—were created by the Brahmans who never treated the agrarian and industrial production process with any spiritual and civilian dignity.

AGRARIAN REVOLUTION AND IRON SMITHTING

Two agrarian instruments that brought about a revolution in conjunction with leather ropes and trained bull power were the iron blade (called *karru* in Telugu) and the bullock cart wheel belt. The iron blade was fitted to the plough so that the plough could furrow the hard soil and make seeding possible. The *karru*, along with the wooden plough, brought about a revolution in Indian tilling technology. The ironsmiths made a host of other iron instruments like the spade, the crowbar and water-drawing buckets which formed a part of the agrarian technology. But of all these instruments, the key instrument that brought about the agrarian revolution was the *karru*. The ironsmiths went on increasing the designs of these agrarian technological instruments, carefully observing their applicability.

The second most revolutionary contribution of the ironsmiths is the 'bullock cart wheel belt' which is known as the *bandi girra patta* in Telugu.

The making of the wheel belt is a much more sophisticated engineering process. Only highly trained ironsmiths can engineer this process. Stretching out hot iron rods into very long belts and bending them into round belts and welding them into wheel belts at the village iron hearth was/is a great process happening in our small villages for a long time in history. When I saw this happening before my eyes as a child, I could not believe that a human being could perform such a wonder—but I never heard any priest praising this skill.

The other stage of making the iron wheel belt is to heat it after it is welded and sufficiently cooled down, so that the readymade wheel belt widens, based on the physics principle that heated iron expands. This hot expanded belt is set on the wooden wheel, and a heavy amount of water is poured on the hot iron belt so that it condenses itself and remains tightly attached to the wooden wheel. Such a wheel, made with the combined skill of the carpenter and the ironsmith, brought about a revolution in the Indian transport system. The key players in this revolution were the ironsmith and the carpenter. The transport revolution that the bullock cart wheel brought about was well recognized by the famous ancient Buddhist king, Ashoka, and he adopted it as the symbol of his state. Quite interestingly, the Hindu tradition never owned the tradition of Ashoka as he was a Buddhist.

This process of making the wheel belt and fitting it to the bullock cart wheel was/is a sort of a miracle for the children who gather to watch the activity in our villages. But nothing about this process is talked about in our school text books, even today. The village children keep watching a great engineering laboratory operating in front of their eyes, without having any opportunity to read about it in any lesson of theory in their school text books. What he/she learns in theory in the school text books is about Rama killing Ravana and Krishna killing his own matriarchal uncle Kamsa, without having any scope to practically observe that war theatre in day-to-day life. Even if we show such war theatres, the children do not acquire any moral and technical strength through these. However, the moral and technical knowledge of children would certainly receive a boost by learning about the process of iron smithing. The Indian ironsmiths have had a long history of such skillful smithing, right from the pre-Aryan days.

This revolutionary transformation of iron into agrarian tools, perhaps, could have been brought about much before the Aryan invasion took place. The wheel of the bullock cart played a more constructive role in the growth of transport facility than the *ratha*, as the latter was used mainly as a vehicle of war by the Aryan war heroes against the native tribes but unfortunately, in all the Hindu books, the chariot became a vehicle of discourse, but the bullock cart was never discussed. Our village children cannot practically observe a *ratha*, about which they read in the books. For the Brahmanical forces, education remained only theoretical in nature, eulogizing their own past. For the Dalit–Bahujans, this education was irrelevant. Their own education process remained practical, and that practical education should have been transcribed into written text, to be read in schools and colleges. But this was never done.

AXE AND SPADE

The other iron instruments that played key roles in agrarian production were the axe and the spade. The axe played a very important role in deforestation and animal hunting. The development of agriculture was essentially dependent on cutting trees and converting the land into cultivable places. The role that the axe played in the hands of shepherds and cattle herders can be seen even in the present day. The axe, in the hands of these communities, played the role of the woodcutter to feed the cattle and goats and of a weapon of self-defence against wild animals. The ironsmiths worked out the technology of axe-making in various models to suit the needs of the people who used the axes. Hundreds of such models exist in our villages even today.

The spade played a key role in preparing the land for cultivation and irrigating the crops. It was, along with the iron crowbar, the most essential agrarian technological instrument in North and South India, assisting in the construction of tanks, canals and agricultural field *bunds*. In working out this technology, the ironsmiths designed the engineering and technological systems that suited the digging of Indian soils the best. The spade along with the crowbar was responsible for constructing tanks, digging wells, structuring canals, and so on. The Hindu gods and goddesses not only did not talk about and relate themselves to these processes, but they were also constructed in a mode that negated all these processes of the smithing industry. For example, a well-known Hindu Brahman God Parashurama uses the plough and the axe as weapons of war, but not as instruments of production.

SMITHING AND SOCIAL INTEGRATION

In this smithing process, the leather sacs that the leather workers (the Chamars, the Madigas, and so on) made, plays a very significant role along with other aspects of technology that go into the making of the complicated iron smithing. Initially, the first blowpipes were completely made of leather. Subsequently, wooden planks were used as supporting structures to the leather blowpipes—the valve system, as we have seen, was built into the sacs in order to absorb air into the sacs. The sac system that pushed air into the hearth to produce enough heat to melt iron was therefore a by-product of the scientific knowledge system of the Madigas, the smiths and the carpenters, as the blowpipes combined in themselves the knowledge of leather, wood and iron. On occasions like this, inter-caste technological connections were established. But quite sadly, inter-caste marriages among these castes were also prohibited by Brahmanism.

However, the iron smithing science put the Indian civilization on its legs as it helped to construct a whole range of wood technology for improving the process of production in India. Let us now turn to the integrative technology of wood-carpenting, which was never examined by the historians of Indian engineering as that was seen as a mundane Shudra activity.

CARPENTER'S ENGINEERING SKILLS

The carpenter's work requires tremendous craftsmanship. The most revolutionary outcome of the carpenter's engineering is the plough, which could furrow the land with the help of bull and buffalo power. As we have already seen, while the West was a land of horse power, India was (is) a land of bull and buffalo power. The carpenters had to work out a model ploughshare that could be handled by human beings whose physical strength was never allowed to go beyond a certain point by the Brahmanical forces, as their food resources were deliberately kept meagre. Brahmanism had a whole range of literature to keep the producers poor. Neither the ploughmakers nor the ploughdrivers had enough food at any point of time in history, for the Brahman writers, who lived a 'life of leisure', also developed sufficient tricks to keep the toilers of the society poor. It was the motive of acquiring a perpetual leisure-centred life that forced them to work out powerful spiritual methods of control.

The early search for wood which could be moulded into a plough needed a careful study of the nature and character of trees, and such knowledge is still available with the shepherds. The carpenters also took the help of the ironsmiths to construct necessary instruments for moulding the wood into a plough. The plough that was carved out by the carpenters, the iron rod that the ironsmith fitted to the plough, and the Mala mode of training of the bulls and the buffaloes to use their strength for production resulted in the development of what is called 'agriculture'. While the Brahmans, the Kshatriyas and the Vaishyas remained out of this basic agricultural process, the other communities within the Shudra, Chandala and the Adivasi layers of the society had a scope for exchange of knowledge because of their agrarian links. The Brahman house became a house that despised agriculture. The carpenter's house, on the other hand, became a social junction where all castes could meet and discuss the knowledge of the human life-blood, that is, agriculture. Even today, in many villages, the smith and carpenter houses serve as great *addas* wherein discourses on agricultural knowledge are disseminated. No Brahman pundit associates with this kind of discourse. It is an *adda* of the Shudras and the Chandalas, whom the Brahmans hate the most, and this *adda* was the source as well as the site of sharing of information of the techno-economic knowledge systems of the productive castes of India.

The second most important contribution of the carpenter was that of the construction of the wooden parts of the bullock cart. If the ironsmith constructed the iron instruments of the bullock cart, the entire woodwork was done by the carpenter. The technically most skillful aspect of the carpenter's engineering was in the construction of the wheel and the body of the cart. Constructing the whole body of the cart itself required skills and knowledge systems of an advanced nature. Making the wooden junction (known as *buddi* in Telugu), for which the wooden plates are linked to give the wheel its round shape, involved not only skill but also a great degree of imagination on the part of the Indian carpenters. The Brahman simply discounted such knowledge, because if such knowledge was recognized, it would demand a highly respectable spiritual status. The making of the wooden wheel is an advanced process of carpenting, and this was available in India in abundance by the time King Ashoka ruled.

The third major human requirement that the carpenters' knowledge system constructed was the wooden house. The earliest mode of technology of house construction was that of carpenting wood to erect it into humanly habitable houses. Of course, the technology of constructing houses developed gradually, starting from the Adivasi stage of the Indian civilization, but once the engineering skills of the carpenters expanded, the technology of house construction acquired some sophistication. Most of the present models of house construction have their roots in the engineering skills of our carpenters. From the single elephant pole houses (known as an Enakarra house in Telugu) that exist even today in central India to the multi-storied houses of Kerala and Kashmir—all were the brainchildren of our carpenter community.

While the carpenters also developed an expertise in the knowledge of space and time related to construction of houses, the Brahmans introduced the superstition of the *muhurtam* (fixing the times for house construction) and *vaastu* (spiritual intervention in shaping a house) into the house construction process. Even now, the Brahman involves himself in this process of house construction in the form of fixing the *muhurtam* and deciding its *vaastu*, only to make money by undercutting the knowledge of the carpenters and the modern brick-and-cement technicians (*maistris*). A Brahmanic mind does not understand the historical truth that neither the Indian Adivasis, Chandalas and the Shudras, nor the Christians and the Muslims of the world base the construction of their house on *muhurtam* or *vaastu*. They believe in constructing a house on a scientific basis, based on the knowledge of the carpenters. The scriptures of the non-Hindu religions do not give much scope to superstition but Brahmanic Hinduism promotes superstition. The science of carpentry could not move into higher stages till it was mediated with colonial modernity. But our carpenters worked out various models of wooden house construction. However, this scientific and technological knowledge of the carpenters did not gain spiritual status in Hinduism.

THE ENGINEERING OF POT MAKING

India was home to some of the earliest knowledge systems of pot making in the world. Pot making was well-advanced by the time of the Indus Valley civilization, which existed much before the Aryans invaded India. Who developed that knowledge of pot making? As of now, there are castes and communities which possess very advanced knowledge of pot making in the Indian villages. Such possessors of pot making technology are known as the Kummaris in Telugu region. Similar castes exist in all other states. A careful analysis of this knowledge system indicates that it has quite ancient roots, perhaps older than the Indus Valley civilization itself. The Indus civilizational system was presumably built on the shoulders of our pot makers—but these skills never found expression in any of the Brahmanic texts.

The knowledge of pot making, at the initial stage, requires a careful understanding of the relationship between soil and the potter's wheel that the Indian pot makers use; they rotate the wheel in order to carve out a raw pot on the running wheel. Who taught the pot makers that soft clay could be converted into a pot which could be used for cooking food, preserving water, oils and other solids and liquids that human beings use for survival?

It is obvious that those who were struggling to use the soil sources in order to improve the human living conditions themselves discovered that soft soil can be converted into clay and that clay can be transformed into pots of various sizes and shapes.

The pot making process on the wheel involves several stages. The first stage is that of converting the soil into clay by mixing in proper ratios of soft soil, ash or saw dust and soft sand. This mixture is worked out by adding the necessary amount of water as the mixture is crushed under human feet. Once the clay is ready, the pot maker places it on the wheel specifically constructed with the combined knowledge system of the potter, the ironsmith and the carpenter. This wheel stands on a wooden (in Telugu region they use *sandra* wood to make the support of the wheel) rotator fixed on a marble stone which has a round whole. The potter keeps on applying greasy oil on the wooden support that keeps the movement of the wheel smooth.

The process of wheel-making itself involves a whole range of engineering skills. It is astonishing to know that the pot makers of India could construct such a wheel in almost pre-Indus times. The wheel, the pot and the technology that goes with these processes could not be constructed with the help of book-based knowledge as no Brahman wrote any text either in the Vedic period or later on the matter—no Brahman pundit thought that this engineering technology needs to be recorded.

The clay placed on such fast-running wheel gets pressed with the finger tips into an initial shape called the *niluvu*. At this stage, the artful operation of the fingers and nails of the potter plays a crucial role. The potter also uses a wet cloth as an instrument to work out a well-designed mouth of the pot. Even to carve out the curls and chains at the mouth of the pot, the potter only uses his nails. Thus, in carving out the *niluvu*, the hands, particularly the fingers of the potters, have played a great historic role. Once this *niluvu* is ready, the potter separates it from the wheel and let it dry for a while so that it can be made into a perfect pot in the second stage of hand work.

This hand work involves skillful handling of the wooden slate, a round stone and dry ash. From this stage, women too enter the process of shaping the pot. There are many women who are experts in this operation. Depending on the size of pot that a given *niluvu* can produce, the potter uses slate, stone and ash to blow up its middle part and shape up its base. The ash is used to maintain the moisture levels while doing the hand work. Once the pot is fully made, it is set to dry for a few days so that it acquires the toughness that can withstand the burning process. The third stage is that of burning all the dry pots in a specific place called the Kummari *vaamu* (in Telugu region), which accommodates hundreds of pots. After the pots are arranged, the *vaamu* is covered with mud so that the heat generated by creating a huge fire in hearth at the bottom of the *vaamu* is absorbed into the pots. After the pots get burnt to a particular level of heat, the *vaamu* is allowed to cool down gradually so that the pot becomes stronger and stable and can be used for all kinds of purposes—cooking, preserving water, oil, grain, and so on.

A variety of pots and instruments made out of the engineering process of pot making are available in our country at present. The primary engineering skills that the pot makers worked out branched out in several directions. Very sophisticated pots are thus made in all parts of the country. Our pot makers are producing highly sophisticated pots that are being used as great pieces of interior decoration. But strangely, no Hindu text recorded this great knowledge system to allow the Indian student community and civil society to benefit from this knowledge of our pot makers. Why were the pot makers treated as inferior beings in the Hindu social order? Their status in the Hindu social order is so low that in many states they are known as the Lower Backward Castes. In the Western societies the potters are highly skilled and have acquired a great name for themselves. May be that is the reason why J.K. Rowling named her most popular children's book series as Harry Potter. Such a cultural system does not exist in the Indian context, as the Hindu culture considered the engineering skills of the potters non-respectable. Hence, a potter could never become a hero in any Indian fictional writing. That is also one of the reasons why Indian writing did not attain any respectable status at the global level.

GOLD AND SILVERSMITHING

Apart from iron, wood and pot making, the artisans of India also possess enormous skills in gold and silversmithing. The knowledge of this engineering, though, was not very useful for the productive process as it constructed a cultural and economic value-based wealth in India. Since gold is the most precious metal and its economic value is the highest, the Brahmans and the Baniyas of India possess the largest amount of our gold reserves. A lot of gold exists in their houses in the form of ornaments. The other castes, which acquired some wealth, also possess some gold in the form of ornaments. However, it is generally believed that the Baniyas, the Marwaris who run all kinds of businesses including that of gold, possess the highest amount of gold in their custody. The principle that operates in our caste-ridden society is that the lower the caste the lower the amount of gold that people of that caste own.

The process of ornament-making has been exclusively practised by the gold and silversmiths of India. They are known as Ausulas or Kamsalis in the Telugu region. The goldsmith's operation in India expressed one of the finest engineering skills of the people involved in the process. Brahmanism, through various writings such as the Manudharma, made it clear that the Chandalas and the Shudras do not have the right to wear gold and silver ornaments—but since the ornament-makers were themselves Shudras who did not distinguish between people, they made ornaments for all those who bought gold and silver to them, on the condition that their own wage is paid as per the agreement. To that extent, thus, the smiths violated the Hindu Brahmanical scriptures.

In the most traditional form of ornament-making, a village goldsmith sets the gold in a small crucible and keeps it in a small coal hearth that he exclusively arranges for that purpose in his own house. He uses a mouth pipe to blow air into the hearth by straining his lungs and keeps on blowing till the gold melts in the crucible. Sometimes, the blowing process takes several hours. This is one of the reasons why several goldsmiths die of lung-related diseases. The smith, then, stretches the melted gold into threads and weaves and moulds that gold into threads of all kinds of ornaments that the Indian people wear on their bodies with pride. Similarly, the smiths also make silver ornaments in the same process by melting silver in the hearth. In the next stage, the smith uses several tools like pliers for cutting and hammers of various sizes to make gold and silver threads. He weaves and bends these threads into beautiful ornaments. In some models of ornament-making, gold and silver are shaped into rods. The way a rod is moulded to make an ornament shows the skill of our goldsmiths and silversmiths.

The ornament-making process is quite complicated and requires sophisticated engineering skills. The smiths of India learnt these skills in a long drawn-out process of self-training. Once the basic training was acquired through regular practice and struggle in the process of work, they learnt many intricacies of ornament-making. Once the knowledge of smithing was perfected by the parents—in most cases by the father (though there have been women smiths in the villages who also acquired smithing skills)—the sons were trained in the profession with great care.

HINDUISM AND ALL THESE ENGINEERING SKILLS

Hinduism treated the entire knowledge of engineering in all these fields as a spiritually undignified activity. Neither the gods nor the Brahman saints recognized these engineering processes as spiritually respectable. In several parts of the country, several of these communities tried to define themselves as 'Vishwa Brahmans' or 'Vishwa Karmas'. In the Telugu country, around the eighteenth century, Potuluri Veera Brahmam organized them into a spiritual sect and wrote a book called *Kala Gyana* (Knowledge of Time and Space), and ordained them into dwijahood on lines similar to the Brahmans, Kshatriyas and Vaishyas. Even then the Brahmans did not give them any dignified spiritual status, equal to that of their own beings. Why?

Even if we exclude the toddy-tappers and the pot makers who did not obtain dwijahood (but both in Kerala and Tamil Nadu the Ejavas and Nadars tried to move in to Hinduhood) the smiths and carpenters who took dwijahood on their own also did not acquire respectable spiritual space, because the Shudra 'feet born' status assigned to them does not allow such a change. Not only they, but all the communities that advanced our engineering skills were also devised equal status. Hinduism as a religion and the Brahmans as priests believed that engineering activity was/is un-Hindu. A careful study of trees and their nature in order to use this knowledge for human needs, as the toddy-tappers did, or as the carpenters did, was seen as Shudra un-Hindu activity. The process of understanding the physical characteristics of iron, gold and silver and the process of engineering that moulded them to become instruments of human use was seen as un-Hindu.

The relationship between all engineering skills and the spiritual domain was seen as inimical. Brahmanism also negated the spiritual relationship between the Hindu gods and engineering activities, as such relationship would push them down the ladder of the society. Neither the *Rigveda* nor the *Bhagavad Gita* speak a word about these tasks in human life. The fact that the children of these social forces are also not allowed to become priests in the Hindu temples even now is a clear indication that they do not have any respect for these skills and the contribution of these communities to the Indian economy. In three thousand years of history and several Brahman writings during such a long period, no recognition was accorded to these skills and knowledge systems. Even after two hundred years of the emergence of Indian English writing, mainly by Brahman scholars, the engineering skills of these communities were never recorded—nor were such skills allowed to become part of our school and college text books. But all these knowledge systems and engineering skills are still there in our villages as witnesses to be seen and improved upon and when the children from these castes get into modern IITs and other engineering institutions, they definitely advance our knowledge of engineering.

Chapter 8   Food Producers

In our long journey of discovering truth, after we cross the civil society of the unknown engineers—discovering in the process that they gave us the knowledge of science and technology that built the mother of all cultures, that is, agriculture—we enter into a Shudra *wada* called the Kapus. The name of this caste emerges from the Telugu word meaning 'watchers of the fields'. Even some English dictionaries define them as agriculturists. In this chapter, we shall examine the contribution of a whole range of castes that constructed their self and being around food production from this very land, by developing a process of tilling (*bhoomi dunnuta* in Telugu) the land to produce the food. All the Shudras in the country, whose social status in Hinduism is even now only that of the 'feet born', irrespective of their economic and political status, had somehow consented to remain at the feet of Brahmanism in the spiritual realm. Some sections of these food producers acquired state titles like Reddy, Rao, Singh, Patel, Patil, Nair, Menon, and so on, in different regions of India. They were/are the biggest beneficiaries of Muslim and British rule in economic and political realms. However, they remain 'feet born' even today in the spiritual realm, without gaining the right to establish a direct rapport with the Hindu gods. They cannot become priests in the Hindu temples, irrespective of their knowledge of Sanskrit. They remain mentally enslaved, in spite of the fact that they have a lot of money at their command—and in some states, political power as well. In the political and bureaucratic realms, the situation is such that the Brahman–Baniya forces control the federal resources and at the state level the Shudra upper castes such as Kammas, Reddys, Patels, Jatts and Marathis, and so on, control power. In India, power is shared by the Brahmanic forces and the upper caste Shudras. The Dalit–Bahujans do not figure anywhere. The Shudra state power, however, is under the control of Brahmanism in spiritual–philosophical realms, across the country. Hence, they cannot play any autonomous role in the Indian system.

SHUDRA FEUDALISM

Quite a lot of people from Shudra caste background embraced Islam and Christianity some time ago in history, because the Muslim rulers gave them the right to land and gave them state titles to add to their names. Thus, the emergence of Shudra feudal lords, who could operate within the spiritual and philosophical control of Brahmanism, owes much to Islam, but not to Hinduism. In non-Hindu religions, they could establish a direct rapport with the prophets and the gods that these religions believe in. If you search for the caste roots of the top mullahs among the Indian Muslims and the pastors and bishops among Indian Christians, most of them come from these agrarian castes. In Sikhism, most of the priests come from the Jat community, which, historically, is a Shudra 'feet born' community without having any rights in the Hindu religion. A very long time ago in history, Buddhism had granted equal spiritual rights to all sections of people. Hinduism, both as a way of life and as a religion in the realm of spirituality, did not grant any rights to any Shudras, irrespective of their economic status. Whatever be their economic status, they cannot have an un-mediated *moksha*. Having constructed the word 'Brahman' as knowledge, they moved on to construct that social group into a caste itself and gradually positioned every other social group in total subordination of the Brahmans. In other words, the 33 million (*muppadi muudu kotla devataltu*) gods that the Hindu texts talk about were food-eaters, but not food producers.

SHUDRAS AND PRIESTHOOD

In the Telugu region, one finds names like Reddy and Rao among the Christian pastors, but there is not a single Reddy priest in any of the famous Hindu temples. Nor do we find a Patel, Patil or Nair in any temple worth the name in their respective states. In other words, their 'feet born' spiritual status has not changed, in the post-independence period. Nowadays, many Reddys can directly negotiate with Allah or Christ, but not a single Reddy can negotiate with 'Brahma', the ultimate God of Hinduism. In Hinduism, even the Shudras have no right to negotiate with God at all. The Hindu gods have become the slaves of the Brahmans and the Brahmans have become the masters of the rest of the human beings in the society. So far, none have succeeded in unsettling their position. It is a master–slave relationship, worked out through spiritual means so that liberation for the slaves becomes impossible. They exist in a state of consensual bondage, thereby granting the Brahmans a role of perpetual mastery. The nebulous fact of the priestly Brahman being poor is an instrument used in order to continue this spiritual hegemony. The Shudras, however rich economically and powerful politically, remain philosophically self-alienated. In no text of Hinduism does the Shudra being exist as a historic being—their physical being and their spiritual and philosophical nothingness do not make them living beings in history.

If we look at the wealth and the political power of some of these castes and think that they have attained a spiritual ordination, we are mistaken. They pretend to be commanding the condescending Brahman sometime with their money or muscle power, but ultimately even the most arrogant Shudra has to touch the feet of the priestly Brahman (*paada vandana* or *paada puja*) because of the so-called spiritual power at his command. The Shudra producers of food do not think that they too can command that spiritual realm. The Shudra self-confidence with regards to the philosophical discourses is so low that it needs to be built from the base. That base, however, exists elsewhere, which they will have to search for. The appalling living condition of the Shudras of India can be aptly described by this proverb: 'a satisfied human being is worse than a dissatisfied pig.'

The spiritual status of a social community depends on its position in interpreting the spiritual books that establish the relationship between God and human beings. Second, its right to communicate with the God within the temple, mosque or the church depends on how that spiritual text represents that community's self. Brahmanical spirituality wrote texts that historically defaced the productive cultural and civilizational ethic of the Shudras, thereby erasing the Shudra self from history. Let us now examine what these spiritual slaves—though not poor economically—have contributed in order to earn that perpetual spiritual slavery, and what it is that makes them unable to understand that they are slaves in the highest realm that humanity has established for its salvation, at least notionally. A word of caution: some diabolical Shudras may themselves argue that they are not interested in spiritual status, but that is an expression of the fear of freedom—an expression of habitual serfdom in the spiritual realm. The philosophical realm and the spiritual realm are very closely inter-connected.

The Shudra castes believe that they are in a position to operate the physical and the political realms, but that leaves them in historical nothingness. I shall construct their philosophical being in their own historical image here.

DISCOVERING LAND AS MEANS OF PRODUCTION

It is possible that the Shudras of India in the pre-Brahman (that is, pre-Aryan) period had realized that land is an agent of production. More particularly, the Shudra women must have realized that like their own womb, which produces a being similar to their own or to the men who cohabit with them, the land too produces new plants that are akin to the existing trees—with similar leaves, similar branches and similar seeds in their ripened state. They must have observed that plants and animals, like them, reproduce beings similar to themselves, and that while in the case of the animal it is the female womb that produces new life, in case of plants the womb is hidden in the land. This understanding of the land was one of the key links in building up the knowledge system of food production. Thus, this mother land (that the Indian Brahmans talk about in a rhetorical manner) owes its development not to the Brahman knowledge but to the knowledge of the Shudra women of India. It owes its development to their hard labour and their unrecorded ability to discover things. The Brahmans of India refused to learn that simple but great truth. This basic truth was discovered by the people of common sense but not by the people of *mantras*. The discovery of this truth, as Hinduism tells us, is not a *maya* (mirage) but a truth that can be seen, touched and realized by everyone and everywhere. It is from this discovery that the process of food production developed.

THE PHILOSOPHY OF TILLING

Once this truth was recognized as a scientific truth, the efforts to till the land began. The philosophy of tilling the land was treated by Brahmanism as a mundane subject, not even worth discussing. It was not considered to be 'knowledge', but a part of *Shudratwam*—work of production, unworthy of consideration in the philosophical realm. But tilling the land is not a mundane task of unworthy beings; it is but a task of constructing philosophy itself. This philosophy of production is the most profound philosophy that the humans have ever constructed. The life cycle of human beings depended on this philosophical basis. Though the philosophy of food production, has its roots in food consumption, once the production started it went beyond the level of mere consumption that the Brahmans understand. Step by step it lead to the process of social development. The Shudra notion of development has an inherent belief in the equality of all productive beings—this is where it stands in opposition to Brahmanism.

The relationship between the philosophy of tilling and the translation of that philosophy into an action is a dialectical relationship. When Gautama Buddha first saw the tilling of land by bulls pulling a wooden plough, he could not believe that such a technological process could operate before his eyes. It was an unknown wonder for him. In his childhood, the tribal republics survived only on *podu* production of grain. The transformation of the production process from *podu* production to plough production was a major revolutionary transformation. This revolution was taking place in the childhood days of the Buddha—for the youth of that generation, the process of tilling by bull was a more miraculous revolution than the computer revolution of the late twentieth century. The Brahmans of India refuse to record the greatness of the Shudra social productivity that has driven the vehicle of knowledge to the logical end of developing the knowledge of tilling. The knowledge of tilling was the first historical knowledge that saw the transformability of earth and nature into a humanly usable system within a limited span of time. They achieved this transformation with their own labour. It was in this process of tilling and seeding that the human being realized his/her humanness and the worth of a being.

The scientific process of tilling the land not only centred around the construction technological instruments like the plough, the yoke, leather ropes, iron rods, the spade, the axe, and so on, but also went beyond that knowledge system. The translation of the knowledge of technology into the praxis of production was a historic achievement of the Shudras. This praxis of production was not an easy, mundane process. It was linked to the skills of handling technological instruments which play with the life of the cattle and the humans who handled that system. The cattle faced very dangerous leg injuries (*kaalu karru*) with the *karru* hitting their leg on account of indiscipline. Injuries could also happen when the animals were indisciplined and kept running here and there with the yoke on their neck. The human being tilling the land could also get crushed in between the plough and the bulls running in all directions with the yoke on their neck. The whole tilling process requires the training of healthy bulls. But the Brahmans of ancient India regarded these animals only as a source of sumptuous meal. Quite ironically, they treated the skilled task of training the healthy bulls as plough drivers as a foolish task. As opposed to the task of training cattle to become productive animals, the Brahmans found the performance of *yagyas*, with their practice of killing these animals, as the most profound form of knowledge. No Indian *rishi* realized in the manner of Jesus Christ that a balanced yoke on the necks of disciplined animals is a symbol of spiritual attainment. Of such a vast number of Hindu gods, not even one talked about the yoke and the relationship between the cattle and human beings—they talked instead about war and war weapons. Rama was described as *purushottama* for killing Tataka and cutting off the nose and earlobes of Surpanakha, the bravest woman in the Ramayana. Krishna was described as Vishwarupa for stealing butter from the Yadavas and for establishing nefarious relationships with Yadava women. Even in grammar books, sentences like 'Rama killed Ravana' and 'Krishna had stolen the butter' have shown the lack of respect for a productive profession. India, as a nation, had lost its direction because of this mode of spirituality. The notion of mother goddesses getting closely associated with productive land as *bhooshakti* (Earth Goddess) indicates the feminist theocratic policy that the Indian Dalit–Bahujan society has constructed. But such feminist philosophical discourses have no value in the Hindu spiritual ideology.

We have seen in the chapter on the productive soldiers that the social forces like the Malas had initiated the whole process of cattle training to begin a bull- and buffalo-centred agrarian production. In sustaining and expanding that system of domesticated cattle to be trained to become productive agrarian beings, the Shudra castes like the Kapus, the Velams, the Kammas and the Reddys played a useful role for a long time in history. Thus, these castes have come to be known as agrarian castes, while living broadly within Shudra culture and economy. As I have shown in *Why I am Not a Hindu*, their transformation into neo-Kshatriya socio-cultural modes is a subsequent development. During the early nationalist period, it was with this Shudra consciousness that the present-day Shudras like Kammas and Reddys organized the Justice Party in South India and a powerful Kisan movement in the North India, like the one organized by Charan Singh, who became the first Shudra Prime Minister, only to be thrown out within six months. Let us see where the actual strength of the agrarian castes lies.

TILLING AS SCIENCE

Tilling the land, after the discovery of the 'plough', had to be done on a highly scientific basis. Tilling has now become a task that all castes interact with, except the Brahman, the Kshatriya and the Vaishyas. For these three

Brahmanical tasks, tilling is, even now, a foolish Shudra task. Let us see what that process of stupidity is.

Tilling the land with the wooden plough, with the help of the power of the yoked cattle, is one of the most scientific and materialist processes that our ancestors have handed down to us. This mode of tilling still dominates the Indian agrarian production. The most brilliant man among the tillers is the one who establishes the first furrow in order to strike a *kondra* (two furrows are ploughed leaving a two and half- to -three metre space in between) by leaving enough space between the first furrow and the second furrow. Furrowing one after the other to completely upturn the land needs enormous skills. It requires mathematical precision as it requires one to leave enough space for cattle mobility and also strike furrow after furrow so that upturning of every inch of the land becomes possible. As the plough gets pushed into the earth and the cattle keep pulling the plough, the plough might encounter stones and the roots of dead and living trees. Indifference on the part of the tiller ends in breaking the plough. If the tilling starts early in the morning, the tiller tills till late evening with absolute alertness.

The tiller's knowledge about the land and its nature and character is a basic necessity to conduct the operation of tilling efficiently. A tiller understands the nature of the soil by examining its very surface itself. An average tiller, who constantly handles the plough, knows the character of the soil in minute details. The tiller has to assess the moisture levels of the soil at the beginning of the tilling process itself. The land must be neither too wet nor too dry to be fit for what is known as 'dry cultivation'.

The farmers (several Shudra, Chandala and Adivasi communities perform the task of tilling) have developed highly sophisticated knowledge in their very communicable languages. If there is a rain, the tillers measure it in terms of ploughability of the land as one or two furrow-depths of the rain (known as *Saaleti vaana* or *rendu Saalla vaana*). A Brahman pundit does not know how to measure the levels of rain—the tiller knows it in its all dimensions. Nor did the social forces who wrote the Hindu scriptures know that this knowledge is central for human survival. Why do the Hindu gods not treat this knowledge as knowledge? There are references to this process in the Buddhist texts, in the Bible and the Quran, but neither the *Rigveda* nor the *Bhagavad Gita* refer to this process even once. Why is it to they did not recognize what the Hindu Shudra culture had achieved (an elaborate system of agriculture and great relationship between the land and the human beings) throughout history? It was because of the negation of agriculture that the Brahmanic culture has become negative and self-destructive. In the absence of the Shudra culture in these books, the

Indian culture, as it is constructed in these books, lives amidst the corpses that are left behind in the wars that the Hindu gods conducted. There is no place for production in Hindu culture as none of the religious texts talk about it positively. The Hindu gods and priests do not give any value to agriculture. The very ethic of Hindu religion is against tilling of land. The Brahman priests do not know that culture does not mean worshipping of war. On the contrary, worshipping production and the forces that engendered production is both spiritual and material. The philosophy of production establishes the relationship between the two. A cultural scenario changes if a god or a prophet is said to have been born in a tiller's family or is said to have interacted with a whole range of productive structures. Since Hinduism is not a prophet-centered monotheistic religion, the Hindus do not have a common literary material (like the Bible or Quran) to evolve a model code of conduct. The ethical fibre of Hindus is weak. Hinduism did not mediate between God and the productive culture of the people, which is the actual source of survival of all the priestly beings.

The tilling process, as I said, was/is a skill-based process. It has to be done in a rhythmic manner. The ploughman has to hold on to the reigns in order to control the trained oxen and guide them to change the direction, control their speed, and so on—this too is a task that requires skill. While carefully looking at the land being tilled, the tiller has to press the plough so that it keeps the land furrowed in a very rhythmic manner. The stick in his right hand keeps the oxen constantly under fear, without leaving any scope for misbehaviour on the part of the oxen. A Shudra differs from the European master, who tortured the slave to produce. The Shudras love even the cattle as they are co-labouring beings. This is the reason why the actual tillers of land have always remained humane.

A tiller's skill in handling the plough is a much more sophisticated task as it needs to be performed in a cool and calculated manner. The driving of the plough is a historic task that needs to be done without creating emotions which produce imbalances in the mind of the tiller. The tiller's psychology, thus, is the very opposite of that of the driver of the war chariot. The driver of a war chariot feels a hysteric emotion—the tiller, on the other hand, is a man with a cool and determined mind. Repeated training in the process of tilling gives him the necessary skill, energy and self-control that is required to keep the activity going day after day, month after month and year after year. Horses, brought to India by the Aryan invaders, were trained only to be the animals of war. They needed to be driven to the war theatre either to kill or to be killed. But driving the plough requires the opposite understanding and the opposite mode of training the animals. It must be done with patience. Both the man who handles the plough and the animals that work on it need psychological training to be cold and determined. The tilling is not a high profile work. It does not grant one fame or immortality that driving a war chariot does. It needs to be done with the conviction of saving the lives of humans and animals. The conviction was/is a historical conviction. A religion that does not give the spiritual and social recognition to this historic task of tilling negates the existential reality of God. Hinduism does that by recognizing only war through all its scriptures starting with *Rigveda*. It passes that ideology of war through *Ramayana* and *Mahabharata*. Take for example the *Bhagavad Gita*, which is said to have been constructed in a theatre of war, Kurukshetra. The spiritual and social morality that this book constructs out of war terrain cannot stand for non-violence nor does it stand for human welfare and positive production. It stands for war and violence. No tiller can take inspiration from this book. Nor does it help in advancing our knowledge about agriculture.

A FEMININE REALM

Agriculture, philosophically, does not operate in the masculine realm; it essentially operates in the feminine realm. Women must have been instrumental in discovering the productive abilities of land. The experience of procreation, as I said earlier, would have helped women in understanding the processes involved in agriculture. The discovery and execution of production is rooted in femininity; war, on the other hand, is a masculine operation both in discovery and execution. What would have happened to Indian agriculture if women were not involved in it at every stage in every season? Women are central in preparing the land for cultivation—for tilling, seeding, weeding, cutting, and so on. Brahmanism has constructed the divine ritual as a masculine realm, where the women have no place. The Indian Shudra and Chandala women are great experts in seeding the furrow. The seeding operation is a highly skilled task. It is done with one's hands and fingers. The movement of the finger is made with great expertise based on the size of the seed.

If the Brahman women were experts in cooking the (divine) food, an act that provides energy to the human beings to consume what has been already produced, the Shudra—Chandala women were/are experts in producing and preparing that produce for consumption as well. Within the realm of females, the Dalit–Bahujan women performed the most self-gratifying productive tasks. Thus, the doubly-exploited Dalit–Bahujan women do posses an experience of a doubly-gratifying life. It is here, in this land, that a myriad wealth of experiences of highly creative social forces lies in an accumulative form—in the form of body and mind of our Dalit–Bahujan women. This nation and the world have not grasped the abilities of these historical social reserves yet. The fact that the Brahmanical books condemned them as ignorant and stupid does not make them historically non-existent people. They were deliberately rendered invisible. The true history of India does not lie in the process of the Brahmanical women writing and re-writing the names of Rama and Krishna, but in the processes of seeding the furrows, weeding and cutting off the crops by the Shudra women. The Brahmanical women were never allowed to understand the significance of tilling and seeding.

Seeding is a highly spiritual activity, because the seed has to germinate and grow into a plant and reproduce its own self. The average Shudra women and men treat the process of seeding with great reverence as the life of the tillers, seeders and of the civil society are dependent on that activity. The seed *gampa* (basket) is decorated with turmeric and neem leaves as and when they are filled with seeds. Once a woman begins to seed, her mind remains focused on the seed and the furrow for hours. The seeder walks behind the tiller, planting the seeds with much more attention than the priest leaves water and grains to propitiate the Hindu gods, setting down the necessary gap between each seed. The woman involved in the seeding process knows that her task is very sacred and tries to keep her body—more importantly, her mind—as clean as possible. If they had been sinners living at the cost of others no seed would have germinated. The source of sacredness lies in building the regenerative power within the human being. The Shudra women have laid the foundation of our sacredness by increasing the productive energy of the plant with their historical involvement in the seeding process.

If women involved in the seeding process are menstruating, or have had sexual intercourse that day, it is never believed to be inauspicious, though bathing goes as a natural part of protection of one's health. The man who tills the land and the woman who seeds has no different values in approaching the productive land, even in spiritual terms. The productive land, in their view, is a mother goddess. If our women were to stop the highly sacred activity of seeding during menstruation, the production would have suffered so much so that both the male and the female population would have perished for want of food. Seeding is a seasonal process, and therefore cannot allow hours and days to go to waste—the three or four day menstrual period is too long in the precious seeding period to allow the women to be rendered untouchable. If the Brahmanical notion of untouchability of the menstruating woman, as practised in the patriarchal Brahmanical realm during a woman's menstrual period, had been practised by the Shudras as well, thereby keeping the Shudra women away from their task of seeding, humanity would have never had crops at all. Men have never been good seeders. If a straight line of crops is an indication of a man's skill, the distance between two plants is an indication of a woman's skill in seeding—a man is no match for a woman in this task. Brahmanism, with its strict rules controlling the lives of women, could not have saved humanity with its prayers alone unless the Shudras had continued with the process of tilling and seeding. However, disrespect to that sacred activity in the Brahmanical spiritual realm has left the nation dull-headed.

All the agrarian activity operates around the notion of the goddess, Mother Earth. The Shudra producers have proved that they produce grain and fruits, and produce their own beings without the help of the Brahmanic spirituality. But the Brahman life could not exist without the help of the Shudra grain and the food resources that the Shudra women produce with hard work, even while menstruating. Menstruation, in their life, is a part of human existence. It is a life process of a human being—both spiritual and material. The relationship between the menstrual blood and human germination is similar to that of the mud in the productive field and the germinating seed that establishes an organic link with the mud. Understanding the organic relationship between the process of nature and humans is the essence of the spiritual philosophy. The so-called spiritual philosophers of the world—more so the Brahman philosophers of India—have failed to understand this truth of life, since no philosopher of the world carefully studied the Shudra experience, especially that of the Shudra women.

DIVINITY AND FERTILITY

The societies that constructed the civil relations around female goddesses have different notions of divinity and fertility. There is no society in the world which constructed as many organic female goddesses as the Dalit–Bahujan society has done. The relationship between the goddesses and the female world is not dependent on the life cycles—neither puberty, nor menstruation serves as a prohibition. The Shudras like the Reddys, Velamas and the Kapus have been closely associated with Shudra goddesses all through the evolution of the human society. In the recent past, there has been an attempt to move away from their Shudraness, which would have self-destructive implications for them.

Puberty and menstruation are a part of the process of human procreation. Unlike the male abdomen, which only possesses digestive capacity, the abdomen of the female has both digestive as well as procreative capacities. This abdomen has the qualities of the fertile land. Among the Shudra social forces, the difference between fertile land and barren land is quite categorical. The barren land does not grow anything within its womb—where there is no life, there exists nothing to die, either. Patriarchal spirituality is similar to barren land spirituality. The female spirituality, on the other hand, is like fertile land spirituality. While tilling and seeding, both the men and women interact with the land, but the interaction of the seeder remains more intimate—deeper and life sustaining. The man's furrowing is an external activity, whereas the female seeding activity is internal and integrative. These days we can find women priests among the Shudras. They can negotiate with the goddesses and the gods directly. As opposed to this historical spiritual process, the infertile men constructed their infertile male god images, and portrayed the fertile women as spiritual untouchables, who cannot even become priests. The interaction of male priests with the male gods is a strange form of interaction, without either of them possessing fertility energy. The Shudra society has a different productive relationship, where women can be priests of male gods and males can be priests of female goddesses. The society, however, gave centrality to women, as it assigned the central role to land in production.

The fertile land grows many things, and many things keep dying there. Death is the source of rebirth. The Shudras—particularly women— know the history of the life cycle very well. That is the reason why, much before the notion of God came into existence, the notion of the Goddess was constructed in the Shudra civil society. The roots of the female Goddess go back to the Indus Valley civilization. This cult of the female Goddess lost its cultural track in the violent patriarchal attack of the Aryans. However, the understanding of the female body as both productive and reproductive is integral to the Shudra agrarian systems in our villages. Both puberty and menstruation are like the productive land requiring to generate some mud out of its own self and producing food out of that mud. One, therefore, cannot hate mud and love only the food that comes out of it. All patriarchal religions erred here, and Hinduism is the most brutally patriarchal of all religions.

WEEDING AS A NON-VIOLENT ACTIVITY

Weeding is a process of both protecting the useful plants for human sustenance and destroying the useless plants that harm the useful ones. The Shudra women (now all Dalit-Bahujan women) were/are experts in the weeding operations. Brahmanism defined weeding as a violent process that takes life out of the plants being weeded out. Of course, all process of cutting (be it of crops, or animals) have been seen as life-taking processes. Cutting vegetables for making curry also involves the process of taking life out of plants and fruits. The Brahmanical forces claimed that since they were not involved in agrarian activities, they were/are free from the sin of taking life away. The process of food production is aimed at a higher sacred act, that of saving the human life. In the process, it involves a contradictory process of taking life in order to save the doubly useful life. The weed is killed in order to save the doubly useful plant which produces grain. This is where the Shudra, Chandala and the Adivasi agrarian masses have gained an accumulated sacredness (*punyam*) by saving the most important human life by producing food. By weeding out all those plants that otherwise would have killed the productive plants (or their productivity would have been drastically reduced), the Dalit–Bahujan communities have approached the production process scientifically. The Brahman pundits failed to explain anywhere what makes this process anti-divine.

The Brahmanical forces, on the other hand, joined in consuming the final product in the form of grain, without participating in any life-saving activity. All productive people in the historical process of production are involved in a dialectical process of generating and regenerating life while simultaneously weeding out the destructive plants. All the Brahmans and Baniyas of India, on the other hand, are involved only in the activity of consumption, which is a self-saving process and involves the cumulative killing of other lives, without participating in the life-regenerating process of planting seeds and nurturing them with water and manure. Though the agrarian masses too involve in the process of consumption, they produce and consume. They do so only after involving themselves in an entire process of regenerative labour. The production of regenerative labour, thus, is spiritually the most pious act that human beings can perform in their life process. Those who do not involve in such regenerative and productive labour but consume the labour power of the producers, without exchanging any other labour reserves that accumulate in their own body, are not only social criminals but are spiritual sinners as well. In this sense, the Brahmans of India are the most sinful on earth, since the beginning of human existence on this planet, no other community is as perpetually away from productive and regenerative labour as the Brahmans as a social community has been in this world. Yet, this community constructed itself as a community that is spiritually pure and socially more knowledgeable. This is a paradox that Hindu spiritual thought brought into operation.

With such communities—the Dalits at one end of the historical productive civil society and the Brahmans at the other end of the historically
consciously constructed civil society—the world is structured with two
perpetual opposites. This opposition of the social forces, as the Brahmanical
existence and writings have constructed, is not based on the Brahmanical
knowledge and the Shudra, Chandala and Adivasi ignorance. It was/is
based on the perpetual Brahmanical possessiveness and the perpetual self-
alienation of the productive masses from their selves. The Shudras like the
Reddys, Kammas, Jats, Patels, Nairs and Lingayats have not realized the
importance of the loss of that historical self. The social communities that
have lost their self in the spiritual realm cannot gain the real self in any
other process—neither by earning money nor by acquiring political power.
The experience of the Shudra castes of India has proved that. They have
not understood how their productive non-violent being was constructed as
the essence of violence, and the violent Brahmanical essence was portrayed
instead in their own mirror, as absolutely non-violent.

The Brahmanical forces justified their non-involvement in productive
labour in terms of the desire to be non-violent, as the productive labour
processes like weeding and cutting crops involves violence against plant and
insect life. However, they never hesitated in killing the Shudras, Chandalas
and the Adivasis in the most brutal manner in the name of protecting caste
dharma. The Hindu Brahman *rishis* instigating Rama to kill Shambhuka is
a well-known tale. The process of taking Shudra and Chandala life, even
in the capitalist era, is a continuous process, as the caste rules became a
part of the market as well. They not only formulated the narratives of the
warrior male gods as divine dispensations, but also constructed the theory
of *dandaneeti* in the realms of the state and the civil society. They wrote
narratives that show production as a sinful activity and prayer—*puja* in
particular—as a spiritual activity.

For the Brahmans of India, human life was/is much cheaper than the
life of plants and flies—human beings must learn not to be like them. At
the same time, the world should learn many things from the Shudras,
Chandalas and the Adivasis for the simple reason that they are social
communities who have spent enormous amount of labour to produce
food for the consumption of the world, without finding some place in the
spiritual realm of the consumer. The supplier's being was constantly shown
as a sinful being, and the consumer's being as the sacred being. Apart
from feeding the Brahmans, Baniyas and the Kshatriyas for millennia,
the Shudras, Chandalas and the Adivasis also produced in order to feed
the Muslim rulers and the British ruling classes for centuries. None of the

consuming classes, however, paid the producers back. The social forces most indebted to these producers of grain are the Brahmans. The struggle against the Brahmans, therefore, is a struggle for historical debt repayment. This indebtedness is not merely material, but it is also ethical and spiritual.

CUTTING CROPS AND CONSTRUCTIVE LABOUR

The weeding process, in a subsequent phase, leads to the cutting of the crops. Cutting of the crops was/is treated by the Brahmanical forces as taking of life in a more brazen form. The Shudras and Chandalas, who were involved in large-scale crop-cutting, knew that both cutting crops or cutting fruits from the plants and trees involves taking life of the plant or of the fruit in order to resolve the contradiction between human life and the nature in which they are living.

The sacrifice of the life of the plants and the fruits is an inevitable aspect of the process of maintaining human life. There is an inherent contradiction between the human life and nature, in which human life definitely has a higher purpose. The purpose of positive use of natural resources to suit human needs is a divinely ordained purpose. For example, in the Bible—in Genesis—God says in clear terms that He has created plants, fruits, animals, birds, and so on, for human consumption. Therefore, human beings love to work to increase nature's bounty and use it for human survival. The contradiction between human life and nature must always be resolved in favour of the human being.

Human existence is comprised of different stages of the Darwinian 'struggle for existence', which combines both the processes of evolution and revolution. The first stage of this struggle for existence constituted the taking of animal life to progressively preserve the human life. Eating of fish, beef and other kinds of meat came into existence as part of the struggle for existence among the native Adivasi, Chandala and Shudra social forces. By the time the Brahmanical Aryans came here the native people were non-vegetarians. Gradually the Indian masses grew out of non-vegetarianism and moved onto combining cultivation with eating of fish and meat, including beef. Vegetarianism was brought into operation in order to overcome cannibalism, but not the practise of eating meat. On the other hand, the huge killing of humans by the Aryan invaders under the leadership of Indra and Brahma, as they figure in the *Rigveda*, could have been to fulfill their cannibalistic appetite. It is a well-known fact that by the time Buddha began to mobilize animal power for agrarian production, the Aryans were beef-eaters. From that day, to this date, the Brahmans of India have not laid their hands on the tools of agrarian production, thereby showing how anti-agriculturalist they were and still are. While the Shudras developed an expertise in using productive tools, the upper caste Hindus developed an expertise in using the weapons. The Mahabharata shows that Drona and other teachers like him were willing to teach the usage of war weapons to Pandavas and Kauravas, but they were not interested in teaching nuances of agrarian production.

Even in the post-industrial modernity, the Brahmans of India claim to be vegetarian non-violent social forces, while continuing to consume, without having an intercourse with agrarian production. This is a diabolism of the Brahmanical variety. The Brahmanic community survives through the consumption of human labour, by systematically sucking the Shudra, Chandala and the Adivasi blood in the form of their labour power that is invested in all fields of production. It is in this background that we must understand the danger of vegetarianism and the Brahmanical refusal to participate in the process of crop-cutting. In fact, crop-cutting is only to pave the way for regenerating yet another round of productive crops. It is meant to bring into being more living things, which serves the cyclical purpose of continuation of human and animal life. Brahmanism constantly stood against this process.

The crop-cutting process, thus, has been an activity of regenerating life. The crop is cut, and in the place of the mature and dying crop a re-growth of fresh crop is worked out—again with the involvement of Shudra labour. The Shudras and the Chandalas have not realized and asserted upon the significance of their involvement in this regenerative activity. The Brahmans of India have never been involved with this process of regeneration of life, but at the same time, they continue to claim that they are the most useful people on earth and are, therefore, *bhoodevtas* (Earth God).

THE SHUDRA–CHANDALA ENVIRONMENTALISM

If a tiller, while tilling the land looks at an aeroplane going over his head, he knows not that every such plane will carry at least one Indian environmentalist from one metropolis to another. Not a single environmentalist, however, has any relation of kinship with the builders of environment on earth. In the Christian world, a baker conducted experiments as to how to reduce the emergence of smoke from the bakery, and tiller (Tiller has been a common surname in Western practice) worked out ways and means to discover the relationship between the smokeless bakery and the increased greenery and productivity of the land that s/he tilled, seeded and grew crops on. Both of them theorized that experiment through the textual knowledge that they acquired by reading a common spiritual text, the Bible. More than the Bible, that world has allowed human beings to create new knowledge through writing, almost for centuries, reflecting the real experience of the producers themselves. But no Hindu book reflected the real experience of the producers, though many Indian Hindu or so-called secular environmentalists draw quotations from Hindu texts to prove that their environmentalist theories are nationalistic and rooted in the soil!

Not only do the present-day Brahmanical environmentalists do not have kinship relations with the builders of the environment, but they also, on the contrary, possess backgrounds that hated the builder of the environment as the abusable Shudra, Chandala and Adivasi. In the non-Hindu social contexts, the builder of the environment (agriculture) shared a blood relationship with the theoretician, because there was/is no prohibition in the establishment of kinship relations between the baker, the tiller, the shepherd, the potter, the pastor, and so on. Those working in the bakery, tilling the land and leading the prayer meeting in the church thus had (have) intimate social intercourse. More often than not, the members belonging to one family branch out into several such fields. Brahmanical Hinduism does not allow this to happen. No names of the theoreticians relate to the work and labour that he or she is theorizing upon. The Brahmanical environmentalists speak about environmentalism without their toes ever touching the soil and their fingers ever touching the factory tools ever since their ancestors migrated to this land and turned into 'Brahman' (knowledge). The modern media is at the feet of these Brahmanical environmentalists, with the press carrying the smell of their non-sweaty bodies to every nook and corner of the world. The tillers (the Shudras, Chandalas and the Adivasis) on the ground do not know how to deal with this form of environmentalism. This form of environmentalism appears to be as progressive as Gandhi's—a revered Baniya leader—regard for cows, despite the fact that the Bainyas lost track of their relationship with cows and buffaloes after they ceased to be agriculturalists in ancient India. All these environmentalists believe that cows are sacred and buffaloes are sinful. After drinking their coffee made of buffalo milk (as the cow does not produce much milk in India), they go on an environmental voyage of cow protection. So far, no food producer has ever contested the theories of Brahmanical environmentalism. That is the reason why the Brahmanical environmentalists can fly in their jet planes while the real protectors of the environment—the food producers—do not have food to eat.

Some of the environmentalists carry on with their so-called secular agenda in their language, while not bothering about the social structure that Brahmanism has built, that never allowed any secular relationship between the environment builders and the consumers of the environmental resources. How can a methodology conditioned by Brahmanism be 'secular', given the fact that Brahmanism has historically stood against that mode of integrative environmentalism where humans, animals, birds and other living beings can live in collectivity in order to grow crops and trees and develop a collectively habitable environment? To achieve that, secularism must encompass not only religions but also castes—the latter is more important in the Indian context. For cow nationalism, and also for cow environmentalism, the coexistence of buffaloes does not constitute a secular economic agenda. Even the secular environmentalists think that the buffalo is sinful and the cow is a sacred animal, but they never think of the buffalo as an animal which is the source of our health and environment. Whatever happens to buffaloes does not bother them because in their childhood upbringing, the cow was said to be a sacred animal by their (un)holy parents. It was while drinking buffalo milk that the Brahmanical society constructed the cow as a sacred being. Even the environmentalists did not see any link between this kind of cow nationalism and Brahmanic environmentalism, as they all share some common roots in the anti-buffalo ideology of Hinduism.

The environment is being destroyed in India because Brahmanism constructed a philosophy inimical to the environment, wherein the Brahmans would not involve themselves in the processes of food production and physically working with nature, which should be a necessary aspect of one's childhood training. To change this process, the Shudra producers should redefine their spiritual and socio-economic self as a life-regenerating, and therefore, sacred, great and non-violent self. Things would change once we accept that the concept of 'Brahman' is socio-economically criminal and spiritually sinful.

The Shudra forces cannot liberate themselves from the historical bondage of spiritual slavery until and unless they demand spiritual equality. They cannot enter the phase of modernity though physical wealth and political power existing and operating within the hegemonic framework of Brahmanical India, because such modernity stands in total opposition to Brahmanism. The two central preservers of Brahmanism are the historically evolved Brahmanic spiritual culture and the business economy of the

Baniyas. They now take up the space in the temples, the businesses, the bureaucracies, the realm of art and literature and the non-resident Indian social base as well. All these centres operate from a perspective of negative nationalism. We shall, in the subsequent two chapters, see how the so-called nationalist Brahman–Baniya castes have worked out the institutional mechanisms in order to keep the Indian Shudra, Chandala and Adivasi masses enslaved in the next millennium as well.

Chapter 9   Social Smugglers

Our long journey across the civil societal terrain of the Adivasis, Chandalas and the Shudras gave us an understanding that the socio-economic, cultural, spiritual and philosophic life of these communities has enormous potential of reshaping India in their own image. That India will be entirely different from what it is now. After crossing this beautiful social terrain of the Adivasi, Chandala and the Shudra castes we enter into a caste called Vaishyas, who are known as the Komatis in the Telugu region. This caste operates in the realm of business all over India, as it is their spiritually sanctified profession. Though small in number, a major part of the market economy that operates outside the non-Muslim, non-Buddhist, non-Pharisee, non-Sikh and non-Christian market economy is in the hands of Indian Baniyas, who also bear the name of Marwaris, Sethis, Guptas, and so on. Quite a lot of business economy that operates within the market, the civil society and in their families is considered spiritually sanctified *guptadhana*. The highest amount of gold and silver reserves in India, apart from liquid cash, exists in their houses with the clear sanction of the Hindu religion and also the approval of the modern state system. The inequitable distribution of wealth has continued even after independence; the ownership of private property is largely confined to certain castes. The Baniyas used this state fully to their advantage to amass wealth in various forms.

WHAT IS SOCIAL SMUGGLING?

I have characterized, as the very title of this chapter shows, the Baniyas of India as social smugglers. The concept of smuggling is normally used with a sense of taking away wealth/goods and commodities across the boundaries of nations without any legal sanction. The advanced learner's dictionary defines smuggling as 'taking some thing secretly and in defiance of rules and regulations'. How does the Baniya business get characterized as smuggling? Business began as a process of exchange of goods and commodities during the feudal mode of production in other parts of the world. The first open competition in the civil society among individuals cutting across communitarian lines came into operation with the process of business itself. In the European context, the children of the servants and also of vagabonds entered into business, which, in their context, was based more on individual entrepreneurship rather than on communitarian/caste entrepreneurship. Since the feudal lords looked down upon the business activity, the youth from the rest of the civil society found an opportunity to start businesses on competitive basis. The spiritual society did not impose any restrictions on the process of business enterprise.

In India, the social process of the emergence of business took place on altogether different lines. The caste system constructed social blocks to the process of free enterprise. The Hindu religion intervened and assigned even the process of business to a community called Vaishyas. In ancient India, the pre-business Baniyas called the Vaishyas in the Hindu texts were characterized as field supervisors. Later on, with the sanction of the Hindu texts, they were promoted as exclusive traders. It was done by drawing spiritual boundaries around the Baniyas as well as other communities and by denying rights to handle the trade economy to other communities. The Hindu religion sanctioned exclusive rights to some communities and assigned exclusive duties to other communities. The Brahmans sanctioned to their own selves an exclusive right to deal with divine agencies and they also sanctioned an exclusive right over business to the Baniyas. The Brahmans did this while sanctioning themselves the exclusive right to draw upon that wealth through spiritual means. With this contract between the Brahmans and the Baniyas, they too were sanctioned the spiritual right of dwijahood. In this contract the other communities were never a party. With the emergence of a *dwija* Baniya caste, who agreed to be their spiritual subordinates, the Brahmans acquired a permanent base of social wealth for their human and spiritual consumption of national wealth and resources.

BANIYAS AS A BUSINESS CASTE

With the emergence of the Baniyas as an exclusive business caste, the Brahmans did not have to depend on only the Kshatriyas for accumulation of wealth. As pro-production Vaishyas turned to permanent business and usury, capital mobilization slowly became an anti-production process and the Baniyas monopolized the process. The Brahmans, with an ideology of a contracted spiritual hegemony (the consent of Kshatriyas and Vaishyas has been given as they too obtained spiritual dwijahood, which was not the case with any other caste) and the authority to sanction license to smuggle grain, goods and commodities only to the Baniyas, retained their spiritual command over the Baniya wealth. For example, neither the Baniyas nor the Kshatriyas had any right to enter into the profession of priesthood. But the Brahmans could easily enter into business or into the realm of politics without any problem. This mode of Brahman hegemony continues till today, as even now the Baniyas have no right to enter into the priesthood, whereas the Brahmans have a right to enter into business in many parts of the country. However, the relationship between the Brahmans and the Baniyas in the age of capitalist globalization seems to be cordial, as they both operate from the strength of the enormous amount of wealth that they have accumulated in the post-independence period in India.

Thus, both the Brahmans and the Baniyas are assured of plenty of socially smuggled wealth for the continuation of their comfortable leisure-centred life around temples, offices, educational institutions, and so on. In the post-independence context, the capital that the Baniyas mobilized by both legal and illegal means allowed the Brahmans to gain the political power to operate without any legal hurdles. Indian law has become virtually that of the Brahmans and the Baniyas. The process of privatization has accrued them even more wealth than what they accumulated in the process of nationalization of institutions. Of course, while building up state assets during the long period of the Congress regime, the Brahman bureaucrats earned more illegal money than the Baniya business caste did. That does not mean that the Baniyas did not make money from the state during that period. Since the Baniya business supplied the hardware for all kinds of government constructions, the Baniyas saw to it that the state is looted in connivance with Brahman bureaucrats and politicians. Thus, for more than 60 years, the state and civil society became terrains of their economic plunder.

Several mechanisms were worked out in order to draw different social boundaries for the accumulation of the wealth that gets generated with the labour power of the Bahujans through a process of so-called business. In the European countries when people began to use mercantile capital to conduct different kinds of businesses, they ensured that social rights were granted to all the classes. However, in India the Baniyas never followed that logic. The accumulation of wealth in India operated within the domain of Hindu ethics. The Hindu ethic has no compassion for the poor, the destitute, the disabled and the diseased. The Baniya capital is ordained to operate in an inward-looking economic operation. Since the Brahmans as *bhoodevatas* (gods on the earth) allowed them to use the Baniya wealth for their own (of all the *dwijas*) *sukha* (pleasure), there is nothing that bothers them in this world. In this world the Baniyas have to make their *dwija* life happy with all the comforts around, and the Brahmans will take care of the other world.

GUPTADHANA AND BANIYAHOOD

The Hindu ethic of wealth accumulation was not for the formation of social capital. It was meant for Brahmanic consumption and preservation in all forms of exclusive private property of the *dwijas*, including in a form of very casteist private property—*guptadhana*. The concept of *guptadhana* was developed by the Baniya economists as a legitimate process of hiding wealth as the state power in certain regions was also being usurped by Shudra rulers. After the decline of the Gupta dynasty, the Shudras became kings in several kingdoms. They had antagonistic relations with the *dwijas* as a social force, which developed a collective emergence after the Baniyas emerged as the exclusive business caste while the Brahmans continued to the exclusive priestly caste. With the emergence of such an exclusive business caste, large amounts of wealth began to be accumulated in individual Baniya houses. Such private family wealth was mostly gleaned through business with the Shudra, Chandala and the Adivasi communities—this property was not under any protection from a state headed by Shudras. The Baniyas thus discovered a perfect method of hiding such wealth underground, with a clear design to hoodwink the state and the civil society. *Guptadhana* is an Indian form of black wealth (money) that has more negative values than normal black money that operates in other countries, as the *guptadhana* was kept underground, without any social use.

Since the Baniya philosophy constructed enormous mistrust among people, the culture of mistrust became part of their own family culture. When it came to *guptadhana*, the father buried wealth without the knowledge of his sons and the sons buried wealth without the knowledge of their parents. The death of either, therefore, led more often than not to the loss of that wealth underground. This aspect of the Baniya philosophy led to another major problem in the Indian society, that of being miserly. .There is a proverb among the Dalit-Bahujans, 'Baniya stingyness does not part with a single pie even if somebody is starving', that is, the Baniyas are not very keen to share their wealth with the other castes. This culture is the very opposite of the culture of sharing of the Shudras, Chandalas and the Adivasis.

The *guptadhana* accumulated in this illegal manner had historically performed two functions: one, it was being accumulated as black money, thereby building up the social power of the Baniya families. In every village, though very small in number, the Baniyas began to enjoy special privileges as they developed an expertise in the art of the bribing the state officials to avoid the tax net of the state. One who commands the state machinery through bribe money wields more power in the civil society than the one who submits to the state laws and operates within the ambit of that law. Even thieves do not touch these parallel systems, as they too are afraid of the consequences. In such situations, thefts, quarrels and contentions take place among those who operate within the ambit of the state laws. Even for local thieves, thus, a Baniya house appeared to be an unbreakable house.

Second, the *guptadhana* served to accumulate usury capital without having any state or religious controls on interest rates, and so on. In religions like Islam and Christianity, the religion itself imposed restrictions on converting any private capital into usury capital. The religious ethic also imposed moral limitations on the interest rates and the methods of recollection of loans. But the Hindu Baniya economy has no such moral restrictions. Such immoral Baniya usury accumulation destroyed the capital accumulation process of the peasant economies. If any peasant family managed to start a business by effort, the Brahman-Baniyas organized a social boycott of such families. Such Brahman-Baniya schemes worked to condition the consciousness of the Shudras. Hinduism, thus, went to all extents for building up *guptadhana*.

The Mughals and the other Islamic rulers, during their reign treated this process of negative accumulation of *guptadhana* as a part of Hindu religious customs. They did not realize that the Brahmanic laws were not applicable to all believers equally, thus could never be defined as 'religious' laws. Because of the inward-looking communitarian worldview of Islam, the Islamic rulers failed to understand that the caste-based Indian system could not be defined in terms of religion at all. In fact, they constructed the term 'Hindu' and applied it to all those who were outside the pale of Islam,

Christianity, Zoroastrianism and Buddhism (who were more organized into definite religious communities). The Muslim rulers did not interfere with the caste system and considered caste hierarchy to be a God-given institution. Since the Muslims believed that what is there in a religious book is God-given (as they believe in the case of the Quran), they also considered the usury accumulation of the Baniyas to be divinely ordained. Thus, the notion of the 'Hindu religion' is a Muslim construction—in, of course, a negative sense of the term 'religion'. The Muslim rulers did not ascribe a sense of dignity to the word 'Hindu'. This negative term was given a positive dimension in the early nationalist period.

BANIYAHOOD AND CORRUPTION

Only the British, who had undergone several secular revolutionary movements in the European society, understood that the so-called Hinduism had neither religious character nor a communitarian living process, as made evident by the caste-based social structure. However, by the time the British came to India, the Brahman–Baniya exploitative economy had established itself very strongly. The Brahmans and the Baniyas were willing subordinates to the British system, under the condition that the British would not seek to destroy the system of caste hierarchy, upon which was dependent the survival of these two castes. Though the British imposed restrictions on the *guptadhana* mode of accumulation of wealth, they did not abolish it because the Baniyas corrupted the individual British officials and saw to it that their accumulation of *dhana* (wealth) and the conversion of that *dhana* to *guptadhana* continued unabated. The Baniya expertise in this process has made the culture of corruption a part of Indianness. The self of a caste, thus, has been imposed on the nation itself.

The personal letters of many wives of the British officials show that the newly-acquired corrupt lifestyle of their husbands began to corrupt their family lives. Some of the British women divorced their husbands because of their corrupt lifestyles in India. Such a corrupt life was unthinkable in the Christian ethic. For these British women, such corrupt life went against the family norms and ethical relationships that had been formed within the larger civil society of Christian ethic. The central point, however, is that there is no business community in the world that can match the Baniyas in corrupting the state machinery and operating business by 'walking over the law'. Even now, they are masters of this practice. The Indian capital is finding it difficult to overcome corruption as the Baniya capital in our markets has made it a systemic process. R. K. Gupta and R. K. Jain, the two middlemen who were recently caught in the Tehelka tapes case, are good examples of Baniya corruption and the institutionalization of this corruption in post-independence India.

The concept of Hinduism, used in a derogatory sense by the Muslims, began to be used in a definite religious sense only after the British began to introduce reforms into the caste system. When some of the British officials began to impose tax laws on the Baniya–Brahman accumulation of *guptadhana*, the Brahman writers began to defend the practice of accumulating *guptadhana* as a religious practice, where the British were asked not to interfere. As we see even today, once a particular practice is constructed as a 'religious' one, the state no longer interferes in its functioning. The Brahmans, thus, wrote many books and interpolated into old books, and many negative ideas were inserted into Indian literature to show that social smuggling was a spiritually sanctioned method of doing business. The literary construction of the images of these two castes as 'great and dignified' is part of the ideological conspiracy of Brahmanism. As the Kshatriyas became marginalized in the context of the emerging constitutionalism in the modern period, the Brahmans and Baniyas operated as twins of historical negation. This negation resulted in the socio-economic stagnation of India in a manner that no other nation in the world could witness.

GANDHI, NEHRU: BANIYA–BRAHMANHOOD

This is not to say that the Brahmans and the Baniyas had no contradictions among themselves. Such contradictions expressed themselves during the period of the religious formation of Jainism, and also during the Buddhist revolution. The Vaishyas, by and large, supported the Jain and the Buddhist movements in the face of opposition by Brahmanical Hinduism. At that time, the Brahmans had refused to grant any respectable spiritual status to the Baniyas. Even today, the Jain community mainly constitutes Baniyas. During the nationalist period, Gandhi became a major mediating point between the Baniyas and the Brahmans, but finally this contradiction was expressed in the form of the murder of Gandhi by Nathuram Godse, a representative of the Brahmanic forces.

However, Gandhi stuck deep social roots among the masses as a skillful representative of Brahman–Baniya Hinduism. The Brahmans, under the leadership of Jawaharlal Nehru, realized that the modernist post-independence national economy can accommodate Brahmans in bureaucratic capital and Baniyas in the business capital. Thus, for 60 years after the independence, the construction of a so-called 'modern' India took place with the strategic enrichment of the Brahmans and the Baniyas, under the supervision of the Nehruvian state. These two castes have become pan-Indian monopolist castes in the political, spiritual, bureaucratic and business structures. The Sangh Parivar, which helped Nathuram Godse in killing Gandhi, realized over a period of time that the Brahman-Baniya interests lie together, as the caste-centred liberal democratic state provides enough scope for both communities to acquire a lot of wealth. As the classical Kshatriyas became marginalized, the Brahmans and the Baniyas began to operate from all centres of power. They, thus, operated in collusion and subverted the system in their interest by systematically maneuvering the Dalit-Bahujan consciousness. They succeeded in their joint effort. Thus, wealth and power in post-independence India belongs almost entirely to these castes, leaving some regional power and capital to the Shudras. The Shudras also did not challenge the Brahman-Baniya power as they too developed vested interests in the local capital of the linguistic regions.

As I said earlier, in the medieval period, the Baniyas established very powerful methods of undercutting the power of the state to collect taxes, even though the state was controlled by Shudra kings. The Baniyas, with the spiritual sanction of the Brahmans, avoided payment of taxes in all forms and one of the most powerful methods they used was hiding the accumulated wealth—gold, silver and coins—underground. *Guptadhana*, thus, was legally not only criminally-earned wealth as it was hidden underground but could also never become wealth that was socially useful. Even in the post-independence period, the Shudra rulers who emerged in certain linguistic provinces did not break the medievalist monopoly of the Baniyas on the business and of the Brahmans in the temples.

The *guptadhana* was accumulated not only to avoid tax payments—which is a practice of the Baniyas even now—but also to see that no Shudra, Chandala or Adivasi could lay their hands on that wealth. As a result, India has enormous underground wealth, more than any other country in the world. In several excavations, such wealth was found, and a lot more lies under the layers of Indian soil. Even now, many Baniyas do not keep their wealth in the banks—a lot of wealth is buried underground. This mode of hiding wealth, without making it available for any other investment, was also part of the Hindu ethic. The *guptadhana* was buried underground not only by the Baniyas but by several Brahmans as well. They issued spiritual sanctions to powerful Shudra kings not to dig out such *guptadhana*, as that would invoke the anger of the Hindus and might result in a *shapam* (curse), which has the spiritual capacity to destroy them. No selling of indulgences during the height of corruption in Christianity in the medieval period could match the *guptadhana* of the Hindu ethic. The *guptadhana* was a specific Baniya mode of de-mobilizing the economy. It was a process of social retrogression that caused enormous economic destruction. At no point of time was socio-economic reform allowed to set in motion, in order to change this retrograde economic structure of the society. The possibility of excavating such wealth for collective social use was never examined by the Indian economists, because many Indian economists came from the Brahmanic background. On the contrary, the possession of *guptadhana* was considered an honourable practice in the ancient Indian society—and perhaps even now—and the Baniyas could hide the largest amount of money under the ground. Baniyas also added a surname 'Gupta' (meaning 'secret') to their own names; till date several Baniyas bear the name Gupta.

MODES OF SMUGGLING

The universal laws of business demanded that buying and selling should be an open, publicly verifiable activity. Social boundaries were not drawn in the taking up of this activity, thereby providing the individual with the scope to enter into this anti-feudal profession. The earliest occupation that allowed an everyday basis of social intercourse of people from all backgrounds was business in non-Indian societies. In India, the Brahmans, with the connivance of the Baniyas stipulate social boundaries to smuggle the grain and goods/commodities without framing any socially interactive exchangeable laws of business. What was exchanged between the Dalit-Bahujan masses and the Baniyas was not through business transactions, but through the means of social smuggling. The social wealth that is generated within the larger social boundaries of all Adivasi, Chandala and Shudra communities was smuggled out without proper payment of price. In ancient and medieval periods, no one from any other community was allowed to enter into the enterprise of business. During the nationalist period, the Shudras managed to make some space for themselves in the operation of businesses, but their businesses did not last long.

One of the essential methods that the Baniyas as a caste used to acquire wealth was that they perfected the art of using 'lies' as an instrument of business. The practice of using lies as a process of life was developed and used widely by the Brahmans in the process of building a Hindu ethic. The theory of *karma* had been evolved as a part of this process of making lies a part of Hindu propaganda. When the operationalization and institutionalization of telling lies expanded from the spiritual realm to business, the masses were pushed from a situation of loss of spiritual identity to deprivation in the realm of economics as well. In Europe, the Protestant ethic opposed many methods of spreading lies, and that paved way for genuine growth of capitalism. In Europe, such processes emerged from the womb of the Protestant ethic itself. In India, the Baniyas left the Buddhist ethic and embraced the Hindu ethic by virtually negating the positive values of business that had been evolved over a period of centuries. Under the spiritual guidance of the Brahmans, they became an inward-looking community and turned the enterprise of business into, as the Dalit–Bahujans say, a 'lie trading process'. For instance, a Baniya never makes the purchase price public—it varies from one customer to other. While buying, the Baniya offers lower prices to lower caste sellers; while selling, on the other hand, the Baniya asks for higher prices from his lower caste buyers. The practice of telling lies was (and still is) used as a powerful instrument to exploit the productive masses and generate consent for the prevalence of such a variety of prices.

The exchange between the Baniyas and rest of the non-Brahman society was/is not legally or socially contracted to fix the prices openly. Historically, the Shudras, Chandalas and the Adivasis were not supposed to know the selling price and the buying price. The rural proverb, that in a Baniya market 'while buying it is fire market and while selling it is forest market' (*konabote korivi ammabote adivi*), indicates that on either occasions, the non-Brahman buyers/sellers had little knowledge about how the prices were being fixed. The Brahmans and the Kshatriyas did not operate as buyers because the Brahmans received goods and commodities in the form of *dakshina* and the Kshatriyas in the form of collection, not as state tax for the common good, but for their royal expenditure. Thus, Baniya business never possessed the character of social service. It continues till date to operate within the realm of social smuggling.

Yet another form of social smuggling took place in the form of establishing usury capital by maintaining a deceptive mode of accounting. The Baniya economy evolved a method of collecting geometrical interest from all categories of civil societal forces. It is probable that they had given some concession to the Brahmans and the Kshatriyas as they fell within the *dwija* spiritual mode of life, but there is a lot of evidence in the villages to support the fact that the lower the caste of the borrower, higher would be the interest collected. This mode of social smuggling of the wealth generated in the society by the Baniyas left the productive masses with no economic energy. This form of economic exploitation on the part of the Baniyas started in the ancient period and continued through the medieval and the modern period. It is because of this kind of exploitation that the Dalit–Bahujan castes could not retain any surplus with themselves.

Social smuggling also operated through the use of deceptive measurements in the village economy. A Baniya is known for using two forms of deception in order to smuggle wealth right in the presence of the seller. The first is through manipulating the rod of the scale, and the second through pasting tamarind below the plate of the *taraju* (weighing machine), which leaves the buyer deceived. They also do not hesitate to cheat while buying. The entire process is known as *dandekottuta* (deceiving the buyers and sellers by manipulating the weighing machine) in Telugu language. Baniyas use similar methods in every state, and the Dalit–Bahujan masses have several proverbs that speak of these Baniya techniques.

BANIYA CAPITAL IS NOT A MERCANTILE CAPITAL

One of the socially accepted laws of the European 'Christian feudalism' was that the business of the feudal economy was supposed to have a system of open transactions. The class-based social structures allowed social mobility within the market. The most important thing in the whole process of business was that the price structure was based, to some extent, on the labour power consumed for the preparation of the commodity. Though Marx said that the labour power utilized in the making of the product was never taken into consideration by the bourgeoisie, labour power was taken into consideration to some extent in all class societies. In caste-based systems, however, labour power expended by the labour force has no social respect at all. When labour does not have any dignity in the society, its economic value becomes a lot cheaper.

In a class economy, the social position of the buyers and the sellers could change—in other words, an erstwhile businessman could change his position to become a labourer, and a labourer could become a buyer of labour or a businessman. The availability of a mobile social structure changed the economic position of the people. This social mobility also framed the terms of business in a different way. The buyer and the seller in non-Baniya markets are equally respected social beings. The Baniya business of India differs entirely as it is structured in caste terms, with an in-built immobile social system conditioned by the Hindu scriptures. Legally and structurally, only the Baniyas could operate business. Of course, the Brahmans did possess a right to operate businesses as well, but that right was considered to be below their spiritual status by the Brahmans themselves.

This kind of closed Baniya business disallowed any social basis to institutionalize the mercantile capital in India. The Baniya mode of business and accumulation of capital negated the formation of a socially useful capital. A Baniya, by definition, is not an entrepreneur but one who squeezes money from his buyers, whose social interest is in accumulation of capital for self-perpetuation and spending it on the so-called self-salvational spiritual processes of Hinduism that only served to dehumanize them even further. Huge amounts of money, thus, were invested in temples and also on the day-to-day consumption of the priestly class, but not in the generation of socially useful wealth. Perhaps no other religion in the world has wasted so much food as much as the Hindu religion has. The Baniya accumulation was/is the main source of such wastage of food resources. A large amount of the Baniya business capital has been wasted on *yagas* and *yagyas* instead of on human consumption. But no amount of spiritual expenditure and wastage of humanly useful wealth could save the epicentre of the Baniya exploitative capital—Gujarat—from the disastrous earthquake on 26 June 2001. It became their doomsday. This is the place where biggest amount of money and food that could have been otherwise consumed by human beings was spent on the Brahmanic spiritual activity in the post-independence India. This Baniya state enforced vegetarianism as a way of life, even among the Shudras. But nothing could save the state on that disastrous day. Though natural calamities are a by-product of environmental shifts, a human society builds enough strength to face calamities only through a process of spiritual, economic and political democracy. The Brahman–Baniya state of Gujarat did not possess the internal strength to withstand such calamities. *Guptadhana* does not contribute to the strength of the society—socially distributed wealth alone possesses the capacity to become the strength of a society.

NON-INDUSTRIALIST DRIVE

Because of such spiritual wastage and caste-centred nature of capital, the wealth accumulated by the Baniyas did not become the base of industrial capital in India. Industry, essentially, is an anti-caste institution. It pushes society into urbanization; it brings anti-caste institutions like hotels, cinema halls and other institutions into existence. In the nineteenth century, when the British were pushing the Indian economy towards industrialization and urbanization, the Brahmans and Baniyas of India were strongly against such a process. The Baniya economy was opposed to industrialization in the same way as the Brahman spirituality was opposed to the education of the Dalit–Bahujan masses and women. The twin processes of opening up education to the Dalit–Bahujans masses and investing in industries were accepted by the Brahmans and the Baniyas only when they worked out ways to keep these institutions caste-centered. Slowly, when the Baniyas started the textile industry, they did not employ Shudras and Chandalas in them. Though gradually employment was given to the Shudras, at no stage were Dalits employed in Baniya-owned shops and factories. This was one of the main arguments of Ambedkar when the question of supporting the working-class strike, lead by a Brahman communist, Dange, came up for discussion. Surprisingly, the Brahman communist also thought that Ambedkar's demand for respectable employment of Dalits was not an acceptable demand.

The mercantile capital that evolved into industrial capital in Europe broke all social barriers. But the Baniya capital in India sustained caste inequality as the Brahmans wanted them to move in that direction. In this atmosphere, if the British had not established their own industries where all castes were allowed to take up jobs, we would not have had even that slow growth of urbanization in India. In a historically caste-centred closed economy, an indigenous development of industrialization and urbanization would have been impossible.

Baniya business stood as a barrier to industrialization because it was inaccessible to the public sphere—capitalism could not have developed in India unless there had been social interaction between labour and capital. The British made an attempt to bring about some sort of social exchange by establishing factories wherein labour and capital could interact without considering the caste basis of the labour. In the Hindu social order, labour was always located among the. Dalit–Bahujans and capital in the Baniya families. When the labouring section of the society wanted to educate their children in the same school as the capital-owners, they were met with stiff resistance from the Brahmans and the Baniyas, as that would lead to a revolutionary change in the system.

SINFUL CAPITAL

In a capitalist enterprise, business is not a sinful activity—but the Baniyas of India turned business into a sinful activity. A Baniya believes that telling lies is a part of his business. Accumulation of sin through lie-based business has tremendous impact on their psychology. Hence, the Baniya business class has upheld the rather unusual spiritual practice of investing money in the *hundis* (coffers) of the Hindu gods, which, in turn, reaches the priestly Brahmans. For example, the Tirupati temple located in Andhra Pradesh receives huge amounts of business money as donation to God. This money gets reinvested in Brahmanic consumption. There are several Hindu temples which receive more than 10 crore rupees per annum. Most of this money comes from the Baniya accumulation. This money is accumulated, as the temple economy generates a 'sinful capital' that does not have to be accounted for either to the government or the society. Whatever accountability is there is merely on paper—in reality, the temple committees are formed to manage the money collected through donations. They do not invest it for fulfilling broad social needs.

Baniya business has always negated accountability. Gods such as Kubera and Ganapati were constructed in order to turn even spiritual accountability into a mockery, as both these gods reflect accumulation of money, usurpation and gluttony. In several proverbs in the Telugu language, Kubera is known for fraudulent accumulation of wealth. Other nations condemned such figures whereas the Baniyas of India worship them. The story and the popular figurative image of Ganapati are well-known. He sits with his huge stomach and an elephant face, with a lot of food items kept around him. For a long time, he was worshipped only by the Baniyas and the Brahmans. Only during the nationalist period was the worship of Ganapati expanded into the Shudra civil society. The celebration of Ganapati festival by the rest of the communities only legitimized the Baniya mode of social smuggling. One only has to see in order to believe how the Baniyas and the Brahmans constructed gods and devils in the spiritual realm in order to retain their social, economic and cultural hegemony. In the process, the masses were made to consent to the humiliation on an everyday basis. As a result of such manipulation of the mass consciousness, the Indian state and civil society lives in a spiritually and morally justified world of corruption. Corruption is a culturally validated system in India. It was/is made as ethical as the caste system was/is.

The officialdom of the state does not collect a reasonable amount of tax in receipted form from the Baniya business caste, as such money would go to the state exchequer. All the officers would rather collect bribe money from the Baniyas and make personal profit. The Baniya businessmen quite openly encourage bribery, as the amount that gets paid to the corrupt officials is much less than the amount they need to spend on properly accounted for taxes. Bribe money and Baniya accumulation have a common ground of illegality. Such a corrupt economy must be seen as part of the process of illegal accumulation of capital by the Baniyas. Such a process also allowed illegal political capital that got siphoned into the hands of the political parties. Thus, the traditional *guptadhana* has turned into an illegal exchange of money between the corrupt business community and immoral political and bureaucratic agencies. Brahmanism covers this process with a spiritual garb. Such vast illegal and immoral transactions that take place in the Indian economy create a social basis of sinful living.

One of the methods to overcome such a deep-seated sin is to go around innumerable temples and investing money on the process of 'sin washing'. This process involves huge amounts of travel and unethical constructions of temples on all sorts of public places like streets and roadways. Most of the travelling done by Indians is not tourism for accumulation of knowledge but pilgrimage for washing the sins accumulated in the process of living a caste-based immoral life. The number of deaths in India due to accidents while travelling is, perhaps, the highest in the world–this is due to the fact that the number of Brahmans, Baniyas and other corrupt bureaucrats and political forces who carry out this practice of undertaking pilgrimages in order to wash away one's sins is the highest in the world. The social smugglers believe that sin cannot be washed through prayer alone, as it is done in other religions. The Brahmans invented a method of worship through money, and the Baniyas were there to spend the socially smuggled money on the temples. Thus, the Indian temples, till this day, remain the playgrounds of these two corrupt castes.

In the post-independence India, a political Brahman like Nehru said that corruption serves as a lubricant for the Indian political system. This is because Nehru knew that the social basis of the Brahman–Baniya economy is basically illegal. The political formations that took shape in the Indian democracy were strongly oriented towards the Brahman–Baniya ethic. The modern westernized democratic state cannot impose all democratic values of legality on basically sinful, corrupt capital that began to accumulate after independence. The democracy that emerged on the social basis of spiritual democracy (the Christian ethic) and the economic basis of capitalist legality (the capitalist ethic) was superimposed on a spiritual fascist social system and the Baniya economic system. Nehru knew that the Gandhian mode of morality and his own mode of socialism were euphemisms that could allow the operation of the Brahmanical politics and Baniya economics, without facing much resistance from the Dalitist schools. The communist and socialist leadership, that has the same Brahman–Baniya background, shared all the anxieties that Gandhi and Nehru were experiencing. No school of thought headed by the Brahman–Baniya leaders attempted to pose a challenge to the Baniya mode of accumulation of business capital and Brahman mode of accumulation of spiritual capital. Not a single book critiqued these socio-economic formations.

The Brahmanic communist argument that India would have developed into an indigenous capitalist country if the British were not to establish their colonial rule has no basis. They never examined the anti-capitalist social basis of the Baniya *guptadhana* economy and its relationship with the caste boundaries that stood as stumbling blocks to the growth of the mercantile capital, which would then move towards industrial capital. At no point of time in Indian history, before the British came to India, did the guilds operate with free exchange of labour and capital. The Brahmans and the Baniyas as civil societal forces never allowed the formation of such guilds. To some extent, the British broke the *dakshina* and *guptadhana* base. The state headed by Kshatriyas, and even the Shudras, did not have the political strength to overrule the Brahman–Baniya dictate. The Muslim rulers, who never had an agenda to break the caste rules and mobilize the *guptadhana* into industrial capital, could not have pushed the economy towards a process of growth of indigenous industries, as it happened in Europe. If the British were not to establish colonial rule in India, the Indian capital base would have remained at the stage of *guptadhana*.

BANIYA NATIONALISM

There is some difference between the way the Baniya nationalist consciousness and the Brahman nationalist consciousness was constructed. Throughout the period of Muslim rule, the Baniyas of India had to face the emergence of a Muslim business class, which had strong spiritual and egalitarian community bondages. The Muslim business egalitarianism attracted a lot of Dalit-Bahujans to Islam, as it shared its capital assets communally. Since the Baniya mode of accumulation is exclusivist, it was hated by the Dalit-Bahujan masses. The Dalit-Bahujans call it 'sinful accumulation'. While the Baniya businessmen were conservative and did not develop the literary and cultural diabolism of the Brahmans, they stuck to their Hindu mode of business, which did not believe in selling leather goods, meat and fish products, commodities that some Shudra artisans produced, like pots, wooden structures, and so on. But the Brahmans negotiated with Islam and the Urdu language in a clever and diabolical manner. It appears that because of the strong Jain formations among the Baniyas, a stronger vegetarian cultural conditioning operated in the Baniyas than in the Brahmans. Even during the Muslim and the British rule, the Baniyas seem to have stuck to their Jain–Hindu tradition of vegetarianism. Though during the British period the Baniyas seem to have spread themselves to all parts of the country except the Kerala region, where the strong Christian and Muslim waves did not leave much space for their Hindu-Jain centred business, they did not transcend the possessive business ethic they built for themselves. That is the reason why till Mahatma Gandhi emerged from this community as a leader, writer and commentator on the Indian civilization, culture and policy, the Baniya community did not produce either a literary figure, or a cultural reformer.

Historically, the Baniyas operated as buffers between the Brahmans and the Kshatriyas. Whenever Brahmanic assertion was under threat from the Kshatriyas, they joined the Kshatriya camp and tried to carve out a space for themselves. But their image had acquired enough autonomy under the shade of Gandhian nationalism. Though Gandhian nationalism operated as a buffer between the capitalist modernity and retrograde *guptadhana* business of the Baniyas, it was a period of gaining a pan-Indian identity and social legitimacy for all the Baniyas of India. The Baniya expansion took place from early 1920s to 1948, during the peak period of Gandhi's operation at the centrestage of Indian politics. Interestingly, during this period the Baniya capital tried to overcome the *guptadhana* retrograde accumulation of capital and began to invest in industrial economy as competitors to Parsee progressive capitalism. The emergence of the Birla group of industrialists and the Goenka group of paper barons using the political space that Gandhi provided for the Baniyas marked a different phase in their history.

The Pharisee capitalism, with the Tata group as its epicentre, has many progressive characteristics. The Pharisees believed in conducting open business and integrating dignity of labour into their market system. Their surnames, like Palkiwala, Doodwala, Tarkariwala, Daruwala, Lakadawala, and so on, indicate that carrying the *palki*, selling milk, vegetables, liquor and cutting wood are socially respectable positions. They believed in constructing something positive out of all occupations that were constructed by the Hindu Brahmans and Baniyas as undignified, negative and untouchable. Mumbai became a progressive capitalist centre because of the Pharisees. It was in competition to the Pharisee capital, that believed in open business and productive reinvestment and had challenged the retrograde Brahman-Baniya capital that the Baniyas of the Mumbai region became more open. But for this competition with the Pharisee industrialists in the Mumbai region and in the rest of the country, they would have remained an absolutely closed community. The emergence of the Birla's in building up the multi-commodity industry and the emergence of the Goenkas as newspaper managers became very handy for Gandhi to re-negotiate with modernity.

Gandhi had an enormous capacity to construct a sacrificial image of himself and develop a pre-modernist, simplicity-centred mass base. As Sarojini Naidu herself expressed, the Baniya strategy of 'living a fairly costly' vegetarian life, while Birla planes were carrying him and his milk-producing goats and the newspapers produced by Goenka popularized his semi-naked image to the masses, worked very well. This was the period in which the Baniyas repositioned themselves in Hinduism, almost erasing the difference between Hinduism and Jainism. The fundamentalist vege-tarianism got Hinduized as the Brahmans took to vegetarianism in the post-Sankara period. Gandhi himself constructed a powerful modern Hindu vegetarian idiom that went against the historical tradition of meatarianism of the Shudras, Chandalas, Adivasis and pan-Indian masses. With Gandhi at the helm of the Congress and at the helm of nationalist movement itself, and the Birlas, the Goenkas, the Mafatlas, and so on, entering into the domain of positive capitalism, the Baniyas began to transform from their position as social smugglers to that of social investors. The Brahmans had no way but to grant them good spiritual status, except for granting the position of priesthood in the temple. One interesting thing about Gandhian Hindu nationalism (Gandhi's nationalism was essentially Hindu nationalism) and the Birla mode of Hindu capitalism was the construction of temples and the selling of *moksha* in the capitalist market, which acquired legitimacy only in India and that too only in Hinduism. Now, we have Birla Mandirs in many places in India, which are doing good business. Gandhi used Delhi as a centre for political-spiritual propaganda, and this is where he was killed by the Brahman fundamentalist, Nathuram Godse.

The Brahmans of India, particularly the Chitpavan Brahmans of Maharashtra developed a serious opposition to the Baniya expansion in every field under the shadow of Gandhi. They thought that the hegemony that Baniyas were establishing in Mumbai and Delhi might pose a serious threat to their educational and spiritual hegemony as well. The Brahmans negotiated and renegotiated their relations with the Kshatriyas as they were rulers and builders of alternative systems like Jainism and Buddhism. The Brahmans succeeded in gaining a consensual superior position against the Baniyas in historical terms. With the emergence of Gandhi as an unchallenged leader in India, the Brahmans faced a crisis in terms of their historical status. Gandhi's status and popularity posed a serious challenge to the hegemony of the Brahmans as the dream of independence was about to be realized. After the death of Gandhi, the Brahmans established an unchallenged control of the Nehruvian 'secular' Brahmanism. The Brahmans of India wanted a Brahman to rule, irrespective of his ideology. After Gandhi's

death, only two Baniya leaders emerged, and they were Ram Manohar
Lohia of Uttar Pradesh and Potti Sriramulu of Andhra Pradesh. Of the
two, Sriramulu went on an unto death hunger strike following the sacrificial
strategy of Gandhi, and Lohia remained a bachelor to build Gandhian
socialism. He also remained a staunch enemy of the Brahman, secular
Nehru. In this process, the Brahman–Baniya socio-spiritual and economic
relationship was reworked to suit the post-colonial state and society.

GANDHI FAILED TO CHANGE BANIYAS

Gandhi was one of the most popular and important moral philosopher
that the Baniya community of India produced. Against their Baniya ethic
of conducting a lie-based *guptadhana* business, he talked about 'truth'
becoming the process of life. As against their wasteful expensive life, he
preached simplicity. Borrowing from the Jain Vardhamana Mahavira, he
lived in an ashram, wearing only loin-cloth and talked about the eating
simple food. He was killed by the representative of the Brahmanic forces
of India for preaching the un-Hindu ethics of simplicity and truth-telling.
Finally, of course, he has come to be known as the father of the Indian
nation. Yet the Baniyas of India, true to their historical nature, did not
own him. Why?

If you visit any Baniya house in India, you will discover that Gandhi's
photograph does not hang from their walls. Even in Gujarat, where he
was born and brought up, Gandhi's photo is not a household symbol of
heritage. He is not their revered hero as Ambedkar is the revered hero of
the Dalits of India. The Baniyas did not adopt Gandhi as their hero because
Gandhi stood for frugality. They worship gods like Ganapati and Kubera
because both the gods stand for accumulation of wealth and gluttony. As
opposed to Gandhi's frugal eating habits, the Baniyas of India are known
for the heavy consumption of rich vegetarian and sweet food products. If
somebody takes a survey on the total amount of food that the Baniyas of
India consume, it might emerge that though small in number, the Baniyas
of India consume the second largest quantity of food consumed by all
Indians. Their consumption will be next to that of the Brahmans. Their
day-to-day lifestyles in terms of the places of residence, use of ornaments of
gold and silver, clothes, cars and other moveable and immovable properties
point to the fact that they are totally anti-Gandhian. Having come from
this caste, Gandhi talked about loving people of all castes, but in their
day-to-day life many Baniyas hate people of all other castes, even after
60 years of Gandhi's death.

HISTORICAL DILEMMA

Baniyas as a buffer caste between the Shudras and the Brahmans in the modern period have always had a historical dilemma with the caste system. They themselves were agriculturists and cattle herders in pre-Buddhist period. They had love-hate relationships with the Shudras and Chandalas. When Gandhi took up the anti-untouchability campaign by mobilizing money from Baniya capitalists, the Brahmans saw it as a threat to their *Varnadharma* system, strategically built by their ancestors like Manu and Kautilya. (The texts written by Manu and Kautilya advised the state to give the stringent punishments to people who violate the rules and regulations pertaining to *varna* system.) For all these reasons, there was a serious tension between the Brahmans and the Baniyas as long as Gandhi was alive. The two major English newspapers that represented these two communities, *The Hindu* and *The Indian Express*, have differing assessments of Gandhi's role. *The Hindu* marginalized Gandhi and did perhaps subtly favour Nehru. Baniyas, in terms of colour, carried more genes of the Dravidian race with them. Even in an Aryan-dominated place like Bihar, the Vaishyas possessed more Dravidian racial features. In the south, the Baniyas are darker than many Shudra castes. For these reasons, the Brahmans of India do not have any marital relations with the Baniyas, even though the Baniyas carry the banner of Brahmanical Hinduism on their shoulders as faithfully as the Brahmans do. As of now, they do not have the right to become a priest in any Hindu temple, and do not have the right to represent the Hindu scriptures. The Brahmans do not interfere in the business practices of the Baniyas. There are tensions between these two castes but they negotiate their differences so that a substantial amount of wealth remains in their control at the expense of Dalit–Baniyans and Adivasis.

Chapter 10   Spiritual Fascists

After we cross the Baniya civil society we enter the Brahman civil society. In any big village of India or a town or even a city, the Brahman *wadas* remain quite marked. They look different in many ways. Even in villages, one can see the absence of productive tools around their houses. In terms of wealth, in each village and town they seem richer than any productive caste that we have discussed in earlier chapters. But, in some villages, as the Shudras, such as Reddys, Kammas, Jats, Nairs, and so on, emerged as feudal lords, they challenged the economic authority of the dominant class—Brahmans. Their dwellings look like the dwellings of colonizers as opposed to that of the rest of the people, who look like the colonized. They somehow do not look like the sons and daughters of the soil—this might be the case because their relationship to the soil that they live on is not the same as the one that the productive communities have. Since they hated soiling their hands for centuries, their relationship to the soil appears very inimical. Their appearance, the way they decorate their houses, the arrangements in front of the house and at the back of the house make their beings what they are—different from others. Their households contain vessels, jars, copper and steel containers that deal with spirituality and cookery. In some states they look physically different; in some they are physically and mentally different. They construct a living environment that makes them look different and live different. Wherever they physically look similar to others, they make themselves up to look different so that the physical difference is maintained. This physical and mental otherness was constructed quite deliberately. Being the other of India, far away from the rest, with a feeling of being above all has become part of their mental make-up. In West Bengal and Orissa, Brahmanism got intertwined with feudalism, thus negating the possibility of emergence of the Shudras.

THE BRAHMAN BODY AND MIND

Historically, the Brahman body was supposed to look distinctly different. This principle applied to both men and women. Apart from wearing the sacred thread, they applied different kinds of pastes on their foreheads and dressed up differently to indicate their identity as Brahman. Similarly, women have their own markers to be specified as Brahman. The way they dress, the way they do their make-up clearly indicate to the observer that they are Brahmans. They believe philosophically and culturally that they should look different. Though that trend is changing to some extent, the notion that a Brahman should appear 'different' is an in-built cultural characteristic of a Brahman. That mental make-up of consciously being different is the first step towards establishing a caste culture. This caste culture emerged with the Brahmans and became a part of every caste. Many castes constructed their physical beings as different from one another.

The Brahmans have an exceptional sense of self-love. They hate the Shudras, Chandalas, and the Adivasis as much as they love themselves. They have some affinity with the Baniyas but there are differences even among these two castes. In terms of housing, for instance, the Baniyas normally live in better houses. The Brahman houses vary in shape and size. They do, however, wish to possess better houses than that of all other communities. A Brahman *wada* anywhere in India (and not just in the Telugu region) does not appear as a dwelling place of ordinary human beings with work-roughened hands and bony bodies to any Shudra, Chandala or Adivasi who might pass by. Though the Brahman houses were made to appear divine, there was an element of cunningness in that construction. That very appearance of divinity was meant to differentiate and construct people as unequal.

The soil around the Brahman houses does not have the productive essence, because the Brahmans do not allow it to be so. They prefer instead a soil that loves *yagya* fire with *ghee* all around instead of bearing fruit and producing crop. The soil smells of a variety of food items, full of *ghee*. The more modern a house is, the fatter it is, full of consumer goods. In some villages, towns and cities, the Brahman *wadas* are quite big in size.

The soil around their houses is forced to become barren. Of course, in some cases there are gardens around their houses. The gardens that the modern Brahmans grow are so selfish that they do not constitute any crop that serves the need of all human beings. A modern, postcolonial Brahman house hates crops and loves gardens. Their aesthetic does not believe in an egalitarian mode of sharing fruits and flowers. The flowers are meant for the consumption of the Hindu gods, and the fruits are meant for their own consumption. Not a single productive tool can be seen in any Brahman house—they are, however, full of godheads with tremendously violent symbols all around.

The Brahmans claim to be a non-violent community, but in reality it appears as though the Brahmans and violence were born twins. The apparent claim of being priests in the temples, where no animal sacrifice was/is involved, hides the fact that they worship violence itself. No community in the world worships violence with as much passion and involvement as the Brahmans do. But that passion is hidden underneath the notion that they do not even involve themselves in the killing of a chicken or a sheep in the temple. Worshipping violence and condemning the productive work built a culture of living in psychological violence, which has now become part of their spiritual ethic. The nation suffered an enormous amount of unrecognized caste and cultural violence historically because of the violent Brahmanical psyche and the spiritual ethic that it built. As the structural violence of Brahmanism is defined as non-violence, it might take generations to retrieve the notions of violence and non-violence from that historical process.

In rural areas, some Brahman houses might look poor, but with the money that they earn around temples as *dakshina* there is no dearth of *pulihora* (rice cooked with tamarind paste), *daddhojanam* (rice cooked with milk and sugar), *perugannam* (rice mixed with yogurt)—all are divine food items—and of the basic comforts of life. In various parts of India, they constructed their own institutions. Many Brahman families have their roots in the Indian zamindari system, which emerged out of the *agrahara* (landed property granted to Brahmans)—the first mode of private property in India. If you look at urban areas, Brahman life varies from prime ministerial life to bureaucratic bunglows, professorial villas, police superintendent quarters and huge priestly houses. The largest number of cars, scooters, refrigerators, washing machines and second largest amount of gold reserves of the country are undoubtedly in Brahman houses. Though the Indian aeroplanes are owned by the Indian government and by private corporations like Jet or Kingfisher Airways, they are all virtually the property of the Indian Brahmans, who constitute the basic air-travelling caste/class of India. The highest number of human beings who enjoy living in air-conditioned houses and travelling in air-conditioned coaches are Brahmans. How has a caste, which does not even constitute 3 per cent of the Indian population, come to own so much power, property and wealth? How does a caste that claims to live a life of sacrifice lives a life of luxury? More than any thing, how have they come to control the Indian institutions? The answer lies in Brahmanism. What is their social essence? Do they, as caste, live a life of sacrifice or of luxury? Any observer with common sense can make out that their human essence is the embodiment of luxury and self-love. The cultural connotation of sacrifice does not appear to exist around their modern beings. Why and how did they evolve in that form as a caste? The answer is simple. They constructed themselves as exceptional species—the Brahmans in the image of their own god: Brahma.

BRAHMANISM AND SPIRITUAL FASCISM

The word 'Brahman' has three modes of use. Interestingly, all the usages are constructed by the Brahmans themselves. This is only one social group in the world which constructed its own self in an exalted mode of exceptionalism. The Jews in the ancient period constructed themselves in spiritual exaltation, but they did it as a nation. All communities and social groups were part of that spiritually exalted nation. That nation was created out of their enslavement by the Egyptians. Their God came into their life as a liberator of slaves from the master. The Jews never constructed themselves as gods on earth. Though the Pharisees, who constitute the highest core of the Jewish priesthood, constructed themselves as exceptional beings, they were subjected to a revolutionary reform after the spiritual revolt of Jesus. He ensured that the Samiritans (Jewish untouchables, leather workers) and the Gentiles (tillers of soil, carpenters, fishermen, and shepherds) had equal access to God. He was crucified for bringing about this revolution. After this revolution the Pharisees became farmers and the farmers became their pastors. The Brahmans, on the contrary, performed this exalted mode of self-construction to exclude others from the realm of God for the longest time in human history. This strategy was part of their historical cunningness. In this process, they worked out the meaning of the word 'Brahman' to keep themselves above history, which, for them, is an instrument of magical games.

The Brahmans seem to have derived the word 'Brahman' from the name of their god Brahma. The idea that Brahmans are superior beings was constructed by the Brahman classes themselves without deriving any divine essence from their God. Brahma, as an Aryan invader, was a killer of native Indians. They transformed the name Brahma into a caste of specific cultural essence–Brahman. Subsequently, they adopted that adjective as the name of their caste. Second, they defined the word 'Brahman' to mean 'knowledge'. The contours of that 'knowledge' are not wide enough to include all that goes with the word 'knowledge', as many philosophers and linguists of the world have used it–the knowledge of seed, fruit, bird, animal, soil, water, air, body and soul, and so on. None of the latter became a part of that word as the Brahmans defined it. Knowledge, astonishingly, was defined in terms of knowing Brahma, a euphemism again used to refer to their own caste self and to their war hero–Brahma. Goddess Saraswati is often regarded as goddess of education and learning. As per Hindu mythology, she was a daughter of Brahma but later became his wife (many scholars, including Ambedkar, have made this point). In ancient times, women did not have access to education, thus it is difficult to accept the idea that a woman could be the goddess of education. The Brahmans wrote a set of books called the Vedas, which are essentially books that worship war. They constructed war as an essential embodiment of life of every ruler. They used education as a means to construct their entire philosophical realm. They made that field exclusively theirs.

The most powerful instrument that human beings discovered to transform their selves is education. This instrument–both reading and writing–was not only under Brahmanical control for a long time, but also misused by the Brahmans to their own advantage. They even wrote books called the 'Brahmanas'. Though these books were assigned secondary status to the Vedas, they played a critical role in assigning the Brahmans an exalted social position. These books helped in strengthening the Brahmanic cultural realm and sanctified the oppressive practices of the Brahmans.

The three terms 'Brahma', 'Brahman' and the *Brahmanas* etymologically have their roots in the name of an aggressor migrant social group called the Brahmans–the most violent of all social groups–who became a per-manently dominant source of the earliest colonization of the Indian mind. The colonization of the minds of the productive masses is more harmful than colonization of national economic resources for a particular period of time. If the productive resources are colonized, a revolt against such colonization becomes possible–but if the minds of human beings are colonized, as happened in the case of the Dalit-Bahujans of India, it becomes difficult to liberate the mind for a long, long time. This is what happened in India.

The word Brahman, thus, originated as the name of a caste/clan and from there it transcended to godhood, was then transformed into a definition called 'knowledge' and was ultimately translated into books called the Vedas and the *Brahmanas*. All these concepts, in essence, refer to one caste: Brahman.

Thus, Brahman was the first caste to have been constructed. This construction was done by the Vedic priestly social group. This caste then worked out the boundaries of all the other castes. The other meanings of the word 'Brahman' are also derived from the exaltation of their self into an exceptional self. It was this self that was (and still is) superimposed on the religion called Hinduism. Hegel, the synthesizer of world philosophies, said in the *Lectures on the Philosophy of World History* (1975, translated by Johannes Haffmeister; New York: Cambridge University Press) while writing on India, 'If a Brahman is asked what Brahm is, he answers: When I fall back within myself, and close all external senses, and say Om to myself, that is Brahm.' He understood the fact that Hinduism is nothing but Brahmanism, and it is a mystical mode of constructing a religion. He further said,

> The Hindoos will not tread upon ants, but they are perfectly indifferent when poor wanderers pine away with hunger. The Brahmans are especially immoral. According to English reports they eat and sleep. In what is not forbidden then by the rules of their order, they follow natural impulses entirely. When they take part in any public life they show themselves avaricious, deceitful, voluptuous.

Hegel discussed the day-to-day lives of the Brahmans. He did not discuss the spiritual realm. The real spirit of their spiritual life lies in the spiritual realm. They constructed their fascist spiritual realm in order to achieve this selfish goal through spiritual means.

THE HINDU IMAGE IS BRAHMAN IMAGE

The essence of Brahmanhood is the most selfish of all human essences. It is one that constantly exalted the caste-self as the true representation of the Hindu divinity on earth. For any external observer, Hinduism is nothing but an institutionalized image of the Brahman self; although some people say that it is a religion that encompasses all the castes. The Hindu books are authenticated by Brahmans, regardless of the name they exist in. They themselves constructed their spiritual self as a fascist self—unreformable and untransformable. At the same time, the authors of spiritual fascism also constructed the others as low, inferior and ignorant. Their brand of spiritual fascism was institutionalized through their books, through their philosophical constructions and the practices of their everyday life. Unlike the political fascism that we know about, again in relation to German Aryanism, the Brahmans constructed fascism in the spiritual realm so that they could generate long-lasting consent from the subjects of that spiritual fascism. Since the Brahmans did not allow the mental faculties of the subjects of spiritual fascism to develop properly, people could not comprehend the essence of spiritual fascism. They institutionalized that process quite early itself—as early as that of the writing of the *Rigveda*. Thus, the *Rigveda* was the first fascist book in the world and the Brahman social forces were the first fascist social group that began to operate in the spiritual realm on this earth. This mode of construction of spiritual fascism had serious implications for the global knowledge system itself. Since the knowledge systems of vast social masses of India were arrested for centuries without allowing them to explore new areas of knowledge, the world also lost a great source of human innovations.

Thus, the institution of caste in India was born with the word, which later transformed into the name of the caste itself—Brahman. The country's tragedy started with this word, with that name, with those books and with that understanding of God itself. The descendants of the same self-loving and other-hating people exist as the Brahman caste. Though this caste has been undergoing some changes, it did not radically restructure itself to suit the modern notion of equality. This form of Brahmanism continues to play havoc in a nation that has had a history of much stronger productive roots than Greece, Egypt, Israel and China in the ancient times. A nation that the pre-Brahmanic masses have built by their sweat and blood is now rendered into a position of helplessness. This nation is suffering in the grip of the same Brahmanic people, without any hope of liberation for centuries. The Shudra, Chandala and the Adivasi masses, whose knowledge and contribution we have examined in the preceding chapters, were rendered to be their permanent slaves because of the one weapon that they used: 'Spiritual Fascism'. That is the reason why I characterize the Brahmans of India as spiritual fascists. This characterization reflects the historical experience of people who built a nation that does not belong to the social mass that built it. It is because of Brahmanical spiritual fascism that the productive masses were alienated from their own self and from their nation, even as the nation was alienated from them at the same time. Colonialism could make roots in the Indian subcontinent because the country was plagued by two institutions: caste and spiritual fascism.

SPIRITUAL FASCISM AND POLITICAL FASCISM

The concept of fascism has its origin in the Italian and German dictators—Mussolini and Hitler—evolving a theoretical and practical understanding during and between the two world wars. Today in the realm of political philosophy, the concept of 'fascism' has come to be identified with Hitler, who worked out a notion of Aryan racial superiority that planned to control and suppress the rest of humanity through the means of political fascism. Since political fascism had to operate in the realm of the state and the visible power structures of the political society around the state apparatus, it was easily detected. The political fascism that the German Aryans constructed was like a white snake in green grass. Its danger to the world was easily understood by the Euro-American political agencies and the life of that Aryan political fascism was cut short by the Euro-American democratic and socialist forces. The gravest victims of that fascism were Jews, who once were liberated by Moses and who later themselves oppressed the Israelite Samaritans and Gentiles. After the coming of Jesus, they became a spiritually reformed force—even then they lost their nation and spread across Europe and America. The German Aryans, under the leadership of the political fascist Hitler, persecuted and killed several Jews. It was these Jews who produced the best brains in socio-spiritual and scientific fields. The best examples of these are Jesus, Karl Marx and Albert Einstein. The Brahmans of India lived in totally opposite conditions. They controlled every aspect of a big country for more than three thousand years. Once they occupied India after the Aryan invasion, they never left this land. They remained the most stable priestly class in the world. Yet they produced a miniscule number of world-class intellectuals who could influence global thought in any field of knowledge. The spiritual fascism that they built destroyed them, and also the entire nation. The world never realized that spiritual fascism is far more dangerous than political fascism.

The development of genuine socialist thought in Europe and America was resisted by the Aryan political fascism with all the strength at its command. A major historical tragedy in Europe was averted with the killing of political fascism in Germany and Italy. But the modern world is living with a much more dangerous, but almost undiscovered 'green snake in green grass'— namely, the spiritual fascism that the Brahmanic forces of India had constructed around the same Aryanism, almost five thousand years ago. This spiritual fascism has survived for long, but it faces a stiff competition from Buddhism, Christianity and Islam in the era of globalization. The socio-cultural equality and humanitarian spiritual life of other religions attract many educated Dalit-Bahujan people, who seek to satisfy their spiritual hunger. The spiritual fascism that Brahmans of India established does not have any internal mechanism to reform itself as other religions could in the course of their evolution and growth. This spiritual fascism constructed the most dangerous disease of the world—human untouchability. Millions of Shudras, Chandalas and Adivasis thus suffered almost irreparably for centuries because of it. This practice of human untouchability and the theory of natural inequality that Brahmanism constructed by making the Shudras as the unequal partners of Hinduism will put the religion on the course of its own demise in this era of globalization and social democracy.

SPIRITUAL FASCISM AND LABOUR

The dignity of labour should be the ethical and existential reality of a society. One of the main characteristics of spiritual fascism is that it kills the productive ethic of a society. It constructs a consciousness of indignity of labour, wherein even the notion of God keeps operating around indignity of labour. All religions, except Hinduism, have combined spiritual democracy with dignity of labour. Hinduism, thus, is the antithesis of the very ideology of religion. The Brahmans hated productive labour, and along with that they hated the labouring social forces.

Great prophets like Christ and Muhammad came to spread the message that labour was the will of God Almighty. The Buddha too saw all energies in the labouring human agency. The Brahmans, on the other hand, claimed that they were *bhoodevatas*, who can produce everything without labour. But they produced nothing but the energy within themselves to consume the labour power of others. In a spiritual fascist society, labour does not remain a dignified re-energizing process of life but becomes a self-negating process. Spiritual fascism does not believe in humanizing the labour process and dehumanizes it instead. The process of building up the knowledge of science and technology is considered to be the task of condemned beings who possess no social dignity. The relationship between the spiritual—the divine— and the humans in a spiritual fascist environment is not mediated by production. The divine in the Brahmanic mode of life is not a companion in the process of digging roots for food, carrying the carcass for burial for the well-being of the environment, or rearing the sheep, goat and cattle for improving the living conditions of people. The Brahmans constructed spiritual theories in their literary texts which claimed that the Hindu God will do everything. God, in this understanding, does not stand for a particular kind of philosophy. In fact, most of the times the Hindu gods are represented as war heroes (for example, Hanuman, Ganesh, Ram). It is here that Brahmanism divorced itself from the realm of spiritual democracy and adopted spiritual fascism as its philosophical essence, whereas the other three schools—Buddhism, Christianity and Islam—adopted spiritual democracy as their philosophical essence.

GENEALOGY OF SPIRITUAL FASCISM

The Brahmans were a small group of people who came to India as a part of the Aryan aggression, a few thousand years before the British came as the colonizers of modern Indians. The Brahmans decided that they should be exclusivists, and established themselves with the weapon of violence. Mahatma Phule, in his famous book *Gulamgiri* (slavery), has shown that the figure of Parashurama—who killed several thousands of men, women and children—bears testimony for the inhuman violence that the Brahmans were capable of indulging in. Most of the Brahman organizations that have come into existence in the post-Mandal era have declared Parashurama as the symbol of their civil war (of the 10 incarnations of Vishnu, only Parashuram and Vamana were said to have been born in Brahman families. Parashuram was an extremely violent person). As they settled down in this land and built a culture of theirs parallel to the culture of the productive social masses, they did not automatically become nationalists. Nationalism is a concept of all freedoms—a core part of that freedom is spiritual freedom—that evolved out of the spiritual democratic theologies and practices of people. Nationalism is not just geography-centred—it is in fact more centred around freedom. But the essence of Brahmanic life is against human freedom and is structured in spiritual fascism.

It started with the first book of the Brahmans—the *Rigveda*. In a section called the Purushasukta, the *Rigveda* says, 'His mouth became the Brahman; his arms were made into the Warrior, his thighs the people and from his feet the servants were born' (see *Rigveda* published by Penguin in 1994). In other words, it says: the Purush called Brahma created the Brahmans from his mouth, the Kshatriyas from his shoulders, the Vaishyas from his thighs and the Shudras from his feet. This is the theory of the creation of the four varnas. It was in this theory of varna that Hinduism constructed a theory of natural inequality of human beings. This is where spiritual fascism originated.

This theory was made coterminous to the process of divine violence. The *Rigveda* itself provides enough evidence that Indra, the hero of the invaders, killed hundreds and thousands of indigenous people. The indigenous animal of the Dravidian masses was the buffalo. For them, it was not only a milk-giving animal but was also a symbol of black beauty and spiritual equality. The Aryans, on the other hand, preferred the white cow as a source of food as well as ritual sacrifice. The cow was also projected as a symbol of Aryan racism. As the Aryan racism transformed into spiritual fascism and violent vegetarianism, the cow was also constructed as a symbol of Hindu cultural nationalism. They constructed the beautiful black people as ugly *Rakshasas* and the beautiful black indigenous milch animal, buffalo, as a devilish animal. The cow was portrayed as *Kamadhenu* (animal that provides food and wealth without working for such a wealth). The buffalo, on the other hand, was shown as the Vahana of Yama (the vehicle of devil of death). Brahmanism thus constructed the most useful as devilish and the most deadly as divine.

Brahmanism saw Buddhism as its enemy, as Buddhism established a democratic *sangha* system to grant equal opportunities to all. It also saw Gautama Buddha as a dangerous spiritual force who had constructed an anti-Brahman spiritual civilization. They did not rest till Buddhism was driven out of India. B. R. Ambedkar (see *Revolution and Counter Revolution*, vol. 3) has shown how the Brahmans completely destroyed Buddhism. He was of the opinion that although Islam played an important role in weakening Buddhism, but even before that, during the reformist campaigns by the Hindus in the post-Adi Shankara period, Buddhist monasteries were destroyed and monks were killed. Periyar Ramasami argued that the Dravidians have been denigrated as untouchables by the Brahmans. There are some commonalities between the Dravidians and the buffalo: both are known for their productive abilities but are despised by the upper caste Hindus. The Aryan–Dravidian tension was once again expressed around the Rama Sethu issue in 2007. A living representative of Dravidians forces, M.K. Karunanidhi of the DMK described Rama as an imaginary figure, thus challenging the very existence of the Aryan hero Rama. The Aryan Hindutva forces such as the BJP, RSS and VHP issued a *fatwa* to kill Karunanidhi. The Dravidian forces retaliated by attacking the BJP offices in Chennai and other parts of Tamil Nadu. Finally, the anti-DMK agitation ended. Brahmanism tries to create civil war situations whenever their culture is in crisis.

Brahmanism, thus, entered into a contradiction with everything natural and productive, and also Dravidian. It negated the black beauty, black sturdiness and the black sacredness. Its books constructed *shlokas* (couplets from scriptures) of Aryan barbarism as the most natural, divine and spiritual. Such developments might be understood in light of the fact that they took place in the underdeveloped conditions of ancient India. But surprisingly, even after the negative characteristics of Aryanism were exposed after the destructive consequences of the Hitlerite agenda, the Indian Brahmanic forces did not give up the theory of Aryan superiority and greatness. When the BJP was in power, establishing such Aryan hegemonic structures became a part of the strategy of the ruling Brahmanic forces. It tried to bulldoze the religions that tried to establish spiritual equality, irrespective of the race and caste of Indian people.

Now in our own times, Christianity and Islam—that have established spiritual democratic structures after Buddhism got weakened in India—are under serious threat. As the Brahmanical forces of India are spreading across the world, they may negate the positive spiritual and social cultures of the world and establish the hegemony of the spiritual fascist cultural ethic across the world. If the world underestimates the dangers of spiritual fascism, it can do so only at its own peril. The world must understand how and why the Brahmans, who are a very small community, could establish the reign of spiritual fascism in India. We, therefore, must examine the strength of spiritual fascism in detail and in all its modern dimensions.

CONTEMPORARY BRAHMAN LIFE

To understand Brahmanical spiritual fascism, which they constructed over a period of time, we must examine the contemporary modes of Brahman life. Today, Brahmans exist as *sadhus*, *sanyasis*, priests and pundits in the spiritual realm. They exist as politicians, bureaucrats, teachers, doctors, engineers, military men, writers, T.V. and radio artists, and so on, in the societal and socio-political realms. They do not gather food and participate in food standardizing processes, as our Adivasis do. They are not a part of any institution where subaltern science operates; they do not perform any productive work. They do not exist in the fields of washing of clothes and shaving of body. They do not exist in the realms of meat and milk production, do not exist in any process of social engineering and do not exist in food production. If there are some exceptions to this rule, that does not make much difference in history. Their history is not the history of participation in all the above mentioned processes—the history of production. They remain away from all these humanly loveable and essential practices of life because of their 'spiritual libido'. This spiritual libido operates in a mode of heavy indulgence of spiritual self-love. In this spiritual libido, one's own body is seen as exclusive and it operates in its own self and against its own self.

A Brahman, no matter what his realm is, operates in exclusivity. The Brahmanical act of *puja* and offering prayer is thus as exclusive as the act of a human being easing out of company in order to relieve oneself. The act of *puja* has been conceptualized as a private, indoor affair, which does not have any positive public sanctity as it is not meant to be productive. It is a process of self-gratification of a community that has always considered itself exclusivist. The Brahmanical indulgence in *tapasya*, *yagya* and *puja* is not related to human welfare and therefore does not operate in social collectivity but in exclusivity. Similarly, the modern Brahmanical operations in the fields of politics, bureaucracy and industrial entrepreneurship (which is a domain they have become a part of late) are as exclusivist as the *tapasya*, *yagya* and *puja* were/are. Their notions of collectivity were lost because of their own self-indulgent actions. Thus, not a single operation of the caste expresses a collective consciousness. Hinduism could not become an evangelical and integrative religion because the Brahmans operated in the Hindu spiritual realm and made it the domain of one caste. Brahmanical superstition sustained other forms of superstition among the tribals, Dalits and the Shudras, leaving no scope for internal reform.

THE HINDU TEMPLES AND BOOKS

In this process, the Brahmans began to use the institution of the temple not as a place of social solace for the hardworking productive masses but as an institution of mobilization of money, food, gold, silver, and so on, for the consumption of their caste. They worked out various mechanisms of *dakshina* in order to acquire wealth through the temples. Thus God, in their worldview, is not satisfied with prayer alone—he should be offered wealth in all forms. Lately, they have even campaigned for the cutting of human hair at the temple and are making money through its sale. These days the food production, processing and packaging industries have been diversified, thus multi-cultural food items are being offered to the gods.

Building huge temples that are not accessible to all human beings has become a Brahmanic mode of spiritual business. Dalit–Bahujan labour power, skills and knowledge of sculpture are taken as free commodities while building the temple, and once the magnificent structure is erected it is taken over by the Brahmans and turned into an exclusive zone for tasks that are hardly related to the universal notion of prayer. In the so-called act of *puja*, they offer a variety of food items to the idols. The idols inside the temple thus become the instruments of sucking the blood of the poor, innocent and the gullible. The temple is not a place of simple prayer where every corner is wide open for human occupation, so that one may relieve themselves of the day's burden, or fear and anxiety. It is, instead, a place of hiding gold, silver and food items for the private use of the Brahmans. It is in this process, that the social bond of the Brahman caste grows stronger, establishing a perfect communication between one another, like that of a gang of bandits who remain united in order to succeed in theft. It is a theft through spiritual means, where the temple becomes a place of hiding while disallowing others to interrogate the spiritual theft that takes place everyday. For instance, the Sri Venkateshwara Temple at Tirupati is a Hindu Brahmanic temple that collects the highest amount of money in India through *dakshina*, offers human hair for sale, and collects money, gold and silver from the corrupt thieves and innocent masses alike. In the process, they have turned God into a corrupt being. Nowhere else in the world has God been turned into such a corrupt entity. The Brahman priests sell certificates for heaven to the most corrupt people in lieu of money, gold and silver. Murderers can buy peace at this temple by giving huge amounts of money. While they continue their murderous activities, the priests perform special *pujas* for money so that murderers can keep murdering and rapists can keep raping women again and again. *Puja* in such temples becomes a method of sanctification of exploitation, murder and rape. They are also constructed to be places where the flesh trade can take place.

The Hindu spiritual books are written to suit this whole process. They are written in an exclusivist language—Sanskrit. Those books also do not talk about human equality in the spiritual realm. They do not talk about human compassion. They talk about killing, working out war strategies and molesting women. The gods need Rambha, Urvasi and Menaka to dance for their pleasure. They cut the nose and earlobes of women and send pregnant women to forest. (In the *Ramayana* Surpanakha's nose was cut and Sita was sent to forest. This is an example of the male chauvinistic attributes of the Hindu gods.) The gods steal the clothes of women while they bathe; living with women outside the wedlock (Krishna and Radha) earns no spiritual indignation. The romance of the ordinary mortal in the field, in the forest and in the bedrooms is inscribed onto the divine realm, as the Brahman priest needs to see everything in that book. The notion of heaven itself is constructed as a realm of pleasure. The Hindu spiritual books are not simply male chauvinist books but books of war, wine (*soma*) and women in the most dehumanized form of narratives.

No Brahmanic spiritual book discusses human relations in their normal form. These books do not talk about child care. They do not frame the rules for nursing the old and the sick. They do not talk about treating the sick by applying medicine. They do not contain stories and parables about human achievements and failures. Neither the Hindu gods nor the Brahmans fail in their day-to-day life—the failure is attributed to the Shudras, Chandalas and the Adivasis. The Brahmans succeed all through. It is perhaps here in these books that we may find the clue to the historically successful Brahmanical deceptivity, from the ancient age to the modern, from kingships to democracy and from feudalism to the Brahman variety of socialism. And herein lies the source of the failure of the Dalit–Bahujans of India. The books they hardly read arrested their social mobility, and the temples they never entered arrested their spiritual and social liberation. It is in this subtle manner that the Brahmanic spiritual fascism operates. How does the political fascism of the Hitler match this mode of spiritual fascism? This is the mother of all fascisms, born in the Aryan invasion of ancient days. The poverty, hunger, illiteracy and destitution of the social masses amidst Brahmanic wealthiness is a standing testimony of this mode of fascism. Here humanness is killed in cold blood.

PHILOSOPHICAL UNDERPINNINGS

The real epicentre of spiritual fascism are the *sanyasis*, *rishis* and the *sadhus*. A *sanyasi* is an unmarried Brahman, a campaigner of Brahmanism. In ancient India the *sanyasis* operated in the name of Aryadharma and Sanatanadharma, and in the medieval period they operated in the name of Advaita and Vedanta. Now, in the modern age, they have adopted a new name for themselves called Hinduism. This term was coined by a Muslim scholar, Alberuni, in a derogatory sense, but the Brahmans adopted it. Brahmans dislike innovation but plagiarize ideas if it helps them in attaining their goals and objectives.

The *sanyasi* campaign is an exclusively Brahmanical occupation of propagating the law of segregation of humans into castes—any transgression of this law, which the Brahmans made themselves and imposed upon the others, would lead to, as Hegel said, the 'knocking down' of such transgressors by the Brahmans which takes place with an approval of the Hindu gods. The *rishi* is not a cleanly shaven and cleanly bathed being. He is an unclean person with fully grown hair all over and unwashed clothes who, paradoxically, constructs a philosophy of self-purity. There are several forms of rishihood. Many such forms were in display at the time of the Kumbhamela in 2001. There is the naked rishihood with full-grown and unwashed hair all over the body. The hair on their head gets coiled and pig-tailed, and is sometimes as long as two and a half meters. Their hair keep sweeping the roads as they walk. These *rishis* (most of them are only males) looked like fully grown apes as they displayed their naked body to the world. Their presence hurts the sensibilities of public morality because they were allowed to display themselves, without any inhibitions, by the BJP governments at Lucknow and Delhi. Another form is the half-naked rishihood, where the upper part of the body remains uncovered. The five Shankaracharyas live in this form and also the temple priests. Gandhi used this form to bring the Brahmans of India to his side, and succeeded in the strategy. But he was killed by a Brahman. The killer can be condemned, disowned but in reality, a Brahman decided to kill the 'Other'—a Baniya— because he had attained a more important position.

The *sadhu*, clothed in saffron *kurta* and *dhoti*, is yet another product of Brahmanical deception. They collect not only food resources but also wealth in a massive scale from the general public. The *sadhu*'s collection of food and wealth through begging is a legitimate activity in the spiritual realm of Brahmanism. They neither preach, nor teach the masses, but they do indulge in the spiritual smuggling of goods and commodities for a life of full-scale luxury in private and of simplicity in the public. At times they even run into deeper forests, preferably that of the Himalayas, wherein they indulge in self-suffering penance called *tapasya*. This *tapasya* is not meant to grant spiritual liberation to the human mass, or to construct a knowledge system of human liberation, but to construct the so-called sacrificial structure of the hegemonic Brahmanism. The Hindu *sadhus* are not Catholic saints and Buddhist monks living among the masses, eating their food and teaching them the religious morals they believe in. The *sadhus*, essentially, are involved in assuring themselves of a place in the other world—heaven—which is described as a place of pleasure.

One of the strange forms of *tapasya* still survives today. It is a funny spiritual activity that involves long hours of upside-down posturing of ones body—sometimes burying one's neck deep in the sand and ultimately dying a death of self-torture. It does not involve teaching, reading or communicating anything to the community. Many Oxford, Cambridge and Harvard-returned Brahmans have written books about the greatness of these form of Brahman spiritualism, including that of naked *sanyasi* Brahmanism; this is a truly shocking aspect their intellectualism. Brahmanism injects an anti-reasoning consciousness into an individual born into a Brahman family, right from the childhood—this consciousness transcends the individual and been inscribed upon the national self itself. Every so-called great Hindu has only praised this socially disconnected institution.

Classical Brahmanism tells us that these *sadhus*, *sanyasis* and *rishis* had written the ancient Brahmanic books. They obviously constructed these texts to legitimize their parasitic lifestyles of living off the productive castes. One cannot even believe that they wrote books in the ancient period, because in our own lifetime not a single Brahman *rishi*, *sanyasi*, or *sadhu* wrote any book that influenced the society in any significant way. Even if we take their own history of writing from the days of Raja Ram Mohan Roy, not a single *sanaysi* wrote any book on either spirituality or sexuality, as Kautilya or Manu or Vatsayana did. The only book that Dayananda Saraswati wrote—*Satyardha Prakash*—may be said to belong to that category, and we know how bad a book it is. It is bad because it envisions building an Arya Samaj. But they do not realize that while trying to build an Aryan nation, Hitler ended up building a fascist state. If we follow the Aryan nation theory, then we would not be able to see the world from an alternate perspective. Nonetheless, all the spiritual books of Brahmanism were constructed in the names of the Brahmanic *sadhus*, *sanyasis* and *rishis*. They are propagated in a manner that portrays them as the most respectable of all books. The culture that was sought to be built through the propagation of those books was essentially Brahmanic, which saw production as undignified. Not a single person talked against untouchabiltiy, not a single person talked against human inequality. Not a single book talked about the spiritual significance of food production, or sheep, cattle and goat herding as divine. Instead, they portrayed all those who are clean, who participate in productive work as unclean, polluted beings who need to be away from the Brahman body, from the *puja* ritual and the temple. A Brahman *rishi* or *pujari* feels more comfortable while interacting with a Brahman than the people from other castes. The *punyam* (piety attained by performing puja) that is generated in that intercourse is meant for the self-gratification of the Brahman, who is a human being who never wishes the well-being of others.

Normally, prayer in all other religions is a public affair, involving the masses. The Brahmans, however, negated that process and made it a purely secret, self-indulgent process. The *rishi* goes further and further into the forest where he cannot even smell another human being. He interacts only with the Brahman—no Shudra or Chandala is allowed anywhere near his vicinity. The Hindu god Brahma does not appear to possess any of the qualities of Jehovah or Allah, either—while Jehovah and Allah have the desire to liberate all human beings, irrespective of their caste, class, race or gender, Brahma has an agenda of liberating and salvaging only the Brahmans. Brahma, as a god, is not universal but meant for one caste alone.

The concept of God has come into human life in order to liberate the slaves from their oppressors and to ensure the well-being of all human beings. The concept of Brahma, on the other hand, was worked out to enslave people and oppress them perpetually. The Brahmans worked out a method to mediate with God to produce spiritual fascism to suppress the Shudras, Chandalas and the Adivasis of India. The Brahman priests constructed the notion of *mantra shakti* that kills others who violate the Brahmanic codes. For example, the cutting off of tongues of the Shudras and Chandalas for reading the scriptures, cutting off of their hands for writing a book or pouring lead into the ears of those among them who listen the Hindu scriptures being read are just few examples of the Brahmanic code. There are many such spiritual fascist codes against women as well. Although these codes are not practised any more but the implication of these codes effects people in one form or the other.

The spiritual process that Buddha, Christ and Muhammad upheld was the liberation of all human beings who approached them—as the Islamic proverb goes, 'Muhammad went to all mountains to teach them but the mountains did not go to him to learn.' In Hinduism neither the god nor the *rishi* goes to anyone except a Brahman. If some Shudra or Chandala approaches that Brahman, he does not allow him to be alive, but kills him then and there (this is not practiced any more). But Buddha, Christ and Muhammad went to the lepers. They went to those who were suffering with AIDS (in those days this disease must have been there, but not known by this particular name), those suffering with tuberculosis, and cured their diseases. This is not to claim that the mere touch of any human being like Buddha, Christ or Muhammad cured actual diseases—but they gave everybody the necessary confidence to face the disease and applied medicine. They codified principles that pronounced that God treated the diseased as equals.

God, in Buddhism, Christianity and Islam is an unknown entity who works for the well-being of the oppressed, and in doing so he does not look at the race, caste, class or gender of the human being in question. But no Hindu God or *sanyasi* respects human beings as human beings. With a brazen Brahmanism, the Brahmans claim in their books that God only touches the Brahmans, and so the *sanyasis* too will touch only the Brahmans. The temples are the spaces where human untouchability is practised. The Shudras, Chandalas and the Adivasis are hated and abused, and if any of them attempt to approach a Brahman *rishi* or a *sanyasi*, they are cursed to death. In Brahmanism, God was/is not a democratic being, but a fascist being. The *sanyasi* was/is not a democrat, but a fascist. The *pujari* was/is not a democratic being but a fascist being. If a Shudra,

Chandala or an Adivasi, who has been a victim of this mode of spiritual fascism, comes up and claims that for the survival of the society, for the society to acquire a spiritual and social democratic character, the notion of God must be transformed, the *sanyasi* reformed and the *pujari* changed, what will the Brahmanic judiciary say? Perhaps it will declare contempt of the Court, as the Indian courts constitute the very same people who adore all that is inhuman as divine. In the Brahmanic realm, a Shudra writing a book becomes an act of contempt, a woman shouting a slogan is an act of contempt, and so on. Let alone human beings—even if a buffalo asks for the status of a cow, both in the constitution and also in real life, the buffalo would be sent to jail. In the mind of a Brahmanic judge, it is the *sanyasi* who operates in the form of judicial knowledge. In Brahmanical knowledge, a cow can be a constitutional animal, but not a buffalo. Who said so? Brahma. He is a white being as a god, and the cow is a white animal. The buffalo is a bad black animal only worth using for milking—white milk—but not to institutionalize its life in the Constitution. This is the essence of spiritual fascism. Such a spiritual fascism is campaigned for by the institutions called temples, *rishis*, *sanyasis*, and so on. Brahmanism opposed humanism right from inception. No thinker from the Brahman community tried to dismantle the spiritual fascist base of the Hindu society. Spiritual fascism is propagated in the name of dharma.

CONSTRUCTING SPIRITUAL FASCISM

The Brahmans constructed a spiritual realm for all, but the handling of it was made exclusively their own prerogative. They alone deal with God. They alone talk to God. Very surprisingly, in the very first book that the Brahmans wrote in the name of God—the *Rigveda*—they said that they alone were born from the mouth of God. The other social forces were born from God's shoulders, thighs and feet, respectively. Of course, the vast Dalit and tribal masses were not even born from that divine body. Here, God does not have enough ideas to construct people in his imagination. In the Brahmanic realm, God is a physical entity but not a philosophical entity. Rendering God into a physical entity that does not have ideas to construct the world in an imaginative manner is, in itself, an uncreative exercise. In a Brahmanic mode of thinking, the mind has no value—only the body does. In this process of giving utmost importance to the body, but not to the idea, a Brahman constructs the notion of bodily pollution. In all great religions, the body and the soul have dialectical relationship. But since the idea has no role to play in Brahmanism, the perpetual engagement with the body has become a self-promotional and other-destructive process of living. Although the Brahmans claimed that they are the storehouse of knowledge but they remained worshippers of the physical entity of God (idol worshippers). Unlike religions like Christianity and Islam, they did not become worshippers of the philosophical aspect of God. None of the philosophers from the Brahman community could spread his influence outside India. In fact, whenever any philosopher emerged from the other communities, they tried to undermine his influence. For instance, Brahmans tried to oust Buddha (a tribal) from India; Gandhi (a Baniya) was used by them as a stepping stone for attaining power and position; and Ambedkar (a Dalit) was ignored by them for a long time and ultimately accepted as an idol of lesser importance.

As I said in *Why I am Not a Hindu*, they talk about the body being *kshanabhanguram* (only that lives for a minute), but body gets all the priority and the idea and knowledge of the world gets no priority in the intellectual debate. A Brahman does not believe in debate at all. In the world where debate does not find any place, the physical force—violence—gets the central place. It is in this process that the concept of *danda* was constructed as a central theme of Hindu religion. Religions as social organizations emerged to enlarge the organized social base of people. Religious institutions like *viharas*, churches and mosques were places of human congregation where people shared their pleasure and their pain. The slave had the opportunity to tell the master that God was observing the torture that was being inflicted upon them. The masters, at least in a *vihara*, a church or a mosque, had to listen to the slaves, as all human beings at that place were considered equals. The Brahmans, on the other hand, worked out a spiritual institution called the temple. All cannot meet here. There is no notion of equality before God. Many lives were lost for stepping inside the temples. Killing around temples became a common practice as these institutions were worked out as the exclusive places of the Brahmans.

If we see the social practice of discourse and debate among the Adivasis, Chandalas and the Shudras, the concept of *danda* does not exist there. Resolution of any conflict is made possible through debate and discourse. Unlike this, in Brahmanism, all conflicts are resolved only by war. Thus, the figures of Brahma, Indra, Vishnu, Rama, Parashurama and Krishna were all constructed as warrior gods. Neither in the Dalit–Bahujan notion of godhood nor the Buddhist, Christian or Islamic notion of godhood does killing the other have any role. Spiritual fascism alone constructs killing—danda—as the natural process of divine and human life.

ARYANISM AND SPIRITUAL FASCISM

True spiritual thought in the world emerged out of the democratic discourses of people. In such a thought process, God is the most imaginative of beings. The Indian Brahmans, on the other hand, negated all processes of human imagination. Their understanding of nature is negative. Their understanding of animals is negative. Finally, their understanding of human beings is negative. This negativism seems to be the generic character of Aryans as a race. There is a commonality in the minds of Indian Brahmans and followers of Hitler: one constructed the spiritual fascist ideology in the ancient period and other constructed the political fascist ideology of the modern period.

The Aryan race has an unusual psyche. They do not believe in human equality. This is clear from the written views of Dayananda Saraswati, a so-called liberal Aryan Brahman, and Hitler, the German Aryan fascist. Dayananda in his book *Satyarth Prakash* (translated by Durga Prasad; New Delhi: Gyan Prakashan) says, 'A Brahman should marry a woman of Brahman order, a Kshatriya, of the Kshatriya, a Vaishya, of the Vaishya, a Shudra of the Shudra' (p. 36). What is the reason behind prescribing this mode of intra-*varna*/caste marriages so strictly? He says, by quoting the Aryan sages, that 'it is the only course which makes persons (pure)...preserves the purity of their race. There will be no bastard in any class' if this method is followed in marriages. The marriage by choice system that major religions like Buddhism and Christianity had brought into practice is seen by Dayananda as an institution of producing bastard children. Even for schooling 'to regenerate the twice-born classes (the present day Brahman, Kshatriyas and Vaishyas) should send them (their children) to respective seminaries'(39). It is a known fact that Dayananda Saraswati called his organization the Arya Samaj. This name itself is racist. To understand why the Aryan race wanted to maintain its purity we should turn to Hitler.

Hitler, in his book *Mein Kampf*, builds a theory that maintaining racial purity is a mechanism that nature itself worked out. In all sexual intercourse of species, even in a natural process, engagement with dissimilar species is avoided. He tells us that a mouse indulges in sexual relations with only similar mice and horse engages with similar horses only. In such a natural intra-species sexual engagement, the higher race retains its purity. According to him, of all the human races, the Aryan race is the best and hence it should maintain its racial purity. Hitler being a European Aryan, unlike the Indian Brahmans, rationalizes his argument and builds a theory in order to build an Aryan fascist civil society and state. Hitler, being a political fascist while operating within the Christian ethic of spiritual democracy, does not go for spiritual justification of his thesis. As a close ally of the Italian fascist Mussolini, who tries to use the Machiavellian secular thought to achieve his fascist goals, Hitler constructs a much better theory than the Indian Brahmanic Aryans did and still do.

The Hindu Brahmanic writers established the spiritual fascist ideology in the ancient period and this ideology was drawn into the political realm by the Nazis. If we go by the literary texts, the concept of superman was present in the *Rigveda*. It is, therefore, obvious that 'Hitlerism' lies in Hindu Brahman thought and its essence got constructed in the ancient times. Aryan Brahmanism laid a much stronger foundation for fascism in the world by constructing the spiritual supremacy of the Brahmans, because like Dayananda Saraswati, the Brahmans considered themselves as the carriers of Aryan racial superiority. As the roots of Hitlerite political fascism lie in Hitler's German Aryan racism, the roots of Brahmanic spiritual fascism lie in Indian Aryan racism. The implications of the Brahmanic Aryan racist spiritual fascism were/are more dangerous than that of Hitlerite political fascism. Hitlerite political fascism ended within a short time by pushing the world into World War II. It is a fact that in the World War II, the world suffered a great deal. It is equally a fact that this fascism was detected by the West itself. But because of Brahmanical spiritual fascism, the world—if we compute in historical terms—suffered much more than what humanity had suffered because of World War II. The sufferers and losers in the process of institutionalization of the Brahmanic spiritual fascism were not the Indian Dalit-Bahujans alone—the whole world suffered because of its general impact on the human mind. While the crippling of the Dalit-Bahujan mind, for centuries, negated the whole process of scientific thinking in this country, that negation also affected the global knowledge systems as a creative social mass was kept out of reading and writing of its social and scientific experiments that we discussed in earlier chapters.

THE DIFFERENCE BETWEEN SPIRITUAL AND POLITICAL FASCISM

Political fascism eliminates a certain number of targeted people. It declares war on the targeted people or nations. Such a targeting can be countered either with a similar war, as the socialist and democratic forces had done against Hitlerite fascism, or it can be countered at the political level. But spiritual fascism of the Brahmanical variety controls the thinking process of human beings for thousands of years, as it has done in India. It kills the mental and physical growth of millions of people as they are not allowed to see the light of God and the light of the book. In fact, the image of God itself is constructed as the enemy of most docile human beings like the Dalit-Bahujans of India. In all other religions God relates himself to the human process of food production, organizing human relations around productive tools, and establishing cordial relations among human beings, but in Hinduism, the Brahmans have divided people on the basis of community and caste. The Buddha, Christ and Muhammad, great prophets in whose name religions have come to be established, are hated by the Brahmans. The Brahmans constructed their own divine images, which became the source of spiritual fascism. The tasks assigned to such Brahmanic Gods are that of conducting wars, killing people and spending time in the company of women. In this mode of spirituality, the human beings who toil for the welfare of the whole society are considered *adharmic*, whereas eliminating them is the task of the *dharmic*. If the positive people try to learn the spiritual truth through the means of education, they are either killed or maimed so that they would be permanently immobile. Unlike in other spiritual modes of life, the poor and the destitute are not sympathized with—they are treated instead as unwanted creatures, who need to be condemned as unworthy to live. The spiritual fascists do not believe in providing succor to the poor and the needy but believe in putting them through pain, humiliation and agony. The agony of others is constructed as the pleasure of God. Thus, God becomes a torturer here, like a sadist policeman in a police station.

A shockingly negative psyche has developed among the Brahmans, who enjoy life only when the others are suffering. They hate the pleasure of all. They hate all human beings except those on the same social pedestal as they are. The rich and racist whites in the West exploited the poor and humiliated the blacks and sexually abused their women, but there was human compassion and an understanding of pain somewhere in their heart. There was a constant desire in their hearts to take all human beings towards equality, and share the pain and pleasures of life among all human beings—this desire was responsible for many changes. This realization of the equality of the black and the white was rooted in the Christian idea of God and their repeated readings of the life experience of Jesus Christ. Their spiritual book, the Bible, says that the rich will pay penalty in the other world. There is a notion in that book that God stands by the poor, the ignorant and the suffering. Hence, the rich and the exploitative social forces are forced to ask self-searching questions. It was such a spiritual heart that changed the political mind of racism. That heart was always missing in the being called the Brahman.

This is not to say that spiritual inequality did not exist in all societies, or that some people did not enjoy life at the cost of others. Such notions and practices exist in many societies. But Brahmanism treats inequality and suffering as necessary—as divinely ordained. Brahmanism worked towards this inequality. No Brahmanical writer, thus, wants to talk about inequality of castes. The difference between political fascism and spiritual fascism is that political fascism states in obvious terms what it thinks. There is the possibility of changing a political fascist. The spiritual fascists, on the other hand, do not say what they think. They are like snakes which always keep awake but pretend to sleep. They have adopted a life of permanent pretension. Their life process itself is hypocritical. When fascism combines itself with hypocrisy and operates in a spiritual mode, it becomes impossible for the others to know what is operating through one's mind. The mind of such beings operates like the devil's work shop. It always aims at somebody's suffering. It derives pleasure out of the suffering of others.

THE MIND OF SPIRITUAL FASCIST

The Brahman mind did not develop through the normal human processes of hunting, fishing, digging roots, plucking fruits and finally entering into deeply embedded intercourse with nature, by producing things out of its womb and by engaging itself in labour. In positive religions, spiritualism emerged out of a constant struggle with nature. The need for the notion of a god emerged more in order to win over nature rather than to win over other human beings. The Hindu religion was evolved by the Brahmans to win over other human beings, with the mediation of a violent God. Nowhere does labour and struggle with nature figure in the Brahman life and nowhere does suffering become the life process of the God they constructed in their own image. If God created people in his own image in other religions, in Hinduism it was God who was created in the image of a Brahman. That made the course of Hinduism totally different from that of other religions. As a result, Brahmanism did not allow other religions like Buddhism to survive here and did not allow the human mind to develop in a rational manner, where it could mediate between spirituality and science on a humanitarian plane.

The Brahmans characterized themselves as people of knowledge. They claimed that they constructed the Indian spiritual thought out of their knowledge. Let us compare them with a very knowledgeable community, which was also the source of a major school of spiritual thought in the world—the Jews. The Jews constructed the notion of Jehovah and Jesus

Christ became the source of another major religion—Christianity. They also produced the most powerful scientific and investigative brains of world, like that of Spinoza, Einstein, Columbus, Karl Marx, and so on. The Brahmans have not produced a comparable social force either in the spiritual realm or in the scientific realm. Why?

The Jews developed their notions of the divine, discovered their prophet in Jesus Christ and constructed their knowledge of sciences and social sciences based on the experience of productive struggle with nature. Their concepts evolved out of a tremendous amount of suffering, but not from torturing the other. They did not evolve out of violence, but out of a torturous course of sacrifice for the sake of the whole humanity. They evolved out of physical labour, in accordance with the Hebrew canon. While talking about their conditions, Will Durant says,

> ...barred by the feudal system from owning land, and by the guilds from taking part in industry; shut up with in congested ghettoes and narrowing pursuits, mobbed by the people and robbed by the kings; building with their finance and trade the towns and cities indispensable to civilization; out caste and excommunicated, insulted and injured;—yet, without any political structure, without any legal compulsion to social unity, without even a common language, this wonderful people has maintained itself in body and soul... (Will Durrant, *The Story of Philosophy*. New York: Simon and Schuster)

Do the conditions of these people resemble the conditions of Indian Brahmans in any way? Did the Brahmans suffer at any time without having any property in history? Did they live in ghettoes at any time in history? Were they ever robbed by any section of Indians, or was it they who robbed others for centuries? In fact, the Jewish life resembled the conditions of the Indian Dalit-Bahujans. Will Durrant further talks about the education system of the Jewish students that requires every (Jewish) student to acquire some manual art. Labour was the most respectable process of life. They believed that 'work keeps one virtuous, whereas every learned man who fails to acquire a trade will at last turn out a rogue' (Will Durrant, *The Story of Philosophy*. New York: Simon and Schuster). This was a dictum of every Jewish family.

All Jews believed in hard physical work, hence they combined productive work with spiritual activity . The Brahmans of India did the very opposite. They became learned to become manipulators of the system. The labour that produces fruits of sustenance was constructed as undivine. The main difference between the two ancient communities is that the Jews worked out their knowledge through labour and sacrifice whereas the Brahmans worked out their knowledge through violence, sex and parasitism. This mode of immoral spirituality has constructed the ethical values upside-down. Those who are the most humane were pushed to the margins of the civil society, and those who are the most inhuman are kept at the helm of affairs of the state and civil society. This spiritual process has very deep implications on the Indian psyche itself as the Brahman became the model being for every educated person, even in the modern post-colonial India.

THE BRAHMAN PSYCHOLOGY

No study has been conducted to understand the psychology of the Brahmans. There is a marked difference between the psychology of the productive communities and that of Brahmans. A Brahman, by the very process of childhood formation, does not acquire a creative mind and the physical and mental boldness to confront the hostile nature that they are born into. Their essential training is about recitation of written material, right from their childhood. Whatever written material the Brahmans produced was centred around building upon the ideology of spiritual fascism. It is a psychology of generating fear and insecurity within one's own self. A Brahman, by training, is made to be timid. There are many proverbs within the Dalit–Bahujan civil society that say that 'Brahmans and timidity are born twins'. The social source of this timidity is rooted in their withdrawal from encountering nature in its rudest and crudest forms. Nature is an economic force of multi-dimensional energy. At the same time, it is a brutal force that knocks down those who work to exploit it. In the struggle against nature, in other words, in the struggle to transform that nature into a utilitarian social essence, human beings confront all kinds of danger. This is true of all other species too which operate within the principle of the survival of the fittest. While cutting a tree, the human being encounters the danger of that very tree falling on the cutter himself/herself.

In fighting against the animals, the fighter himself or herself is in the danger of getting attacked by that animal. The wood-cutter and the animal hunter combine physical strength with constantly improving mental knowledge to overcome the dangers of life. A Brahman, for generations, remained away from such physical and mentally re-energizing struggle with nature. Thus, a Brahman family does not have the day-to-day experience of transforming nature into humanly usable commodities.

As a result of this withdrawn life, a Brahman lives in constant fear of struggle and experiment with nature and matter. When I first heard that a Brahman envisions an earthworm to be a snake, I just could not believe the amount of fear of nature that they carry with them. Why are they, as a community, so afraid of nature? Courage and confidence is developed in human beings during struggle with nature from childhood. Courage does not materialize in any human being in the course of the struggle with a book. By reading a book one cannot gain practical experience. A book only broadens the understanding of human beings. Brahmans projected the ancient books—particularly the Vedas—as everything. The Brahman communitarianism operates like the communitarianism of penguins or sheep, which hardly builds the energy for individual struggle for survival. The Brahmans, who were aliens on Indian soil, developed that model of the community right from the formative stage of their migration. Even among animals, staying too much with the flock is a symptom of the constantly haunting fear for one's life, which does not allow any individual enterprise. Even hunting and grazing by animals expanded their knowledge of the animal kingdom. The process of hunting and grazing among animals take place with the individual enterprises of animals, within their broad social collectivity. But Brahmans did not allow any individual enterprise in their own social collectivity. They carried the underdeveloped animal instinct of penguins and sheep into human beings. And that instinct is being sustained by regenerating the same instinct in members of their group from childhood onwards.

Like animals and birds, each human race developed its own instincts. Work ethics, notions of morality and immorality, beauty and ugliness differ from race to race. While explaining the racial differences in the perceptions of beauty in his *magnum opus*, *The Origin of Species*, Darwin says,

> I may first remark that the sense of beauty obviously depends on the nature of mind, irrespective of any real quality in the admired object; and that the idea of what is beautiful, is not innate or unalterable. We see this, for instance, in the men of different races admiring an entirely different standard of beauty in their own women. (p. 185)

Different racial characteristics of the human beings construct the instincts of the human beings differently. A careful study of the instinctual psychology of the Aryan Brahman race and its comparison with that of the Germanic Hitlerite Aryan instinctual psychology indicates that parasitism and worship of violence are the innate instincts of these two communities, which share the same racial characters.

Brahman instincts have a strong tendency towards self-love and hate for others. That instinct was formed as a consequence of the Brahmanical culture of negating production of food, and they acquired the characteristic of parasites. The Brahman community constantly looks at its own self with an innate fear that was formed out of its parasitism. All parasites suffer from a constant fear of individualism. Parasitism and individualism are antithetical to each other. Thus, we witness an instinctive fear of death in the parasite the moment it disjoins itself from its support structure. It coils around the support structure at every step, disfiguring that very structure in the process, killing it bit by bit. This is because the basic quality that distinguishes the plant–animal kingdom from human beings is the process of production of food from the earth. The Brahmans, as a community, shared the animal instinct of not being able to produce anything from the earth. This human caste differs from all the other social communities that emerged into a larger civil society, ever since human beings evolved out of the ape and formed the human communities all over the world. This unusual instinct of parasitism forced the Brahmans to construct a social process of spiritual fascism that became the fortress of its parasitism.

Weak beings evolve more powerful violence-centred methods in order to survive as living beings. This is more so in the case of human beings. Of all the human races, the Aryans have displayed the greatest tendency of constructing violence-oriented theories for their survival. The German Aryans and the Indian Aryans (the core of which are the Indian Brahmans) share many common features like that of worshipping violence. The Mongoloids, the Jews, the Dravidians and the Australoids have shown a different tendency. These races acquired the innate physical and mental strength to change the environment more with the use of labour instead of violence. They were never inclined to depend on violence. The Buddha (let there be no misrepresentation here—the Buddha was not an Aryan, but belonged to the Sankhya, which is a Mongoloid tribe) and Jesus Christ are two great examples as representatives of the Mongols and Jews who changed the course of human history without resorting to violence at all. Both of them are non-Aryans. The Chinese, the Japanese and the Jews have shown tremendous mental and physical energy in using labour power to transform their socio-economic conditions. They have also developed a tremendous capacity to undergo suffering and have developed enormous creative skills and recuperative mental and physical skills that would allow them to come out of suffering. The emergence of China in the modern world almost from nothing, Japan's techno-economic empowerment and Israel's ability to rebuild itself was based on the Mongoloid and Jewish racial characteristics of these people. Our journey through the Dravidian Dalit–Bahujan productivity and their ability to suffer and sustain, in the preceding chapters, has shown that but for the Vaishyas and Brahman cultural parasitism, India would have been a different country altogether. We have seen in history that the personally weak kings survived by building up a strong army and more powerful weapons (for example, Pushyamitra Shunga was a weak Brahman king, but with the help of a strong army he could expand his state). If Pushyamitra Shunga was an example of ancient Indian/Aryan racist ruler, then Hitler was an example of German racist ruler. If Hitler was an individual symptomatic expression of the Aryan race, he was personally the most timid ruler that human history has ever witnessed. To overcome that personal timidity and insecurity, he built an army and weapons that moved towards killing the others. But there is a self-destructive aspect to that strong desire for the destruction of the other. The self-destruction of such social forces, of course, with an intention of the destruction of the whole humanity itself, is historically known. The Brahmans of India and the German Aryans carried that instinct very strongly with them. And that resulted in generating an army of political fascism in Germany and of spiritual fascism in India. Fascism and extreme timidity are two opposite sides of the same coin. In the case of the Brahmans, it was their timid nature and their non-energetic mode of community behaviour that led them to the construction of an array of gods of spiritual fascism. Envisioning an earthworm as a snake and constructing a fortress of spiritual fascism around themselves are part of the Brahman community's historical evolution. This psychology had serious implications not only for India but for the whole world.

THE IMPLICATIONS OF SPIRITUAL FASCISM

The Brahmans have yet another psychological instinct, that of imitation. Since parasitism is their historical weakness, for the sake of survival, they depend on imitative knowledge rather than on creative knowledge. This is clear from their role in the ontology of language. The Pali language was originally constructed based on people's productive interaction with nature, much before the Aryans came to India. Sanskrit was imitatively expanded, without building any creative vocabulary. As a result, however divine that language was claimed to be, it could not survive. The Brahmans themselves moved into English the moment the British introduced that language. But they failed to use that language for a creative and liberative purpose. For almost two hundred years, they used English for imitative learning. Statistically, the Brahmans—with their long interaction of 200 years—constitute the largest number of English-speakers in India.

Their contribution to English, however, is nothing but imitative speaking and imitative writing. The best English writers, like Salman Rushdie and Arundhati Roy, come from non-Aryan non-Brahmanic background (religionwise, one is a Muslim and the other is a Christian). Not that these two writers contributed something original, but they developed Indian English into a more creative form than all the Hindu Brahman writers put together. As they did with Sanskrit, Brahmans also used English for the purpose of Dalit–Bahujan enslavement. In this, they betrayed an instinctive possessiveness towards any language they learnt, which is why they jealously guarded the English language and did not teach it to the native productive masses, even though they themselves were taught the language by Christian missionaries who came from Europe. The upper caste Brahmanic churches have shown the same tendency. Thus, the social parasitic forces suffer from two important problems. First, they do not allow the language to expand itself to more and more creative areas and to a larger number of people. Sanskrit suffered from this possessiveness of Brahmanism and Indian English has suffered from the same possessiveness of Brahmans of Hinduism—and also Christianity—in the last two hundred years. Second, they disconnect any language they possessively own from its interaction with the production process. This they have done with regard to Sanskrit and now they are doing to English.

The fact that the Brahmans received education from the Christian missionaries, with its emphasis upon sacrifice, proves that the Brahmans, as a caste, learn everything in their own interest, without allowing their spiritual fascist self to transform. The highest number of people who learnt English and other branches of Western education from Christian missionary schools and colleges are Brahmans—hardly a handful of Brahmans from this convent-educated group converted to Christianity. A Brahman house is like a cuckoo's nest—it trains it's children in such a manner that no school can transform them from the Brahman mode of existence. The childhood formation in the Brahmanic households takes place in the form of a frozen superstition. No Christian missionary school can break that frozen Brahmanism. The Brahmans who became Christians also carried that psychology into Indian Christianity. They used English to Brahmanize the Christian missionary system, which started working only for the sake of money but not for the sake of liberative values that Jesus left behind in his crucifixion. The Brahmanic childhood formation thus has both genetic and social characteristics of non-transformability. It is also proved that when any institution or structure comes in the way of their spiritual fascist mode of living, they simply attack them, without bothering to consider their own benefits from such institutions. From Raja Ram Mohan Roy to Radha Krishnan to Arun Shourie (a modern Brahman writer who worked out the strategies of attacking the Christian missionaries and churches in the recent past) to any average Brahman youth in modern India who has acquired English and Western education, they have not shown any qualms in constructing a theory of missionary education being dangerous. This is part of the instinctive behaviour of Brahmanism. The very same people whose labour power they consume are treated as untouchables for centuries. A parasite uses a thing only to destroy it. These days they use English for furthering their goals and objectives but sooner or later they would destroy it.

The modern world faces a serious danger if Brahmanism remains what it is. As I said in *Why I am Not a Hindu*, a powerful school of Dalitism should encounter Brahmanism and a massive transformative discourse has to be deployed on the Indian soil. But such an attempt to deploy Dalitism will not be allowed easily. The attempt of the Dalit-Bahujan forces to introduce a transformative discourse and knowledge system that mediates between faith and reason—in other words religion and science—and the Brahmanic resistance to that process may lead to a civil war that Brahmanism did not allow in India at any point of time in history. To avoid any resistance to their mode of parasitic living, they created the caste system that fortified the spiritual fascist mode of life and kept the Indian productive masses in complete subjugation. In post-independence India, a section of Dalit-Bahujan forces have come to realize this historical process. This, combined with the process of globalization in all walks of life and new conditions for confrontation with Brahmanism are being created in every sphere of Indian life. In this atmosphere, a civil war may emanate in the socio-spiritual and political life of India as the organizations like the Rashtriya Swayam Sevak Sangh (RSS), Vishwa Hindu Parishad (VHP) and the Bajrang Dal (which is their military wing) have been very clearly leaning in that direction. A political party like the BJP may aid and abet that process. In the next two chapters, we shall examine the role of intellectual goondaism and the symptoms of civil war.

Chapter 11   Intellectual *Goondas*

After our journey through the Brahman *wada*—from where emerged the spiritual fascist philosophical realm of Hinduism—we have to make a survey of the intellectual realm, which played a very important role in mauling the Indian system. Even to understand the future of the larger capitalist and post-capitalist stage of the world, we have to make an assessment of where we stand intellectually and of the nature and the character of the intellectual class that has emerged in the caste-centred Hindu civil society and state. In an age of the so-called 'knowledge society', where intellectuality is going to play a very significant role, we should see what kind of a relationship is possible between productivity and intellectuality. So far, the mode in which the intellectual realm has been constructed in India, in my view, is unique. The activities of the already existing dominant intellectual realm of India can be characterized as intellectual goondaism. Let us, therefore, see how the caste system led to the formation of intellectual goondaism in India and what it actually means.

The word *goonda* is a specific Indian word. It denotes either some individuals or a small group of people, who, through exercising their muscle power, control the rest of the civil society in localities and regions. A *goonda* can be either male or female, but usually it is the male *goondas* who are visible owing to the patriarchal social structure of India. *Goondas* browbeat people to extract money, grain and other forms of wealth, but in order to perform that task quite legitimately they establish hegemonic power structures within the locality, mainly through coercion. Through that coercive hegemonic system, the *goonda* ensures that the collection of resources takes place with ease. He, thus, collects as much material resources as possible from the subjugated people. A *goonda* does not end his activity there. He manages the state agencies, the civil authority and the police so that they do not interfere with his authority. He sends out private threats to public functionaries within the state by citing some instances of his misdeeds, such as that of killing such functionaries or raping their women, so that the state functionary keeps himself out of his operations. This mode of goondaism could be characterized as street goondaism. The street *goondas* by and large come from the Shudra civil society.

SILENCING THE VICTIM

More significantly, the *goondas* operate by silencing the victim with a fear of life, safety and modesty. This process of silencing the victims is a carefully crafted act. Since the purpose of the *goonda* is to extract wealth for his livelihood and luxury, he consciously crafts the method of circulating and withholding information in a selective manner. First, a *goonda* spreads several rumours about his power—physical, mental, as well as organizational. Second, information regarding his weaknesses, like how many times he was beaten or defeated by the rival or neighbouring *goondas*, or what kind of weaknesses and diseases he suffers from, are systematically hidden from the people. The quantum of his collections, his own distribution to state officials, his arrests, his diseases, and so on, are the kinds of information that are not leaked out to the public out of the fear that the *goondas* hold among their subjects may weaken. Thus, a *goonda* is an organizer and synthesizer of several dimensions of his goondaism. A social survey of such *goondas* of streets, *mohallas*, and areas indicates that they come from the Shudra/ Dalit-Bahujan communities. There have been writings about such *goondas* in Indian literature. But there are another kind of *goondas* who emerged, again, only in the Indian context—nothing has been said or written about them so far. They can be characterized as 'intellectual *goondas*'. The intellectual *goondas* have done more damage to the socio-economic, political and civil societal life processes in India than the street *goondas* could do.

Though the concept of goondaism appears to be modern, it existed all through, ever since the Indian society began to operate as a civil society. *Goondas* do not evolve along with the society by contributing to its growth—they grow out of it like cancerous cells in the human body.

They emerge as accidents, but they remain either permanently or for a long time in the society. Though the state emerges as a result of the conscious actions of the productive people, the *goondas* involve themselves in it in order to use it for their advantage. They are not the state, but the state is theirs. The masses build the state and the *goondas* use it. The civil and the state institutions slowly go under their control. This kind of evolution of *goondas*, both street and intellectual, seems to have a common ground. But in fact it is not so. There is a subtle difference in the way they have evolved. That difference is very clear in India. Because of the very nature of Hinduism, the intellectual *goondas*' command over the state and civil society is majestic and all pervasive.

The intellectual *goondas* work out their strategies very systematically. They control the state. In India, the modern democratic state has been seized by the intellectual *goondas*. The civil society is manipulated by their socio-spiritual and political machinations. They make the civil society believe that they are the most learned and most concerned about the other, in spite of the fact that the 'othering' of the productive masses is an essential condition of their intellectual existence. They present themselves as the most selfless of all. The civil society is thus made vulnerable, owing to the theories that they keep constructing. To operationalize the agendas of the intellectual *goondas*, the spiritual fascism that had been institutionalized in India, becomes an excellent instrument. The social base of the intellectual *goondas* is spiritual fascism, and the masses, including street *goondas* are completely subdued through the mechanism of spiritual fascism because it works in the name of God. The intellectual *goondas* constantly regenerate the consciousness of spiritual fascism as a necessary condition of the society.

The Indian intellectual *goondas* are far more organized and far more powerful than all other *goondas* put together. In order to take history away from the makers of history, the intellectual *goondas* have put up a barrier between history making and history writing. The makers of history are told that they cannot write history. They show that the writers of history should be from a separate caste. That caste should not interact with the productive social forces, should not have any idea about the tools that were responsible for making the history and should not share their food and their bed with the makers of history. The intellectual *goondas*' names, social manners and cultural symbols would be entirely different from that of the masses who make history. Many a times the intellectual *goondas* appropriate the knowledge produced by the productive classes and attribute it to themselves. As I have discussed earlier the mathematical expression zero was discovered by the cattle herders and shepherds but Aryabhatta claimed that he had discovered zero. Similarly, many of the Ayurvedic medicines were discovered by the Dalit-Bahujans but the Brahmanic writers appropriated their knowledge. Since the Shudras, Chandalas and other Dalit-Bahujans were not allowed to write books, they were not able to document their knowledge. While writing history, the intellectual *goondas* also ignored the culture, skills and customs of the productive classes—their history is a mirror of their goondaism. The same principle applies to the writing of history of the Indian women. The best example of this is Vatsayana's *Kamasutra*. It is projected as art but, in actuality, it degrades women. A woman's human essence and sensibilities have no value whatsoever in this text. Women are assigned a cultural role of protecting and preserving the caste hierarchy in the name of chastity, cultural convenience and tradition. The intellectual *goondas* have built an iron curtain between mental labour and physical labour and portrayed themselves as exclusively endowed with the highest mental faculties. The productive masses are assigned exclusive physical labour, though such a division does not exist so categorically. Thus every relationship is arranged as per the convenience of intellectual *goondas*.

ELIMINATING THE OPPOSITE IDEA

One of the main functions of intellectual goondaism has been to eliminate the opposite idea that comes into existence, particularly in a written form. Elimination of radical or rational thinkers at each stage of a given society took place in many societies and in all religions. But the intellectual *goondas* in India, with the help of spiritual fascism, eliminated the opposite idea itself. Elimination of idea of the opponent, even if it was/is the most socially relevant and universally valid idea, became the primary function of intellectual goondaism. For example, the universal idea that all human beings are equal before God was eliminated in India by the enforcement of spiritual fascism and intellectual goondaism. Hence, all the ideas that were generated in the productive society remained at the level of the productive masses alone. They worked out their praxis with the help of those ideas. If those ideas were to receive a written expression and were synthesized into a coherent philosophy, India would have been a country of more powerful thought than many European countries because of the fact that India has far more ancient civilization of production. But at the stage of the formation of written script the Indian productive idea was intercepted with spiritual fascism and intellectual goondaism. The idea that rice production is possible in an enormous quantity with the intervention of human labour was pre-Aryan. The idea that skin could be converted into leather and that leather could be transformed into commodities is pre-Brahmanic; the idea that a buffalo can be domesticated and trained to be a milk-giving animal is pre-Brahmanic; the idea that clay can be transformed into a pot is pre-Aryan and pre-Brahmanic. All these ideas would have been codified, synthesized and developed in subsequent periods but for the intervention of the intellectual goondaism that developed in India.

The basic skills of the productive communities in themselves do not make a full-scale modern system. But the fact that all these communities constructed, synthesized and developed that knowledge of production itself is a historical resource. At a particular point of time, because of the intervention of the negative anti-production social forces, that knowledge began to stagnate. These negative forces have their origins in spiritual fascism, but in order to diversify their activity outside the realm of spiritual fascism they produced a powerful force of intellectual *goondas*. These intellectual *goondas*, by using the modern state, modern communication channels, civil societal structures and finally, the English language, have spread into every nook and corner of the world by now. In the ancient and medieval period they operated by exclusivizing Sanskrit language. In post-independence India, a section that emerged from the same social force may talk of secularism, socialism and pluralism, but in fact, all of them share the common ground of spiritual fascism. They operate within that very philosophy, and the fact that fighting against it did not become their agenda for three thousand years makes their intent clear. And as long as they do not cut their umbilical cords to detach themselves from the blood and body of spiritual fascism, they will not be able to see the importance of spiritual democracy and the productive ethic in everyday life. They do not understand the productive skills of the productive castes. Millions follow the spiritual fascists and intellectual *goondas* in India—their twin schools of thought have succeeded in India because they overpowered the masses so thoroughly. They have made the productive masses not to believe/trust their own self, their historical energies and their ability to set the intellectual *goondas* aside and run the system on their own. Intellectual goondaism has destroyed the self-confidence of the society. And that is where spiritual fascism and intellectual goondaism have succeeded in making this nation impotent. And it poses the greatest danger not only to India but to the whole world in the future.

Intellectual goondaism survives on the threshold of the silence of the productive masses. But such a silence is manufactured through the process of goondaism. First, they coerce them to be silent; second, they project that silence as consent and finally that consent is constructed as consent given consciously to serve their interests. They have developed symbols that construct the life processes and the essence of the productive culture as a blot on the entire nation, even though it was these very life processes that built the nation in the first place. In contrast, they project the culture of intellectual goondaism, as the most representative culture of the nation. The productive knowledge of the masses is said to possess much less value than the word power of an intellectual *goonda*. They propagated, for example, that the word 'Om' repeated in a Brahmanic manner produces miracles. No other spiritual agency ever propagated such a theory. And in the whole history of Brahmanism and of entire India, the pronunciation of the word 'Om' did not produce food for the people and did not provide them with equal opportunities. The result of such a miraculous language constructed by the intellectual *goondas* was that some very small communities and castes became very rich and influential. The rest of the castes and communities were forced to suffer through hunger, poverty and illiteracy. Intellectual goondaism legitimizes such a situation with a theory of *karma*. Those who pretend to not believe in the theory of *karma*, while having been born of intellectual goondaism, do not talk about the spiritual fascism which is an integral part of their own roots. They want us to believe that a society can change its branches without changing the roots.

WRITTEN WORD AS LIE

The written word is propagated to be an embodiment of truth by the forces of intellectual goondaism. And the right to engage with the written word is claimed to be exclusively theirs. The written word is used as an instrument of constructing the philosophical foundations of spiritual fascism. The idols, temples, books and institutions were constructed by the intellectual *goondas* as per their convenience. They had exclusive access to these institutions and sources of power. Then the intellectual goondaism begins to operate as an octopus that engulfs the social essence of the masses that exist around it. India, as the most ancient society, has produced two gigantic octopuses which are eating the very vitals of the society—spiritual fascism and intellectual goondaism. There have been interventions of spiritual democratic schools at times, but as fate would have it, the adaptability of the intellectual *goondas* is quite strong, and at each stage they have overcome even the most powerful interventions. The reasons for prolonged sustenance of both spiritual fascism and intellectual goondaism lie in the total loss of the self-image of the subject masses. The intellectual *goondas* either killed the agents of spiritual democracy or co-opted them. They were allowed to exist autonomously by organizing the masses around their own self-respect. This is a technique well suited to the world of goondaism. Even the street *goondas* do the same thing—either the rival force has to be killed or they must be co-opted within the main *goonda* gang. The difference between the street *goondas* and the intellectual *goondas* is that the intellectual *goondas* do this in relation to history itself. The street *goondas* only destroy the social energy of a small section of the society around themselves, but the intellectual *goondas* kill the historical energies of nations. India is a good example of this process.

The intellectual *goondas* want to talk in the voice of the other. The other is shown whenever necessary as part of the *goonda*'s soil, his religion but certainly not of his caste, as that tears the curtain that separates the masses and the intellectual *goondas*. The intellectual *goondas* maintain a studied silence about the very instrument of oppression, because even a discourse around it would weaken that very instrument. For example, they made caste as an instrument of use but not of theoretical discourse. Once it is made a subject of theoretical discourse, it will begin to be deconstructed.

One of the key efforts of the intellectual *goondas* is to avoid the deconstruction of their self, their own history and their ideology. Because they know that deconstruction opens their body—both individual and social—that was constructed as pure, and displays the pollution within. That itself leads to a reconstruction of the self of the other. That reconstruction of the self of the other leads to reconstruction of the whole society itself. If the 'unpaid teachers' ask for the wage of their historically invested labour in constructing the food culture that this country is proud of, the intellectual *goondas* get irritated and dismiss them as stupid *vanavasis*. If the 'subaltern scientists' ask for their share in the national production, they laugh at them. If the 'productive soldiers' ask for their place in history, the intellectual *goondas* beat them down with the help of much more advanced weapons that their gods are holding. If the 'subaltern feminists' claim that they laid the stepping stones of male–female equality, they instigate their own women to counter it as an absurdity of history—feminist history. If the 'social doctors' claim that they have the right to patent the knowledge of health science, including the science of surgery, they instigate the foreigners to fight against such claims and then sell the patent to a foreign country for a paltry amount. If the 'unknown engineers' who built the technological base of India claim that they are responsible for building the great monumental buildings, dams, tanks and artifacts, they brush it aside as nonsense. If the 'meat and milk economists' say that they should decide as to what place a buffalo should have, a cow should have, a sheep should have and a goat should have in the national life, they run them down as unworthy people who have no right to decide such important issues. If the 'food producers' say that they should have the right to decide the prices of the food grains they produced, they laugh at them, as if the animals themselves are asking such questions. They use the labour of all these categories as unmindfully as they use the dustbin around them. To do all this skillfully they use intellectual *goondagiri* as a modern instrument as well. The modern communication network is being used as yet another instrument to operationalize their intellectual goondaism to their advantage.

THE INSTITUTIONAL GOONDAISM

One of the characteristics of intellectual goondaism is that it builds institutions in its own image. These institutions are said to belong to all, but they remain under the control of the intellectual *goondas* themselves and they must operate under their own hegemony. First, they see to it that every such institution should come under the influence of spiritual fascism. An overarching cultural conditioning of the institutions and the individuals that operate in them is worked out. Since the whole process gets structuralized in the realm of religion and spirituality, the social forces that are objectified under the thumb of spiritual fascism and intellectual goondaism—the objectified other—are not able to see the self-alienation process under way.

The training ground of intellectual *goondas* is spiritual fascism itself. Their childhood formation, the *upanayana* and *gurukula*, or the entry into a modern school and the lessons that they learn are systematically structured to make them intellectual *goondas*. One of the main elements that prepares the psyche of an educated man to become an intellectual *goonda* is that as part of their childhood training, they are told that they, even as children, are different from that of the rest of the children. The story narratives they are taught and the socio-psychological setting they are supposed to work out for themselves should be different from the rest of the civil society. Take, for example, consuming vegetarian food: it is not based on individual taste of the child or on the condition of the health of the child, but on what is known as the caste-culture of the people involved. In order to make them different, vegetarianism was constructed as a spiritual institutional process. Vegetarianism is not a universally accepted and practised spiritual food culture. They constructed it as a counter-culture to the Buddhist mode of egalitarian food culture, and through the means of intellectual goondaism established it as a part of the institution of 'purity' and reduced the people of universal food cultures—the Dalit–Bahujans—to the status of impurity. The Brahmanic children, who grow up in that kind of atmosphere, need to produce spiritual fascism in the spiritual realm and intellectual goondaism in the intellectual realm. The direction of that training is to hide the truth in all spheres of life. It was/is aimed to show production as pollution and consumption as purity; universal food habits as barbarianism and reactionary underdeveloped food culture as civilization; straightforwardness as ignorance and deception as truth; labour as ruggedness and leisure as dignified. They pretend to have constructed an all round philosophy. But that philosophy is in fact one of consumption, war and sex, of a negative ethic that constructs social walls, which do not allow hybridization of the human mind and body, the knowledge system, the scientific skills, including that of kinds of production and food culture. This philosophy pits one group of producers against the other; it pits one technological instrument against the other; it pits one human skill against the other. It finally makes the producers fight against each other in defence of the spiritual fascism and intellectual goondaism. A street *goonda* needs to fight the enemy himself face to face, but an intellectual *goonda* makes his enemies fight among themselves so far as the physical battles are concerned. The mental battles he fights himself. But he confronts the masses—whom he keeps on oppressing—through the means of his intellectuality and unethical notion of the divine. The moral realm that this class has constructed is unusually selfish both for personal ends and also for caste ends.

As a result of intellectual goondaism, the most ancient institution—religion—here acquired the role of social disintegrator. Hinduism, as a religion of social disintegration, did not allow the human collectivity to grow as it happened in other religions, where intellectuality became a collective property of the whole community that did not fragment into castes. This religion, for centuries, was used as a weapon of de-mobilization of mass energies and even in the beginning of the twenty-first century this negative religion is being used as a perpetuator of spiritual fascism. Though the intellectual *goondas* understand the relationship between Hinduism and capitalist underdevelopment and the total incapacity of the social system that operates around it to build a new society where equality becomes possible, they remain totally silent about it. Those who gained some sophistication among them argue, quite sheepishly, that all the underdevelopment that India as a nation suffers from has no relationship with religion. Some may even invoke, most uncreatively—as a part of their recitational culture (the pundits believe in mugging up and reciting but not in creative reading), their historical method of acquiring knowledge—that Marx's theory of base and superstructure is applicable even to India. For them, no critique of the Hindu religion is required. At least some such 'base-superstructure' theoreticians know that the Dalit-Bahujans of India are the upholders of the world's most 'suppressed science'. Once that suppressed science breaks out of the grasp of the octopus of the spiritual fascism and intellectual goondaism, it possesses all the energy to build the Indian society as one of the most prosperous and most egalitarian societies, one that would bring Marx's dream of communism to reality. This is because the essential ingredient of that dream world is the productive creativity of the masses. Productive creativity and scientificity are as dialectically related to each other as spiritual fascism and intellectual goondaism are. Historically, it is an established fact that productivity and scientificity can kill spiritual fascism and intellectual goondaism, and cremate both of them. Since they have survived too long in this country, they have done enough damage. Even in this globalized world, the intellectual *goondas* want spiritual fascism to sustain along with their own gains from economic globalization—but they oppose cultural globalization. Their political hegemony over the masses, even though they do not have their creative energies—as the nationalist or Marxist or democratic scholars of the other countries have shown—depended on the spiritual fascist roots.

As of now the nation, as a larger socio-political entity, suffers from enormous weaknesses. It has failed to make its civilizational, cultural, political and economic vitality express itself and its strength has not been felt by the world because of the non-creativity of the intellectual *goondas*. As their self-interest and not the national interest (which in essence means putting mass knowledge on the highest pedestal) worked its way and the self-interest of some castes and communities received centrality in the sphere of the construction of national knowledge, but that knowledge never reflected the true national spirit. Many European commentators, having interacted with such negative intellectuals, have said that India has never formulated its national spirit. The fact that the national spirit of India is hidden in the unwritten knowledge system of its productive masses, who combined in themselves spiritual democracy and socio-economic productivity, is never understood. The political realm that the intellectual *goondas* have constructed is not based either on any historical imagination or on the positive and contending speculations of historic social forces. Only intellectuals who put the people's interest above everything—above their own interest—can synthesize their knowledge, their experience, their skills and the historic essence of their nation into a holistic and powerful national self. The intellectuals who turned into self-reflective beings have never constructed a powerful nation. India has suffered from this process more than any other nation in the world. The nation is constructed in the image of spiritual fascism and intellectual goondaism. In the intercourse of these two agencies, democracy was born as a weak and constantly suffering structure. Even that was in the beginning superimposed by the colonial rulers who, unlike the spiritual fascists and intellectual *goondas*, have a historical angle of human equality. But the post-colonial India is struck with the twin problems of the lack of a scientific temper and the dignity of labour because of the intellectual goondaism that the national institutions are steeped in. The nation has thus lost 60 precious years, even with a formal democracy and constitutional governance in place, without achieving the basic ideals of social democracy. Since the intellectual *goondas* are in control of every institution without even having a formal agenda of socio-spiritual reform, the nation's ability to negotiate with other nations is minimal.

Political leadership in India has been mostly seized by the very same forces, who have come from the very same background. They have established very close nexus between spiritual fascism and political demagoguery. Though elections take place on regular basis because of the pressure from below, the political leadership has managed the system in a manner that does not let it slip away from their hands. The intellectual *goondas* operate with a systematic network base of temples, religious congregations, educational institutions, employment bureaus, and so on. Intellectual goondaism operates from mainly three branches of the institutional structure: from educational centres, from bureaucracy and from the institutions of jurisprudence.

THE EDUCATION

Educational institutions are the nerve centre of either change or stagnation of a given nation or socio-political system. The spiritual fascism that used to be cooked in the *gurukulas* transferred itself to the modern education system in various forms. Because of the intervention of British English education, the mind of spiritual fascism was reframed in tune with the modernist agenda and English was allowed to replace Sanskrit, again within themselves. A co-habitational relationship was worked out between home and temple-centred Sanskrit prayer and the school-centred English language. Most of the Brahman children were trained to be comfortable with the diabolical relationship of 'temple Sanskrit and school English'. The Christian institutes—schools and colleges—that started teaching the Indian non-Christian social forces thought that they were serving God by teaching the children of the Brahmanic castes, who were being taught the alphabets of spiritual fascism every day at home. Quite surprisingly, the lifetime bachelorhood of Christian nuns and fathers was/is been/being invested in educating the children born within the structures of spiritual fascism, who learn(t) English keeping their heart and soul in the realm of spiritual fascism itself. The Christian institutions never realized that they were violating the code of their God Jehovah and their prophet Christ, that they should educate the poorest of the poor and cleanest of the clean by heart. And that constituency was available only among the Dalit–Bahujans all over the country. They never realized that by educating the community that itself was/is the source of global sin, they were preparing the future English-knowing spiritual fascists and intellectual *goondas* who could perpetuate inequality but never work for the equality of spiritual, social and economic life processes, given their background. They never realized that they were preparing a global network of spiritual fascists who could prepare the ground for the rape of nuns and killing of priests. The Christian institutions have committed a grave sin against God by educating the believers in perpetual spiritual fascism and intellectual goondaism. Now, the only way to wash that sin is to turn all their educational institutions towards the unpaid teachers, subaltern scientists, productive soldiers, subaltern feminists, social doctors, the meat and milk producers, and so on, where the gods/goddesses live for their solace.

Unfortunately, the entire education system in this country is ridden with intellectual sophistry. The government and private institutions have negated the dignity of labour, scientific temper, spiritual and social democracy and intellectual honesty. They have fed into the system a disbelief in reason of all forms. Since the basic education is dishonest, coupled with spiritual and social fascism, even the higher education that some of the Indians receive abroad cannot disconnect them from the roots that evolved in their childhood formation. Some of the educationalists of India won some of the best awards for hiding the truth rather than for speaking it out. The truth was elsewhere with the masses as they were making shoes, washing clothes, grazing sheep and tilling the land, and that truth largely remains undiscovered till this day. The education system, thus, is entangled in dishonesty, un-productivity, spiritual fascism or fundamentalism, and it has become a real training ground for intellectual *goondas*. It is from here that the intellectual *goondas* are sent into two other branches—bureaucracy and judiciary.

THE BUREAUCRACY

From recruitment to the execution of bureaucratic operations, intellectual goondaism has become the ethical value. Ever since the constitutional government began functioning, the Brahmanical forces made the Indian state institutions their own. First, the recruitment agencies were captured. The intellectual *goondas* defined the realm of knowledge in their own life experience, and the books their ancestors wrote in opposition to the productive knowledge of masses were projected as the embodiment of knowledge.

The setting of questions papers and the evaluation of answer scripts in examinations have also traditionally been done from the point of view of the community of the intellectual *goondas*. The vast productive field, in which the Dalit–Bahujan children are trained, were ruthlessly avoided in the knowledge system and the examination that accompanies it. Silencing of the truth that production is the bane of the Indian society, and the communities that produce should become part of the examination for the selection of the administrative social force—this has to be made an ideology of the recruiting authorities. The ethics of the selection process is now centred on self-preservation, but not the development of the system as a whole. The linguistic symbols invoked in the question papers are carefully chosen from the lifestyles, food habits and narratives of the intellectual *goondas* and the spiritual fascists. All of them are chosen from their existential experience and from the books written by the intellectual *goondas*. The interview boards are carefully constituted in order to manipulate the selection of the candidates in the interest of spiritual fascism. The forces that operate in the state sector know very well that if the modern constitutional state is allowed to slip from the hands of spiritual fascism, the state will marginalize the religion and cut down the roots of spiritual fascism itself. The spiritual fascists operating from temples and other institutions realized that the possibility of growing capitalism, coupled with the mass education that the constitutional governance introduced, might unleash a total crisis in the camp of spiritual fascism. Hence, the spiritual fascist network has used its intellectual *goondagiri* to man all institutions, from district-level civil and police administration, to above. The most inconvenient factor in this process is the principle of reservation for the SCs and the STs and the OBCs. The spiritual fascists grumblingly compromised with it, but saw to it that the production-based knowledge of the Dalit–Bahujans could not be brought into the administrative apparatus.

The Indian Administrative Service (IAS) has been very conveniently converted into the Indian Brahman Service (IBS), and the Indian Police Service (IPS) has been converted to the Indian Political Service, where again the same ideology was made operational, as the political structure at Delhi is completely under their control. The physical presence of these small castes which are trained in spiritual fascism and which have no knowledge of the whole productive realm is only one dimension of the problem. The problem of constructing such a bureaucracy is deeper. The top officials in the administrative apparatus do not have critical knowledge of the social forces. Spiritual fascism and intellectual goondaism thus began to operate through the file system, and became structural in allocating finances and implementing programmes. The main agenda of the bureaucratic agencies is to see that education, especially English education, does not go into the hands of the productive masses.

For spiritual fascism, corruption is not only common but quite integral to the life process. The social forces that make living outside the production process naturally live in corruption, which is an integral part of the constitution of their selves. As we have seen in an earlier chapter, parasitism breeds corruption as a natural process. More and more corruption is necessary in order to have a tighter grip on the system, and once the state apparatus is in their hands, legitimizing corruption becomes a part of the administrative process itself. The rhetoric of anti-corruption is an eyewash to hoodwink the Dalit–Bahujans. Spiritual fascism, intellectual goondaism and financial corruption go hand–in-hand. They have evolved a very powerful mechanism to use the public office for private purpose. Sixty years of constitutional governance has legitimately transferred the national wealth from the state exchequer to the private bank accounts of the Brahmanic forces for the comfortable family life of the intellectual *goondas*, who started operating from state institutions. The life of the productive masses, whose labour, skills and restless effort has gone towards building the wealth of the nation, is struggling between modernity and a medieval mode of existence. If the children of the productive masses had received the very same English education as the children of the bureaucratic classes, with a syllabus that emphasizes upon the dignity of labour as an essential component of learning, the productive ability of India as a nation would have increased greatly in the past 60 years and the very basis of the productive science would have changed. But that would have also challenged the very basis of spiritual fascism and intellectual goondaism. The intellectual *goondas* sitting in the bureaucratic structures have stalled that flow of education, relating to the productive technology and have promoted the culture of corruption.

THE JUDICIARY

With the establishment of the constitutional government and separation of powers, the judiciary has acquired an almost divine status. In a society of spiritual democracy and caste-free culture, the social forces which have had their linkages with the productive fields would have gone into the judiciary, where objective interpretation of law would have become possible. Now the Indian judiciary is totally manned by people whose childhood formation took place in a cultural environment of spiritual fascism and whose educational upbringing was done in an atmosphere of intellectual goondaism. As of now, the social source from which Indian law derives itself is spiritual fascism. The sources of the diabolical discourse of law are in Sanskrit, and the discourse taking place in the courts is in English—the subjects of the discourse, therefore, can understand nothing while in the court. Neither the material that the judge refers to nor the citations given by the lawyer reflect the laws that operate in the day-to-day life of the disputants. The moral base of a majority of judges and lawyers is in spiritual fascism. The moral base of the majority of disputants is rooted in un-Hindu productive ethic, which varies from spiritual democracy to spiritual anarchism. In this situation, the role of the judges ceases to become one of developing the legal science and becomes manipulative instead.

The law itself was not allowed to emerge from the experience of the masses and the customs and conventions of their own social evolution. The social life processes and the customs and conventions of the spiritual fascists were first written in the Sanskrit books. Later on, these very customs and conventions were codified into so-called laws, which were defined as the Hindu laws. Thus, the essence of spiritual fascist life was codified as law and that law rules the roost even today. The social relations, the marriage and divorce customs of the Dalit–Bahujan masses were never allowed to become the reference point of courts. Thus, the difference between a court and Hindu temple was rendered so marginal that the spiritual fascism manufactured in temple was very conveniently exported into the judicial centres as well. This is where the legal jurisprudence of India remained uncreative. It never served as a reference to any other legal system of the world.

The judges sitting in the Indian courts have an innate dislike for the cultural life of the productive masses of the nation. They do not own the juridical history of productive masses—the juridical history that belongs to them is the very opposite of that of the productive masses. The secular law that became the norm of the modern juridical systems of the world in an environment of spiritual fascism and intellectual goondaism transformed into a legal process of self-aggrandizement of spiritual fascists. They saw to it that the very legal institutions go against the interests of the productive masses, who have made hard productive work as the essential condition of life. Because of his biased worldview, a Brahman judge treats the Shudra and Chandala criminals with contempt. Starting from the *Rigveda* to the *Grihasutras*, the *Arthashastra* to the *Dharmashastras* and even the *Bhagavad Gita* condition the mind of the judges to mock the productive masses as they are referred to as Shudras, Chandalas, or as Rakshasas or Vanavasis. The Indian Constitution and other secular laws that have been derived from the colonial yet secular/rational mind of the lawgivers appear absurd to most of the judges sitting in the higher courts. The affairs of the masses, the judge believes, are not worthy of being debated in the judiciary; not worthy of being a part of the temple culture of Hinduism; not worthy even of being politicized—the Brahmanical gurus like Kautilya and Manu did not consider the Dalit-Bahujans to be political animals at all. Even in Gandhian language, whom the judges often quote—if not out of love for Gandhi then out of a desire for legitimacy—the Dalit-Bahujans masses are *daridra narayans*. Gandhi argued that the poor are children of Vishnu. He appealed to them to suffer the poverty but not to revolt against the rich. Gandhi realized that the poorest of the poor in India come from the Dalit-Bahujan background and the richest of the rich come from the Brahmin-Baniya background. He wanted to maintain the caste-class status quo. For the Brahman judges this theory of Gandhi is very useful and handy. The God, that the judges believe in, does not love the *daridra narayana*. The poor are born poor and the untouchables are born untouchables because of the subject's *karma* in an earlier life. The judge, like Gandhi, thinks that at the structural level there is nothing that they can do for the poor. Something can be done only at the superficial level, even that too to see that the poor do not revolt. They, therefore, evolve all kinds of legal methods to avoid such civil wars taking shape in this country, as that would overthrow the hegemony of their children and grandchildren in future.

A nation, where a vast majority of the population is excluded from the judicial institutions cannot claim to deliver justice to all citizens. The productive masses have been beyond the pale of the judiciary because it has the power to deliver judgements that determine the life and death of people. In this case, the life blood—the productive being—of the nation itself is kept out of the judicial process. The language of merit and experience that the judiciary boasts of is in fact a language of intellectual goondaism. When this language is spoken from the court, it acquires the power of translating itself into law. The police, the political authorities and the civil society, including the productive being whose essence has been constructed as meritless, ignorant, innocent and unhistorical himself/herself, is made to believe that (s)he really is so. The language of the productive beings has no meaning in the court, in the state structure and also in the larger civil society. The language of intellectual *goondas* has made the otherwise creative and sensible productive beings disbelieve themselves. Particularly, the juridical goondaism leaves them no confidence whatsoever. Their labour power, which possesses the capacity to produce, has been discounted; their language, which established excellent human relations between all human beings and their artistic abilities that produced the artifacts, culture and civilization of the nation have been rendered without value by the judges, bureaucrats and educationalists in their respective institutions. Their very potential has been portrayed as a lack of potential with the help of one single instrument—intellectual goondaism. All this has led to an enormous lack of self-confidence among the productive masses. Even the best of the Dalit–Bahujan minds could not convince the Brahmanic mind that the tools that the Dalit–Bahujans are operating with are productive, creative and regenerative tools. The hope that the reading of a document like the Indian Constitution changes the judges to become real impartial judges is a historical misjudgement of the spiritual fascist and intellectual *goonda* mind. A thorough de-Brahmanization of that mind alone may help in repositioning it, but that process needs the filling of these institutions with such judges whose childhood formation took place in the productive environment.

THEIR WRITINGS

In the social milieu of spiritual fascism, the evolution of intellectuals went on almost unprecedented lines. In the intellectual realm, the spiritual fascists seem to have thought that the educated people must emerge as intellectual *goondas* who can perfect the art of controlling the mind of the subjects. It is an innate desire to negate every democratic process in the human life. In the modern context, the modern institutions were meant to be handled by such intellectual *goondas* who can make them centres of money-making and not of delivering service. There is no notion of delivering service to the productive masses in this intellectual realm of spiritual fascism. If there is any thought of service at all in them, it is that of self-service. The texts they wrote reflect the politics of spiritual fascism and self-service.

The ancient Brahmanical texts show the inhuman social beings—the Brahmanical castes—as great, akin to God himself. For instance, in the *Ramayana*, Rama sends Sita to the forest on the suspicion of sexual impurity.

Here, the writer of *Ramayana* used a Chakali's man's statement of accusation as the cause behind the realization of Rama's self-respect in relation to his wife's sexual immorality. I have shown in the chapter 'Subaltern Feminists' that of all male beings, the Chakali men are the least male chauvinist, because their mind and body has been de-gendered. The Kshatriya men are by training and day-to-day practice masculine brutes, as the Brahmans are. The writer and the propagators of the Brahmanical narrative portray the positive being as negative and vice versa. Hence, the Chakali man in the *Ramayana* is projected as the source of suffering of Sita, who is portrayed as a meek feminine being. Both the Chakali man and the Kshatriya woman have something in common—both are agents of historical suffering as their beings were caught up in the cobweb of spiritual fascism, where negation of women was as strong as that of the lower castes. The morality that emerged out of the *Ramayana* is made concrete in a sentence that became part of modern grammar books in order to show the relationship between subject, object and predicate—Rama killed Ravana. The national, divinely constructed mode of predication is killing. The moral message from the *Ramayana*, thus, was that by killing other human beings one can become a part of moral predication of the just being.

In the *Mahabharata*, Krishna is said to have been a Yadava. In the Hindu representations of Krishna, he has been shown as one preoccupied with the act of sex, as a thief of butter and a stealer of the clothes of bathing women, and a very cunning war general. The social training of the Yadava men does not equip them to perform such inhuman tasks. Except for his status as a cattle herder, which is a part of the economic character of the 'meat and milk economists'—as I have shown in a preceding chapter—all the characteristics that Krishna possesses are that of the Brahmans and the Kshatriyas. The Yadavas, in the entire history of their community, have shown themselves incapable of doing what Krishna did. Yet another sentence in the grammar book that was a part of our school curriculum and that emerged from Krishna's life experience is—Krishna has stolen the butter. The moral code that emerges out of the *Mahabharata* is, therefore, that stealing anything is just and divine as long as the object being stolen belongs to the Dalit-Bahujan community. This morality of Vedic and Puranic Brahmanism was propagated as positive and sustainable from the time of the Gupta period. The intellectual *goondagiri* of that period developed the culture of *guptadhana* and the *Kamasutra*—and they are shown as the attributes of Hindu Golden Age.

In the medieval period, Adi Shankara and Ramanuja reworked this mode of spiritual fascist ideology into a Vedantic philosophy. This Vedantic philosophy wiped out Buddhism from India and paved the way for the invasion of several Middle-Eastern rulers. All the Hindu intellectual *goondas* who destroyed the ethical strength of India acted like dogs hankering for bones around the Slavic and Mughal rulers, but at the same time protected their intellectually immoral philosophy around temples and the civil society. They did the same during the British period. In nineteenth and twentieth century they produced their modern intellectual *goondas* who laid down the modernist foundation for the survival of spiritual fascism. Raja Ram Mohan Roy, Aurobindo Ghosh, Vivekananda, and finally, from our universities, S. Radhakrishna, belonged to the same school of thought. Their intellectual goondaism is a discourse that lies in its silence on a barbaric practice like human untouchability and Shudra slavery. They did not see a single virtue among the millions of these communities, which were producing their food, their milk, building houses and establishing communication systems for them. In other words, the labour power of the productive mass was the life blood of these writers and thinkers. Their so-called voluminous writings do not recognize the existence of the Dalit–Bahujan masses and thus marginalizes their history and culture.

The history of the Brahman caste, on the other hand, shows that right from the days of Kautilya, Manu and Vatsayana, they were capable of diabolical behaviour. Our own times provide numerous examples from among them, where many such characters exist as intellectuals. As a part of the design of spiritual fascism, the caste background of even the divine figures is declared. This is because the ideology of spiritual fascism operates on the arch-pin of caste. In the Vedas, the *Ramayana* and the *Mahabharata*, the caste background of the central figures like Brahma, Indra, Rama and Krishna are mentioned. The caste background of the *rishis*—all of them are Brahmans—is mentioned. As I said earlier, caste is central to the texts of the *Rigveda* and the *Bhagavad Gita*. The intellectuals who wrote these books did not intend to liberate the social forces that were enslaved by the kith and kin of the very writers.

In other societies, though the spiritual book writers themselves came from the rich and powerful background, they developed an innate desire to liberate the poor, the suffering, the meek, and so on. Every writer in other societies has shown some philosophical vision. In India, the book writers—mostly Brahmanical forces—have shown an enormous fear of freedom. No book suggested that all human beings are equal before God. This is the most dangerous philosophy that was ever created within the sphere of religion. The Hindu religion was the only religion that negated the very purpose for which a religion came into existence. Intellectual goondaism, which is a socially mobilizing institution, was established as a social disintegrator. The religion was developed in a manner that made it not only exclusivist and self-loving but also inimical to the entire humanity. For example, in both the so-called epic texts there is a systematic display of spiritual fascism and intellectual goondaism. The writers constructed certain images around certain castes. Nowhere does the *Bhagavad Gita* reflect the sensibilities of cattle herders and sheep grazers, shoe makers, cloth weavers, food producers, and so on. The *Ramayana* does not reflect the culture of the Valmikis, in whose name that book was deceptively written. The foundations of intellectual goondaism were laid upon such historical deceptivity that masked the disjunction between the contents of the texts and the socio-economic direction of the authors and their social background. The intellectuals, though they appear to be bold, are, in fact, very timid. They cannot own what they say. Their statements are attributed to the victims of intellectual goondaism, even though the content of the text is in conformity with the logic of spiritual fascism and intellectual goondaism. This is what the *Ramayana* and the *Mahabharata* are. The intellectual forces that used these texts during the freedom struggle and subsequently knew very well that these texts are the source of social inequality and social strife. Yet they were not only projected as nationalist texts, but as the texts that need to be revered by all the castes.

The intellectual *goondas* have mauled the possibility of social change and development in India for a long time, in a systematic manner. They are mainly from Brahmanical backgrounds. Some of them are from other castes, mostly Shudra, but they too follow the foot steps of the intellectual *goondas*. The intellectual *goondas* who emerged from the background of spiritual fascism do not generate knowledge but work out the ways and means to own it and patent it. In this case, they did not use legal means to patent it—they used spiritual means. Having patented it, they use it as a resource of life. The intellectual goondaism operated through the spread of the information that protected their interests and constructed the image of their victorious self and that of others in a manner that laid the road for their success. Any *goonda* is essentially not a creative man. He does not explore all possibilities of life. Since goondaism as a process of life itself is based on violence—social or spiritual—the *goonda* tries to perfect that art of using violence. Intellectual goondaism links violence with divinity. The street *goondas*, who are by and large Dalit-Bahujans, do not link their power to that of someone outside themselves, but the intellectual *goondas* work out theoretical models in an abstract mode, and always operate by keeping themselves out of the process. The social controls are shown as natural/divine, while he himself is the beneficiary of the mechanism of that social control.

Normally, the intellectuals integrate productive knowledge with spiritual, social, economic and political knowledge. Intellectuals in the non-Brahmanic context have traditionally understood the truth at the cost of their own self, their own being. Intellectuals emerged from two kinds of social bases all over the world—one from the philosophical realm and the other from the spiritual realm. In the ancient period Socrates, Plato and Aristotle emerged from philosophical realm and Jesus from the spiritual realm. In India, the Buddha emerged from a combination of philosophical and spiritual realms. But all of them stood for telling the truth and for that they were ready to pay a heavy price—that of their own life. In the Brahmanic tradition, there is no such intellectual who tried to stand up for truth. This is because in the very negation of production, which is a process of truth generation, the Brahmanical intellectuals practised a mode of goondaism on an everyday basis. Once they left the path of production and entered the path of spiritual fascism, the truth had to be made the historical victim. And they did that with impunity.

The same tradition produced thinkers like Kautilya and Manu. They could not see the necessity of an integrated life. Whereas Christian thinkers like Cicero and St. Thomas Aquinas, having come from a truly spiritual school of thought, theorized upon the spiritual civil society, law and state on a positive human plane, the Brahmanical scholars failed to develop any positive vision where the relationship between God and the entire humanity was structured in a democratic fashion. It was not based on the social background of the productive masses. The social laws, including that of familial relations and community relations, when interpreted even from a divine perspective, laid a basis for individualism, claiming that every individual has a relationship with the divine. But Hinduism laid an unequal social and legal relationship with the divine, based on caste. No Hindu thinker broke this negative relationship. In the medieval period, Shankara, Madhava, Ramanuja—all operated in the same sphere. No text written by these thinkers paved a way for decasteizing the individual relationship with divine. All modern writers, starting from Raja Ram Mohan Roy to Dayananda Saraswati, from Sri Aurobindo, Swami Vivekananda, S. Radhakrishnan to E.M.S Nambudiripad, who have claimed a reformist agenda for themselves, did not break the fortress of spiritual fascism. All of them came from the background of spiritual fascism, and they reinforced that system through their writings.

Apart from these writers, in the modern times the school of spiritual fascism has produced brazen intellectual fascists like Savarkar, Golwalkar, Arun Shourie, and so on. These intellectuals have shown the traits of Hitlerite theory and practice in their life and works. They have produced books that have not only reinforced spiritual fascism but created an army of fascist politicians and activists who do not have any reformist or nationalist vision, have no feeling for the untouchable, the hungry, the sick, the poor, and so on. This school of intellectual *goondas* that has emerged in this country could not and cannot produce genuine intellectuals who can transform and develop the Indian society. The Dalit–Bahujan community has to produce a galaxy of organic intellectuals who study their own social, economic and historical self in a creative and egalitarian way. However, the end of intellectual goondaism is closely connected to the end or annihilation of spiritual fascism.

Chapter 12   Symptoms of Civil War and End of Hinduism

THE SETTING OF CIVIL WAR

The upper castes, led by the Brahmanic ideological forces, have greatly humiliated the large communities of Shudras, who have come to be known as the Other Backward Castes (OBCs) in the post-Mandal era. The historical humiliation meted out to Dalits is too well-known to be further elaborated here. The OBCs have come under attack in all the public spaces available to the upper castes, starting with the 1990 reservation debate. In 2006 reservation debate, the humiliation reached its nadir. The upper castes have quite consistently claimed that the OBCs are historically meritless. The classical Brahmanical discourse of Shudra brainlessness has revisited Hindu India in a modern form in the 1990s and 2006. If it had just happened in the 1990s, one might have thought that the anti-OBC expression was spontaneous, but its more organized re-emergence in the twenty-first century highlights its pathological dimension. The pattern has been strongly established in history. The Brahmanical forces have not only humiliated the Dalit–Bahujans, but also declared the Dalit–Bahujan professions that we examined in the preceding chapters to be worth nothing but social condemnation. They have mocked the productive professions as mean and unworthy. They have gone on to say that if they are not allowed to become doctors, engineers and scientists in the manner that they want, they will not remain quiet in response, because they do not wish to be pushed to tasks like sweeping roads, polishing shoes and washing clothes by the 'dirty' OBCs—tasks which they believe are meant to be done by the OBCs themselves. The Brahmans, Baniyas and the neo-Kshatriyas believe that they are here to play the role of a priest, a businessman, a doctor or an engineer, or an administrator, and not to till the land, make pots, tend crops or look after the sheep and goat and nurture buffaloes and cattle. They cannot even conceive of taking up a leather-related or cleanliness-related profession. They will rather wage a civil war—this was their message. In 2006, their behaviour in the capital city—Delhi—was brazen and arrogant, and their method of humiliating the other reached its peak. That they wanted to create a civil war was evident in slogans like 'Reservation ke kutte kaise rahenge, SC/ST/OBC ke jaise rahenge' (How do the reservation dogs look like? They are like the SC/ST/OBCs).

Such slogan shouting in a central university like Jawaharlal Nehru University, New Delhi, lead to clashes between the Dalit–Bahujan and upper caste students. In that clash the SC/ST/OBC youth fought a united battle against all the powerful upper caste youth, who have the support of money, market, media and top police officials. Yet the SC/ST/OBC youth succeeded in driving out the upper caste youth, who were humiliating the Dalit–Bahujan social beings. The Brahmanic historians have documented the civil war situations that emerged based on the social humiliations of the upper castes by the British administrators. In one of the earliest uprisings of the Indian upper caste soldiers against the British that took place in 1806, popularly known as the Vellore Uprising, the Indian upper caste soldiers revolted against the introduction of new type of leather hats as headgear in place of the traditional cotton or silk turban and a general order prohibiting the use of caste marks by soldiers. The Brahmanic upper caste soldiers recruited into the British army considered wearing leather on one's head as an act of polluting the upper caste culture and Hinduism. The Hindu Brahmanic soldiers killed 14 British officials and 115 others working in the British army before the uprising could be put down by the massacre of 350 Hindu upper caste soldiers by the British army. We also know for sure that the Sepoy Mutiny of 1857 began on the ground of humiliation of upper caste soldiers, who were asked to open the cartridges which were pasted with cow and pig fat. The Brahmanic soldiers felt that the British deliberately did this to humiliate the upper caste forces, as they were vegetarian.

The question of SC/ST/OBCs being part of that group of soldiers does not arise, because beef was a part of their menu. Thus, the ensuing civil war in India would be based again on caste and cultural humiliation.

In both the 1990s anti-reservation upper caste counter-movement and in the 2006 counter-movement, the Brahmans who are a part of the media—both visual and print—strategized the humiliation campaign. In 2006, they behaved more arrogantly than they ever were in the 1990s. They were pushing the upper caste youth into street battles. The TV channels and newspapers mobilized the youth, provided them with cues and the necessary language to humiliate the mental and physical faculties of the SC/ST/OBCs. The upper caste industrialists and businessmen and women were giving them all the money that these social fascists needed. The highest judicial court—the Supreme Court of India—praised these social fascist youth as Abhimanyus (son of the epic hero called Arjuna, who waged a war against his own relatives; Abhimanyu was killed in the *Mahabharata* war). Thus, the Dalit-Bahujans of India cannot even look up to the modern judicial wing of the state to escape from the civil war situation being created by the upper caste social fascist forces.

WHO CAUSES A CIVIL WAR?

All civil wars in the world have been imposed by the ruling social forces on the ruled social beings, both as a condition of consciousness and as a process of social transformation. Before such civil wars were imposed on the ruled beings, they remained mere subservient beings. They did not organize themselves into a social force. In India, the upper castes have always been a social force and the Dalit–Bahujans have been always mere social beings. A civil war situation has existed in India on an everyday basis, for a long time now. The upper caste social forces have been oppressing, humiliating and exploiting the productive social beings quite consistently over a period of centuries. Since the Dalit–Bahujans were divided into castes, they could not organize themselves into a social force. In order to organize themselves into a social force, their identities need to transform. Can the Dalit–Bahujans turn a social fascist attack of the upper castes into a civil war, which the upper caste forces are ever-ready to fight the moment their authority is challenged at the micro or the macro-level?

There are various options available for transforming the identities of the oppressed castes. They can, for instance, shape political formations to capture political power. But to give shape to a political formation, an organized social base is a necessary condition. The caste system does not allow such a political formation to take shape so easily. The Brahmanic social force can create a crisis in all such political formations from the epicentre of Hinduism. Unless the Dalit–Bahujans organize themselves into a spiritual democratic social force that could counter the organized structure of spiritual fascist social force, they cannot consolidate themselves into a viable alternative. The Dalits and the tribals are on the course of moving into alternative spiritual democratic social systems. That is where their autonomous thinking is strengthened. But the OBCs have not developed such an alternative vision. Their alternative vision may form in the course of a civil war that the *dwija* castes are slowly but surely imposing upon them in the course of the anti-reservation counter-movements. The targeted attack against the OBCs in the 1990s and 2006 has created enough ground for the realization that leaving Hinduism is a necessary option, as it is a preparation for a war of position. Of course, the pro- and anti-reservation debates have already provided a basis for a war of position between the upper castes and the OBCs. However, the OBCs are not very sure about their alternative. They have not yet produced their own commonly accepted organic intellectuals who could turn into icons of civil war as well.

Such icons of the civil war must emerge among the OBCs in the near future. Since the caste system had been created in the name of God, its destruction will also take place in the name of God. When God becomes an agent in the anti-caste struggle, Hinduism as a religion, with the self-centred Brahmans in its command, is bound to die bit by bit. Those who oppress others on a daily and hourly basis—or, in other words, those who wage a one-sided war on the oppressed castes—claim that a civil war would be against the interests of the oppressed masses themselves. But what is not understood by the oppressed lower caste masses is that unless they are transformed from the position of social beings to the position of a social force, their war cannot become a civil war. A civil war is a condition where the war of position (ideological, and so on) is transformed into a war of nerves. A war of nerves is the highest form of war that will assist the overthrowing of Brahmanism. It may even reach the stage of a war of weapons. The whole process depends on the upper caste forces and their mode of imposition of a civil war on the lower caste masses. If the upper castes use weapons to suppress the struggle for equality, the lower caste masses may move into all forms of war of weapons.

After 60 years of the constitutional governance headed by the upper castes themselves, the Dalit–Bahujan masses, because of the principle of 'one person, one vote', have come to the stage where they are capable of waging a war of position. Once this first ground is broken, the other stages too will be reached as the anti-caste struggles progress. Since the anti-caste struggles are perceived as anti-Hindu by the upper castes—the RSS, for instance, perceived the pro-reservation struggle as anti-Hindu—the ideologues and the OBC masses will also realize that their liberation within the fold of Hinduism would be impossible. As this realization increases among the Shudra slaves of Hindu Brahmanism, the Brahmanical forces will not allow the issue of equality to be resolved within the framework of constitutionalism. It will also not allow the issue to be resolved through the means of intellectual debates. A heated intellectual debate is a reflection of a war of nerves. If only the upper castes had any willingness to resolve the problem of caste, the system would have transformed without the social mass resorting to a war of weapons. Historically, the upper castes have suppressed the lower caste masses with weapons, as the Hindu gods' origin itself is rooted in the culture of weapon usage. The SC/ST/OBCs will then have to turn to a war of weapons in the process of elimination of Hindu violence from India. In my opinion, in this whole process, the stage of war of nerves will play a decisive role in the whole process of Indian history.

The transformation of the social masses involves a change in the spiritual position of the historically oppressed masses into a differently organized, and possibly, into a more organized religion than Hinduism—a religion that can culturally and civilizationally look down upon Hinduism. In the process of abolishing caste, the war of nerves needs to be fought at two levels—one at the level of one's own mind, one's family and one's caste, and the other at the level of spiritual democracy vs. spiritual fascism. At both levels, however, one needs to fight in the realm of thought and ideology, winning the ideological battle against the system of consent generation that has been constructed to maim the authority of Brahmanism and casteism over the productive Indian masses. Their self has to extricate the slavish self of the Dalit–Bahujan from within in order to win the battle in a decisive manner. Once the consenting self rejects consent on caste hierarchy, the family units of the Dalit–Bahujans as well as the larger caste units undergo a change in position. That change is in the offing. That is how the pro-reservation struggles are succeeding and the anti-reservation counter-struggles are losing. The pro-reservation struggles are mass struggles and the anti-reservation agitations are class agitations.

The upper caste social forces operate in a diabolic mode. At one level, they wage a constant war on the being of the Dalit–Bahujan. They want the Dalit–Bahujans to keep operating as slaves and semi-slaves, even in the age of political democracy. The caste system sustained itself and survived through the means of spiritual fascism and monarchical authoritarianism in the domain of politics. The Kshatriyaized kingship was a known channel of continuing the Brahmanical authority, in both the spiritual and the political field. Colonialism was a mediator between the two. The first phase—from 1948 to 1989—of political democracy was a period of consolidation of the Brahman, Baniya and neo-Kshatriya coalition. In 1990, a decisive new phase of Dalit–Bahujan era began. This era is conditioned by the conscious efforts of the upper castes to resist change and that of the Dalit–Bahujans to push that change into a situation of civil war. The intellectual *goondas* who operate in the realm of the Brahmanic civil society portray a civil war as something dangerous to the Dalit–Bahujans themselves—at the same time, they constantly wage war against the conscious and transformative being of the Dalit–Bahujans. We therefore need to examine the role of the civil wars that took place in other parts of the world in different phases of history.

WHAT DID CIVIL WARS DO IN THE WORLD?

Because of the caste contradictions and the new consciousness that has started to take shape among the Shudras, Chandalas and the Adivasis, India is now moving towards a major civil war. Hinduism as a religion and Brahmanism as a spiritual fascist ideology are facing a revolt that is likely to lead into a major civil war, one that the Brahmanical forces have avoided for centuries. The difference between class societies and a caste society like India is that the caste society did not allow a major civil war in the past. Such avoidance of the civil war did not do any good to the society. All human barbarities in day-to-day life continued to operate, keeping the Indian society at sub-human level. The class societies, on the other hand, underwent several civil wars, and the socio-economic and scientific development of the world emerged out of that conflict between contending ideologies. A popular proverb in Telugu reads like this: *Mantrasaani modata baadha penchutadi kaani taruvaatha baadha teerustaadi* (in the beginning the midwife increases the pain, but later she provides permanent relief). In the same vein civil wars cause pain, but also develop some permanent solutions to social problems. Nation states were shaped and developed because of the contending ideas and the scientific temper that was formulated in the Western countries in the eighteenth and nineteenth centuries during the civil wars. Civil wars served as harbingers of new knowledge in those countries. Brahmanism worked out several strategies to avoid such civil wars in India. Such an avoidance of civil war at every point of time worked more in the interest of the spiritual fascists and social smugglers. The master/feudal class lords in the ancient West, the feudal lord class in medieval West and the bourgeoisie class in the modern West could not avoid civil wars. Such civil wars led to revolutionary transformation of the poor into the rich and the rich into either the middle class or to poverty. In the spiritual realm, the classical papal class moved into the working class and the forces of the working class moved into the papal class. Such a possibility of mobility of classes enriched healthy competition amongst the Western social forces. In India, Brahmanism killed the scope for such competition by killing the human essence within itself. In the globalized era, when the Brahmanical Hinduism resists radical social changes, a civil war on the basis of caste is on its way. As of now, ours is a weak and unimaginative society. A civil war, perhaps, may make it creatively energetic.

A civil war with a progressive ideology is a necessary evil of every upwardly moving society. Social upheavals with a vision of change to establish better human relations and equality as an essential goal of human beings are necessary evils. The evil of civil war is preferable to the evil of caste degradation of the society. It is wrong to think that in societies where there are no civil wars of progressive mode, there is no blood-letting at all. Indian Brahmanism sustained its hegemony by making the blood flow in abundance, as we have witnessed in Gujarat in 2002. The Brahmanical forces, with a spiritual sanction, killed numerous people raped women; cut the wombs of pregnant women and killed the babies growing in the wombs of mothers, and burnt people alive in hundreds and thousands. The story of Parashurama, the Brahman god, who killed all mothers and all the foetuses of Kshatriyas and Shudras in the wombs in order to safeguard Brahmanism, was not just a mythological concoction. The religious genocide that the Hindu Brahmanical forces conducted in Gujarat in 2002 is an expression of their historical culture. The easy justification of it by the Brahman Prime Minister—Atal Bihari Vajpayee—as a representative of that caste is a part of the blood-sucking culture of that caste. Since religions like Islam and Christianity possess mechanisms of self-defence, the Brahmanical forces allow them to survive, but the Dalit–Bahujans who were divided into many caste clusters had faced many such genocides, without even letting the world discuss such brutalities and blood-letting. Spiritual fascism has survived so long only by conducting constant genocides.

CIVIL WAR AS AN AGENT OF REGENERATION

All European countries had undergone the process of civil war in order to move from medievalism to modernity. Britain, France, America, Russia and China have undergone civil wars in one form or the other. It was in such civil wars that the old hegemonic forces were overthrown and the historically exploited classes and races came to occupy the respectable position in their societies. The Indian civil war would have many similarities with that of American civil war of 1857-58. The Afro-Americans were treated as slaves by the white Americans in a manner similar to the Indian Dalit-Bahujans and their treatment at the hands of the Brahmans. They were as slavish—though not untouchable—as the Dalits of India are. But Christianity, as a religion, granted them the right to spiritual equality. They also slowly gained some rights to education and that right to read a book in the beginning started with reading of the Bible itself. They realized over a period of time that unless a major fight is launched, the right to equality could not be achieved. Thus, the Bible was the harbinger of civil wars to achieve socio-spiritual equality in the West.

A sympathetic white president—Abraham Lincoln—provided the necessary conditions to launch a civil war in America. It was this civil war that shattered the fetters of not only Afro-Americans but also released the socio-economic potential of all Americans. The American war of independence had provided them the political independence and American civil war had changed their race relations. The changed political and race relations had unleashed the productive knowledge systems and allowed unbridled participation of the Afro-Americans and white Americans, with a spirit of collectivity in all socio-scientific experiments. The American society became the most productive society only after the civil war. India was never allowed to pass though such a phase. Having trained in Brahmanism and the books like the *Rigveda* and the *Bhagavad Gita*, no Brahman could take a lead like Abraham Lincoln did in America. Gandhi raised some questions, but they were within the framework of the Hindu spiritual fascist books. When one is trained in spiritually fascist books, one cannot think in absolute democratic terms. Gandhi's limitation was that of his caste. Since he was a Baniya with Jain ethical values in the background, he could not go that far. But no Brahman thinker, writer and ruler in Indian history could think like Abraham Lincoln. The caste they were born in, the spiritual books they read and the divine images they worship do not give them any scope to think about absolute equality of all human beings of their own nation.

The Indian society, in spite of the political freedom it offers, has become stagnant in all spheres of life because of the continuing caste system and the self-aggrandized policies of the spiritual fascists, social smugglers and above all, of the intellectual *goondas*. This impasse has to be overcome. That is possible only when we overcome the historical hurdles created by Hinduism. As Ambedkar predicted, Hinduism is on its way to die out. That seems to be part of the process of revolutionary transformation of India.

BREAKING THE WALL OF SPIRITUAL FASCISM

The Indian society has stagnated for centuries because of caste. In all societies, the civil wars cleansed the dirt from the society. The progressive phase of humanity began with the establishment of religions that accepted the principle that God created all human beings equal. Only Hinduism went against this principle and remains like that till date. As the Indian society has not faced any civil war, its social stagnation has been never broken. The most productive communities suffered indignities all through history. The social layers that suffered indignities must move into a life of social dignity in all spheres, including the spiritual sphere. Even the gods in Hinduism remained discriminatory. In order to change that situation, a revolutionary reordering of the social system is an essential pre-requisite. Even the god must come to the human plane, where he does not discriminate between people, between different castes, between man and woman. The Hindu God created people from his feet, thighs, shoulders and head. In Hindu spiritual thought, human beings were not created out of God's imagination on an equal basis. The spiritual inequality of birth is a negation of all divine laws. Spiritual fascism, thus, was born here. It was constructed in the form of caste. Caste is a spiritual fascist wall between one community and another. Only a civil war can break that wall and establish equality in all spheres of life, including that of spirituality. Thus, a civil war in India is a wish of a god who does not believe in caste.

SHUDRAS AND CIVIL WAR

The educated Shudras of India failed in acquiring a liberative mind. In the first Hindu religious text—the *Rigveda*—they were said to have been born from the feet of Hindu god, Brahma. Brahmans were said to have taken birth from his head, the Kshatriyas from his chest and the Vaishyas from his thighs.

The Dalits and the Adivasis were not born from his body. In the ancient and medieval days of ignorance, that could have been thought to be a curse for the Dalits and the Adivasis. But now, that has become a boon for them. In the North-East, the Adivasis were liberated. In many parts of India, the Dalits are being liberated. That liberation started more decisively with Ambedkar embracing Buddhism with half a million Dalits, and many more of them going into Christianity. In those religions, all of them gained the right to spiritual equality. The Shudras, on the other hand, remained stuck at the feet of the Hindu Brahmanical society without any aspiration of spiritual liberation.

The social forces whose status and socio-spiritual aspirations have remained stagnant do not gain liberation in any sphere of life. Their status, therefore, remains that of the 'feet born' within Hinduism. The position of the Shudras in the Hindu religion is uninitiated. If the Brahmans and the Kshatriyas are twice-born (initiated into Hinduism), the Shudras are once-born (not initiated into Hinduism), they are made into objects in that religion, without having any subjective self of their own. Although they are allowed entry into Hindu temples, they cannot perform the rituals themselves. For that they have to depend on the Brahman priests. The priest does not eat their cooked food. The priest treats them as people unworthy of occupying the position that he holds, because his position is considered to be closer to God. Thus the Shudras have not attained spiritual equality.

All the Hindu religious books are full of abusive language against the Shudras. A community that does not feel angry at books that have historically abused their selves is a community that has not acquired a sense of self-respect. Such a community cannot acquire the capacity for philosophical thinking as well. Philosophical thinking is generated in a process of self-assertion. So far, the Indian Shudras did not develop the philosophical self because they have not developed a full-fledged spiritual self. If the position of the Shudras is ever changed and they are put at the helm of Hinduism, many Shudras would have headed the Hindu temples. In medieval and even in the modern period, the temple is not only a place of worship but also a place of philosophical discourses. If communities are denied the authority to lead the socio-spiritual philosophical discourses, then they remain underdeveloped in the realm of philosophical thought. The Brahmans, who have traditionally headed such discourses, have focused their attention in building an unequal negative philosophy in order to sustain the unnatural institution called caste. As a result, they have not contributed any positive philosophy to the world philosophical systems. The Hindu religious books are entirely written by the Brahmanic intellectual *goondas*, who have hardly any spiritual element in them. Spiritually, there is nothing wrong if all such books are rewritten to establish spiritual equality among people who live within that spiritual realm. But the Brahmanic intellectual *goondas* only tell us cock and bull stories if we ask for the rewriting of the Hindu books and a radical reform of the Hindu spiritual system.

Today, every Shudra has only the right to visit the Hindu temples and take the spiritual blessings of the Brahman priests. If a Shudra goes to a church, a mosque or a *vihara*, would he not be allowed inside by the priests of those religions? Would they not give him spiritual blessings? They would. In fact, they would treat them as equals. Merely allowing the Shudras into Hindu temples or to take the ritual help of the priest does not automatically bind them to that religion. It is only the spiritual and philosophical underdevelopment of the Shudras that keeps them ignorantly happy within that system. When one does not build one's philosophical self, even an unequal relationship with another person would appear natural to them. The Shudras as a social mass constitute good example of blissful ignorance.

The Bible and the Quran or the Buddhist scriptures do not insult the Shudra historical self. If a Shudra approaches any priest from any of these religions, they would perform the religious rituals, and would not insult them. They would not say that they would not touch the Shudra or eat the food that they have cooked. The Shudras were not initiated into Islam, Christianity or Buddhism, and they cannot therefore become priests in these religions, like Hinduism. But these religions invite them to baptize themselves and gain access to equal rights. The Shudras are as un-Hindu as they are un-Christian, un- Muslim and un-Buddhist. This status of the Shudras of not belonging to any universally recognized religion should change. The spiritual fascists, the social smugglers and the intellectual *goondas* do not accept any change in the status of the Shudras. Nor do they allow their position in the books to be changed. The change of that status of the Shudras, Dalits and the Adivasis will also radically change the parasitic, exploitative life of the spiritual fascists, social smugglers and intellectual *goondas*, because it is Hinduism that guarantees the latter the various rights to exploitation.

The Hindu religious texts still contain abusive language against the Shudras. An intellectual rebellion against such abusive Hindu scriptures by the Shudras would have changed the conditions of the Indian nation a long time back. Why are we asking only the Shudras to revolt when the Dalits have suffered such humiliation in history, with more destructive implications to their self than that of the Shudras? This is because the Shudras started to be educated before the Dalits, and in greater numbers. A section of the Shudras acquired more property and stable life, which the Dalits are fighting for now. During the Bhakti movement, the Shudras asked for the right to worship the Hindu gods and the right to enter the Hindu temples at a time when they too were as untouchable to Hindu spiritual structures as the Dalits today are. After the Bhakti movement, the Shudras gained very little within the Hindu religious domain. What they gained was merely the right to worship and entry to Hindu temples. That is the end of it. Their right to be initiated by acquiring a status of twice-born is still unachieved. Their right to read the Hindu texts on spiritual occasions or in a temple is yet to be attained. Their right to attain priesthood remains yet a distant dream of the Shudras in the spiritual realm. Any educated Shudra with a sense of self-respect and with some philosophical vision of his/her own would have initiated a struggle within that spiritual domain for all equal rights.

INDIAN NATIONALISM AND THE SHUDRA SELF

The nationalist struggle that started in the nineteenth century has not changed the spiritual status of the Shudras. Since modern philosophical faculties were not injected into them, they did not realize the importance of the spiritual realm. Mahatma Jotirao Phule rebelled against the Hindu spiritual system. His thought, however, remained at the rudimentary level. Thereafter, no Shudra, even in the modern nationalist period could acquire the basic status of interpreter of spiritual events. Since Indian nationalism was always shown as Hindu nationalism, the Shudras thought that by being within that religion they would gain everything. Many Shudras claimed ownership of Hinduism as their religion and they acquired some national space. They got some land and industrial property, and more significantly, a definite space in the domain of regional political power. But that did not change their spiritual and philosophical position.

Even in the realm of property, business and politico-bureaucratic power within the broad Hindu system, the position of a social group depends on its proximity to the Hindu gods and temples and its priesthood. The amount of property and power that the Shudras control in India is far less than that of the Brahmans, Kshatriyas and Baniyas. So far, the Shudras as a community have not acquired the philosophical capacity to understand this limitation. Their psyche is a historically humiliated psyche, and so far, there has been no realization of that humiliation in them. The Shudra position within Hinduism is like that of a person who is said to belong to an office, even though he cannot sit in a chair in that office. It is like that of a peon, without having any rights to promotion within that office. Assume that that peon has lot of money at home and he/she has lot of power within his locality or within his family. That itself does not make him/her a happy being in the office. Yet the peon seems to be happy with the small amount of salary that he gets every month. The position of Shudras in Hinduism is like that of a peon in an office.

In any imaginative society, such a stagnant and eternally humiliated position of a vast mass of people would have caused a civil war within that society. But the Shudra civil society has not acquired the philosophical vision of revolt as well. This is because its philosophical vision is too weak. They cannot achieve a philosophical vision for spiritual equality, as that desire has not been generated within them. Theirs is a position of historical ignorance and a life of desirelessness. They are akin to the satisfied human beings of Socrates, whom the philosopher considered worse than dissatisfied pigs.

All that they have produced by constructing science and technology stage by stage, as we have seen in preceding chapters—as social doctors, as meat and milk economists, as social engineers, as food producers, and so on—was not recognized by them as science and technology of great historical importance. Their work has not only constructed the basic science of India, but has also contributed towards the development of productive technology and science of the world. But they do not know that their own knowledge is a knowledge that helped the whole of humanity to acquire its civilizational status. Once they know it, they will fight for the recognition of their historical contribution and for receiving their historical due. The Brahmanical society has forcefully kept their contribution out of the annals of history. Civil wars occurred in societies where the slaves realized that they were slaves. Once a slave realizes that he/she is the basic source of scientific knowledge, his/her rebellion gains a greater sense of direction. In India, the Shudras are the spiritual salves of Brahmanism and they have not realized that they are slaves. Because of this situation, the Shudra spirit has remained underdeveloped. When one's spirit remains underdeveloped, the scientific temper also remains at a rudimentary stage. Herein lies the source of national underdevelopment too.

THE SHUDRA BASE AND BRAHMAN SUPERSTRUCTURE

As we have seen in the earlier chapters, the Shudra, Dalit and tribal productive base is responsible for whatever development we have in India. The food we produce, the technological knowhow we have built, and the positive productive human relations that this nation survives with are constructed and developed by the Dalits, Shudras and the tribals. The procurement of food in the form of roots, fruits and meat, food production in various agrarian and semi-industrial manners, working out the functional skills around health science, were built by the present Dalit–Bahujan and tribal social forces. There is no historical evidence to show that the Brahmans, Baniyas and the Kshatriya communities participated in building up this knowledge at any point of time in history. The available textual evidence, the ritual culture they hegemonized in the past and keep hegemonizing in the present indicates that they condemned the productive and health science as unworthy. They have built the Hindu spiritual culture and Hindu business values and the state structure to checkmate the positive productive and humanly interactive processes.

The cultural superstructure that the Brahmans built has remained so anti-civilizational that they structured a religion that is entirely inhuman. Hinduism as a religion went on demonizing the acts of tilling land, grazing cattle, sheep and goat. Making pots, which was an universally recognized and creative act of interaction between the productive culture and the advancing spiritual culture was also projected as an anti-divine activity. This mode of Brahmanical spirituality went against the universal spiritual ethic that organized the civil society into a unified organism to boost production, and create a culture of social cohesion. If we look at the images of gods and goddesses that the Shudra society constructed, as opposed to the images that the Brahman–Baniya society constructed, as I proved in *Why I am Not a Hindu*, they were totally opposed to the Brahmanic spiritual culture. Unfortunately, they did not develop a written discourse around their own spiritual culture. Of course, the Brahmanic violence of cutting of hands and tongues if somebody made an attempt to write that discourse into a holistic philosophy was one reason for its stagnation in the ancient period. But in the modern period, the Shudras have lost speculative philosophical vision as they left the realm to their enemies called Brahmans. Instead of philosophizing their own spiritual and cultural tradition, they began to own the enemy's culture and enemy's religion. Hence, they too undermined their own knowledge base.

The tribal and Dalit–Bahujan spirituality and the god and goddess images were worked out around the productive process of their lives. It was their struggle with nature that forced them to construct the divine images that were production-friendly, as opposed to the war-mongering divine images that Hinduism has created. Thus, the Shudras, who have now lost their distinct identity, have had a strong cultural history of anti-Brahmanism, that is, anti-Hinduism. In countries where Buddhism, Christianity and Islam advanced the economic base and the cultural superstructure, strong inter-linkages and friendly alliances were built. That was the reason why the economic culture and the spiritual culture did not become contradictory to one another. Those countries could easily overcome the Marxist postulation that the religious culture, science and technological advancement would oppose one another and in the process the religion would die out. Of course, the dogmatic Marxist thinkers thought that religion would die out within the course of material and techno-economic advancement. But because of the tremendous labour friendliness of Christianity and Buddhism, the pure materialist schools entered into crisis and those who talked about spirituo-material interactive cultural paradigms—that is, capitalist and Christian and Buddhist markets being sustainable—have proved to be correct as of now. The Hindu religion is the anti-thesis of all global religious cultures. That is the reason why Hinduism produced the most negative institution called caste that went on negating socio-scientific advancement.

If the Shudra, Chandala and Adivasi cultures were to synthesize themselves and advance the Indian civil society, the Indian state would have developed on altogether different lines. The Indian state has now acquired all the characteristics of Brahmanism and the whole socio-spiritual culture of the nation has become anti-developmental. The Shudra philosophy was not only creative, but it was also humanitarian and integrative. If the Brahmanic Hinduism were not to intervene, perhaps the Indian nation would have been much stronger than any Asian nation today. The Shudras have lost that track of progress and have become victims of historical Brahmanism. Now they are unable to come out of that process. The Dalits, having traversed on a much more difficult road and having luckily remained outside the terrain of Hindu Brahmanism, are now on a much better liberative course.

DALIT AND SHUDRA RELATIONS

The Dalits, who realized their historical potential, started a struggle for liberation. They have not only realized the historical potential of their subaltern scientificity and productive soldierhood but also realized that they should attain unmitigated spiritual status of their own. They have also realized that they can overthrow the yoke of Brahmanism. The symptoms of a civil war were expressed among the Dalits in their production of a philosopher of the stature of Ambedkar. All civil wars first produce philosophers who construct a philosophy of the oppressed. That philosophy remains not only creative, but it would also have full potential to kindle a light, a spirit of liberation in the unkindled minds of hard working but enslaved people. Rousseau and Voltaire in France, Frederick Douglas in America, Lenin in Russia, Mao in China emerged as philosophers of liberative civil wars. Ambedkar, with a definite theory of revolt and a vision of an alternative spiritual ideology produced a text of Dalit philosophy which has a liberative message for the Shudras and tribals as well. Ambedkar correctly pitched his battle in the religious field. Unlike in other countries, the Dalits of India lost their natural rights in the spiritual field. To liberate people in the spiritual realm is harder than liberating them in the political realm. With a theoretical vision, he asked for equality within Hinduism and gave them enough time. When he realized that the spiritual fascists would not grant it, and the intellectual *goondas* did not approve of his demand and would not adopt his methods, he embraced Buddhism. The Buddhism that he regenerated in India is known as neo-Buddhism. In neo-Buddhism, the Dalits at once received the right to initiation, the right to read the text within the spiritual precinct and also the right to head the *viharas*. In 1956, at Nagpur, he liberated half a million Dalits at one go. All of them embraced Buddhism. Thus, Ambedkar became the modern prophet of India.

The Dalits who were not allowed to wear even ordinary dresses at once wore the garb of most respected monks. The Buddhist monks are respected not only in India (the Hindu *sadhus* and *sanyasis* are respected only in India, that too only by the *dwijas*) but all over the world. An untouchable in Hinduism flew to the top of spiritual world at the *deeksha bhoomi* of Nagpur. This was the biggest spiritual liberation of a social mass that had so far lived in spiritual darkness. By entering into one of the biggest religions in the world, they acquired global spiritual citizenship. For acquiring global spiritual citizenship, one must belong to a globally recognizable community. The Dalits of India, by declaring that they not only embrace Buddhism but also oppose Hinduism and work towards its death, became a part of that community. This was the first step of the beginning of the end of Hinduism. Dalits took that first step. The Shudras could not take such a step owing to the spiritual slavery that they were living in.

THE NATIONALIST TRAP

Why did the Shudras remain Shudras, without becoming Hindus, as the spiritual fascists and social smugglers had succeeded in becoming? Why did they not begin a liberative struggle? This is where the intellectual *goondagiri* of nationalist Brahmanic forces trapped them. Indian nationalism was constructed in the spiritual image of Hinduism, in which the Shudras hardly had any space. Nationalism offered them some crude economic development and regional political power, which in turn gave them the myth of power, of influence and of transformation. Philosophical life has its roots within the spiritual realm. Both the notion of economic development and political power are structures of *maya* that Brahmanism built around Shudra life. Control over political structures can be automatically gained once the spiritual structure is within control, but mere control over political structures does not lead to control in the spiritual domain. The Shudra society that encompasses the largest number of people in India, thus, lives within a barren terrain of spiritual life.

LACK OF SPIRITUAL CITIZENSHIP

The Shudras might claim that they are Hindus both in the national and international platforms, but that claim is not an authentic, spiritually integrated claim. When neither the book nor the clergy recognize them as fully initiated and integrated Hindus, when their children at no stage in the history of the Hindu religion could head any spiritual institution, their claim is based on false consciousness. This false consciousness has become so pathological in their historical existence that they believe that they own something that is not theirs. Since they believe in a community that does not exist, as a community, their social being has become totally alienated. To put it in Jean Paul Sartre's epithet, their 'Being is Nothing'. If they are satisfied in their life of Nothingness, that satisfaction is that of animal satisfaction.

All communities in the world acquired an advanced level of community consciousness by acquiring spiritual citizenship in a congregative community. This spiritual citizenship provided them with the right to be initiated into a spiritual community on the basis of equality. It gave them the right to read the religious book(s), the right to congregate and the right to lead the congregation on various occasions of social importance. The productive energies of people got sharpened when they were given sanctions of the spiritual community. There, the image of God merely acted as a social organizer. What played the role of a morale booster in the spiritual community was the spiritual citizenship of all classes and races. For a long time, women suffered from a lack of spiritual citizenship, and that has had a historical impact on their socio-political and economic advancement. Brahmanism meticulously avoids the congregative cultural gatherings because it does not want to grant the citizenship to all castes. The historical Shudra effort to push the Hindu religion into a religion of egalitarianism, a religion that is based on spiritual citizenship, met with a violent resistance in which many Shudras died. Shambhuka and Bali are two outstanding examples in the ancient period. They were killed not for asking the right to be kings or rulers. They were rulers and were killed for asking for their spiritual citizenship.

In the modern period, at the pan-Indian level, Charan Singh and Deve Gowda became prime ministers in spite of belonging to Shudra castes, but no Brahman minister, secretary, diplomat or press person ever considered them to be respectable spiritual citizens of their social community. Many Shudra chief ministers buy respect from the Brahman socio-spiritual community out of that haunting consciousness of being a Shudra political leader with a lower social rank than those they are dealing with. They do not possess the false consciousness that they were/are Hindus. If they had come from a minority spiritually integrated community instead, this particular feeling of inferiority, of being an alienated being, would not have existed. A Muslim or a Christian or a Buddhist prime minister, while surrounded by Brahmanic Hindus who take every opportunity to prove them as failures, would fight back against them. A Shudra, with a history of being treated as inferior and living with a lack of spiritual citizenship, a historical sense of being alienated, cannot handle such affairs with adequate confidence.

Education could have led the Shudras to revolt against their current status. They could have even led a civil war in the socio-spiritual realm. But as of now, the Shudra mind is intellectually crippled. It does not see its own humiliated image in the mirror of history. Since Shudras did not acquire a spiritual self, they also failed to acquire a philosophical self. They still depend on Brahmanical philosophy. So far, not a single Shudra has acquired the status of a philosopher, because they have not developed an imaginative and creative self of their own. When a social community cannot develop its own spiritual and philosophical self- image, it cannot construct a philosophy of its own vision. The Shudras of India lack that vision even now. The educated among them are happy with the money that they have earned in modern India. They are happy with the political power they have gained in some regions. They never aspired for philosophical power, which would have come only when they challenged the Brahmanical philosophy. To challenge a negative philosophy, they should have constructed a positive philosophy of their own. It appears that they now depend on the Dalits for leadership. This, in a way, is good thing because this brings the Dalits, who have historically been the most oppressed, to a position of leading the Shudras, who have historically betrayed enough arrogance against them out of mere ignorance. They still remain under the total grip of Brahmanism. This conditioned consciousness of the Shudras postponed the civil war in the post-independence period.

THE DALITS AND CIVIL WAR

The Dalits have enormous potential to lead the civil war in India. The strong liberative seeds sown by Buddhism and Christianity are growing slowly but surely into planthood. The fact that Ambedkar's birthday had to be declared as a national holiday by the Brahmanic rulers is an indication of their strength. They have come to a stage of making what is theirs—what has been ignored as unworthy—national and universal.

This is an indication of strength. Let us not forget that the Buddha, Jesus and Muhammad in the spiritual sphere and Karl Marx in the political sphere became global with a group of committed conscious intellectuals who took up a campaign about them. Among the Dalit Buddhists, there are such Dalits who can make Ambedkar a universal name. He is the first leader whom they can treat as a star in the sky and use him as a guiding light. Furthermore, they have reached a stage where they can dictate philosophical terms to the Brahmans. This act of dictating terms is not only assertive but is also indicative of the direction that the Dalits are ready to take. Their intellectual command is an expression of the inner potential of their social collective.

Those who lead the civil war must establish their moral authority over the enemies. Of the three suppressed communities—the Shudras, Dalits and tribals—only the Dalits have acquired that tone of moral authority. After the Buddha, only Ambedkar could gain that moral stature of being feared by the Brahmanical forces. Ambedkar established a terrain of war from where the Dalits could take the position of war. As Gramsci rightly noted, beginning this 'war of position' is significant to advance towards subsequent victories. They first took the position of war in the spiritual field. This made them quickly move on to the position of war in education and in politics, and in the near future this is going to lead them to a position of war in the field of economics. Once a historically brutally humiliated community knows how to take the position of war and locate its enemy, its liberation is imminent.

From the location of 'war of position', any civil war has to move to a stage of war of nerves. The war of nerves in India has to operate as a war of spiritual ideologies. In a situation of spiritualized political nationalism at the time of freedom struggle, Ambedkar put the Buddha's image as superior and more ethical than that of Gandhi's Rama. His committed followers subsequently counterposed the image of Ambedkar to that of Gandhi with a counter hegemonic moral authority. By the end of the twentieth century, Ambedkar's image had crossed the border of being that of a socio-political leader and entered the stage of acquiring the image of a spiritual leader. Negation of the oppressive spirituality and construction of a liberative spiritual ideology is part of the war of nerves. It can be called a war of spiritual ideologies as well. All spiritual battles are ideological battles. In all such spiritual/ideological wars, establishing the cultural hegemony of the hitherto marginalized social forces that stood condemned by the enemy as inferior and unethical is an essential condition. The Dalits of India have come to that stage where they can inverse the cultural idiom. Once they win that war of nerves, the enemy pushes the process into a battle of physical violence. This, in my view, is nothing but war of weapons.

The Dalits are now in the thick of that war of weapons. The Ambedkarites are being killed, their women are being raped and their children are being burnt alive at many places in the country. They own small economic assets and such assets are being destroyed all over India. In some patriarchal societies rape is used as a weapon against women. Dalit women have experienced the use of rape as a weapon for centuries. The Sangh Parivar's actions in Gujarat are an extension of the atrocities generally committed against the Dalits. During the Gujarat riots many Muslim and Dalit women were raped. The spiritual fascists and intellectual *goondas* even instigate the Shudras to conduct such rapes and murders, and the social smugglers finance that process. The Shudras, thus, are used as objectified weapons of rape and murder. Their minds were ingrained with the immoral ideology of Hindutva. Thus they were capable of such atrocity. Hence they organized the carnage by using spiritual immorality as a weapon of war. The Gujarat carnage of the Brahmanic Hindutva forces, thus, is an expression of the religious civil war that Hinduism has started to see that India does not undergo any spiritual transformation. Brahmanism feels threatened with the presence of Islam and Christianity and the rekindled Buddhism.

In a majority vs minority war of weapons, the minority—as the Muslims of India did—turn to bombs. The Muslim ethic allows the use of grenades and human bombs as weapons of war, but not rape and burning of a foetus by ripping open the mother's womb. If the bomb as weapons of war is not properly guided or suppressed with brutal military power of the state, it turns into terrorism. This process has become very clear after destruction of the Babri Masjid in the continuing civil war between the Hindutva forces and the Muslims of India. The Hindu Brahmanic war of weapons has no moral angularities. Following Kautilya, a Brahman thinker of ancient India, the Hindu forces aim at destroying the enemy in all possible ways by using all immoral weapons. This meant enormous suffering on the part of the Dalit-Bahujans as they stood on a higher moral pedestal as followers of the Buddha and Ambedkar. So far, they have not resorted to the rape of upper-caste women as a weapon. Ambedkar fought Brahmanism all his life, and he married a Brahman woman and treated her with dignity. But there is no Brahman leader in the country who married a Dalit woman and treated her with dignity and respect. I am told that many Brahman and Baniya leaders of the VHP and the Bajrang Dal were gleefully involved in the rape campaigns of Muslim women in Gujarat. In entire Gujarat, one does not find a single Brahman or Baniya man who married a Dalit or Muslim woman and treated her with respect. That is the cultural and humanitarian difference between the Brahman–Baniyas and the Dalits and the Muslims. The Shudras have not reached the Dalit level of maturity in terms of their cultural self. They still operate as cultural agents of Brahmanism as they still function as the feet of the Hindu society that is guided by the Brahman head.

Some Brahman writers try to argue that the 'kicking feet' (that is, the Shudras) are responsible for the atrocities against the Dalits. They do not see the role of the head in moving the kicking feet. The leaders who lead the civil war should know whether their target should be the kicking feet or the head that guides the feet, pointing out the targets and determining the speed in which the kick will be delivered. Those who see the kicking feet as the enemy say that there is a historical inimical relationship between the feet that kicked and the objects of that kicking. If one tries to establish a friendly relationship with the head of the person who delivers the kick, the targets of the civil war go wrong. Ambedkar knew and elaborately theorized that in any system, the head is responsible for the functioning of the organs. That is the reason why he made Brahmanism responsible for all the ills of Hindu society. Subsequently, many Dalit leaders followed that ideological framework of Ambedkar. Of course, there were and will be some elements of aberration in that scheme of thought which would make the feet responsible for the type of directions that the head was giving—but such theories do not change the course of a civil war.

The course of the Indian civil war is a far more tortuous one than of any of the civil wars that took place in the Western nations. First, the Brahmanical Hindus pit one caste against the other so that the unity of all oppressed castes becomes impossible. Second, they make it appear bloodier than any of the civil wars that took place in the Western countries. They keep on discounting the tortures, deaths and the rape of the Dalit-Bahujan castes and show only their so-called sacrifices in situations like anti-colonial struggles. Even in those struggles, the sacrifices of the Dalit-Bahujans do not become part of history. The history of India so far has been written upside down. In this book we have seen that only when the condemned self of the tribal, the Dalit or the Shudra is allowed to stand on its own feet does the world would be able to acknowledge their contribution to science. In the Brahmanic history, they have been portrayed as stupid, ignorant and unskilled social forces who need to be under their command. Turning history as it exists now over its head alone can show the truth as it really is. In any civil war, the truth itself becomes a weapon of war.

In this civil war, if the targets are located properly, the weapons of war can be used against the proper targets. If the killers are spoken to in their own language, they claim that they have been abused. If one attacks them with their own weapons, their hegemony slowly begins to die. This death, according to their hegemonic discourse, would result in the end of history. Following that logic, the process of death of Hinduism began with the war of position, and also the war of nerves that the Dalits of India started from the time of Ambedkar himself. So far, the various manifestations that this process of death of Hinduism takes have not been analyzed and understood in an adequate manner. The so-called rise of militant Hinduism is in fact one such manifestation of the of Brahmanic Hinduism. The Hindutva mode of militancy is not a reformative, self-changing militancy of vision and wisdom. It is in its last stages and would wither away soon. The present state of Hindutva mode of militancy can be best summarized through this proverb: 'Sacche paamu kerosene poyagane tokaadinchi natlu'(a dying snake wags its tail when some kerosene is poured on it).

THE END OF HINDUISM

Internally, the process of Hinduism's death has gained momentum with the emergence of the Rashtriya Swayamsevak Sangh (RSS) and its Hindu terrorist network. In history, whenever the Brahmanical forces sought to organize themselves in the name of one religion and one culture while the oppression of the Dalit–Bahujans remained at the same level, it lost ground to other religions which began to occupy the Indian landmass. When Brahmanism tried to occupy all of India while keeping the productive masses totally oppressed, they turned to other religions that offered them equality. That is how Buddhism supplanted Hinduism in the ancient period. The Sanatan Dharma is an older form of modern Hinduism that believed in violence and war. In the ancient period, Buddhism became an important religion in the sub-continent. Later, in the medieval period, Hinduism lost out to Islam. In the modern phase, ever since Christian missionary activity started in India, Hinduism has been facing a serious crisis. Every time it used its violent mode of spiritual fascism as a mechanism to survive, it became weaker and weaker. Whenever the Hindu forces gained political power, they used violence as an instrument to eliminate the other religions. This is what they did against the Muslims and the Christians after the BJP came to power at the centre. This is because it fears the existence of other religions because the tribals, Dalits and the Shudras might embrace them, leaving the *dwijas* to their own fate. Communities that have been historically parasitic simply die of hunger once they are left by the slaves en masse.

Except for its success against Buddhism in ancient India, violent Hinduism did not succeed in rooting out any other religion from India. It did not win the battle against Islam in pre-British India. Islam expanded and occupied the Hindu land, creating three independent states over a period of time—Afghanistan, Pakistan and Bangladesh. This brand of Hinduism now treats Christianity as its most dangerous enemy. However, Christianity has been expanding in the North-East and the South beyond the expectation of the Hindutva forces. It can easily defeat Hinduism because of its internal spiritual democratic structures. Because of casteism and the lack of internal strength, Hinduism surrendered to Islam when the Muslim warriors invaded, which then surrendered to the Christian colonial rulers. There is every possibility that it will die in the near future, as it does not have the ability to transform to evolve itself into a religion of one people.

THE ANCIENT REVOLTS AGAINST HINDUISM

The Indian society in the pre-Buddhist period survived not as a Hindu society but as a caste society. Both Pali and Sanskrit writers called it *Varnavyavastha*. The attempts to impose *Sanatan Brahman Dharma*, which essentially means the imposition of the hegemony of the spiritual fascists on the entire Shudra–Chandala social mass, were resisted by many forces. To oppose that, the Jain and Buddhist revolts occurred, and slowly, Buddhism dismantled the social basis of *Sanatan* Hinduism. The Brahman campaigners were lazy, parasitic vagabonds who did nothing. They roamed about here and there taking the name of *rishi* or *sanyasi*. They were unethical and superstitious humans who consumed all the food resources of the society without participating in any productive activity. As they began to be organized with the help of codified spiritual fascist books, serious revolts occurred in India, first in the form of Jainism and later in the form of Buddhism. That was the first attack against Hindu spiritual fascism. All modes of fascism have a tendency to die and be reborn. Hinduism died in three phases and was reborn three times. It died during the Buddhist period and was reborn. It was substantially weakened during the rule of Muslim rulers and slowly re-equipped itself to rise to its former strength. It was undermined during the British colonial rule and was revived during the nationalist period. It became more and more organized and strengthened during the last 60 years of independence. These 60 years were real golden period of the spiritual fascists, social smugglers and the intellectual *goondas*. But the most important thing is that at no stage did it work for the abolition of caste and the total synthesization of all castes into a congregative community of spiritual equality. This is the central death wish of Hinduism.

THE CONTEMPORARY PHASE

In this present phase, however, it is facing a challenge from the Dalit-Bahujans, who have acquired a consciousness of spiritual equality. Its present phase of remobilizing itself in the face of challenges from Christianity, Islam and Buddhism seems to push it towards its own death once and for all. If the Dalit-Bahujan masses overcome their historical spiritual primitivism, they will walk into different religions that grant them spiritual equality. The claim of Hindu religious leaders, that it is a great religion that commands two nations—India and Nepal, particularly a big nation like India—also comes to an end. At best, some Brahmans and Baniyas might still remain a part of it, leaving it in a status akin to Judaism and Zoroastrianism.

We all must remember that because of its spiritual fascist nature, Hinduism could not become a cross-country religion like Buddhism, Islam and Christianity. It remained within the subcontinent more as an oppressive religion and could never become a liberative religion. From the period of Raja Ram Mohan Roy to the present, as the Brahmanical forces began to organize the oppressed castes into the modern Hindu religion, without granting them the right to priesthood within that religion, it has failed to reform itself quite radically. The expansion of Islam, Christianity and Buddhism has been taking place as the Dalit-Bahujans want to move into a congregative cultural community. When the capitalist market is alienating the human self in the market, the need for increasing communitarian cultural bondages in the public sphere is also increasing. As Marx predicted, religion is not dying with the expanding base of capitalism. On the contrary, the need for an egalitarian religion is increasing. India is a very good example where as the capitalist market and the notion of equality are expanding, movements towards spiritually democratic religions like Christianity, Buddhism and Islam are also increasing. By the end of the twentieth century, three Muslim nations (Afghanistan, Pakistan and Bangladesh) emerged within the sub-continent which were occupied by the spiritual fascists. The rebirth of Hinduism in those countries is impossible. The fourth Muslim nation—Kashmir— is going to be fully born in the near future. The possibility of several Christian nations emerging in the North-East in slightly distant future is also inevitable. Within the larger Indian provinces, the Dalit-Bahujans have no respect for Hinduism. Their movement towards the three global religions in order to acquire their global spiritual citizenship is a clear indication of the shrinking space of Hinduism. In the fourth phase of its campaign, after the birth of the RSS, Hinduism is quite decisively working towards its death in its desire to acquire global status without even granting the right to spiritual equality to its claimed members.

As I examined in detail in *God as Political Philosopher: Buddha's Challenge to Brahmanism*, Buddhism challenged Brahmanism in all spheres in the ancient period and destroyed it in many areas. It also destroyed the social basis of Hinduism. Whenever the Brahmans of India tried to organize Hinduism without establishing a spiritual democratic system, it got wiped out. In the pre-Buddhist period, the ancient Hindu Brahmans wrote Hindu books like the Vedas, *Vedangas* and the *Upanishads* to control the productive masses. The spiritual democratic Buddhism organized a campaign to wipe out Hinduism by granting spiritual rights to all those who embraced it. After the great emperor Ashoka embraced Buddhism, he undertook a massive campaign for the spread of Buddhism. As I have said earlier, Ashoka was the first evangelical leader in the world who sent scores of people, including his own son and daughter, to spread the message of Buddhism. Ashoka succeeded in spreading Buddhism to the whole of South Asia and South East Asia. The Buddhist books were written and distributed among the masses. The Buddhist states were established with a massive mobilization of people of all castes into the socio-spiritual realm and also to run the state apparatus. The Buddhist state and civil societal initiatives succeeded in achieving very high levels of production. Dignity of labour of all castes was restored. Because of the massive anti-violence campaign that the Buddhist state and civil society took up, the violent Hindu structures were weakened. A large-scale willing participation of the socio-scientific forces of all castes led to the development of several historical monuments and art centers like Ajanta and Ellora. For example, huge statues across the world, from the Bamiyan Buddhas to the Sri Lankan, Tibetan and Chinese statues, were carved out in the process.

Redoubled production of food grains with the positive participation of the Buddhist monks and civilian masses advanced an economic revolution in Asia. The transport system advanced with the development of bullock carts and horse drawn buggies. That was the context in which Ashoka adopted the wheel of a bullock cart—Ashoka Chakra—as the symbol of the state. That was the period in which most of the Buddhist *viharas* were built. That was the period which may truly be called the Golden Age of the Dalit-Bahujans in ancient India. And that was the period of darkness for Hindu Brahmanism. The Hindu Brahmanic forces used all their violent methods to counter the Buddhist middle path. Yet the caste system was very much weakened by the Buddhist advance. Medical science was advanced. The first university of India—Nalanda—was established. The Brahmans of India were not pleased with these developments. They organized several attacks against all the Buddhist educational centres, as they were educating the Shudras and the Chandalas as well. They went on preaching violence as the only way out. The way the RSS, the VHP, the Bajrang Dal and the BJP are openly preaching violence ever since they killed Gandhi, killed thousands of Muslims, destroyed the Babri Masjid, killed scores of Christians in Kandhamal, Orissa—including the innocent nuns—and finally conducted the Gujarat campaign, proudly preaching the virtues of Hindutva violence, shows that their mode of violent Hinduism is at its dying phase. This violence is a part of Brahman culture—the fact that it has been unleashed upon the tribals and the Dalit-Bahujans for a long time in a systematic manner alone will lead Hinduism to its self-immolation.

Hinduism re-equipped itself in the ancient period by writing two most violent and brutally Brahman books of the time—Kautilya's *Arthashastra* and Manu's *Dharmashastra*. The titles of both these books are misleading. In reality, the former was a book of political aggrandizement of Brahmanism and the latter was a book of social aggrandizement of Brahmanism. As we examined in the chapter on intellectual *goondas*, the Brahman scholars have always written diabolical books in the name of other castes. The *Ramayana* and the *Bhagavad Gita* are two good examples of Brahmans writing books on war in the name of Valmiki and Krishna. But fortunately the most dangerous books—the *Arthashastra* and the *Dharmashastra*—were written in Brahman author's names, with a clear assignment of their self to these books and to their contents. After these books were written, the brutal Brahman state of Pushyamitra Sunga was established. This process gradually led to the establishment of the Baniya state called the Gupta kingdom.

The Brahmanic nationalist writers at the time of the freedom movement propagated this era as the Golden Age of India. It was during this period that the spiritual fascists carried out their strongest campaign to construct the indignity of labour. Occupations of all castes were not only rigidified, but they were also institutionalized to function as per the wishes of the Brahmans. The Buddhist productive ethic and egalitarian values were attacked as spiritually untenable and socially destructive.

From this period up to the campaigns of Adi Shankaracharya the most violent attacks took place on Buddhism. The most powerful religion of the world was annihilated in its own birthplace and all its *viharas* and collective and congregative worship centres were occupied violently by killing several monks. The process of occupation of the *viharas* was carried out in a manner similar to which they destroyed the historic Babri Masjid in 1992. All the Buddhist monks, women and children were killed, just as they killed thousands of Muslims in Gujarat in 2002. Whether a massively spread out religion like Hinduism, which has a vast establishment of temples, and its blindly superstitious followers will ever be obliterated is something that remains a serious doubt in the mind of a modern Dalit–Bahujan, Muslim, Buddhist, or Christian. The answer to such a doubt may be located in Indian history itself. The Indian subcontinent has seen the rise of Buddhism and its fall under Hinduism's massive assault. Similarly, the end of Hinduism in this modern phase of aspiration of equality of all castes seems to be quite decisive, even though it might be very bloody as well. All trends indicate that Hinduism is sinking within the Indian mainland.

Hindu nationalism is not the nationalism of all castes and communities. The 60 years of independent India have proved that it is essentially a *dwija* nationalism, and the Brahmans and the Baniyas profited in the nationalist period in a criminal manner. The mobilization of the Sangh Parivar and the *dwija* accumulation of wealth and power are a sure indication that one nation, one people and one culture is a slogan to hoodwink the aspirations of the Dalit–Bahujans. In order to see that the spiritual democratic religions do not mobilize them, the Brahmanic forces started attacking all the religions. Fortunately, this is a phase of globalization of all modes of life, including the spiritual mode of life as well. The Hindu nationalists are trying to impose the Brahmanic vegetarian food culture and the dead Sanskrit language on the masses who are looking towards globally integrative food, dress and linguistic cultures. This is what makes Hindu nationalism negative—it will drive them towards the death of their own religion.

THE COURSE OF END OF HINDUISM

The course of the death of Hinduism, on the surface, appears to be very difficult. For some it might appear even impossible. It has scores of basic books that construct its philosophy. During the freedom struggle and later, these books have been commented upon and propagated about at a massive scale. For the last 60 years in schools and colleges, millions of students were made to read these books as great books. A number of brain washing campaigns have been conducted through the media. The Brahmanic newspapers have been established to propagate the greatness of Brahmanism. Radio networks have been used to propagate the so-called greatness of the Hindu books, its languages and the Brahmanic culture. Now the TV networks are being used in a big way. This brainwashing process has affected the educated Dalit-Bahujan masses in a substantial manner. Since all organized religions have come into being with a discourse around the book—education—it is the educated who have continued the religious propaganda and discourse. The nationalist period used education as a tool for Hindu propaganda. Is it possible to render so many Hindu books irrelevant at this stage of Indian history? Is it possible to deconstruct the Hindu sensibility of the Dalit-Bahujans, which injected a historical inferiority complex among them?

Hinduism has thousands of temples across the country (I am referring to the temples headed by the Brahmans only). These temples have millions of floating visitors. The Shudras constitute the largest number of visitors to these Hindu temples. All these temples have enormous gold and silver wealth. The priestly castes act as a cohesive unit and because of their spiritual prowess they have been able to indoctrinate servility in the masses. Their main aim in having such an organized life is to see that other religions do not liberate the Dalit-Bahujans and their exploitative methods continue unabated. Hindu nationalism was meant to serve this very purpose. The Hindu temples are, thus, exploitative institutions. The Tirupati temple of Andhra Pradesh, the Jagannath temple of Orissa, the Guruvayur Krishna temple of Kerala and the Somnath temple of Gujarat are examples of such wealth and splendour. Most of the wealth was acquired through systematic and subtle exploitation of the socio-spiritually ignorant Dalit-Bahujan communities by the Brahman priestly class. The children of the productive masses were denied food, education and the elementary facilities of life. In the name of facilities for gods and goddesses, the Brahmans enjoyed perhaps the most luxurious life of all the priestly classes of all the religions in the world. These historical accounts need to be settled in the civil war.

How does a civil war handle such huge temples that draw the very innocent Dalit–Bahujan masses, wherein they spend all their resources for the benefit of the Brahmanic castes?

Even if we leave aside the Dalit–Bahujan temples, the Hindu temples occupy millions of acres of land. No other religion has as many temples as Hinduism has. If Hinduism ends, what happens to all these temples? The Brahmanical writers projected the history of these temples as Indian history. They had never bothered to examine the productive skills of the people. They have not treated the productive culture of the people as culture at all. Several books describe the *puja* process that goes on in the temples—that too the mere act of food consumption of the Brahman priests—as the culture of India. How is all that to be dismantled?

Before the nationalist movement, most of the Hindu temples were places of visit for the *dwija* visitors alone. They were empty structures being maintained by local rulers and visited by only the Brahmans, Baniyas and the Kshatriyas. The Dalit–Bahujans seldom visited them. The Brahmans were fed on a day-to-day basis with very good food and were given huge amounts of landed property by the local rulers to maintain their families with wealth and riches. While the Brahmans were making money through exploitation inside the temple, the Baniyas were accumulating wealth by establishing their businesses around the temples. Many Shudras also started visiting the market places near the temples. The Bhakti movement of the Shudras gave an impetus to this process. As the places surrounding the temples were slowly becoming towns and cities, these two castes became rich as they constructed their exclusive spiritual theory barring people from all other castes from entering priesthood and business. The mass contribution to the Hindu temples came from the Shudra masses through the taxes paid by them, but they did not even have the right to head temples. The Brahmans and Baniyas mobilized more and more wealth around the temples in the post-independence period by propagating the Hindu nationalist myth. It, therefore, must be understood that the Hindu temple system operates more as a centre of exploitation of the Dalit–Bahujan masses than as a centre that provides spiritual satisfaction to the Dalit–Bahujan masses. The moment the Dalit–Bahujan masses stop going to these temples, their income dries up in little time. The Brahman–Baniya economy, on its own, will collapse as a house of cards if the rug under Hinduism is pulled by the Shudras.

All over the world, religion was the source of accumulation of landed property by the priestly class. But religions such as Christanity, Islam and Buddhism reinvested the wealth accumulated by the priests in welfare activities. Hinduism did not do it in the past and is not doing it even now.

In Hinduism, it is the source of business and politics. The moment the mass trips to the Hindu shrines are reduced, the business around the temples collapses. If the productive millions stop going to the Hindu temples, the Brahman *dakshina* economy collapses. Once Hinduism is weakened at the temple, it gets weakened in the civil society, which then leads to the collapse of its control over politics. Brahmanical control over every field, therefore, begins to crumble. And as the Brahmanical control over every sphere becomes weaker and weaker, the Dalit-Bahujan masses rise. Unlike other religions, Hinduism has never given equal opportunity to all. There is no scope of a Shudra, a Dalit or a tribal to move upwards in the ladder by remaining in Hinduism. Therefore, it is also very difficult to retain them within that religion.

As Hinduism begins to collapse, the other religions begin to gain ground in equal proportion. If Buddhism grows in India, it has a legitimate right to claim all the assets of most of the old Hindu temples, as they were originally Buddhist shrines. Once the Brahmanic books are rejected at the school and college level, the mass media in the modern context of globalization has to toe the market line. As the Dalit-Bahujan consciousness begins to shift, the mass media begins to shift its position and alternative mass media begins to come into operation. The *dwijas* themselves begin to throw away their so-called sacred thread, as that would become a marker of attack in the civil war period. Let us not forget the fact that when the Brahmanic forces attack the Dalit-Bahujans, the lack of the thread on one's body serves as the marker for identification and humiliation. Many Dalit-Bahujans despise the sight of a man with a thread across his body because it symbolizes the power that a Brahman possesses vis-à-vis other castes, but the Dalit-Bahujans cannot protest against the Brahmanic castes fearing backlash. It is this thread that operates as a marker of discrimination between the Brahman and the Dalit-Bahujan. In the ensuing caste civil war, these markers will become sources of attacks and counter-attacks. Through these attacks and counter-attacks centering on these markers, the language of intellectual *goondas* would change. Only a civil war situation, with massive attacks on the so-called markers of purity, can radically change the language of purity and pollution. In the communal riots between the Hindutva forces and the Muslims, the circumcised penis and the traditional Islamic beard were markers of attack. When attacks on the Sikhs were conducted in 1984, the Sikh beard and turban became the markers of attack. When the Hindutva forces in Gujarat conducted the attacks on Christians, the cross became a marker of identity of the enemy.

MARKERS OF HEGEMONY

The *dwija* markers, unlike other religious markers, are not markers of difference. The Muslims, Christians and Sikhs bear markers of their religion to highlight their difference from other religions. But the *dwija* forces wear markers of dwijahood to humiliate the productive people, whom they describe as Hindus on one hand and humiliate on the other. The humiliation is both contemporary and historical. In other religions, all markers of religion can be used by all those who belong to that religion, whether they are rich or poor. Since the Brahmanical forces portrayed the thread around their body as divine and sacred, the Shudras and Chandalas, at different phases of history, asked for the right to bear the same markers. The Brahmanical forces responded to this demand with the most brutal of punishments. The culture of having markers of superiority for a group of people within a religion, markers that become instruments of social humiliation, can be changed only when the markers are attacked and negated. The humiliation within a particular religion, which claims vast masses to be belonging to that religion, engenders more brutal struggles. The humiliated psyche remains vengeful for a long time. Hinduism is one religion that has constructed such a deep vengeful mind in social layers, over a period of centuries.

Because of consciously constructed caste hierarchy, the *dwija* markers were never attacked, in spite of the fact that the others were denied them and at the same time humiliated for not possessing those markers. The Dalit-Bahujans miserably failed in their historical efforts to acquire the right to bear the same markers and attain equal status with the Brahmans and the Baniyas. What one fails to achieve by begging one can achieve by negating, by deconstructing and attacking that marker of superiority so that it ceases to exist. They should then be treated as markers of social barbarity. Even the whole theory of social plurality, advanced by a section of the so-called secular Brahmanic intellectuals does not realize that in a truly plural society, the cultures of difference of different groups of people must also have the social status of equality. The whole language of purity and pollution in relation to the Shudra, Dalit and Brahman cultures is a violation of the principle of social plurality. The civil war has to reframe the social discourse on all fronts.

The religious hegemony of Hindutva is different from that of other religions. The Brahmanic caste hegemony over other castes is a negation of the historical evolution of social plurality and religious equality. Social plurality essentially operates around cultural plurality. All differing cultures, irrespective of the number of people involved in that cultural system, must be given equal status. Religion should guarantee that equal status. The right to cultural autonomy in a mutually respectable cultural plurality operates on the model of right to citizenship. Irrespective of an individual's wealth, age, sex and height, the citizenship principle operates on the basis of equality. If social pluralism was to operate in its modernist democratic ethic, all caste and religious cultures and social ethics must have equal textual and socio-psychological status. For example, the Pharsees in India have a respectful and dignified social status within India. No Hindu text constructed the Pharsee cultural self as an inferior self. In all ancient Hindu texts, on the other hand, the Dalit–Bahujan caste cultures were shown as barbaric, and many modern and contemporary texts have shown the Muslim and Christian cultures as inferior as well. The Brahmanic arrogance has its roots in the caste system—a civil war alone can deconstruct that historical arrogance.

Any counter-cultural movement has to attack such markers of hegemony without any compunction. All civil wars in the world attacked the symbols of the ruling classes that constructed the social self of the working classes as unworthy of being respected. The social self of the working classes was not allowed to occupy any position of power—particularly any spiritual position. When the working class attacked all those markers of humiliation, the very history of exploitation and oppression began to undergo a radical change. The royal/feudal caps, dress codes, peculiarly made out shoes that they alone were entitled to wear, were attacked in all European civil wars. The leisure-based ruling classes all over the world built cultural symbols that dehumanize the working classes. The working classes in the civil wars repositioned their counter-cultural hegemony so that they too can acquire cultural confidence. In India, the Brahmanic markers have never faced an attack that seeks to deconstruct them. Hence there is cultural confidence among the Brahmanic forces, who know their selves are protected by the violent divine images like Brahma, Vishnu, Rama, and so on—that is why they keep on worshipping them. It is easier to continue exploiting the victimized self when the victims of exploitation are forced to worship those divine images that are complicit in their exploitation. Therefore, for the Brahmans and the Baniyas of India, it is easier to exploit the Dalit–Bahujan than the Muslims and the Christians, because the latter do not allow any exploitation in the socio-spiritual realm. It is for this reason that the Brahman–Baniyas want to continue the caste system, because it gives them enormous confidence, to continue exploitation with spiritual justification. It is this confidence that needs to be shaken in the caste civil war.

In the Indian civil war, cultural conflict remains central. The enemy's dress code, spiritual symbols, food culture, linguistic notions, modes of housing that the Brahmanic forces constructed as spiritually superior, and the interior decorations that the Brahmanic houses consist need to be critiqued in a systematic manner. The religious cultural mode of life of a community is reflected in the lifestyle of the women of the community. The Brahmanic women's dress code, make-up, life within the house, life at the spiritual space and in the civil society remain the key areas that have sustained the cultural hegemony of Brahmanism. The anti-Brahmanic civil war has to attack all that is Brahmanic and Hindu, because the entire cultural idiom of Hinduism is built in the image of the Brahman man-woman life and relations. All the Brahmanic modes of life were standardized to humiliate the productive culture and further the hegemony of the parasite culture. The image of the productive mass, their idiom, their man–woman relations, their dress code, food habits and linguistic expressions—all were constructed as spiritually unworthy and culturally unfair. The civil war must put the culture of the productive mass at a hegemonic position and degrade all that is Brahmanic. The lives of the productive masses have their own parallel to everything that is Brahmanic, but the productive masses have been forced to believe that their day-to-day cultural life is inferior, and therefore unworthy of history and public discourse.

Our detailed examination of the cultural history of the Adivasis, Chandalas and the Shudras shows that they have a more creative and productive history of science, technology, medical, engineering skills and social life processes. They have historically been unpaid teachers, subaltern scientists, productive soldiers, social doctors, subaltern feminists, social engineers, meat and milk economists, food producers, and so on. These forces constructed the modern Indian nation with their sweat and blood. The Brahmanic temple, the Brahmanic idols, the Brahmanic architecture, the Brahmanic food culture, the Brahmanic art and ideas have grown by sucking the blood of all these productive masses. In the civil war the productive masses have to claim all that is lost in Hindu Brahman history.

IS END OF HINDUISM INEVITABLE?

All great religions reformulated their own self when they faced revolutions from the oppressed social masses, but Hinduism perfected the mechanisms of suppression of all those who asked for equal rights. Hinduism essentially is the cult culture of the Brahmans and the Baniyas. A cult culture with an underdeveloped mind does not understand the meaning of social equality, let alone economic equality. The competing cultures of religions like Islam, Christianity and Buddhism and the forceful imposition of political democracy by the British have given rise to a seemingly operative democratic political system in India. The Brahmans and the Baniyas compromised with the notion of political democracy because this system would allow their hegemony to continue unabated.

Ultimately, what made the Brahmanic forces accept the present form of democracy was that it did not require them to be involved in the production process of the nation, thereby ensuring their hegemony. They linked both nationalism and political democracy to Hinduism with the help of books written by the spiritual fascists. The nationalist self was constructed around the notion of Hinduism. To keep the Hindu sentiment alive, constant communal riots were created against the Muslims and Christians. The Dalit–Bahujans were forced to a situation where they had to struggle for existence. Since the Brahmanic intellectuals have projected their own life process as Hinduism with all the primitive cults around, Hinduism has not acquired the qualities of a positive religion. In spite of such problems, the Brahmanic forces, ever since the nationalist phase, have projected Hinduism as the religion of all non-Muslims, non-Christians, non-Buddhists, and so on.

As I have mentioned earlier Ambedkar made a serious attempt to reform the Hindu religion. He attempted to make it a religion on the lines of Christianity, Islam and Buddhism. But the Brahmanic forces did not show enough maturity in restructuring the religion. Now, the only alternative left for the religion is to die, as such spiritual fascism does not contribute to the transformation and development of the Dalit–Bahujans of India. The religion also does not allow the positive science to develop within the Hindu social fold because the Hindu essence is anti-scientific. Since the Hindu ethos stood against the ethos of science that the tribals, Dalits and the Shudras developed and condemned such a scientific interaction with nature as spiritually polluting, there is no future for this nation and people if Hinduism exists for long. Historically, as Brahmanism has worked for the underdevelopment of all the Dalit–Bahujans, in this modern phase they all have to fight for the dismantling of Hinduism, as that alone paves a way for their liberation. At this historical juncture, the end of Hinduism seems to be inevitable, as its own builders have a strong death wish. A religion that does not wish for spiritual equality ends up with a death wish. The priestly Brahman caste will be responsible for the death of Hinduism in the modern period, because it is this caste that brought into existence the institution of caste in order to oppress the social masses. In the modern world, all such oppressive structures must die soon so that the oppressed masses are liberated.

Brahmanism as a social system is more dangerous than AIDS. AIDS can be destroyed by discovering a medicine, but Brahmanism will have to be destroyed only with a constant and long-term struggle against it. Brahmanism has killed millions of people in its long survival. The civil war that will take place in India will perhaps be the last major civil war in the world, which will involve the liberation of about seven hundred million people from the most primitive form of slavery, that is, spiritual slavery. The Africans and the Latin Americans were taken out of spiritual darkness during the expansion of Islam and Christianity, and also during the colonial and pre-colonial periods. But significant sections of the Indian Dalits and Adivasis and the whole of the Indian Shudras remain in spiritual darkness under the brutal suppression of Brahmanic spiritual fascism that no other people of the world have experienced. Even this dark spot of the globe, as a result of an inevitable civil war, will see the light in the future to come.

Chapter 13   Conclusion: The Post-Hindu India

The process of the end of Hinduism, as we have seen in the earlier chapter, begins a new phase, a new era in Indian history. The caste civil war that operates in various modes and forms releases enormous energy, which has been spiritually, morally and socio-politically suppressed ever since the end of Buddhism, after Adi Shankara's counter-revolution took place in India. The Brahman thinkers kept India a very backward nation and innovative thought was never allowed to develop and advance. Since the productive and creative masses were suppressed for so long, they could not come to terms with their own productive and creative energies even after the establishment of a democratic nation. The process of the end of Hinduism begins to bring the whole range of hidden energies of the Dalit–Bahujans and Adivasis of India to the fore. The end of Hinduism does not mean the end of India, as some Brahman writers and media propagandists want us to believe. In fact, the end of Hinduism means the end of spiritual fascism. Spiritual fascism suppressed rationality and sustained a system that left the body and the brain of the society undernourished, ridden with superstition, attitudes of self-negation and cultural hegemony of the anti-productive castes. The beginning of the end of Hinduism will be a new beginning for India.

The historical disengagement of Dalit–Bahujans from education began to undergo a radical change with the entry of Muslim rulers, and more substantially, with the establishment of British administration. It took a somewhat radical turn with the establishment of a democratic state with a constitution written under the leadership of the great liberator, Ambedkar. As we have seen in the previous chapters, the Hindu religion and the caste system that it brought into force destroyed the scientific temper of the social mass of India. With the end of Hinduism, the re-energization of India begins in multiple realms of Indian society. The science and technology that the productive masses nurtured for so long will take a new life.

The self-realization of the historical Dalit–Bahujan energy was not only rekindled with the entry of English education into the Dalit–Bahujan communities, but also began to grow in a social environment of equality. The post-Hindu India, as I visualize it, will undergo a radical and a re-volutionary change in a much speedier way. The spiritual fascism that the parasitic Brahmanic social forces imposed on the Indian civil society, over a period of time, will begin to be replaced by the spiritual democratic structures. The development of the world in social, economic and political fields depends very much on the spiritual democratic structures that Buddhism, Christianity and Islam have established. As I have shown in *Why I Am Not A Hindu*, though there are a number of spiritual democratic institutions like the Dalit–Bahujan spiritual practices and small religions like Judaism, Sikhism and Zoroastrianism, the future world will be shared only by three major spiritual democratic structures—Buddhism, Christianity and Islam. Hinduism as a religion, it appears, will disappear, as no fascist structure ever survives for long. Its place will be occupied by the spiritual democratic theories and practices, leading to the establishment of an egalitarian civil society in India.

WHAT IS SPIRITUAL DEMOCRACY?

Spiritual democracy is a process where the notion of God/Goddess remains accessible to all on an equal basis. Neither the spiritual books and scriptures, nor the priestly social forces can make any distinction in the relationship between God/Goddess and human beings, irrespective of their birth, race, caste, sex, food habits or language. The very notion of God/Goddess and the methods of communication with the God/Goddess must be egalitarian in nature. The race, caste, sex or language of an individual cannot become the source of inaccessibility of the divine and inequality before the divine. Of all the religions in the world, Hinduism has been the most casteist and sexist religion, which has institutionalized all forms of inequalities. The Brahman priests are the most sectarian and casteist of all the clerical classes in the world. They believe in treating all other human beings as spiritual untouchables and are instead comfortable with the spiritual fascist methods that they have evolved. They never went through a cyclic process of change. The Hindu religion is also the most superstitious religion in the world, and this superstitious nature of the religion allows the inequalities to foster.

Spiritual democracy shall not allow such a social force to survive. It must transform them by whatever means into socially positive human beings, who could do any kind of work. A spiritual democracy operates around a book that remains the reference point for all those who want to be part of it. But such a book must remain flexible regarding the basic changes in the lives and thought processes of the social masses involved, and should incorporate many changes that human beings bring about, in accordance with the times. The spiritual inequalities that are integral parts of the books written by social agencies like the Indian Brahmans must be changed to suit the historical contradictions. Neither the Vedas nor the Shastras or the Puranas of Hinduism possess any positive textual character—they never developed any positive human values, either. They do not, therefore, reflect Indian history or the collective spirit of the Indian people. This is true of all books of spiritual fascism, which cannot reflect the culture and the civilization of the productive people. The culture of the Dalit-Bahujans and Adivasis, which remains completely different from the one described in the Brahmanic books, stands as a testimony of this failing of the books in question.

Spiritual democracy came into operation with the intervention of powerful social prophets like the Buddha, Jesus Christ and Muhammad. All non-prophetic religions like Hinduism became structures for free play of violence and inhumanity. The socio-spiritual prophets are agents of moral transformation of societies. That is the reason why the religions that came to be established around prophets like the Buddha, Jesus and Muhammad constructed values that rekindled knowledge of humanism and re-established higher moral values, even if they at times faced moments of crisis. But Hinduism as a religion and the Brahmans as a priestly and intellectual class failed to do the same. They carried, instead, a brutal negativism with them. Only by establishing a spiritual democratic social order and by bringing in positive prophetic visions into their lives, will Indians be able to overcome the negative past and the burden of civilized barbarity.

Spiritual democracy integrates the socio-economic productive ethics within itself for a positive development of the society. It considers labour as an integral aspect of spirituality, thereby empowering more and more social forces involved in services that spiritual sinners like the Brahman priests of India condemned as menial, ugly and unworthy of touch. A priest who lives a life of spiritual democracy does not mind touching a leper, does not mind washing the clothes of people who remain unwashed and does not mind caring for the patients of AIDS. The Hindu Brahmans placed no value on such acts of healing, and in the process did not develop a culture that treats human beings as human beings. For a Hindu doctor, a patient's money is all that holds value, and not his life. A priest trained in spiritual democracy treats soil, dung, dust, animals and birds as worthy creations of the very same God/Goddess that he worships, and involves himself constantly in growing the plants, nursing the animals and feeding people who cannot feed themselves. They do so not out of self-interest, but because their spiritual and moral culture constantly reminds them that the divine power approves of such acts of good human beings. In a spiritual democracy, a healthy man suffers the pain of the ill, as it is essentially a suffering of the social collective. Brahmanism did not allow such a notion of the social collective to evolve in India.

If Mother Teresa is a good example of the spiritual democratic life process, the Shankaracharyas of Hinduism are good examples of spiritual fascism. All the five Shankaracharyas operating from different *pithas* are spiritual fascists. Spiritual democratic discourse disallows any space for spiritual fascism and keeps its doors fully open for the spiritual forces that are involved in the service of mankind by touching everybody and serving everybody. Spiritual democracy does not allow extreme suffering of human beings in the name of God. It does not permit violent modes of divine punishments or human images to be adored or worshipped. There is a close link between not espousing idol worship and espousing book-based prayers. In book-based religions, God remains a universal agent, accessible to everyone who prays to the God/Goddess on an equal basis—on the basis of spiritual democracy. The religions that promote idol worship remain not only socially backward but keep the state and civil society underdeveloped. Idol worship was one of the first forms of worship that evolved in the early stages of human development. Later, mass prayer became a common mode of worshiping God. I think, philosophically speaking, praying to an abstract God is a more mature act than worshipping idols. To my mind, worshipping a book/abstract thought helps an individual to conceptualize the philosophical entity of God. In contrast, while worshipping idols people focus on the physical entity. Historically speaking, the worshippers of physical entity remained backward and the worshippers of philosophical entity moved forward. The Brahman priestly class of India kept the Indian masses underdeveloped, and the socio-political system remained underdeveloped in the process. This kind of underdeveloped civil societal base does not allow even the state, which is supposed to be a very organized and advanced institution, to establish egalitarian ethic in all spheres of life.

If the first Aryan invasion took place because the indigenous Dravidian race failed to organize itself and develop enough mechanisms of self-defence to contain the violent invaders, the second and third invasions of the Pathans and the British took place because of their advanced religious and civil societal strength as opposed to the Hindu Brahmanic forces. Whereas the caste-ridden, superstitious, idol-worshipping Hindu social order was divided into various categories: touchable and untouchable, Brahmanic and non-Brahmanic castes, the Islamic and Christian societies were very well organized. This is because they had before them the highly emulatable images of Jesus Christ and Prophet Muhammad, who believed in serving the poor and the sick, and provided a model for collective living. Neither Rama nor Krishna can provide such an integrative, social service-oriented model of living. The capacity of the Hindu fundamentalist forces to butcher, rape and burn alive human beings they dislike has been witnessed in Gujarat in the year 2002—it would not be a surprise if they had killed the Buddhist monks in the past in the same way.

The continued worshipping of the idols of Brahma, Vishnu, and so on, without allowing a universal book to emerge, is an indication of an undeveloped mind. There is no positive principle containing spiritual democratic elements in either Vedic or Vedantic philosophy, because spiritual fascism in one form or the other is embedded in them. Killing human beings in the name of *dharma* is a devilish, and not a divine act. For example, the Hindu Rama and the Muslim Osama Bin Laden are two poles of spiritual violence. One is a figure of Hindu mythology, and the other derives his philosophy from the Islamic myth of *jihad*. Such forces might be adored and worshipped by certain social elements for their own historical reasons, but those who worship or adore such divine or human figures are bound to find themselves entangled in spiritual fascism. Islam can overcome Bin Laden by invoking the spirit of Muhammad, but Hinduism cannot overcome the cult of the killer Rama because it remains a cult of violence, without having evolved itself into a religion. The history of Hinduism has proved that again and again.

In a spiritual democracy, the divine figure does not need weapons to handle the world, like Rama did, nor do they want human beings to act in the manner that Osama Bin Laden did. Spiritual democracy, as the Buddha, Jesus and Muhammad in three different historical phases have shown, resolves human problems through discourse and debate, and not through violence. The divine images constructed around violence—from Brahma to Krishna—have established negative values. There is no space for such values in the realm of spiritual democracy. The values of violence in the divine discourses or in human life do not build a society that can construct a positive philosophy. Such a society can only develop a negative system of thought. We have witnessed before our own eyes how people who have internalized violence through divine means can kill those whom they conceptualize as their enemies. The maiming and murder of Dalit–Bahujans throughout history and the massacre of Muslims in Gujarat are results of such internalization of violence.

Universal social conditions operate in the realm of spiritual democracy, thereby allowing human beings to change from one faith to another or read one spiritual book and another. One communicates with God while praying in a spiritual place which no one is barred from entering—unlike the Hindu temples, where the Brahmans have prevented the Dalit–Bahujans from entering. The relationship between this God and people is democratic, and not fascist. The notion of God, as it emerged in societies plagued with the problem of class, was democratic, at least in the realm of the divine. The notion of God in a caste-ridden society on the other hand negated all the positive values of religion and led to the emergence of spiritual fascism. It rendered millions of people socially crippled and forced them to remain ignorant and poor and illiterate for centuries. The fear of spiritual death destroys all human initiatives—that is what has happened to the Dalit–Bahujan masses of India. Now, the Dalit–Bahujans are willing to obey every command of the Brahmanic forces. They have achieved a state of total self-negation. This is the essential aim of spiritual fascism, and Hinduism has achieved that in India in its long existence on this land.

A political system in itself cannot change a society conditioned by spiritual fascism. The society has to go through a process of interaction with positive spiritual democratic systems in order to build its primary confidence and create an educational base. There have been Shudra states and so-called great Shudra kings in India in the past. But they surrendered to the dictates of Hindu spiritual fascism. Hence, even now, the attainment of mere political power by the Dalit–Bahujan forces will not radically change the social basis of spiritual fascism. The spiritual fascist basis of the society must be replaced with a spiritual democratic system.

Spiritual democracy, as a philosophical system, provides one with a language of philosophical discourse in every day life. The moral philosophies of the world have emerged in the process of building up spiritual democratic ethics. Some ethics have become a part of textual discourses and some exist in the common sense knowledge of the people. Such common sense knowledge is invoked in the day-to-day life of the people. This is true for the lives of the productive masses of India. The Brahmanic forces did not integrate this common sense knowledge into their spiritual texts. Spiritual democracies have made such knowledge a part of their religious books, but Hinduism has remained a moribund fundamentalist superstitious institution, thereby never allowing the human mind to grow on positive lines. Thus, all its books reflect only the spiritual fascist knowledge of Brahmanic forces. It did not integrate the people into a cultural ethic of respecting a human being as human. Human beings who were socio-spiritually positive were condemned as culturally backward and human beings who were culturally negative were praised as people of great knowledge. All Hindu saints, sadhus and sanyasis are spiritual fascists. Knowledge in the Hindu books is turned upside down—the forthcoming spiritual democracy will have to set it in the right order.

In the new spiritual democracy, the notion of God/Goddess will come to be associated with people who produce food for all, who makes pots and take care of cattle, sheep and goat, and so on. People like the Brahmans, who treated other human beings as socio-spiritually untouchable, will be made accountable for their historical sins in the social court of human beings. The judgement of the masses will be treated as the judgement of God/Goddess, as the very notion of God/Goddess was developed in the image of humans who happen to be producers of ideas and wealth for the well-being of all human beings. The Brahmans of India have violated this law of humanity and of nature, and constructed devilish principles that denounce productive human beings as untouchable. In the spiritual democratic society they will have to pay the price of history. This is the common message of all three great builders of the world's great spiritual democratic religions—the Buddha, Christ and Muhammad.

SPIRITUAL DEMOCRACY AND FOOD CULTURE

Spiritual democracy does not discriminate between different food cultures. Spiritual fascism, for example, facilitates the hegemony of vegetarianism over the practice of eating meat or beef. In a spiritual democracy on the other hand, notions of the divine are related to all positive, health-centred food habits of the people. Neither beef nor pork is prohibited food, nor do they pose hurdles in one's becoming a priest of a temple. Hinduism destroyed the overall health of the Indian nation by spiritualizing vegetarianism. No great prophet—the Buddha, Christ or Muhammad—imposed restrictions on the food habits of people.

Only Muhammad asked his people to avoid eating pork, but even he allowed the consumption of pork under exceptional circumstances. It is possible that Muhammad came by this measure out of his concern over the consumption of human excreta by pigs. This situation, however, has changed now—the farms raising pigs have developed mechanisms to raise them purely on grain. Thus, even Muslims can overcome the classical dictum of Muhammad, as he provided several exceptions for every prohibitive dictum. All prophets constructed certain principles that survive beyond time and space, while there are other principles specific to a certain time and space that can change. Muhammad, as the last of the three great builders of the spiritual democratic institutions, had evolved more humanly practicable principles and he left a definite text that could be interpreted for more positivist evolution of the human society. He was the first feminist who worked out time and space specific man-woman relations.

Muhammad allowed a man to marry four times at a time when male members of the society were scarce in number, owing to the deaths of men in wars, and so on—in other circumstances, monogamy is the norm. By applying the same principle, we can now come to the conclusion that in opposite conditions, where more women are available against fewer men—for whatever reasons—polyandry is also spiritually valid. So far, even in the Muslim world, which follows the advice of Muhammad, the Quran has been interpreted one dimensionally to suit the interests of the patriarchal society. Thus, following Muhammad's view, this is wrong, because according to Muhammad it is the condition that determines the norm and not the other way round. If polygamy is spiritually valid in adverse situations, then so should polyandry be, while monogamy should prevail in ordinary circumstances. As Muhammad's first wife was a businesswoman herself, Islam allows any woman to take up any job. He was the first prophet who accepted the de-gendering of labour in his own lifetime. Similarly, if pigs are raised in a farm where they eat only grain, they are as eligible for human consumption as cows, camels and other animals are. This is the essence of spiritual democracy. It provides space for the progressive interpretation of religious principles, as the prophets have shown in their lifetime with their own interpretations of the spiritual democratic ethic. Prophet Muhammad opined that all human beings should dress in a manner that covers all the parts of the body. This principle was designed for the protection of the human body. The principle then was used to condition the women to cover themselves and wear the burkha. The situation in Islam, however, is bound to change, because no spiritually democratic society can allow man-woman inequalities to operate for long.

No images of gods or goddesses can be linked to exclusively meat-eating or beef-eating cultures. A human being's body and mind develops better in a composite food culture. Cultures of food have also evolved in the process of human evolution, and the religions that evolved in the same course absorbed all the different food cultures of people. Spiritual democracy endorses a composite food culture. The Chinese, Japanese and other people from the Far East eat many varieties of food that people of other geographical regions dislike. I am certain that the Christian and the Muslim people of the countries in the Far East have far more universalistic food cultures than that of the Christians and the Muslims of other continents and regions. Hinduism destroyed the collective cultural evolution of Indians. By segregating the different cultures of food, the Brahmans destroyed the possibility of the emergence of a coherent social collective in India. The emphasis that God likes only vegetarianism is a part of the process of strengthening spiritual fascism. The Hindu gods like Brahma, Vishnu and Rama and goddesses like Laxmi and Saraswati in the ancient period were eaters of beef, but the South Indian Brahman Shankaracharya transformed them into vegetarians. The Brahmans and the Baniyas as castes and Gandhi as their modern representative campaigned for a nationalist vegetarianism. As a result, the Indian agrarian economy became vegetarian, leading to a great loss of health and energy.

The Dalit–Bahujans of India kept the universal food cultures alive amidst their cultural settings. They were condemned by the Brahmanic forces as uncultured Shudras and Chandalas, which is but an instance of the truly cultured people being portrayed as uncultured while the uncultured enjoy the status of being cultured. Several Dalit–Bahujan communities, in order to overcome the social humiliation of being non-vegetarians have turned to vegetarianism, but even that could not earn them socio-spiritual equality. Only in a post-Hindu India can all the Shudras and the Chandalas turn to their universal food cultures with a sense of dignity. The universal food cultural reservoir of Dalit–Bahujans can become a great insurrectionary mechanism in the cultural development in post-Hindu India.

The process of offering food to images and idols of gods and goddesses is a process that denies food to needy human beings. Positive spiritual processes in the world thus evolved a method of offering prayer to the God and food to the needy and the poor—it is for this reason that no advanced religion allows the offering of food as a part of the spiritual process. Buddhism, Christianity and Islam do not allow the wastage of food through such means. Only Hinduism evolved a method where food is offered to the stones and wooden images, while being completely indifferent to the people who starve. A religion that continues to believe that the images of the gods and goddesses actually consume the food offered to them is not a civilized religion. Such a practice can only be said to be of a primitive cult of underdeveloped social forces. Spiritual democracy provides enough scope for the abolition of offering food to rock, steel, iron and wooden idols. It helps human beings to overcome the primitive modes of worship and transforms them into higher cultural beings who could use prayer as a method of obtaining spiritual satisfaction. The Brahmans as social forces did not allow rationalism to grow along with increased education. They combined superstition and education to construct a negative social base for religion. India, as a nation, suffers because of this negative role of education. To transform education into a positive rational socio-spiritual process of life, Brahmanism has to be abolished before it destroys the global positive ethics. Indian education system has to be de-Brahmanized through a positive means of introducing courses on dignity of labour. Reservations in all educational institutions are only the transitional means to displace Brahmanic forces in them—it is for this reason that by and large, all Brahmanic forces oppose all forms of reservation in educational institutions. As they are not positive intellectuals, they understand the dynamics of their displacement from every institution. They resist any positive change. As we have seen in the chapter 'Symptoms of Civil War and End of Hinduism', the Dalit-Bahujans should push that course to a logical end so that it leads to the end of Hinduism itself. That is the only course available to the Dalit–Bahujan masses to make their own selves dignified and to save the positive systems from Brahmanism.

IDOL WORSHIP AS UNDERDEVELOPMENT

Idol worship, whether of the Hindu mode or of the Dalit-Bahujan mode, is not only an underdeveloped version of the relationship between the humans and the divine, but also a process that denies the possibility of development of abstract thinking. The social process of reading books, of interpretation of the words and sentences written in the books handed down by the positive prophets in the process of evolution of different religions is totally absent among the Hindus and also the Dalit–Bahujans. The Dalit–Bahujans developed several positive spiritual cultural processes, modes of singing and dancing, cutting across castes. They possessed an uninhibited food culture, which included the consumption of beef, pork, meat of various kinds as well as vegetarian food. The Adivasis constantly developed new food habits. All societies can still learn from these social forces. Hindu Brahmanism did not leave anything positive for human progress. Many of the food cultures that have been destroyed and rendered completely non-existent by Hinduism need to be reworked and developed to suit the socio-economic life processes of the productive masses. Many things that have been lost must be retrieved and many things that survive with the stamp of Brahmanism need to be destroyed. The process of idol worship is one such negative aspect that the Dalit–Bahujans carry in their cultural realm.

The difference between idol worship and book-based prayer is that book-based prayer transforms every house into a centre of education through the means of religion. Religions that allowed women to read the spiritual texts to do their daily prayers would make every mother an educated person. Idol worship increases fear among people. This is particularly true when an idol worshipper is worshipping a divine image that holds a weapon (like Rama), or one that is known for its capacity to kill (like Narasimha, Durga, Kali). These images, by spilling blood, generate a sense of fear in the idol worshipper—or alternately, prepare the idol worshipper's mind to be cold and calculating and capable of great brutality. The best example is the mind of the average Brahman in India. Having worshipped the idols of the killer gods everyday, the Brahman mind has acquired several criminal qualities that would justify human brutality and ill-treatment of other human beings. When the god's image itself is presented as a killer, criminality becomes a socially acceptable condition. No caste community or individual who inflicts brutality upon other people can realize the suffering undergone by the victims. Brahmanism is an ideology of victimizers. It does not believe in learning through the experience of suffering itself, as they Brahmans themselves have never suffered—instead, they made others suffer by executing all kinds of cunning designs.

The Dalit–Bahujans, despite their enormous positive, productive and technological skills, failed to break out of their underdeveloped spiritual ethic and idol worship to move into the higher mode of book-based prayer, which would have, to a large extent, transformed the status of their literacy and education. All educational trainings are based on practice. The Brahmanic idol worship and *mantra*-based recitational culture arrested the social consciousness of the masses, binding them to idol worship and not allowing them to read any spiritual or secular book for thousands of years. In the process, they arrested the spread of education among all Shudras, Dalits and Adivasis and bound the Indian civilization to a state of primitivity. For the ideology of self-perpetuation of the Brahmans of India, the sustenance of primitivism in the society is a necessary condition. It is for this reason that they adopted recitation and not reading as a form of knowledge. As a result, the knowledge of the Brahmans in the present-day educational institutions is recitational. They did not allow the Dalit–Bahujan communities to even become a part of that recitational culture. The creative and productive masses thus remain backward in reading and writing and in elevating their scientific knowledge into written texts, where they can be transferred from one caste to another. In this process the creative energy of the nation itself has suffered.

Idol worship and the divorce of the productive masses from the practice of reading spiritual books is an ideal condition of arresting social transformation. Confining the Hindu spiritual books to Sanskritic poetry was an instrument of spiritual goondaism. Spiritual goondaism did a lot of damage in the very formation of the Hindu spiritual system. When the values of spiritual goondaism became a part of the system of modern education in India, the very notion of merit was turned upside down. A mapping of this infiltration of spiritual goondaism in the realm of modern education invariably generates discourses on the merit of the Brahmanical castes and the meritlessness of the Dalit–Bahujans, as we have witnessed in the 1990s Mandal debates and the 2006 OBC reservation debates. The Brahmanic civil society operates in the primitive mode of recitational knowledge, and does not understand what is knowledge and what is not. Since its spiritual ideology itself operates in the primitive ideology of idol worship, it cannot operate in the modern or post-modern realms in the domain of education, simply because the spiritual realm infiltrates into education as a means of culture. The childhood formations of the Brahmanic civil society condition their thinking to negate positive philosophies, even in the twenty-first century. A nation can be built as a strong nation only when the productive culture is integrated into the national culture. Hinduism as a religion and Hindu intellectual goondaism as an instrument of propaganda has so far made the nation walk on its head. While all the other spiritual societies are re-writing their codes, the Hindu spiritual society continues to hang on to primitive idol worship. Every Brahmanic intellectual occupying a space in the modern institutions has been conditioned by his Brahmanic upbringing, and therefore operates as an intellectual *goonda* with respect to the productive mass. This condition can be changed only when the primitivist Hinduism—which is on the course of its demise—actually dies.

The relationship between societies that have a spiritual democratic base and India that has a spiritual fascist base, will remain unequal. Any human being who reads a book to appeal to God will develop a more mature personality than the one who worships an idol. The culture of worshipping idols leaves one without any imaginative capacity. The absence of an abstract God allows no scope for constantly imagining His abilities—the idol thus puts an end to human imagination. It is for this reason that the Brahmanic intellectuals also did not acquire imaginative skills. The transformation of India remains very slow because its intellectual class operates as a class of *goondas*. No intellectual *goonda* can produce a higher level theory on their own. They merely read and recite the theories produced in the spiritual democratic societies. It was this intellectual goondaism that stalled the basic transformation of India when all the spiritual democratic societies were transforming over time.

Idol worship keeps people spiritually ignorant. It is impossible to interpret the discourses that are generated in the social communities that practice idol worship because idol worship does not leave any scope for new thinking. The first human being who fought idol worship in the world was Isaiah. After him it was the Buddha. Jesus Christ and Muhammad followed that tradition. The Indian Brahmans negated this evolutionary process and stuck themselves to the pre-Isaiah mode of idol worship. If any Shudra opposed idol worship, such a person was brutally done away with. Their books—the *Rigveda* to the *Bhagavad Gita*—were full of descriptions of the physical elements of their war heroes, whose images could be easily worked out into idols. These books reflect only the spiritual fascist tradition of the Aryans and not the spiritual proto-democratic traditions of the Indian people. The positive socio-spiritual ethics of the Indian masses—as we have seen in the preceding chapters of this book—are the true upholders of the culture of the Indian people, which has evolved for over a thousand years. But even among them, there is no culture of abstract thinking because of their adherence to the primitive practice of idol worship. If these masses overcome the practice of worshipping the idols of their gods and goddesses as well as the gods of Hindu Brahmanism, they can evolve into one of the most powerful communities of the world.

SPIRITUAL DEMOCRACY AND MARRIAGE SYSTEM

Modern marriage system of all societies is, by and large, conditioned by the culture of religious institutions that govern those societies. Unless the marriage system is also democratized, that is, it is based on the choice of young men and women, the family relations would not get democratized. If family as a primary institution of life is not democratized the civil society would not get democratized. Amongst Hindus and Muslims most of the marriages are arranged by the parents. The girl and the boy do not play any significant role in this decision. Since the spiritual fascist culture of Hinduism revolves around caste, and the marriage market operates within the boundaries of caste, this has a long-term impact on the mental and physical growth of people who live in the Hindu caste and marriage system.

Spiritual fascism has imbued the system of marriage with negative values. It has become a cultural noose around people's necks. The marriage system has become centred around caste and *gotra*, and the choice of the bride and the groom plays no role at all. Spiritual fascism has not allowed rational choice to operate in the marital relationship of men and women. All the positive marriage mechanisms that evolved in different tribal communities were negated once they entered the multi-tribe and multi-caste village systems that were governed by the Brahmanic ideology. Since the caste system is central to spiritual fascism, it sought to sustain that system by abolishing the process of marriage by choice that exists in many small spiritual democratic structures. The mechanisms that abolished forms of choice marriage in India were worked out by the Brahmanic forces, as they could not have sustained the caste system without that arrangement. Spiritual fascism brought in *sati*, child marriage and permanent widowhood in order to establish permanent authority of the husband over the wife in life as well as death. In the modern times, though many Brahmanical reformers have tried to abolish some aspects of the negative marriage system—*sati*, child marriage—but since they all adhered to the basic tents of spiritual fascism, the caste-centred marriage system remains intact.

The post-Hindu society needs to work out its marriage forms in a creative manner. Though the notion of love marriage has been talked about, the concept of love is mythical. The only objective way of abolishing caste-centred marriage is to adopt various methods of marriage by choice. However, the scope for marriage by choice increases only when spiritual fascism begins to die. Along with dismantling boundaries of caste, the food culture of people should also reach the universal level. It is possible for individual likes and dislikes to exist within the large, universally available family-level food culture—individual choices of food do not create disharmony in family relationships in the way that spiritually-sanctioned segregation of food cultures does. This segregation of food cultures of different communities conditions the tastes of the children and the youth to be accustomed to differing food habits, customs and cultures. Thus, the table fellowship between individuals is restricted. Once the table fellowship is restricted or banned, a free space for the social interaction of young minds is closed. This closes all avenues of marriages of choice.

The selection of partners for marriage and friendship between young men and women requires a space where they can constantly interact. Spiritual democratic institutions of similar belief would provide such a meeting ground. Though schools and colleges play their own role in providing a ground for choice-making, the minds that are brought up in an environment of spiritual fascism are not helped very much by school and college-level interactions. Furthermore, a large number of young people in India do not receive school and college education, even in the twenty-first century. The spiritual place is the best ground of interaction for people in villages and urban spaces. Since the spiritual realm is what influences culture in the most powerful way, there is no equivalent alternative to spiritual democracy in India, which provides the maximum choice in many aspects of life, and marriage in particular.

LIFE STYLES AND SPIRITUAL DEMOCRACY

Spiritual democracy allows enormous freedom in the dress code of people. Most of the dress codes were evolved to suit different geographical conditions. But the Hindu religious thought worked out certain modes of dress codes that were very oppressive and socially irrelevant. The Hindu *sanyasis* and priests adopted semi-nakedness as the spiritual dress code. Sometimes a *sanyasi* or a Hindu priest lives around temples with just a loincloth around his waist and keeps the rest of the body naked. This is a very repulsive dress code for a priest in a public place. No divine force ordained that a priest should not be fully dressed. The Hindu priestly class did not bother about the protection of one's body and the social dignity of men and women. The *sari*, in case of a woman, is an undignified dress as some parts of the body remains uncovered. In winter, such a mode of dressing does not protect women's body at all. Second, this dress code was meant to construct the figure of a Hindu woman who would be a sexual doll in the hands of Hindu men. Though Islam has provided full dresses for men and women (*kameez* and *pyjama*), the fundamentalist imposition of the *burkha* and the confinement of the lifestyles of women goes against the spiritual democratic ethic of the modern world. Is it spiritually wrong for women to wear trousers and shirts, as men do? What is ethically valid for men is also ethically valid for women. God does not condition the human dress code—neither does he discriminate between men and women, even in terms of dress code. No spiritual book of Buddhism, Christianity or Islam prescribes any such dress code for women or men. If a religion keeps its priests or people semi-naked or naked, then it cannot be modernized.

God is an entity of civilizational progress not primitivism. But this progressive essence of God is missing in Hinduism. The Hindu books are not spiritual books, and the Brahmanic forces wrote them in the interest of their own patriarchal Brahmanism. Hence, whatever is written in the Hindu books cannot be taken to be spiritually valid at all. The Hindu books are a byproduct of spiritual fascist minds. A thorough deconstruction of that mind has to take place. Spiritual democracy allows freedom in dress patterns. The post-Hindu India will have to evolve many such dress codes. Symptoms of such patterns can already been seen in India today.

For the dress code, spiritual fascism conditioned the hairstyles of men and women in a spiritually fascistic manner. The Brahmanic priestly class in the ancient period—in pre-Buddhist days—did not believe in the practice of cutting one's hair or shaving one's head. The Brahman *sanyasis* roamed about with their long, unwashed, dirty hair. We have seen their prototypes in the Hindu Kumbha Melas, where the *sanyasis'* dragged their hair across the ground while displaying their uncovered bodies. Many of them had rubbed ash all over their bodies. It was an ugly sight and a display of spiritual barbarity. Normally, the apostle's image is projected onto that of the God. The Hindu Brahmanic desire for a semi-naked self is projected onto the Hindu gods. Hence the images of the Hindu gods appear rich and semi-naked. There is hardly any scope for creative transformation of the image of God in Hinduism. The Hindu God, thus, is a killer, a semi-naked, a sexist and a patriarchal fundamentalist being. The relation between Hindu men and women is unequal and uncivilized.

Spiritual fascism developed a code for female dress style and hairstyle to suit the male taste, demanding that they wear clothes that expose and keep their hair uncut and long. At the same time, the Brahmanic men who started interaction with the West adopted the European style of short hair. A so-called secular Brahman lives a spiritual life of idol worship and intellectually remains within the realm of recitation. He adopts the Euro-American lifestyle on the outside, but the inner self remains Brahmanic. Primitivism in mental framework and modernism in outward appearance is a part of the cultural deceptivity of Brahmanism. It uses the scientific skills of the Dalit–Bahujan mass for its own well-being, but at the same time denies it legitimacy. We know very well that no spiritual democratic text constructed a rigid code of dress style or hairstyle of men and women. The whole evolution of the hair-cutting science of the barbers shows that human beings remain healthy and beautiful with a trim hairstyle. This principle applies to both men and women. Similarly, the washing of clothes by the Chakalis is used by the Brahmans for their well-being, but the science of washing is denied the legitimacy it deserves.

The concept of beauty is a constructed one. The notions of beauty change from one social condition to another. Buddhism and Sikhism espoused different hairstyles, as a part of their spiritual life. The Buddhists, just like the Jain tradition, adopted the practice of shaving the head and face of men and women (only the head for women) in order to expand the notion of cleanliness of the body. Hinduism, on the other hand, adopted the style of full-grown hair with an unshaven face as sainthood. But the temple priests would have a clean shaven head with a *pilak* (tuft of hair) at the back of the head. All the Shankaracharyas adopted the priestly Hindu hairstyle as a necessary spiritual condition. Every thing has a fixed form. The interesting thing is that even if a Shudra, Dalit or an Adivasi is willing to adopt a similar hairstyle, they will not be allowed to head the spiritual institutions. Spiritual fascism changes norms from caste to caste and community to community.

Women's hairstyle in India was conditioned by spiritual fascism, which ensued the dictate that they should have long hair as a part of Hindu spirituality. Over a period of time, a notion has been developed that long hair for women is also a part of the Hindu notion of beauty. Thus, the hairstyles of people now have both the dimension of spirituality and of beauty. These assumptions are both historically and culturally wrong. Both Indira Gandhi and Mayavati have proved the falsity of these assumptions, underlining the fact that a short haircut is not only acceptable but also has enormous value in terms of beauty.

The barbers, with their tremendous knowledge of human health, would tell us that short hair has enormous significance for our health. Spiritual democracy allows human beings to learn from the positive and negative experiences of communities around the world. In China, the new dress code for women following the same style as men and short haircut seems to have improved the condition of women's health. Most of the women in the West—where the Christian ethic operates—have been opting for similar styles. Plurality in dress codes and hairstyles is common in several countries. This includes the spiritual domain as well. Take, for example, the dress code or hair style of a Christian pastor while preaching from the pulpit. He can preach in any dress and wear any hairstyle he desires. This is not possible in Hindu religion because every thing is pre-determined and controlled by a caste—the Brahmans. That keeps every thing undemocratic and underdeveloped. Individualism has no place in this spiritual operation. Is the adoption of a plural lifestyle spiritually wrong? No God or Goddess put any condition for dress codes of men and women or their hairstyles. All dress codes and hairstyles have been humanly constructed. All the dress codes and hairstyles that create oppressive conditions for women and men should be allowed to transform into egalitarian modes. Very visible distinctions between men and women in dress codes and hairstyles impose patriarchal distinctions in the work ethic and behaviour patterns of men and women. Egalitarian lifestyles also improved the labour efficiency of women in public spaces. In post-Hindu ethical systems, plural lifestyles will also acquire spiritual legitimacy.

The post-Hindu women will go for a radical restructuring of their dress codes and hairstyles so that they do not need to spend a lot of time in the maintenance of their bodies. While Hinduism remains primitive in conditioning women, Islam too remains medievalist in its suppression of women. Spiritual democracy liberates women in several ways. Thus, the deepening of spiritual democratic ethics within religious communities over the world may resolve many issues that the feminist discourse has raised. The question of sexual division of labour could also be sorted out without much difficulty if the spiritual democratic process is strengthened in the civil societal structures. The world has not overcome the man–woman differences because of the embedded patriarchal structures within the religious societies. Spiritual democratic religions like Buddhism, Christianity and Islam will have to wage internal struggles to change their existing undemocratic systems, lifestyles, and so on. Hinduism has no ability to internally reform itself—it can neither resolve caste inequality nor liberate women in a meaningful way, and can therefore only slowly wither away.

The control of the female sexuality by the male forces in the name of spirituality does not have any divine spiritual sanction. The guidelines of the great prophets are so flexible that as times change, the lifestyles of the people must change. The notion that men and women are unequal is a patriarchal construction. Spiritual fascism went further and took away the priestly class/caste from all modes of productive activity and positive man–woman relations. Spiritual democracy opposes the anti-production values of all spiritual fascist forces. For both men and women, constant interaction with nature—which has enormous productive ability—alone improves the knowledge system of people. In addition, the constant and creative interaction within the civil society between men and women lays the foundation for new thinking. When a religion establishes the condition that those who interact with production cannot become priests, that religion has a tendency to de-link production and spirituality. Such a religion cannot help the society to develop its economic conditions as well. Nor does such a religion allow any space for meaningful dialogue between sexes within the social womb of that religion. The social masses like the

Indian Dalit–Bahujans, who suffered social horrors because of a religion like Hinduism, must realize that they need to make a comparative study of the spiritual democratic structures and the spiritual fascist structures that came into existence in various parts of the world. People must adopt democratic modes of thinking and adaptability so that at each stage they can reformulate their being.

SCIENCE AND SPIRITUAL DEMOCRACY

Spiritual democracy leads to a synthesis among science, technology and spiritualism. Religions like Christianity and Buddhism have been through several ups and downs in history and have allowed science and technology to develop. The Islamic societies experimented in the realm of science and technological innovations in their early stages, but they gradually descended into stagnation. The Hindu society, of course, never allowed any scientific innovation to take place because of its spiritual fascist essence and also because of the social stagnation that was a direct result of the caste system. As I had mentioned in the introduction if we divide the globe into four spiritual-cultural worlds and examine how spiritualism and science have mediated with one another in history, we can come to an understanding of the place of the Hindu world in the realm of science and technology.

The far-eastern world belongs to the Buddhist cultural realm. This was the first spiritual world that moved away from the culture of idol worship. Though the Buddhists worship the image of Buddha, their mode of spirituality moved away from the Hindu mode of primitive multiple idol worship and superstition. It expanded from India to the far-east with Ashoka's evangelical campaign on Buddhism. From China, it spread to several far-eastern countries. The earliest scientific discoveries took place in the Buddhist world.

The West—starting from Israel and moving upwards to Europe and America—and parts of Africa belong to the Christian spiritual cultural realm. This is the second world that established a firm spiritual ideology of human organization that began to synthesize higher science with spirituality. The middle-east, from Saudi Arabia to Indonesia, belongs to the Islamic cultural realm. This is the third spiritual world that had established its links with its past and repositioned the tribal communities living in deserts in relation to God, book and science. India and Nepal belong to the fourth world, the Hindu cultural realm, which continued to exist in multiple forms of spiritual primitivism and continued to operate within the realm of the anti-science spiritual organization of Brahmanism, caste and untouchability.

The Buddhist world—China—discovered the compass, paper, the printing machine and gunpowder in the earliest phase of scientific discoveries. Japan added other modes of scientific and technological knowledge in subsequent years in competition with China. The Christian and Islamic expansionists made use of the Buddhist discoveries of the printing machine and gunpowder to expand and organize their spiritual messages. Of course, in the process they also expanded their empires. Their spiritual and political expansion was based on their usage of science and technology in every field of life. Evangelism, which is a positive ideology of inclusive spiritualism, spread across the world as a part of this process. Quite interestingly, when Christianity and Islam started expanding, Buddhism died in India. It also did not adopt an aggressive evangelical posture in other countries. The Hindu primitivism and anti-science spiritual fascism was responsible for the confinement of Hinduism within India and Nepal. After Christianity stabilized in Europe, though with some tension, it allowed modern science to grow alongside organized religion. Starting with the discoveries of Copernicus, Galileo and Newton, their discoveries moved on to the discovery of electricity, the radio, locomotives, the aeroplane, the computer and the modern chip. During the protestant revolution many people were persecuted who argued against the authority of the Church. However, because of these movements many leaders like Martin Luther, and so on, emerged. This led to the re-interpretation of the Bible. Hindu religious texts like *Rigveda and Bhagavad Gita* have not been scrutinized so minutely. In the Hindu society very few scientific discoveries took place, and whatever discoveries were made by the Dalit–Bahujans remained stagnant because of spiritual fascism.

The Islamic world began its journey of mediating with science by developing the science of stitching clothes and discovering the social science of the ancient texts of the Greeks. The Islamic world also developed a strong culture of honest enterpreneurship, while upholding an egalitarian spiritual value. The greatest contribution of the Islamic discoverers is the discovery of oil in the sandy deserts. Once the Islamic world discovered oil in its most unproductive lands, the face of the earth changed quite radically. In business and exchange of money, the Islamic world's contribution is interest free exchange of liquid cash and egalitarian exchange of goods and commodities. As of now, the Islamic world is in a stagnant position as it became rigid in its interpretation of the Quran.

As opposed to all these discoveries, the Hindu world remained completely anti-science. The Brahman scholars neither became adventurers nor allowed any adventurous mind to emerge from the Shudras, Dalits and the Adivasis. The Hindu society has not produced any major scientist or thinker whose research has influenced the global knowledge system. We can get an idea of how India as a Hindu nation, without the intervention of Islamic and Christian culture in the early and late modern periods, would have fared if we compare India with the purely Hindu Nepal. Since the Islamic and the British rulers of India de-Brahmanized the nation in certain areas, India is in a slightly better position than Nepal. However, even the post-colonial Indian Brahmanic mind remains uncreative and dependent on Christian and Islamic thought with a false consciousness of its own merit. Even now, it remains so unscientific and anti-egalitarian that it refuses to learn from the productive people of India. Though its knowledge is based on imitation, it believes in its own excellence, when, in fact, it does not understand that scientific excellence and Brahmanism are mutually exclusive of each other. Indigenous science and technology can develop to the stage of self-discoveries only in the post-Hindu phase, where the Dalit–Bahujan forces will occupy all the centres of education.

The Hindu Brahmans, so far, have not produced path-breaking scientific experiments within their own social realm. They adopted the results of scientific experiments that the Christian, Buddhist and the Islamic societies developed. In a society where a religion seeks to instutionalize inequality and anti-productive ethics by constructing something like the caste system, an autonomous civil societal ground for scientific experiments cannot be created. The fact that many great scientists were also deeply spiritual people living in the spiritual democratic civil societies is a good source of understanding this relationship. No society can construct an innovative social base for great discoveries unless the foundation of that society is structured on spiritual democracy. The Hindu priests, including the Shankaracharyas, use computers and cell phones, but they cannot prepare a social ground for the discovery of such advanced technology. A mind that believes in human untouchability cannot create an educational ground for the Hindu children to learn scientific thinking in the *muttas* and the temples. Even the secular institutions controlled by the Brahmanic forces cannot produce the knowledge of basic science. As I have shown in earlier chapters, if those who have constructed the scientific base of India are seen as untouchable in socio-spiritual realms and unworthy in the educational realm there is no way in which basic science can develop in India.

Any Hindu man or woman who has received some recognition in the field of science and literature was educated in English medium schools. But even then, the Brahmanic training of their childhood worked to keep them in an underdeveloped scientific culture. As a result, many of them operate as intellectual *goondas* as they do not have any respect for productive science. This fact has been established during the nationalist period, the 1990 Mandal struggle and in all the debates on caste and race, including the most recent, 2006, OBC reservation debate. Unless these intellectual *goondas* are marginalized in every sphere of life, they will not allow indigenous science to grow.

The scope for the development of science and technology lies in the creative interaction of spirituality, productivity and scientificity. Hinduism, as a religion, negated all positive interactions with these three processes. The fact that no child trained in the production system, with a positive interaction with nature, was allowed to become the head of a temple or of a spiritual centre is enough indication that the Hindu religion has no ability to synthesize human creativity, religion and scientificity. The Hindu temple institutionalized the values of greed and gluttony, without any respect for productivity. This is the reason why the children of the Adivasis, Dalits and the Shudras were not allowed to head the temples or *muttas*. Many Shudra leaders have become chief ministers and even the prime minister, but even their children do not have the right to become a priest in the Hindu temples. Though the Dalit–Bahujan productive cultures are positive cultures that developed the embryonic science and technology systems of India, they have been conditioned by illiteracy and Brahmanic hierarchical culture. The Brahmanic forces did this by a systemic denial of education to the Dalit–Bahujans. No advanced system of knowledge was synthesized in India because of Hinduism as a controlling agency. Globally recognizable civilizational systems have not developed in India. As of now, the Dalit–Bahujans are in the process of destroying the Hindu ethic. They are expanding the social base of spiritual democracy and scientificity. If the Hindu–Brahmanic obstacle is removed, the productive social mass shall acquire an educated and enlightened mind that can synthesize spiritualism, productivity and scientificity.

SPIRITUAL DEMOCRACY AND POLITICAL DEMOCRACY

While political democracy has its roots in tribal republicanism, the actual establishment of political democracy took place where spiritual democratic practises were established as a civil societal norm. The actual establishment of its political democracy in its modern form was based on the ethics of spiritual democracy, which became an integral part of the modern notion of democracy. The modern democratic process was institutionalized in the West because of the fact that the people who experienced spiritual democracy in the church became intolerant of social and political in-equalities, both in the state and the civil society. The slave and the master were equals in the church. The church and the Biblical language showed them that the notion of equality before God was the essence of Godhood, and therefore, a new understanding of egalitarianism in law emerged in the society. Thus, the roots of rule of law could be traced back to spiritual democratic practices in the Western churches. If the Bible was the first book in the world to say that all men (and in this it was patriarchal) are equal before God, the *Rigveda* is the first book to say that God created all men (even within the patriarchal social system) unequal. The Brahmans, the Kshatriyas, the Vaishyas and the Shudras were constructed as unequals in the divine book of the Hindus. Oddly, God himself was a Brahman who decided who should be at the feet and who should be at the head. As I said, the roots of spiritual fascism lay here in this so-called 'spiritual' book. The Quran, that came several centuries later, also declared that all men (Islam too was patriarchal in nature) are equal before Allah (God). But the Islamic world did not go for political democracy, as the Islamic religion did not allow serious internal debate within the religion. Thus, a spiritual society that does not allow contending ideas to reformulate the state and civil society would not allow scientific experiments to take place in that society. That is why Islam could not compete with Christianity. However, Islam can reform itself if it overcomes these lacunas. In Hinduism there is no scope for improvement because it is a spiritual fascist religion and there is no scope for individualism in it. The pre-condition of the creation of a world of equality is the abolition of Hinduism, as that established the principle of divine inequality.

In India, the believers and practitioners of spiritual democracy (the Britishers were Anglican Christians) superimposed political democracy upon the country. The contradiction between a spiritual fascist civil society and political democracy has been expressed time and again. Once the spir-itual fascists come to power, even through the means of popular election, they can easily undo political democracy, as Hitler did in Germany. Such attempts are afoot on everyday basis but the masses are resisting them with great difficulty. Political democracy operating upon a spiritual fascist social base may collapse any moment. It is a historically verifiable fact that political democracy stuck its roots in nations where spiritual democracy operates at the base of the society. In India, the spiritual fascists are very unhappy with the political democratic system coming into operation as it begins to raise fundamental questions with regard to the very structure of spiritual fascism itself. Thus, the post-Hindu India will have to safeguard the political democracy that the colonial rulers, with their background of spiritual democracy and humanism, have handed down to us. For the last 60 years, political democracy survived in India because of the Dalit–Bahujans, who have a strong desire for democratic equality, and because of the Muslim and the Christian minorities who had to support the democratic institutions because the spiritual fascists might establish a fascist state. In this respect the Indian Muslims are different. They have a close linkage with their historical blood brothers and sisters—the Dalit–Bahujans. The spiritual fascists are always opposed to political democracy, because they perceive it as essentially dangerous to their interests. They see it as an impracticable system because at some stage their hegemony, even in the Hindu spiritual realm, will be overthrown.

The recent developments indicate that the spiritual fascists, social smugglers and the intellectual *goondas* will always declare that what truly matters to them is their faith in spiritual fascist practices, and not in the democratic state and the rule of law. The spiritual fascists declared a war on the Muslims and the Christians in order to destroy the fragile spiritual democratic base that these communities have provided to Indian political democracy. The intellectual *goondas* thus have repeatedly claimed that the productive castes have no merit. Though political democracy survives with the strong support of the Dalit–Bahujans, the Adivasis, the Muslims and the Christians in India, it has a weak base in the spiritual and intellectual realms.

Once the Muslims, who are themselves non-believers in the tradition of political democracy, move away from voting out of fear of riots that happen on the eve of every election, the others will also withdraw their support to the political democratic structures. Mass consciousness in the Indian villages is still under the control of Brahmanism to a large extent—but as we have seen in the preceding chapter, if there is a caste civil war, the Indian democracy will be protected. A civil war is inevitable. The twenty-first century is moving towards that direction. The incidents of the last leg of twentieth century—particularly the Mandal and the anti-Mandal debates and the OBC reservation debate of 2006 and Gujarat and Kandhamal carnages have shown the direction.

THE AGENDA OF POST-HINDU INDIA

The first major agenda of post-Hindu India is to build a ground-level spiritual democratic basis. For this the Dalit–Bahujans of India have to move towards a religious structure that guarantees their right to spiritual equality and move into systems that guarantee equal spiritual rights. For that, the

Dalit-Bahujan civil society must muster the courage and confidence to fight Brahmanism and idol worshipping within themselves, because the Dalit-Bahujan castes have also not moved out of Brahmanical idol worship. Without moving away from the primitive cult culture of idol worship and slowly entering into positive book-based prayer system, the Dalit-Bahujan society cannot challenge Hindu Brahmanism. Dalit-Bahujan illiteracy, ignorance and bondage to Brahmanism will not be demolished unless it realizes the organic strength of its scientific and technological systems. Though the Dalit-Bahujan food culture, work culture and democratic man-woman relationships work as a positive social base, in order to build India in their own image, they should move into an advanced spiritual democratic system. Unless they do that, they cannot realize their inner potential and cannot displace the Brahmanic forces in all walks of life.

The Brahman scholars put a trap around the Dalit-Bahujan scholars by projecting a dead language like Sanskrit as the language of Indian culture and civilization. In fact, the entire Shudra and Chandala societies and their histories do not exist in any Sanskrit text. They need to be constructed anew. For that, English is the best-suited language, as it provides us with the global methodological experience and also communicates whatever we write across the globe. The Dalit-Bahujan scholars should also have global exposure in order to unleash their creative faculties. This will also help in liberating the Dalit-Bahujan masses from the shackles of spiritual fascism.

The oppressed people must choose a language that changes the social position of the oppressors and the oppressed. If all the children of the Dalit-Bahujans learn English, they can synthesize their productive knowledge with higher science and technology. The Brahmanic writers would say that such a step would be dangerous for the nation, for our languages and our culture. But if one asks them why their own children are learning English from the age of three, they are shocked because their design has been exposed. The moment they realize that their Hinduism is going to die and the Indian masses are going to embrace spiritual democratic systems, their designs begin to crumble. The Dalit-Bahujan intellectuals need to play an important role in promoting the English language amongst the masses. Spiritual fascism would begin to end when English becomes a mass language.

The food cultures that the tribals have evolved, the scientific processes that the Dalits have worked out, the productive skills that the Shudra/OBCs have developed will gain a different basis in post-Hindu India. Synthesization of their knowledge systems with global scientific knowledge systems will not only elevate their status but will also change their socio-economic position altogether. As we have repeatedly discussed, the Brahmanical Hinduism has forced vegetarianism on the nation. But that goes against the history of the Adivasis, Shudras and the Chandalas. Even now, these masses enjoy beef, pork and other kinds of meat, but they have lost the courage to speak about it. They have lost the courage to speak proudly about their own culture. As their food culture gets synchronized with that of the larger world, they can declare their food cultures as far more superior than the food culture of the Brahmanic Hindus. At the same time, they can also learn lessons in cooking, eating and maintaining a clean environment from the global cultures.

Modern spirituality has to combine itself with scientificity if the spiritual institutions have to run on spirituo-scientific lines. A religion that does not teach its members how to be clean and how to work its institutional structures on modern lines makes its people second grade citizens of the globe. A religion that remains so patriarchal that its men do not even learn to wash their plates and do not even think of washing their own clothes can only reinforce patriarchy of the modern type. Whether a socio-spiritual domain is anarchic or not must be judged on the basis of the productivity of that society. Normally, a lazy society characterizes dynamic societies as anarchic. We can see the Brahmanic people propagating such a lazy discourse regarding the West now. But in terms of knowledge of socio-spiritual, economic and cultural life processes, we must examine how the West combined spiritual democracy, social democracy and political democracy.

We see in our own lifetime that the most unproductive Brahmanic social force attacks the Dalit–Bahujan male–female relations that operate in the productive fields, in the village environment, in the cultural practices where men and women dance together, as anarchic. Brahmanism taught Indians to see the relationship between man and woman only in terms of sex. But it never understood that the relationship between man and woman has more to it than the sexual relationship—it is also about the production of collective ideas, of spiritual and social ideas, and goods and commodities for the survival of the society. The sexual relations are biological, innate and procreative, but they do not begin to operate between every man and woman the moment they interact intimately on socio-cultural and economic terrains. Christianity has come to understand the broad contours of these relationships much better than any other religion in the world today. If the Christian world was anarchic, it could not have produced so many dedicated and committed generators of wealth and ideas in all fields—science, engineering, medicine, social science and human values.

A positive religion constructs positive institutions that allow all kinds of experiments. It might produce in the process some negative individuals and social forces that oppose such positive human experiments, but it will slowly and surely overcome such individuals and institutions. Hinduism has always remained the enemy of critical theory, so much so that it did not produce a single critical theoretician in its entire history. The post-Hindu India will produce an array of theoretical and scientific thoughts. India then will be in the race for equality with all the far-eastern and Western countries.

ECONOMIC DEVELOPMENT

Economic development is based on the condition of the mind of the people involved in the process of development. The spiritual realm helps to frame one's mind, either towards the direction of development or as an impediment in the process of development. Spiritual democracy allows the society to advance, even in economic spheres. On the contrary, spiritual fascism does not allow the society to advance in economic spheres.

It has been established that historically, the Buddhist countries have had a combination of the principle of welfare with that of monarchy, and that has been done in India during Ashoka's time. After that period, the Indian subcontinent became a nation centred on Hindu spirituality, and it slowly became a stagnant country, as the Hindu spiritual authorities consistently remained anti-production and anti-humanitarian. The Hindu process of life did not believe in the distribution of any spiritual resources. It went against the building of the scientific temper of the people. The Buddhist countries like China, Japan, and so on, gradually expanded the Buddhist positive spiritual ethic and scientific interaction with nature. One can see the striking contrast between the Buddhist China and Japan on the one hand and the Hindu India and Nepal on the other. From the days of the discovery of gunpowder to the experiment of Cultural Revolution in China, the interaction between the spiritual democratic realm and the development of socio-economic thought has been inter-linked. But as Ambedkar pointed out, Buddhism did not become a book-based religion that could be a mediator between spirituality and science. With the composition of the Bible as the first book of religion, that too in prose which could be understood by all human beings who could read, the role of religion in human life underwent a radical shift. The religious democratic process from that time became an agent of economic development.

The Bible, quite interestingly, talks about all aspects of life. A major portion of it discusses economic activities like sheep-breeding, cattle-rearing, pot making, carpentry, leatherwork, fishing, cultivating the land, and so on. For the first time in human history, it put labour in the centre of spiritual life. Here, God was involved in producing wealth by doing productive work. Thus, he was a liberator of the oppressed classes and the slaves. The Bible condemned the exploitative rich as unworthy people who cannot go to heaven. With the Bible's denunciation, the exploiters and the vulgarly rich began to be seen as sinners. Hinduism developed a very opposite notion of wealth. Social smugglers like the Baniyas and spiritual fascists like the Brahmans, however rich they might be, are seen as divinely ordained to be rich, and the poorer communities, like the Dalits, Adivasis and the Shudras have been condemned as sufferers of their *karma*. While Christianity seeks to provide enough scope for the poor to be liberated, Hinduism has tied the poor down to be poor forever. The Quran, like the Bible, provided the poor enough scope to become rich. Even a bitter critic of Christianity like Karl Marx had to admit in his famous book, *Economic and Philosophical Manuscripts of 1844* , that in the period of the development of capitalism, the owners of capital were the liberated slaves of yesteryears. He said,

> But mindful of their contrasting origin, of their line of decent, the landowner knows the capitalist as his insolent, liberated, enriched slave of yesterday and sees himself as capitalist who is threatened by him. The capitalist knows the landowner as the idle, cruel, egoistical master of yesterday...

Though Marx attributes that change to the industry, the social root of that change lies in the spiritual democratic ethic that Christianity established. The life of Jesus as a hardworking carpenter was a symbol of the possibility of the liberation of slaves and of the building up of an economy which attributes spiritual dignity to labour. Hinduism, till today, has not allowed a single Dalit-Bahujan slave to be liberated, and labour, which is the real capital hidden in the human body, remains spiritually undignified and disrespectful.

The struggle for the establishment of spiritual democracy and a constant struggle to develop the material resources of life shifted from Asia to Europe with the establishment and expansion of Christianity in Europe. The spiritual democratic environment and the continuous reading of the Bible went on changing the relationship between the slaves and the masters, between the feudal lords and the serfs. The Church began to draw slaves and serfs into its fold by changing the social relations in a big way. In this process, the historically hardworking and oppressed forces gained social status. They participated in the process of production, with more and more enthusiasm, and won over nature in such cold terrains as that of Europe and America. The struggle against oppressive nature and oppressive human beings who used and interpreted the Bible for their advantage went hand in hand. After the seventh century the Biblical societies were suffering from stagnation within the Christian spiritual realm as there emerged many selfish forces within that realm. However, it had to undergo a radical restructuring with the emergence of Islam, which tried to combine radical development and total spiritual fusion of people. To overcome that challenge, the Christian spiritual realm underwent a revolution by allowing Machiavelli, Copernicus, Newton, Einstein, Darwin, Marx and several other radical thinkers to construct a secular philosophy, economic thought and scientific vision to transform the European society.

It is this combination of spiritual democracy and socio-economic and political thought that made the Western society what it is today. Most of the scientists read and re-read and interpreted and re-interpreted the Bible to work out the science of development. The Bible, as a book of spiritual democracy, and Jesus Christ as a supporter of equality, combined with the dignity of labour lead to enormous discoveries by the organic intellectuals who came from the social womb of the producers of food, the shepherds, the tanners, the carpenters, the potters, the tillers, and so on. The feudal authoritarianism of Papal authorities was checkmated by the intellectuals who emerged from the working class.

In India, the Hindu hierarchy of caste and the hegemony of the anti-productive Brahman-Baniya castes have continued unchanged. The spiritual books, starting with the *Rigveda*, remain anti-production and pro-indignity of labour. Hinduism has continued to oppose scientific innovations. Economic development has no basis in the Hindu spiritual and social life. India and Nepal have suffered from ignorance, indignity of labour and a lack of scientific temper because of the stagnation that is the inevitable end product of spiritual fascism. The movement of India into the post-Hindu phase alone can release the forces of production and scientificity. India will then develop as a nation of great wealth and virtues. The Dalit–Bahujans and Adivasis will move into a new life of equality in all spheres in the twenty-first century. The new consciousness of the Dalit–Bahujan social forces points towards that development quite clearly. Let us hope that this century is a century of their dreams and a century of realization of those dreams.

Glossary

aadabokilla	womanly
aadatanam	femininity
aare	a needle used to stitch leather *chappals*, shoes and other commodities
adda	a place for discussion; gossip
adharmic	unjust people
Advaita Brahminism	a school of Brahmanical thought developed by Adi Shankara. Often it is interpreted as monistic system of thought. It put primacy on Shiva rather than Vishnu
agni	fire
agrahara	the land given to the priests and the temples by the ruling classes; the Indian Brahman priests came to own large tracts of land under this system, thereby becoming the first ever landlords in India
ayacut	an area of irrigated land in a particular village or town—in Andhra Pradesh, all the irrigated land under a particular tank, for instance, is known as the *ayacut* of that tank
bandi girra patta	bullock cart wheel belt made of iron
bhikkhu	male member of a Buddhist *sangha*
bhikkhuni	female member of a Buddhist *sangha*

bhoodevta	Earth God
bhooshakti	Earth Goddess
bhoomi dunnuta	a process of tilling the land
Brahmanatwam	Brahmanism
buddi	Telugu word for wooden junction of a bullock cart wheel
bund	a heap of soil and stone meant to check the flow of water from a tank or canal
Chakalatwam	the life and thinking process of the washermen's community. The Chakalis believed in the washing of clothes for human use, as it not only keeps the human body and environment clean but also increases the production of food and other commodities for the prolongation of human life. The human civilization has grown because of the contribution of washer men and women of India.
Chakali	Telugu word for the caste that washes clothes; an individual member of the caste
chakamukha rayee	the fire-producing stone, along with cotton and the iron pieces that are always kept with a cattle-grazing Yadava. The collective combination of this is called 'fire producer'
Chaki revu	dhobi *ghat*—site where the washing takes place
chandala padartha	Untouchable material
dakshina	the money given to a priest for conducting a ritual
daridra narayan	poor, exploited people of India
daruvu	an activity that generates pleasure through laughter or through other forms
deeksha bhoomi	the place in Nagpur where Dr B.R. Ambedkar embraced Buddhism
dhana	wealth
dhobi	the North Indian word for a Chakali
daddhojanam	a divine food item
dandekottuta	deceiving the buyers and sellers by manipulating the weighing machine
dharmic	just people

dora	landlord
dwija	twice born
dolu	big, roundish drum played while hanging it to the neck of the drum player with the help of a rope
Ejava	same as Gouda in Andhra Pradesh or toddy tappers in Kerala
Enakarra	Telugu word for single elephant pole used in building houses
erramatti	red soil
gaddi	a raised platform where the landlord sits. It symbolizes feudal hierarchy
gampa	basket
gela	tender growth at the neck of the tree, from where toddy flows out
ghat	the washing place at streams and tanks
Gollas	the caste that reared cattle, sheep and goats
goonda	a specific Indian word denoting some individuals or a small group of people, who, through exercising their muscle power, control the rest of the civil society in localities and regions
gopalakas	cattle grazers
gotra	people who share the same lineage
gooda	a leather belt stitched to the foot-sized leather base for holding the foot to the *chappal*
Gouda	Telugu name for a caste that specializes in toddy-tapping—same as Ejava (Kerala) and Nadar (Tamil Nadu); the individual member of the caste
grihaprastha	Brahminical term for *Samsaratwam*
guptadhana	an Indian form of black money; the money is often hidden at secret locations by the Baniyas
gurukulas	centres of education/schools in the ancient period
gutam	wooden or iron rod with a wide and strong bottom that is used to crush the leather and to soften it so that it can be moulded as necessary

jaggu	small musical instrument that can be played by hand
jihad	liberation
kale kambali wala	Prophet of the Black Blanket; referring to the Prophet Muhammad
kaalu karru	means that if there is a lack of coordination between the bull and the tiller, the iron blade (*karru*) would injure the bull's foot
Kapu	the name of a agrarian caste in Telugu; the name of this caste emerges from the Telugu word meaning 'watchers of the fields'.
karma phala	fruits of all labour and knowledge
karru	plough tip rod
kolimi	ironsmith's forge
kondra	the process of ploughing two furrows, leaving a two-and-half- to-three metre space in between
kshanabhanguram	something that only lives for a minute
kumkum	red powder used by Hindu women and men during religious functions
Kummaris	the caste that made pots
kummari kunda	potter's pot
Kurumas	a caste community; same as the Gollas
Lathangi	creeper; a thin and frail woman
Madi	a wet piece of cloth that the Brahman and the Baniya women wear while cooking in their houses. It is a torturous course that these women suffer in the name of religious purity
Madiga Dandora	is an organization started by the Madigas of Andhra Pradesh under the leadership of Krishna Madiga. This organization intends to ensure that the benefits of the reservation policy should be divided amongst the Madigas and the Malas of Andhra Pradesh on the basis of their population composition
maistrees	brick-and-cement technicians
mamsaharam	the practice of eating meat
mangali	that which is good and positive
mangala kathi	barber's knife

Mangalatwam	barberhood
magatanam	Masculinity
Mangali	Telugu word for the barber caste
martole	a sharp and roundish iron needle, big in size, with which holes are made to the leather in a required size so that leather threads can pass through the whole
mohalla	locality
moksha	spiritual liberation
moku	instrument used to climb toddy tree
muhurtham	the time fixed for house warming ceremony or marriage by the priest
muppadi muudu kotla devatalu	33 millions gods of Hinduism
mutta	is a place of worship for the followers of the Virashaiva cult
mutthadu	instrument used to climb toddy tree
Nadar	same as Gouda in Kannada or toddy tappers in Tamil Nadu
niluvu	the initial form of the pot shaped by the pot maker
paada vandana/paada puja	touching the feet of a priest in a public place
padakollu	are wooden sandals that are worn by the Hindu saints
palki	a palanquin, generally used in marriage
palugurai	Telugu word for a soft stone used by the barbers; constant rubbing against this stone, along with the leather sheet, leads to the semi-sterilization of the barber's knife
paraloka prapti	entering heaven
perugannam	a divine food item made of curd
pilaka juttu	tuft of hair that the Brahman priest maintains in his clean shaven head
punyam	sacredness
Purush	primordial man
purushatwam	same as *magatanam*
purushottama	the supreme being; one of the names of Lord Rama
pulihora	a divine food item made of tamarind sauce
Post-Hindu Nationalism	is an alternative stream of nationalist thought which runs counter to all the nationalist discourses that the upper-caste

Hindus working in all kinds of organizations and institutions—secular, communist, and so on—have constructed so far. Post-Hindu nationalism looks for its roots in Dalit–Bahujan class and it hopes to build this nation on productive, creative and scientific lines.

rampe   wide-edged knife that is used to cut leather in different sizes

ratha   chariot

rishi   saint

saadhu   same as *rishi*

Samana Brahmans   they devoted themselves to a life of saintliness and self-renunciation. They disregarded rites and rituals inculcated by Brahmans

sambhandalu   relationships

samsari   a disciplined householder

samsaram   familyhood

Samsaratwam   a philosophy that believes that God did not ordain bachelorhood for human beings. It does not associate sexual act with either purity or pollution. One can get married yet work as a priest in a temple or any other religious institution

Sangha   monastic association of ordained Buddhist monks and nuns

sanyasam   sainthood

Sanyasatwam   a philosophy that believes that celibacy is essential for attaining salvation

sati   a custom prevalent amongst many upper-caste Hindus whereby the bride was forced to die on the funeral pyre of her husband

shakaharam   vegetarianism

shapam   curse

sheela   Telugu word for chastity

shloka   couplets from scriptures

soma   a drink prepared from the nectar of toddy trees

sudakam   a Hindu practice where the family members of the recently deceased are treated as untouchable to others for eleven days; they are also supposed to remain on the outer side of the house and sleep and eat there. Only close relatives are allowed to cook food for them. This practice emerges from the fact that the dead body itself is treated as untouchable

Shudratwam — the philosophy of the Shudras that respects physical work as part of human productive life. It believes that soiling the hands is a part of human existence

sukha — pleasure

sura — intoxicants

tapasya — a form of meditation practised by the Hindus

taraju — weighing machine

teedgal — soft stone used for sharpening the knife whenever its edge gets rough

tilak — is a mark of auspiciousness. It is put on the forehead with sandal paste, sacred ashes or *kumkum*

upanayana — a sacred thread ceremony

ungutam — a leather ring stitched to the *chappal* to grip the big finger of the feet

vaamu — a specific place where the pot maker burns all dry pots, accommodating hundreds of pots

varnavyavastha — caste system

vasthu — spiritual intervention in shaping a house

Vishwarupa — the universal form revealed by Lord Krishna in the *Bhagavad Gita*

yagya — a ritual practice in which Brahman priests recite *mantras* and pour ghee in the fire altar to evoke blessings of the gods

yagya mandapam — the special place built for the performance of the Brahmanic Hindu *yagyas*

yagya kumbham — the place where *yagya* fire burns—it is around this *kumbham* that the Brahman priests sit and pour the *ghee* into the fire; it is the heart of the *yagya* activity

About the Author

Kancha Ilaiah, a passionate social activist and author, is a Professor at the Department of Political Science, Osmania University. He is a major figure in the ideological movement against the Indian caste system and has been instrumental in internationalising Dalit-Bahujan issues. He was born into a Kuruma Golla (an 'other backward caste') family and grew up in a small South Indian village. A prolific writer, he has authored several books and regularly contributes articles to national newspapers and magazines. His book *Why I am not a Hindu–A Sudra Critique of Hindutva Philosophy, Culture and Political Economy* (1996) is a bestseller. He has also authored *God as Political Philosopher: Buddha's Challenge to Brahminism, The State and Repressive Culture, Manatatwam* (in Telugu), *Buffalo Nationalism: A Critique of Spiritual Fascism, Turning the Pot, Tilling the land: Dignity of Labour in Our Times* and *The Weapon of the Other: DalitBahujan Writings and the Remaking of Indian Nationalist Thought.*